CHANGE THROUGH INTERACTION

Social Psychological Processes of Counseling and Psychotherapy

STANLEY R. STRONG
Virginia Commonwealth University

CHARLES D. CLAIBORN
University of Nebraska at Lincoln

1807 1982

175 YEARS OF PUBLISHING

A Wiley-Interscience Publication

JOHN WILEY & SONS

New York   Chichester   Brisbane   Toronto   Singapore

Copyright © 1982 by John Wiley & Sons, Inc.

All rights reserved. Published simultaneously in Canada.

Reproduction or translation of any part of this work
beyond that permitted by Section 107 or 108 of the
1976 United States Copyright Act without the permission
of the copyright owner is unlawful. Requests for
permission or further information should be addressed to
the Permissions Department, John Wiley & Sons, Inc.

This publication is designed to provide accurate
and authoritative information in regard to the subject
matter covered. It is sold with the understanding that
the publisher is not engaged in rendering legal, accounting,
or other professional service. If legal advice or other
expert assistance is required, the services of a competent
professional person should be sought. *From a Declaration
of Principles jointly adopted by a Committee of the
American Bar Association and a Committee of Publishers.*

Library of Congress Cataloging in Publication Data

Strong, Stanley R.
  Change through interaction.

  (Wiley series on personality processes, ISSN 0195–
4008)
  ''A Wiley-Interscience publication.''
  Includes bibliographical references and index.
  1. Personality change. 2. Psychotherapy. 3. Counseling. 4. Psychotherapist and patient. I. Claiborn,
Charles D. II. Title. III. Series. [DNLM: 1. Counseling—Methods 2. Psychotherapy—Methods. 3. Interpersonal relations. 4. Attitude. WM 420 S924c]

  RC480.5.S727   616.89'14   81-14631

  ISBN 0-471-05902-1   AACR2

Printed in the United States of America

10 9 8 7 6 5 4 3 2 1

To our wives,
Ina-Jeanne and Barbara

Series Preface

This series of books is addressed to behavioral scientists interested in the nature of human personality. Its scope should prove pertinent to personality theorists and researchers as well as to clinicians concerned with applying an understanding of personality processes to the amelioration of emotional difficulties in living. To this end, the series provides a scholarly integration of theoretical formulations, empirical data, and practical recommendations.

Six major aspects of studying and learning about human personality can be designated: personality theory, personality structure and dynamics, personality development, personality assessment, personality change, and personality adjustment. In exploring these aspects of personality, the books in the series discuss a number of distinct but related subject areas: the nature and implications of various theories of personality; personality characteristics that account for consistencies and variations in human behavior; the emergence of personality processes in children and adolescents; the use of interviewing and testing procedures to evaluate individual differences in personality; efforts to modify personality styles through psychotherapy, counseling, behavior therapy, and other methods of influence; and patterns of abnormal personality functioning that impair individual competence.

IRVING B. WEINER

University of Denver
Denver, Colorado

Preface

The analysis of counseling and psychotherapy as processes of social influence has received increased attention in the last several years, and *Change Through Interaction* is intended to further stimulate and advance the analysis. This book broadens the social influence framework as applied to counseling and psychotherapy and introduces a relatively new point of view that integrates impression management, attribution, internal consistency, and objective self-awareness theories from social psychology with communication theory and identifies the functions of clinical theories in facilitating people's efforts to change. Many of the notions presented are controversial. We even disagree with each other on many points. Yet we believe that the controversial nature of the material reflects the exciting and nascent stage of the social influence approach to therapy. We hope the ideas will stimulate further research and theory development that will result in greater understanding of therapeutic processes.

Change Through Interaction is intended for all who wish to better understand the processes of change in counseling and psychotherapy. Counseling and clinical psychologists interested in theory and research on the processes of change in counseling and psychotherapy will, we believe, be stimulated and provoked by the ideas presented and will find the material useful in generating research and theory development on therapy processes. Advanced students in clinical and counseling psychology should find this book similarly useful. We believe that the material will benefit practitioners as they seek to deepen their understandings of the art of therapy and will encourage them to expand their approaches and experiment in their efforts to help people change. Finally, social psychologists should find the application of their concepts and research to the applied social psychology fields of counseling and psychotherapy of interest, and some may be intrigued enough to pursue research and theory development on the processes of counseling and psychotherapy.

Our major emphasis is on accounting for change with variables that arise in the interaction between practitioner and client. We consistently argue that change does not arise from the internal processes of the client, as most clinical theories of counseling and psychotherapy posit, but rather from forces generated in the interaction. We recognize that both explanations of change are in part true but believe that the therapeutic process can best be understood and made amenable to research and improvement in a pragmatic sense by focusing on interaction variables, variables over which counselors and therapists have considerable control. The explanations of change that are posited by most clinical theories are seen as necessary aspects of the process of creating change rather than as scientific explanations of the process of change.

Another underlying theme is that people are viewed as the centers and sources of action, as proactive agents who act to control their environments rather than as reactive pawns of environmental manipulation. This view of people arises from recent notions of causal attribution as a tool of interpersonal control and of interaction behaviors as efforts to manage impressions. The view is also congruent with our experiences with clients in therapy and as living beings. This view results in some relatively new and unexpected ideas on the nature of change in the therapeutic encounter.

In Chapter 1, a brief history of change through interaction in the West in the last 2000 years is intended to reveal the principles of how change is stimulated in interaction and the functions of belief systems in the change process. Chapter 2 presents a theory of change through interaction. The presentation is uncompromising, straightforward, and unqualified even though we know that it is speculative. The rest of the chapters present research results that elaborate the implications of the theory and apply the theory to the process of stimulating therapeutic change. Chapters 3 and 4 review much of the domain of social psychology relevant to interpersonal interaction—Chapter 3 within the context of internal consistency theory, and Chapter 4 within the context of impression management theory. Chapters 5, 6, 7, and 8 focus explicitly on the processes of change in therapeutic encounters, bringing to bear the theory and the implications of the research just reviewed. Chapter 5 proposes that therapeutic change is best seen as spontaneous compliance and identifies aspects of the process that make spontaneous compliance the likely outcome of therapy. Chapter 6 systematically explores therapeutic methods for stimulating change in individual counseling and psychotherapy and analyzes their impact in light of theory and research on change through interaction. Chapter 7 presents an interactional framework for group counseling and psychotherapy, identifies the dynamics of change in groups, and describes therapist strategies for operationalizing the dynamics. Chapter 8 presents an interactional framework for family and couple counseling and psychotherapy, identifies the dynamics of family formation, self-regulation, and transformation, and describes methods for stimulating therapeutic changes in family functioning. Chapter 9 describes therapeutic psychology, both counseling and psychotherapy, as in the midst of revolutionary change from frameworks based on a linear cause model and intrapsychic concepts to frameworks based on a circular cause model and interactional concepts. The chapter presents in final form the interaction concepts and therapeutic interventions evolved in the previous chapters.

Each chapter is written to stand on its own, yet concepts are systematically developed from beginning to end. A reader more interested in application could well begin with Chapters 6, 7, 8, and 9 and work through the other chapters as concepts are needed to elucidate points of interest. For most readers, we recommend taking the material in the order it is presented and ask them to persevere through points they disagree with, for the ideas evolve and mature as they go from theory to research to application.

We are grateful to many colleagues who have directly and indirectly contributed to the development of the concepts presented in this book. Elliot Aronson and Karl Weick introduced the senior author to social psychology, and their continuing influence is apparent. Lyle Schmidt has played a key role for both of us in the development of our thinking about the application of social psychology to counseling and psychotherapy. A group of students and colleagues at the University of Nebraska worked closely with us in a two-year research seminar that resulted in the development and enunciation of many of the concepts presented in this book. Another group of students in a research seminar at Virginia Commonwealth University stimulated the further development and expansion of the ideas as presented in the last three chapters of the book. Thomas McGovern of Virginia Commonwealth University generously read and made helpful suggestions to the chapter on group counseling. We are indebted to the American Psychological Association, Lawrence Erlbaum Press, Lyle Stuart, Pergamon Press, and Simon and Schuster for permission to reproduce figures and quote passages. Finally, we thank Rosa Bradley, Michaele Moore and Craeg Strong for expertly preparing the final manuscript.

STANLEY R. STRONG
CHARLES D. CLAIBORN

Richmond, Virginia
Lincoln, Nebraska
December 1981

Contents

CHAPTER 1

A Brief History of Persuasion and Healing

Counseling and psychotherapy are the arts of change and healing through personal interaction. Through intimate conversation, people find relief from distressing feelings and disabilities, new strength and vitality in relationships with others, and direction and purpose in living. The remarkable curative powers that flow between persons in interaction have been known and relied upon in human society throughout recorded history and doubtless before it. How can simple conversation have such salutary effects on participants? What principles and guidelines can aspiring practitioners of counseling and psychotherapy follow to enhance the benevolent effects of their artistry?

Answers to the above questions can be sought by examining the nature of the interaction between the participants in conversation. Concepts of influence and change through social interaction can be drawn from social psychology, communication theory, and the history of healing and change through interaction over the last 2000 years in the West.

PERSUASION AND HEALING

Jerome Frank's *Persuasion and Healing* (1961) initiated the analysis of psychological helping as a process of social influence within the interaction of sufferer and healer. He analyzed healing in primitive societies, religious healing, and modern practices of psychological helping and concluded that healing and change were a function of belief, ideology, charisma, and ritual. Most important is the sufferer's belief or faith in the effectiveness of the healing procedure. ''The apparent success of healing methods based on all sorts of ideologies and methods compels the conclusion that the healing power of faith resides in the patient's state of mind, not in the validity of its object'' (Frank, 1961, p. 60). The personal charisma of the healer and the belief he or she transmits in his or her system reinforces the patient's faith and expectancy to be healed. Finally, common to all healing methods is a distinct ritual that has the function of informing the sufferer when the healing is to occur and that flows from and reinforces the ideology of the method of change.

1

If faith and belief in the curative powers of factors in an ideological system are major determinants of the effectiveness of psychological helping, then approaches to psychological healing should reflect the ideologies and values of the society in which they are embedded. In this vein, Frank pointed to the authoritarian approaches to helping that have emerged from the Germanic and Russian cultures as opposed to the democratic and individualistic growth approaches that have emerged from the American culture. An appreciation of the dramatic impact of the zeitgeist or ideological system in which psychological helping is embedded can be obtained from an examination of the ideologies of healing and change in Western society over the last 2000 years.

IDEOLOGICAL HISTORY

The last 2000 years can be divided roughly into three periods, distinguishable yet overlapping. The periods begin with the Age of Faith, which continued dominant through around A.D. 1500 (Durant, 1950). During this time, behavior was believed to be controlled by conformity to the will of God, either through the spirit of God acting in the person through the mystery of faith or, in pre-Christian philosophies, conformity to the law of God. Illness and peculiar or antisocial behavior were the results of possession by foreign powers, agents of the devil, and were consequences of living in and being part of a fallen world controlled by evil. The highest reality was located outside of the self and the social system. Humanity was studied within a theological perspective as children of God (Lowe, 1976).

The second period, the Age of Reason, began with the Renaissance and held full dominance until the late 1800s, a bit after the publication of Darwin's work on evolution (Durant & Durant, 1961). The Age of Reason dawned at the end of the Middle Ages when "the locus of subjective reality gradually shifted from witches and demons, which were external to man, to human reason, which was within him. Thus metaphysical reality advanced from the hereafter to man's immediate life as divine reality was placed within the mind of man, a person Riesman fittingly describes as inner-directed" (Lowe, 1976, p. 74). In this tradition, behavior was a function of people's rational faculties that were available to them to keep their passions in order, within a universe of clear design and mechanical perfection. Natural law ruled all. People were gifted by God with faculties for controlling the self and understanding all else in creation. Erratic and antisocial behavior was due to physical malfunctioning of the body or mind, as well as willful villainy and mischief. Evil was personally caused rather than the demons' work.

The Age of Reason was also the age that spawned science; the highest pursuit was uncovering natural law. Within this pursuit were the seeds of destruction of the Age of Reason—as the natural laws of the universe were pursued, people's views of themselves began to shift, and the idea that people might also be subject to natural law began to emerge. Darwin's *Origin of Species*, published in 1859, was a direct attack on the view that people were a special part of creation, not themselves subject to natural laws but, rather, endowed with special qualities of reason that overrode natural law. The publication in 1890 of William James's *Principles of Psychology* and, in 1900, Sigmund Freud's *Interpretation of Dreams* marked the demise of ideologies of humanity as set apart and in control of its own destiny and the beginning of the notion that outside social forces have strong effects on the internal functioning of people.

The Age of Socialism, beginning with James and Freud's works, is upon us today and is dominated by the idea that persons are social creatures controlled by their environments. People are removed from their lofty positions as free agents with self-determination. The perception of social reality as the major determinant of behavior is becoming more accepted, and the idea of people as individual islands unto themselves is less central in our thinking. The individual is viewed as a social being, subject to the actions of others. He or she is other-directed. The doctrine of psychic determinism is losing ground, and the doctrine of external forces, especially cultural relationship forces, is gaining prominence. Persons' abilities to adjust to others are becoming the criteria for health. Indeed, the recent emergence of social psychology and notions of social influence and interaction is but a sign and part of the zeitgeist.

Spiritism

An understanding of psychological helping requires an understanding of the West's Judaeo-Christian heritage, especially Christian doctrines, because of the profound impact of the Christian church's complete dominance of western culture for 1500 years. While many persons of the West are not Christian today, none can escape the effects of the 1500 years of church dominance. In this light, our investigation of psychological healing practices begins with the Christian tradition. The most complete descriptions of healing in the Christian tradition are contained in the New Testament, especially in the four Gospels and the Book of Acts. The Gospels, for the most part, are accounts of the three years of Jesus' ministry written on the basis of personal acquaintance and the oral traditions that carried Christian teachings for the first hundred years or so. The Book of Acts describes the activities of the disciples for the first several years after the Crucifixion and has an origin similar to the Gospels.

Jesus was born into a deeply religious culture, one with strong traditions of their God working miracles and delivering his people from their enemies. The period he lived in was one of great expectancy for God to send a Messiah to deliver the nation from the domination of the Romans. The society was governed by religious authorities and had numerous groups dedicated to particular expressions of the Hebrew faith. Jesus began his ministry by preaching that the time of deliverance was now and the kingdom of heaven was at hand, and he blended into his preaching many healings and miracles:

> He went round the whole of Galilee teaching in their synagogues, proclaiming
> the Good News of the kingdom and curing all kinds of diseases and sicknesses

among the people. His fame spread throughout Syria, and those who were suffering from diseases and painful complaints of one kind or another, the possessed, epileptics, the paralyzed, were all brought to him, and he cured them. (Matthew 4:23−24, *The Jerusalem Bible*, 1966).

There is no way of knowing what diseases and sicknesses are referred to in this or other passages. Probably, the diseases described covered a wider range of afflictions than the same labels would today, and the causes were diverse. Certainly the practice of medicine in that day was primitive.

Jesus was preaching a message well fit to the spirit of the time, and the ideology included the expectation of signs and wonders through God's Chosen. The following are some of the healings:

1. After he had come down from the mountain large crowds followed him. A leper now came up and bowed low in front of him, "Sir," he said, "if you want to, you can cure me!" Jesus stretched out his hand, touched him and said, "Of course I want to! Be cured!" And his leprosy was cured at once. Then Jesus said to him, "Mind you do not tell anyone, but go and show yourself to the priest and make the offering prescribed by Moses, as evidence for them." (Matthew 8:1−3)

2. When he went into Capernaum a centurion came up and pleaded with him. "Sir," he said, "my servant is lying at home paralyzed, and in great pain." "I will come myself and cure him," said Jesus. The centurion replied, "Sir, I am not worthy to have you under my roof: just give the word and my servant will be cured. For I am under authority myself, and have soldiers under me; and I say to one man: Go, and he goes; to another: Come here, and he comes; to my servant: Do this, and he does it." When Jesus heard this he was astonished and said to those following him, "I tell you solemnly, nowhere in Israel have I found faith like this. And I tell you that many will come from east and west to take their places with Abraham and Isaac and Jacob at the feast in the kingdom of heaven; but the subjects of the kingdom will be turned out into the dark, where there will be weeping and grinding of teeth." And to the centurion, Jesus said, "Go back, then; you have believed, so let this be done for you." And the servant was cured at that moment. (Matthew 8:5−13)

3. And going into Peter's house Jesus found Peter's mother-in-law in bed with a fever. He touched her hand and the fever left her, and she got up and began to wait on him. (Matthew 8:14−15)

4. That evening they brought him any who were possessed by devils. He cast out the spirits with a word and cured all who were sick. (Matthew 8:16)

The Gospel of Matthew describes 19 additional healings. The healings came out of an ideology that includes the expectation that healing will occur; it also provides a rationale for the sickness and the healing. God acts to heal his people, and sickness is a result of a lack of God's blessing and the action of evil in the world, including possession. The healings came to those who believed the doctrine. It occurred to those who came to the healer or had an intercessor with the healer. Obviously, those who came were especially interested in the doctrine.

Healing occurred when the healer declared it to be so. People were not healed in their houses while oblivious to the actions of the healer. The impact of faith on healing is brought out especially clearly in the following excerpt:

> When Jesus had finished these parables, he left the district; and, coming to this home town, he taught the people in their synagogue in such a way that they were astonished and said, "Where did the man get this wisdom and these miraculous powers? Is not his mother the woman called Mary, and his brothers James and Joseph and Simon and Jude? His sisters, too, are they not all here with us? So where did the man get it all?" And they would not accept him. But Jesus said to them, "A prophet is only despised in his own country and in his own house." And he did not work many miracles there because of their lack of faith. (Matthew 13:53–58)

Later in the account when his disciples fail to cast a demon out of a boy and the boy's father appeals to Jesus to do it, the father is quoted as saying:

> "I took him to your disciples but they were unable to cure him." "Faithless and perverse generation!" Jesus said in reply. "How much longer must I be with you? How much longer must I put up with you? Bring him to me." And when Jesus rebuked it, the devil came out of the boy who was cured from that moment. (Matthew 17:16–18)

It appears that the healing ability of Jesus was tied to the belief of the sufferers, for when they doubted him as they did in his home town, he "did not work many miracles." Also, the greater faith of the boy and his father in Jesus than in his followers seems to have been vital in curing the boy.

A kind of "belief contagion" is apparent in the New Testament. As word of the healings spread, more and more people came and were brought for healing, and the expectancy for healing no doubt also grew. For example:

> When the local people recognized him they spread the news through the whole neighborhood and took all that were sick to him, begging him just to let them touch the fringe of his cloak. And all those who touched it were completely cured. (Matthew 14:35–36)

Several rituals are used to announce the cures in these works. Jesus often touched the afflicted part. He also waved his hand, verbally announced the event, spat on the part, and rubbed spit and dust on the afflicted parts. As his fame spread, cures were effected by touching his clothing. In the Book of Acts, his disciples are reported to heal to the same degree as did Jesus. There also a faith–contagion effect is reported, and many rituals are described as a means of announcing the healings, including all of those used by Jesus and others. For example:

> So many signs and wonders were worked among the people at the hands of the apostles that the sick were even taken out into the streets and laid on beds and

> sleeping-mats in the hope that at least the shadow of Peter might fall across some of them as he went past. People even came crowding in from the towns around Jerusalem, bringing with them their sick and those tormented by unclean spirits, and all were cured. (Acts 5:12–26)

The writer of Acts also reports that:

> So remarkable were the miracles worked by God at Paul's hands that handkerchiefs or aprons which had touched him were taken to the sick, and they were cured of their illnesses, and the evil spirits came out of them. (Acts 19:11–12)

It is also useful to note that the healers were commissioned by some authority before they commenced to heal. Jesus claimed the commissioning of God his Father, and he began his ministry only after the ritual of baptism by John the Baptist. Jesus explicitly commissioned his followers. Jesus summoned his 12 disciples and gave them authority over unclean spirits with power to cast them out and to cure all kinds of diseases and sicknesses: "Cure the sick, raise the dead, cleanse the lepers, cast out devils" (Matthew 10:8). Later, he commissioned his disciples with the breath of the Holy Spirit and by a laying on of hands. The power to heal has been handed down within the Christian church in the same way ever since.

The powerful effects of faith and charismatic healers, the role of a doctrine or ideology accounting for the events, and the role of rituals to convey the healings are all clear in the above passages. If we take the descriptions as factual, at least in large part, we would be compelled to believe the ideology was true, were it not for a charismatic healer 17 centuries later who accomplished much the same healings using a very different ideology. There are some aspects of events described in these narratives that defy psychological explanation and have not been repeated by any other healer. Raising the dead and affecting animals are outside the pale of social influence phenomena. A multitude of other explanations are possible, and one of them is faith in the Christian cosmology.

In the Christian cosmology, both healing and illness are seen as resulting from the activity of outside forces over which the sufferer has no control. The person cannot and does not try to be sick or well, but is to accept the change. Change is not a result of self-control, but is direct. Victims are not enjoined to try to walk, but to walk. The change is not controlled by the will or consciousness. The individual is changed by forces he or she cannot control through the events marked by the ritual. If many of the changes described above were due to faith and social influence, then behavior appears to be to some degree under control of the unconscious, beyond awareness and the effortful self-control emphasized by many change theorists today. Change in spiritual healing involves the person changing directly without conscious effort to change. Persons change; they do not try to change. Reliance on some mechanism of direct change rather than on a try-to-change mechanism is a nearly universal component of the ideologies of change, including the ideologies of modern psychotherapies. In nearly all systems, change is ascribed to principles over which the person does not have direct conscious control.

Appeal to the healing power of God as the method of change was the dominant psychological approach for 1700 years in Europe. The extent of ''superstition'' in the Age of Faith is clearly evident from the following excerpts from Durant (1950) and Durant and Durant (1961):

> Science and philosophy, in the medieval west, had to grow up in such an atmosphere of myth, legend, miracle, omens, demons, prodigios, magic, astrology, divination, and sorcery as comes only in ages of chaos and fear. All these had existed in the pagan world, and exist today, but tempered by civilized humor and enlightenment. They were strong in the Semitic world, and triumphed after Averroës and Maimonides. In Western Europe, from the sixth to the eleventh century, they broke the dikes of culture, and overwhelmed the medieval mind in an ocean of occultism and credulity; Augustine thought that the pagan gods still existed as demons, and that fauns and satyrs were real; Abélard thought that demons can work magic through their intimate acquaintance with the secrets of nature; Alfonso the Wise accepted magic, and sanctioned divination by the stars; how, then, should lesser men doubt?

> A multitude of mysterious and supernatural beings had descended into Christianity from pagan antiquity, and were still coming into it from Germany, Scandinavia, and Ireland as trolls, elves, giants, fairies, goblins, gnomes, ogres, banshees, mysterious dragons, bloodsucking vampires; and new superstitions were always entering Europe from the East. Dead men walked the air as ghosts; men who had sold themselves to the devil roamed woods and fields as werewolves; the souls of children dead before baptism haunted the marshes as will-o'-the wisps. When St. Edmund Rich saw a flight of black crows he recognized them at once as a flock of devils come to fetch the soul of a local usurer. When a demon is exorcised from a man, said many a medieval story, a big black fly—sometimes a dog—could be seen issuing from his mouth. The population of devils never declines.

> The Church struggled against the paganism of superstition, condemned many beliefs and practices, and punished them with a gradation of penances. She denounced black magic—resorting to demons to obtain power over events; but it flourished in a thousand secret places. Its practitioners circulated privately a *Liber perditionis,* or *Book of Damnation,* giving the names, habitats, and special powers of the major demons. Nearly everybody believed in some magical means of turning the power of supernatural beings to a desired end. John of Salisbury tells of magic used by a deacon, a priest, and an archbishop. The simplest form was by incantation: a formula was recited, usually several times. By such formulas a miscarriage might be averted, a sickness healed, an enemy put out of the way. Probably the majority of Christians considered the sign of the cross, the Lord's Prayer, and the Ave Maria as magic incantations, and used holy water and the sacraments as magic rites bringing miraculous events.

> Belief in witchcraft was next to universal. The Penitential Book of the bishop of Exeter condemned women ''who profess to be able to change men's minds by

sorcery and enchantments, as from hate to love or from love to hate, or to bewitch or steal men's goods, or who profess to ride on certain nights and on certain beasts with a host of demons in women's shapes, and to be enrolled in the company of such''—the ''Witches Sabbath'' that became notorious in the fourteenth century. A simple witchery consisted in making a wax model of an intended victim, piercing it with needles, and pronouncing formulas of cursing; a minister of Philip IV was accused of hiring a witch to do this to an image of the king. Some women were believed able to injure or kill by a look of their ''evil eye.'' Berthold of Regensburg thought that more women than men could go to hell because so many women practiced witchcraft—''spells for getting a husband, spells for marriage, spells before the child is born, spells before the christening . . . it is a marvel that men lose not their wits for the monstrous witchcrafts that women practice on them.'' Visigothic law accused witches of invoking demons, sacrificing to devils, causing storms, etc., and ordered that those convicted of such offences should have their heads shaved and receive two hundred stripes. The laws of Cnut in England recognized the possibility of slaying a person by magic means. The Church was at first lenient with these popular beliefs, looking upon them as pagan survivals that would die out; on the contrary they grew and spread; and in 1298 the Inquisition began its campaign to suppress witchcraft by burning women at the stake.

Many theologians sincerely believed that certain women were in league with demons, and that the faithful must be protected from their spells. Caesarius of Heisterbach assures us that in his time many men entered into pacts with devils; and it is alleged that such practitioners of black magic so distained the Church that they travestied her rites by worshipping Satan in a Black Mass. Thousands of sick or timid people believed themselves to be possessed by devils. The prayers, formulas, and ceremonies of exorcism used by the Church may have been intended as psychological medicine to calm superstitious minds.

Medieval medicine was in some measure a branch of theology and ritual. Augustine thought that the diseases of mankind were caused by demons, and Luther agreed with him. It seemed logical, therefore, to cure illness with prayer, and epidemics by religious processions or building churches. So Santa Maria della Salute at Venice was raised to check a plague, and the prayers of St. Gerbold, Bishop of Bayeux, cured that city of the epidemic of dysentery. Good physicians welcomed the aid of religious faith in effecting cures; they recommended prayer, and the wearing of amulets. As far back as Edward the Confessor we find English rulers blessing rings for the cure of epilepsy. Kings, having been consecrated by religious touch, felt that they might cure by imposition of hands. Persons suffering from scrofula were supposed to be especially amenable to the royal touch; hence thename ''king's evil'' for that ailment. St. Louis labored assiduously with such impositions; Philip of Valois is said to have ''touched'' 1,500 persons at one sitting. (Durant, 1950, pp. 984−986)[1]

By the late 1500s, the belief in magical arts was declining, with a bloody exception: this period was the heyday of judicial murders for witchcraft.

Persecutors and persecuted alike believed in the possibility of securing supernatural aid by incantations or similar devices. If one could win the intercession of a saint by prayer, why not the help of a devil by courting him? A book published at Heidelberg in 1585, *Christlich Bedenden vonZauber (Christian Ideas on Magic)*. laid it down as an axiom that "everywhere the whole universe, inward and outward, water and air, is full of devils, of wicked, invisible spirits." It was a common belief that human beings could be "possessed" by devils entering them. In 1593, there was "a terrible panic in the little town of Friedeberg, for it was said that the Devil had taken bodily possession of more than sixty people . . . and had tortured them frightfully . . . even the pastor had himself been seized while preaching." The story of the Gadarene swine (Matthew 8:28–34) pictured Christ as driving demons from possessed person, and had he not given his followers the power to cast out devils in his name (Mark 16:17)? Priests were called upon by their parishioners for a variety of exorcisms—to drive pests from the fields, to still storms at sea, to cleanse a building of evil spirits, to purify a desecrated church, etc. Pope Paul V issued in 1604 a manual for such priestly services. Protestant writers condemned sacerdotal exorcism as magic, but the Church of England has recognized the value of exorcism as a healing rite. Here, as in so many ceremonies, the psychological effect has been good. (Durant & Durant, 1961, p. 576)[2]

Magnetism

The power to heal through social influence remained the exclusive domain of the Church and other practitioners of the supernatural until 1773 when a new approach was introduced by Franz Anton Mesmer (Podmore, 1963). Mesmer's work was the culmination of a long struggle of science and reason against superstition in Europe that began in the early 1500s. In many ways, the philosophies that science and reason introduced are best described as alternative superstitions. But the movement was based on the notion that the world was natural and was guided by natural laws. Events were orderly. In the Age of Reason, it was argued that God had given people free will and intelligence and that they could gain willful control over events. People were, by God's will, spontaneous, free agents guided by reason, while the world was guided by the natural laws set down by an orderly God. Few denied the sovereignty of God; instead, people sought to gain rule over the dominion of humanity in God's order.

The magnetic system was a prescientific theory of the influence bodies have on one another, and it grew out of a fascination with planetary effects on earth events, astrology, and magnets. Magnetism was set down in a rather complete theory by Von Helmont in 1634 and by Robert Fludd in 1637. The theory asserted that the stars worked on the bodies on the earth, that things on earth acted on one another, and that all people had the same particles of influence emitting from them that affected others. Many magnetists asserted that persons could, by power of will, focus their magnetic energies and direct their action on others and on things. Before Mesmer, magnetism was considered to emanate from the spiritual world, utlimately from the Creator. Mesmer's contribution to the theory of magnetism was to completely free the doctrine from the spiritual world. For him, magnetism was strictly a force, an energy or fluid. It was strictly a physical entity.

Mesmer was born around 1734. He was awarded a doctorate at the University of Vienna in 1766 for which he wrote a thesis titled *De Planetarum Influxu (On the Influence of the Planets on the Human Body)*. Mesmer came into public view in 1773 when he claimed to have cured a patient using a new form of treatment that entailed passing magnetic plates over the patient's body. Credit was immediately claimed by the Jesuit Father Hell, a professor of Astrology at the University of Vienna, who invented the plates (Podmore, 1963, pp. 1−2). The controversy raged for two years, during which time Mesmer claimed that the cures were from the action of a special fluid he had discovered which he called animal magnetism (magnetism from living beings) and that they had nothing to do with the plates. In the controversy, Mesmer developed a detailed statement of his position which he drew up in 1779. The essential points of the doctrine are as follows (translation from Podmore, 1963, pp. 38−39):

1. A mutual influence exists between heavenly bodies and living bodies.

2. The means of this influence is a fluid universally spread and continued in such a way as to not leave any void, whose subtlety permits no comparison and which in its nature is susceptible to receive, propagate and communicate all the impressions of movement.

3. This reciprocal action is submitted to mechanical laws unknown until the present.

4. There results from this action, alternating effects which can be considered like a flux and reflux (ebb and flow).

6. It is by means of this operation (the most universal of these that nature offers us) that active relations are exercised between celestial bodies, earth, and the parts that constitute it.

9. There is manifest particularly in the human body, properties analogous to those of magnets; one distinguishes equally diverse and opposed poles which are able to communicate, change, destroy and reinforce; the phenomenon of the dip of the magnetic needle itself is observed there.

10. The property of a living body which renders it susceptible to the influence of heavenly bodies and the reciprocal action of those which surround it, manifested by its analogy with the magnet, causes me to name it "animal magnetism" (magnetism of living bodies).

14. Its action takes place at a far off distance without the help of any intermediary body.

15. It is augmented and reflected through glass like light.

16. It is communicated, propagated and augmented by sound.

21. This system will furnish new elucidations on the nature of fire and light as well as in the theory of attraction and ebb and flow of the magnet and electricity.

22. It will be recognized that the magnet and artificial electricity have with respect to illnesses properties in common with several other agents that nature gives us; and if there has resulted several useful effects from the administration from the latter they are due to living magnetism.

23. One will recognize by the facts according to the practical rules I will establish that this principle can heal immediately sickness of nerves and mediate other sicknesses.

24. That with its help, a doctor is enlightened on the use of medicines; that he perfects their action, and that he initiates and directs the beneficial crises, in such a way as to render himself in charge of it.[3]

Mesmer remained in Vienna until 1778 making many trips around Europe to expound on his discovery. He apparently cured many people of various diseases while in Vienna, including restoring sight to a young woman who had been blind from birth. The girl had been under the care of several of Vienna's leading physicians who questioned the cure and managed to persuade the girl's family to remove the girl from Mesmer's care. It is interesting to note that the girl was receiving a stipend from the Empress because of her blindness, and whatever improvement she had experienced soon relapsed to its former state. Mesmer found it convenient to move to Paris shortly afterwards.

Mesmer found Paris an ideal setting for his work. The city was alive with new ideas, had many wealthy residents in search of entertainment, and was ready for a doctrine of healing devoid of spiritual overtones and cast in scientific terms. To those versed in the emerging science of physics, the theory was fanciful and archaic. To all others, the theory solidifed their notions of the power of magnetism. Mesmer himself was completely certain he had discovered a basic scientific truth, and repeatedly he applied to the Royal Societies of Science and Medicine in France, England, and Germany for investigation and authentication of his discovery.

Mesmer's treatment at first was individually ministered. He met with the patient, performed routine diagnostic workups and treated them by focusing his fluid on them, often touching the part to be healed. Within two years in Paris, he had 70 patients in treatment, 600 places promised, and several thousand applications received (Podmore, 1963, p. 5). To meet the demand for treatment, he devised a group form of magnetism, called the Baquet, and took on students (for a considerable sum) to increase the resources for treatment. Podmore describes the Baquet, from records of the Royal Commissions that investigated Mesmer's claims, as follows:

> The Baquet was a large oaken tub, four or five feet in diameter and a foot or more in depth, closed by a wooden cover. Inside the tub were placed bottles full

[3]This and the following quotes from F. Podmore's *From Mesmer to Christian Science* (1963) is reprinted with permission of Lyle Stuart.

of water disposed in rows radiating from the center, the necks in some of the rows pointing towards the center, in others away from it. All these bottles had been previously "magnetised" by Mesmer. Sometimes there were several rows of bottles, one above the other; the machine was then said to be at high pressure. The bottles rested on layers of powdered glass and iron filings. The tub itself was filled with water. The whole machine, it will be seen, was a kind of travesty of the galvanic cell. To carry out the resemblance, the cover of the tub was pierced with holes, through which passed slender iron rods of varying lengths, which were jointed and movable, so that they could be readily applied to any part of the patient's body. Around this battery the patients were seated in a circle, each with his iron rod. Further, a cord, attached at one end to the tub, was passed round the body of each of the sitters, so as to bind them into a chain. Outside the first a second circle would frequently be formed, who would connect themselves together by holding hands. Mesmer, in a lilac robe, and his assistant operators—vigorous and handsome young men selected for the purpose—walked about the room, pointing their fingers or an iron rod held in their hands at the diseased parts.

The progress of the cures was generally furthered by the application of the operator's hand to various parts of the body, and especially by the pressure of the fingers in the abdomen. And this pressure was often maintained for a considerable time—sometimes even for several hours. The proceedings were enlivened throughout by excellent music from a piano or other instrument. (Podmore, 1963, p. 6)

The effect of the treatment varied. A frequent experience was a crisis, followed by cure. It is most important to keep in mind that crisis is an essential part of exorcism, a dominant healing procedure for the 1700 years preceding the Baquet. In exorcism, as presented in the Bible and practiced even today, the possessed can be expected to be thrown to the floor by the invading spirits, and to grovel about screaming and grunting, often discharging fluid from their orifices. When the exorcism is completed, the person becomes calm as in a deep sleep, and slowly wakes up in a rational state, with little memory of the proceedings. The scene at the Baquet was described as follows:

The tableau presented by the patients is one of extreme diversity. Some are calm, composed, and feel nothing; others cough, spit, have slight pains, feel a glow locally or all over the body, accompanied by perspiration; others are shaken and tormented by convulsions. These convulsions are remarkable in their frequence, their duration, and their intensity. As soon as one attack begins, others make their appearance. The commission has seen them last for more than three hours; they are accompanied by expectorations of the viscous matter, torn from the chest by the violence of the attack. Sometimes there are traces of blood in the expectoration. The convulsions are characterized by involuntary spasmodic movements of the limbs and of the whole body, by contractions of the throat, by spasms of the hypochondric and epigastric regions; the eyes are wondering and distracted; there are piercing cries, tears, hiccoughs, and extravagant laughter. The convulsions are preceded and followed by a state of languor and reverie, by exhaustion and drowsiness. Any sudden noise causes the patients to start, even a change in the music played on the piano has an effect—a lively tune agitates them afresh and renews the convulsions. (Podmore, 1963, p. 7)

Mesmer's fame grew, and the success of his treatment was contagious. Thousands sought his treatment; in 1784 he and his student, Deslon, treated 8000 persons! Examples of patients treated by Mesmer and his students can be drawn from the many accounts of Mesmer's animal magnetism published by those who believed him to be a charlatan or at best misguided, and his firm supporters, usually those who knew first hand of the validity of his discovery through being healed themselves, as well as those who were directly healing others using Mesmer's secret discovery. The following are from Podmore (1963) as he interpreted the reports from the original languages:

1. A girl, 5 years of age who had suffered one year of *"Humeur de Gourme*; violent pains in the side, unable to walk. Accident of the spine was feared." After 9 months of treatment, she is reported cured, following "profuse and long-continued expectoration. After some months the humour discharged by the ear." (p. 12)

2. A boy 6 months of age, whose "eyes were inverted, breathing spasmodic [and] skin livid." His "eyes resumed their natural position, and breathing became easier after treatment by Animal Magnetism for 1¼ hours." After seven days' further treatment "there was a discharge from the nose. Cured." (p. 13)

3. A 2 year old boy, "arm burnt to elbow and skin entirely destroyed," with nine days of treatment, he was "Cured without any drug or ointment. No mark left." (p. 13)

4. "[A] domestic servant who had been suffering for five weeks from severe pains in the head. The malady, of which the cause could not be discovered, resisted all usual remedies. As a last resource, Patillon (the attending physician) counselled a trial of Magnetism, and the patient after some hesitation consented. From the commencement of the treatment, the pulse became softer and more frequent. After ten minutes, the pain in the head was transferred to the muscles of the neck; thence successively to the shoulder, the elbow, and the wrist. The pain was so intense that the patient fainted. She was placed on her bed and the treatment continued. On waking she complained of a severe pain in her wrist, and Patillon implored her to endure for a few minutes longer, in order that the cure might be complete. In effect, she soon went to sleep again under the magnetic finger, and awoke completely freed from pain after fifty minutes' treatment." (pp. 14—15)

5. "[A] lady of the Faubourg St. Germain, who had suffered from severe sciatica following on child-birth: the whole lumbar region was affected so that she could not move without pain. Many doctors were consulted in vain. The patient was unable to leave the house, the general health gave way and the digestion was impaired. Finally, after five years of suffering, she applied to

Patillon for treatment by Magnetism, with the result that after forty days all pain left her, her general health was completely restored, and she was able to go into the world again.'' (p. 15)

6. ''The third case . . . was that of a young girl of eleven, suffering from a congenital skin disease (gale) 'which might be leprous.' All the ordinary remedies had proved useless. After fiteen days' treatment by Animal Magnetism, the skin was changed from leaden colour to white and the scabs had begun to fall off, leaving a healthy skin behind. The treatment was still proceeding, and Patillon was confident of a complete cure.'' (p. 15)

7. ''To these reports we may add the record . . . of a case in which we have a description of the patient's symptoms both from herself and from her physcian, M. de la Fisse, doctor of the Faculty of Paris. The Countess de la Blache has been ill for eight years; for the last fourteen months she has been bedridden, and unable even to rest at ease in bed. Her physician, writing on the 12th of August, 1782, to a near relative described the state of the patient as leading him to fear the worst. She has almost lost hearing, power of speech or movement. She breathes with great difficulty, and that solely by the use of abdominal muscles, the chest remaining quite motionless. Frequent bleedings and the whole resources of the pharmacopoeia have failed to give appreciable relief. The patient is reduced to the last extremity. Immediately after this report, Deslon was called in. Madame de la Blache could not bear to be touched, and it was found necessary therefore to magnetise her from a distance. After two years' treatment she finds herself, not indeed completely cured, but better than she had been for eight years previously: no longer bedridden, but able to move about, and with full use of her voice and senses. Her general health is improved; and three tumours (spuirres) have disappeared under the treatment.'' (p. 17)

8. ''Antoine Santon . . . , valet de chambre to the Count d'Artois, had suffered for six months from rheumatism in the right arm, which prevented him from making use of the limb. Three days' treatment from Deslon sufficed to banish the pain and to restore the use of the arm. Palpitation of the heart, from which he had suffered for four years, was cured at the same time.'' (p. 18)

9. ''An interesting case is that of M. Chauvet, a priest. . . . In early summer of 1778 he had a severe attack of rheumatism which confined him to his bed for three months. Since that date he had never been entirely free from rheumatic pains in one or other arm, often sufficiently severe to prevent him from moving it. In September, 1783, some friends persuaded him to try Animal Magnetism. He went, and was half-persuaded that Deslon was a charlatan when he saw the physician point his index finger at the arm affected and approach his foot to that of his patient. But his opinion changed when, Deslon having placed his hand on the patient's shoulder-blade, there followed immediately a profuse perspiration on the whole left side of the body (where he felt the pain), and on that only. His collar was glued to his skin, and his friends saw drops of sweat rolling down his face. His pain left him at that moment, and he is able a year later to write that he no longer knows what rheumatism is.'' (p. 19)

10. ''Jean Gastal, a scullion . . . , reports a curious case. On a *fete* day a packet of fireworks (fusées), which he was carrying in the pocket of his apron, had exploded. He tried to stop the explosion by pressing the box between his thighs, but made matters worse. He was severely burnt on the lower part of the body.

Deslon on the spot magnetised the thighs, and on the morrow Jean was able to remove the scab and find the skin underneath quite healed. But he had been reluctant to allow the lower part of the body, which had suffered less injury, to be magnetised, and this part was not healed for three weeks.'' (p. 20)

11. "A paralytic who had lost sensation and warmth in the lower half of the body. After eight days' treatment by Mesmer, warmth and sensation were restored.'' (p. 47)

12. A patient "affected with paralysis on the entire right side, was carried to his treatment on a litter. After two months was so far recovered as to discard the litter and walk to the treatment.'' (p. 47)

13. "A young girl nearly blind as a sequel to tumours in the breast. After six weeks' treatment her sight was completely restored.'' (p. 47)

14. "A soldier 'obstrue' in his own words, 'au point de ne plus pense qu'à la mort'; a month later 'ne pense plus qu'a la vie!' '' (p. 47)

15. "A young girl emaciated by scrofula had already lost the sight of one eye; the other was covered with ulcers and attacked by a 'hernia'. Six weeks later she could see perfectly with it; and scrofulous swellings were considerably reduced.'' (p. 47)

Most of the patients reported physical sensations from the healing fluid in the course of healing. Some saw the fluid streaming from the healer's finger or the Baquet rod. Others felt the warm or cold sensation of the fluid as it worked on them. Diseased parts tingled or prickled and patients broke out in perspiration. Patients also reported feeling "an agitation of the blood'' and "the fermentation of humours'' and other manifestations of the fluid's presence (Podmore, 1963, p. 23).

If these reports are credible, a good many persons found themselves rid of many difficult symptoms of various sorts, and many trained physicians found the method to have a beneficial effect on some of their most difficult patients. Further, most of the persons involved, patient and healer alike, experienced unmistakable evidence that the fluid Mesmer had discovered was at work and responsible for the cures. While it is impossible to know how effective the treatment was, Podmore concludes that:

> Of 115 persons whose cases are here recorded nearly half profess themselves to have been completely cured, and of the remainder all but six experienced sensible relief under the treatment. The six exceptions were persons who had not been under treatment for more than a few weeks, and who still continued to attend in hope of a cure. (p. 22)

Surely this rate of improvement is equal to any claimed by psychological healers today.

Mesmer's fame grew contagiously, and large numbers of person sought cures and to be trained in the method. The practice of "animal magnetism'' spread from Paris to the French Provinces, and to all parts of Western Europe in just a few years. The French Academy of Science and Royal Society of Medicine steadfastly refused to officially consider Mesmer's discovery and became increasingly hostile to the point of striking the names of some 30 physicians from their roles for practicing and supporting magnetism. Mesmer made many influential friends among the royalty and in government. At one point, the Queen of France offered Mesmer a stipend to set up a treatment facility for the benefit of the French people. Finally, in 1784, Mesmer's impact on Paris reached such proportions that the French government directed the Royal Academies of Science and Medicine to investigate his claims.

The investigating commissions concluded that pursuing the healing claims of the method through examination of its outcomes with patients was unreasonably difficult, as it was impossible to assess the original state of the problems before treatment and to separate the effects of the natural course of healing and the imagination of the patient from the effects of the animal magnetic fluid. Therefore, the commission gave itself the task of testing for the existence of the fluid. They reasoned that if the fluid did not exist, there could be no beneficial effects from its use. Several of the experiments they conducted reveal much about the processes involved in magnetism. In one study, a young woman was placed behind a closed door, and the magnetist was placed on the other side. The commission members then varied independently when the operator was magnetizing her and when she was told he was magnetizing her. They found that when the patient was told that she was being magnetized, she fell into a crisis. When she was told she was not being magnetized, she remained calm, regardless of the activities of the magnetist.

Benjamin Franklin carried out a similar study. He asked Deslon to magnetize one of several apricot trees in a garden. Then a 12-year-old patient was blindfolded and led into the garden. At contact with the first tree, he "began to sweat profusely" and "fell into a violent crisis" at the fourth tree. Unfortunately for Mesmer and Deslon, the patient was never closer than 24 feet from the magnetized tree. When pressed for an explanation, Deslon attributed the result "to . . . the natural magnetism of the trees, reinforced by his own presence [at some distance from the boy] in the orchard" (Podmore, 1963, p. 58).

The French commission resoundingly condemned magnetism. They reported that not only did the fluid not exist, but that repeated exposure to crisis in the process of magnetism treatment undoubtedly led to the moral degeneracy of the patient. Despite the reports, the application of magnetism to healing continued and spread for the next 50 years. Learned societies continued their staunch opposition to the practice, and as physicians and others were drawn into it, they were excommunicated from their professional societies. Those who practiced Mesmerism formed their own societies and published their own journals well into the nineteenth century. The writings of these early practitioners give clear witness that, in spite of condemnation by all professional societies, the evidence of the effectiveness of the phenomena was so compelling to practitioners as to lead them to dismiss critics, a phenomenon noted today among psychotherapists (Austin, 1961).

As the practice of magnetism spread, the crisis as a necessary part of healing faded from prominence, and other phenomena were noted. Puységur, an early student of Mesmer, noted in 1784 that the phenomenon of somnambulism, an apparent state of sleep, was common with his patients. Mesmer had found it also, but had considered it an interruption to treatment. Also he ignored it because of its uncomfortable resemblance to the effects of witchcraft common only a century earlier. Puységur concluded that the state was highly beneficial to healing because in it the patient was fully open to receive the beneficial fluid from the operator. To increase his ability to aid patients, Puységur magentized a large tree to serve as a Baquet and attached a cord to it for patients to fasten round their bodies. Puységur wrote to his brother that more than 130 persons had gathered around the tree on a single morning. He wrote: "The tree is the best Baquet possible; every leaf radiates health: and all who come experience its salutary influence" (Podmore, 1963, p. 76). As the patients sat, stood, and laid around the tree, Puységur would choose patients and send them into the somnambulistic state by the touch of his hand or the direction of his wand. Other operators found that, in the somnambulistic state under the influence of magnetism, patients could diagnose their own illness and demonstrate abilities and knowledge far beyond their natural abilities, but they had no knowledge of their behavior when they recovered from the state.

Gradually, the learned societies' scepticism about the existence and power of magnetism spread to the populace, and the effectiveness of mesmerism faded. In the 1830s, John Elliotson, a prominent British physician, held a number of demonstrations of magnetism and introduced mesmerism into his practice of medicine. But a few years later, as the public's scepticism took its toll, he wrote:

> I believe I was not wrong; I believe that in what I originally saw, mesmerism played the parts precisely that I claimed for it. It is a wicked error to suppose that I was party to a deception, or to a whole series of deceptions, if you like. But I candidly say . . . that mesmerism, at the present moment, has no power to remove pain. It is a mystery; it had power, and I once saw a leg painlessly removed under its influence; but we are now in another cycle, and it seems to me that there are special periods only in which mesmeric phenomena can be induced. (Fromm & Shor, 1972, p. 30)

What can be concluded from history's brush with Mesmer? Unless we are willing to brand all the writers of the period as liars, it appears that persons were healed of numerous problems through interaction with Mesmer and his students. The healings closely resemble those of the Christian faith healers and exorcists of the previous 17 centuries (extending to today). In fact, in form, Mesmer's approach differed little from the faith healers active in Europe in the eighteenth century. The difference is not in the effects, nor much in the approach to the patient, but rather in the explanation given for the effects. Mesmer's explanation suited the beliefs of his contemporaries, who had become wary of supernatural explanations and were turning to "natural laws" to explain their experiences. Magnetism, electricity, and other natural forces were being introduced into popular thinking. Mesmer's explanation fit the new world people were coming to believe in.

Mesmer's clients came to him for healing, and they believed that he could heal them. As some reported healings, more came to be healed, and many were healed. It is apparent that the patients' belief that they would be healed provided the force for the healing. Mesmer and his students fervently believed in the existence and effectiveness of the special force that they had learned to control, and their belief and confidence undoubtedly went far in mobilizing the belief of their patients.

A phenomenon that the French magnetists labeled "rapport" is evident in the work of the magnetists and throughout the history of psychological helping. Magnetic theory posits harmony in magentic force relationships between bodies such that the flow of force from one body is matched by movement in the other. In accord with the theory, clients responded to the operator's activities in the ritual of the healing process: the events expected by the operator were produced (experienced) by the recipient. The mesmerists' beliefs about the effects of the fluid on the patient were reflected in the productions of the patients (in harmony or rapport) such that when both believed in the operation of the fluid and the effects it would produce, both found the events they expected, thereby confirming to both the reality of the fluid. Mesmer expected his patients to experience crisis, that is, to suffer more before they got better, and they did. The expectation was borrowed from the exorcist tradition of faith healing. Later, others expected somnambulism, anesthesia, and other phenomena. All obtained what they expected. This produces a particular problem in the realm of psychological helping. When clients produce or experience the events their therapists expect, the confirmation of the therapist's theories or predictions does not prove the theory is right, but only that it is believed. Likewise, the fact that a method produces cures does not prove that the philosophy or "scientific principles" on which the system is based is true, but only that the principles are believed by patient and therapist.

Thus, we have a curious truth in the area of psychological helping: finding a phenomenon or scientific principle definitely to be invalid does not mean that the application of the principle by believers will not be effective in treatment; conversely, the ability of a particular approach to achieve remarkable outcomes or to achieve predicted treatment events does not mean the thoery is valid, but only that it is believed. In the area of psychological helping, client and therapist belief that a theory is true is the necessary and sufficient condition for the theory to be effective as a healing agent. Thus we might expect a wide variety of effective therapies—as many as there are notions of truth in a particular culture. Psychological helping is necessarily culture-bound and culture-relative.

Mesmer makes one consider the possibility that the key component of change in therapy is belief. It matters little what the object of the belief is. Unfortunately, science has a history of rejecting effects due to belief as spurious. Perhaps this penchant of science is behind the apparent necessity for practitioners of any system to prove that the tenets of their theory are true. However, it would seem to be more profitable for psychologists to accept the effects of belief as real and powerful. In the material covered so far, few readers are likely to accept easily such powerful effects as the healing of pain, paralysis, tumors, burns, vision impairments, and all the other disabilities encountered in the last few pages as functions of belief. Zimbardo's recent statement "the cognitive control of just about everything" (1969), seems apropos. It is apparent that a key variable in therapy is the intensity and focus of belief.

In Mesmer's system, healing came from the influx of animal magnetism that corrected an imbalance of the same within the client. The process of cure was beyond the client's consciousness and self-control. The client's task was to change, and to accept the change as the inevitable effect of the powerful forces the therapist directed at the client. Self-control was not at issue. It is interesting to note that in Mesmer's system the therapist created the conditions that allowed the client to achieve balance, a balance that inevitably resulted from the therapist's intervention. Roger's client-centered theory of psychotherapy has the same essential outline today.

Hypnotism

As popular acceptance of mesmerism faded around 1840—1850, some scientists searched for more acceptable explanations of the powerful effects they had observed. Most of the practice of healing returned to the spiritual realm, and the practice of spiritism was at a high level by 1850. In the United States, spiritism and mesmerism led to a series of prophets who, in trancelike experiences, received divine revelations and formed cults, many of them centering on healing. In 1867, a prophet named Andrew Jackson Davis wrote *Nature's Divine Revelations,* in which he argued that disease was an invention of the imagination, having no reality in itself. He developed a following of cured persons and established a religious community. Phineas Parkhurst Quimby developed the principle further, and one of his disciples, Mary Baker Eddy, established a healing practice and a religious organization around the principle in about 1880. Her principles of healing were anchored in the works of Christ and the doctrine of disease as an illusion. She and her followers report many healings within the body of the faithful in the organization she founded, the Church of Christ Scientist (Christian Science).

Among the few men of science who dared to investigate the phenomena Mesmer introduced in the face of almost certain ostracism by all the scientific and medical bodies of the day was an Englishman named James Braid. In 1843, Braid published a book titled *Neurypnology, or the Rationale of Nervous Sleep; Considered in Relation with Animal Magnetism.* In it he demolished mesmerism in England and introduced the notion that somnambulism, anesthesia, and other phenomena noted in the practice of magnetism were due to the action of the nerves paralyzed in response to the suggestions of the operator. His work was immediately accepted by the scientific societies of the day in England, probably because it placed the phenomena in the framework of physiology, a growing and respectable body of knowledge and theories. He is considered to be the father of hypnosis, as it has come to be called. Still, widespread acceptance of hypnosis did not occur for some 20 years more.

The work of Jean Martin Charcot finally resulted in the full acceptance in the 1870s of the interpersonal influence phenomena we have now traced over 18 centuries. Charcot was a French physician. He obtained his degree in Paris in 1853 and was appointed professor at the University of Paris. He was also appointed in 1862 to Salpêtrière, a mental hospital for women. Charcot was trained in the new science of neurology. He began to treat his patients with hypnosis, and he concluded that hypnosis and hysteria were neurological phenomena. His careful observations of the progress of therapy led to a theory that the hypnotic trance developed in three stages, released from the patient physiologically as a result of modification in muscular states, reflex movements, and sensory responses. These three inevitable processes of hypnosis were lethargy, catalepsy, and somnambulism. Charcot presented his theory to the French Academy of Sciences and won complete acceptance, no doubt because of his physiological explanation. In practice, Charcot did much the same things Mesmer did. He fixed the patient's attention on one object, and he touched the patient. An essential part of Charcot's induction technique was to tap the client on the head in order to induce somnambulism. Charcot fell victim to the rapport phenomenon we discussed earlier. Because he believed certain events would occur, his patients quietly complied, and this his careful experimental work proved the validity of his assertions, assertions found wanting and absurd by 1910.

A contemporary of Charcot, Hippolyte Bernheim, was converted to belief in the reality of the changes obtained in mesmerism by a French country doctor, A. A. Liebeault, in 1882. While accepting the reality of the effects, Bernheim rejected the magnetism explanation and developed the doctrine of suggestion, which he published in two books around 1884: *De la Suggestion et ses Applications á la Therapeutique (Suggestion and Its Therapeutic Applications)* and *L'Hypnotisme et les Suggestions dans Leur Rapport avec la Médecine Légale et les Maladies Mentales (The Relationship of Hypnotism and Suggestion with Legal Medicine and Mental Sicknesses)*. Liebeault's primary work was published in 1866, and it laid out much of the modern doctrine of psychosomatic medicine: *De Sommeil et des States Analogues, Considéres Surtout au point de Vue de l'Action de la Moral sure le Physique (Sleep and Similar States Considered from the Point of View of the Action of the Moral on the Physical)*. Both men worked at a hospital in Nancy, France, and carried on a lengthy battle with Charcot over the basis of hypnosis, with their view taking the day by about 1910. A fourth man, Pierre Janet, was Charcot's pupil and successor. He accepted the Bernheim doctrine, and hypnotism as we know it today was established.

Dynamism

The Bernheim doctrine postulated an interactional process wherein another's suggestions influenced a person's mental processes and the person's mental processes influenced his or her physical properties. While Bernheim and his colleagues pointed to the psychological processes through which interpersonal influence through interaction operated, the doctrine lacked a healing agent that conveyed the notion of inevitable healing so central to the spiritual and magnetic systems. It remained for another physician trained in Vienna to recombine the power of interpersonal influence and a doctrine of a healing agent in a system that fit the thinking and beliefs of the time.

In 1876, Sigmund Freud was a student under Ernest Brücke in Brücke's physiological institute in the Medical Faculty at the University of Vienna. Freud's ambition was to devote his life to science in the new and exciting area of physiological research. His teacher, Brücke, was bitterly set against the vitalist tradition in physiology and insisted that the physiological processes were due to natural physical forces in the living organism. He believed that a physical-chemical force was the only force active within the organism. This principle was held in equal valence with a newly enunciated law of physics, the law of the conservation of energy.

One year after his graduation, the young Freud reluctantly turned away from his dream of obtaining a university appointment as a research scientist and turned to private practice to support his growing family. He joined the practice of Dr. Joseph Breuer, who was treating hysterics with a new method called *catharsis*. Patients were hypnotized and led to remember the traumatizing incident believed to be the cause of the problem, and thereby their symptoms were alleviated. Using the ideas of energy conservation and the physical basis of all energy in the living organism, Freud and Breuer conceived of psychic events as depending on physical energy that required discharge when the level was too high. In order to learn more abut the basic method of treatment, Freud went to Paris to study under Charcot in 1885—1886. There, Freud learned two important facts. First, Charcot and his students were finding that patients were becoming less responsive to hypnosis, and the effects of hypnotic treatment were beginning to wear off with a distressing reemergence of the symptoms in increasing numbers of patients. Second, Freud found that Janet and colleagues were beginning to think about multiple systems of consciousness, especially as a result of observations that a suggestion given during hypnosis was not available to recall upon awakening. The forgotten suggestion was nonetheless carried out posthypnotically, and patients readily rationalized pseudoreasons for their unconsciously motivated acts. This observation had a profound effect on Freud's thinking. It was the beginning of his system of unconscious forces— forces that lay hidden beneath the conscious mind and form a seething caldron of immense power and are the primary determinants of human behavior (hence the label dynamism). Freud combined knowledge of the latest principles of science, rigorous training as a scientific observer, and observations of unconscious behavior determinants into a therapy system that provided a rationale for psychological change within a context that was believable to the patients and the scientific bodies of the day.

Freud's system struck at the heart of the notion of people as being endowed by God with rationality to conduct themselves and to explore the ordered universe. Instead of conscious and rational determinants of behavior, Freud saw behavior as determined in the unconscious and irrational. Persons rationalized what they found themselves doing rather than determined what they would do rationally. Drawing on the most current scientific thinking of the day, Freud reasoned that patients' problems resulted from some blockage of energy that rendered them unable to deal with current difficulties in living. As less energy was available because of the large amount of energy tied to unresolved psychological events of development, the person was rendered vulnerable to current stress. Treatment consisted of finding and reviewing or reliving the traumatic events or unresolved issues so that energy could be released and applied to current problems. It was thus expected that reworking the traumas of the past would automatically enable the person to deal with the present.

Probably Freud's most lasting contribution to psychological change was method-ological. Because hypnotically induced catharsis was becoming decreasingly effective and many patients were experiencing relapses, Freud introduced the notion that the patient's failure to improve and the relapse of improvement were strong evidence for the correctness of his theory of the causes of the problem. He introduced a "catch 22" clause to mental healing which paradoxically took lack of improvement as proof of his doctrine concerning the reality of strong forces of repression and resistance. Within his system, sudden change was (and is) looked upon as artificial and suspect. Resistance was expected and required of the patient. The dramatic importance of this innovation can be seen in comparing his therapeutic approach to patients who do not improve to that of Mesmer's. For Mesmer, a failure to improve struck a dagger at the explanatory system, for how could a universal fluid not be effective? Perhaps the operator failed to transmit enough of his fluid. Alternatively, the theory is wrong. Clearly, for Mesmer's theory to be effective, it must be used only with those who believe it or who can be persuaded to believe it. Likewise, failure in spiritual healing can only be ascribed to the person's lack of belief, or the unfathomable will of God. Disbelief cannot be used to generate belief. In Freud's system, however, a lack of improvement showed the seriousness of the repression and the patient's strong defenses against the dangerous material at the root of the problem. The more patients resisted changing, the more they were in need of therapy. Thus, client resistance to change became the therapist's means of proving to the patient the truth of the theory. In previous theories, the patient needed to believe in a therapist's theory in order to enter the therapy and receive healing. In Freud's system, the patient must come to believe in the system to get out of the therapy: as disbelief intensifies, the therapy intensifies. This "catch 22" feature is a standard part of methods of change through interaction since Freud.

Freud's second technical innovation was the concept of transference. Freud found that gaining insight into the events constricting the patient's energy supply was not enough. Patients needed to carry out their symptoms in their relationship with the therapist. Thus, behaving toward the therapist as if the therapist were an appropriate target for symptomatic behavior became a central tenet for Freud. The therapist's key task was to encourage the transference, and to frustrate it at the same time by not responding to the client's productions as the client expected. Some expression of transference is also a key component of change through interaction in all subsequent therapies, and it will be discussed in Chapter 5 as the negation paradox.

In Freud's system, as in the spiritism and magnetism systems, change was not a result of the person trying to change, but of the inevitable action of uncontrollable forces unleashed by the therapy. For Freud, change came from the natural equipment of the organism, from its basic processes of energy flow which had been temporarily disrupted by unfortunate earlier experiences. With the therapist's help, energies were released to the psychological processes of the patient, and behavior change resulted from their natural flow, without conscious efforts by the patient. The patient changes as a result of successful therapy. Freud located the healing forces within the person rather than in a universal fluid or the supernatural. Freud's notions that psychological problems stem from unfortunate previous experiences, and psychological health results from unleashed intrinsic processes, are apparent in nearly all therapy systems since Freud.

Freud's system was well suited to the society that spawned it. Freud viewed humans as hedonistic and self-oriented, ruled by pleasure and in need of socialization and restraint, a view that fell well within the basic Judeo-Christian notions of the character of man since the Fall. Yet, the system was "scientific" and thus able to benefit from the high regard for science. Science was regarded as the answer to all mysteries and infallible. The system was based on the then latest principles of science, yet because of its "catch 22" nature and the inferential nature of its basic precepts, it was ironically not open to refutation. In the practice of Freud's system, the effects of rapport were apparent: patients produced the events believed inevitable by the therapist, proving for both the validity of the system.

Freud's system had a life span about equal to Mesmer's. Mesmer's system had major application from 1778 to 1840, about 60 years. Freud's system was the major force in psychological healing from 1900 to 1950, about 50 years. Freud's system is today the major treatment system for psychiatrists and is very influential in clinical psychology, although its use and influence are attenuating rapidly. The scientific community has for some time been attacking the position as unscientific and untestable, and the general populace has been overexposed to its tenets, weakening the system's ability to gain belief and thus heal.

Humanism

Coming out of the Age of Reason and rooted in the Renaissance is a doctrine of the basic goodness of people. People are viewed not only as morally good, but also as endowed with true reason and an ability to rise above and control creation. The doctrine originally tied this goodness to God's creative design. By the twentieth century, the tie was broken. The doctrine exalted the individual and his or her emerging abilities, and it found its greatest champion in Carl Rogers. Rogers was raised in a fundamental Christian home, and he experienced a great freeing and liberation from contact with liberal Protestant humanism as a young man. From this experience, he, like thousands of others in the last 40 years, elected to save souls through counseling rather than through the Christian ministry he had originally planned. In 1951, he published his key book, *Client-Centered Therapy*. His approach fit the American culture and caught on like wildfire in counseling and, later, in clinical psychology.

Rogers argued that people were basically good and were intrinsically self-actualizing as intelligent, moral, realistic, and competent. Unfortunately, in their experiences with others, people's basic tendencies could be distorted, especially by having conditions of worth placed on them that lead them to seek approval rather than actualization. Therapy consisted of creating a nonthreatening, safe, and loving environment in which the person could regain his or her balance and recommence self-growth. Rogers was trained in scientific methods and embarked on several remarkable efforts to provide empirical support for his notions. Rogers captured two strong belief structures in America: the supremacy of the individual and the power of science. He had nearly total dominance over the field of counseling and much of clinical psychology from the mid-1950s to the mid-1960s. While the humanistic tradition remains strong in these fields, Rogers' influence is waning, which no doubt reflects American society's increasing disillusionment with permissiveness and the notion that people are basically good.

Other humanists, such as Albert Ellis, emerged about the same time as Rogers and, while not gaining dominance as quickly as Rogers, they are becoming increasingly powerful on the current scene. Cognitive therapy is based on the notion of the primacy of reason over a person's actions and emotions and is an expression of the Age of Reason. Like Rogers, cognitivists believe that persons experience difficulties because of distorting events in development. Therapy has the function of reinforcing the person's rationality, which will bring the person to change.

Rogers explicitly places change outside the efforts of the client. Change can be expected to occur spontaneously as an outward manifestation of the intrinsic actualization process. Ellis and other cognitive theorists expect persons to behave in logical and rational ways as the distortions of the persons' experiences are removed. The increasing dominance of cognitive and self-control approaches to therapy probably represents the resurgence of the rational view of man following several decades of behaviorism and dynamism, and the recent emphasis in scientific psychology on the cognitive control of behavior.

Behaviorism

Behaviorism, like dynamism, stems from the tradition, late in the Age of Reason, of viewing humans as part of the natural order and therefore open to control and prediction. It draws heavily on the prestige of scientific psychology for its belief effects. In behaviorism, the patient's effort to change is not the cause of change. Instead, the controlling impact of environmental events acting on the person is responsible. The person's behavior is orderly and can be changed through systematic application of scientific principles. Behavioral applications are increasingly emphasizing sources of control within the person, and they seem to be merging with the cognitive approach discussed above.

Socialism

While most philosophies undergirding the process of change through personal interaction since Freud have emphasized the need to free the individual's growth processes from the repressive and distorting influence of socialization, the last 20 years have seen the development of philosophies with opposing emphasis. In the 1960s, O. Hobart Mowrer introduced the notion that many personal difficulties were the result of the individual's undersocialization rather than oversocialization.

He believed that individuals had difficulties because they acted too much on the basis of their selfish and hedonistic desires without sufficient restraint concerning the effects of their actions on others and the long-term consequences of their actions. He proposed that such persons were behaving irresponsibly and were in need of confession, repentance, and renewed effort to behave responsibly. His pronouncements were partially a return to the Judeo-Christian ethic of social responsibility. Because of Mowrer's prestige in scientific psychology and in reaction to the long tradition of permissiveness in psychological treatment, his pronouncements had considerable impact. A few years later, William Glasser presented an approach to therapy that emphasized social responsibility and social reality. His approach has gained increasing importance, especially in the treatment of individuals whose behavioral problems are aversive to others, such as juvenile delinquents, penal inmates, and drug abusers.

Another stream of the emerging socialism tradition emphasizes the human social unit as the primary cause of human behavior. This point of view flows from general systems theory and its emphasis on interdependence and the circularity of cause and effect. Gregory Bateson introduced a systems model for understanding the behavior of individuals, and he and his colleagues are responsible for the development of treatment tactics for individuals in the context of their supporting social system, such as the family (Jackson, 1968a, 1968b). An individual's difficulties in this framework are seen as arising from the individual's efforts to gain control of the system in which his or her behavior is embedded. Treatment consists of stimulating changes in the social system that require the individual to change. As with Mowrer and Glasser, health is seen as behaviors that foster harmonious functioning of the social system, while problems are defined as behaviors that disrupt the social system. An influential writer in this tradition has defined the cause of difficulties as hubris, overgrown individual pride (Palazzoli, Boscolo, Cecchin, & Prata, 1978).

These emerging approaches to psychological helping and change reflect the changing zeitgeist in American society, and they have the function of providing systems that patients can believe and thus providing a rationale for change. The system's view of causes of behavior reflects an important paradigm change in the science of human behavior. Most certainly, it is a reflection of the end of the Age of Reason with its emphasis on the individual and the emergence of the Age of Socialism with its emphasis on the group.

PERSUASION AND HEALING REVISITED

The belief structures that have clothed the social influence process of behavior change through interaction are presented in a time flow in Figure 1. Beginning with the Yahweh tradition, Christian healing and exorcism occur throughout the 2000-year period. Secular approaches begin in 1773 with Father Hell and Mesmer. From Mesmer develops hypnosis, spiritism, and Christian Science. From hypnosis comes Freud, with hypnosis a continuing influence throughout the period. Freudian tradition spawns humanism, existentialism, and socialism. Behaviorism runs

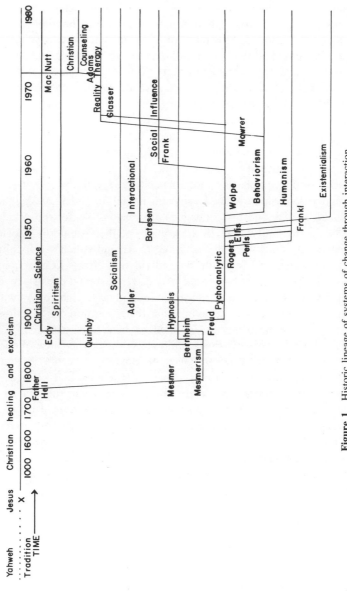

Figure 1 Historic lineage of systems of change through interaction.

parallel to the Freudian tradition. Socialism is seen in interactionism, social influence models, the "reality" therapies of Mowrer and Glasser, and new forms of Christian counseling (Adams, 1970). Many of these practices exist side-by-side in the multibelief culture of today.

The many different clothes of psychological helping in the last 2000 years reinforce Frank's notions about the requirements for change reviewed at the beginning of this chapter. From a historical perspective, the most important requirement for change is the client's belief in the existence of a powerful force that can bring about the required changes in the client's life, a force that is activated in the process of interaction with the helper. It is important that the action of the healing agent have some expected process or sequence so that the sufferer is able to carry through the required change. It is apparent that if the client and helper believe, the events of treatment will occur via the rapport phenomenon and will provide evidence of the reality of the healing agent. If both clients and counselors believe, a system will be effective in helping people change; outcome research will prove the system is valid. Evidence of the effectiveness of a system in helping people change proves that the system is successful in tapping belief and in overcoming disbelief. The evidence does not prove that the system is in some sense objectively valid.

The French commissions appointed to investigate Mesmer were right to eschew investigation of the effectiveness of magnetism in healing as a means for determining the reality of the magnetic fluid. Such exploration of outcome for any system cannot prove its reality, but only its fit with the beliefs of clients. On the other hand, the commissions' conclusion—that because the fluid did not exist, it could not heal—was ill-conceived and misguided. It did heal, as do all the systems we have discussed, given that the participants in the treatments believe. Pragmatically, persons dedicated to psychological healing must be prepared to accept success as the criterion of the utility of a system. The effectiveness of an approach rests on the operation of social influence factors, one of which is a theory that the sufferer will accept. Reasonableness or objective proof of the system is irrelevant, except as such factors contribute to a client's acceptance of the theory. In the Age of Reason and with modern science, reasonableness and objective scientific backing have been important to the acceptance and thus effectiveness of systems. In the Age of Faith, scientific evidence was irrelevant. Today, with widespread disillusionment with science, reasonableness and scientific proof are decreasingly important in inspiring belief.

An effective theory vests the helper with authority or expertness in controlling forces that will work for the client's benefit. The helper is annointed by God for the ministry of healing, or has learned to control basic elements of nature as magnetic fluid, or through study and experience has gained special insights into the nature of persons and their behavior that the helper can apply to the specific situation of the client. The healing force is unleashed through interaction with the healer, and it works beyond and more fundamentally than the usual resources of the client. The client is found to have unexpected internal resources, unleashed energies, or powerful potentialities that drive the patient inextricably to health. Perhaps new forces from the outside are brought to bear, such as animal fluid, reinforcers, or spirits. Operating from such forces, change is uncontrollable. It is the result of forces that work outside of the person's willpower, outside of the person's effort to produce change. Some theories for which rationality is the key belief vest uncontrollable power in the rationality of the approach; rational problem solving *will* allow the person to change. All approaches operate on the principle that the forces unleashed through interaction with the therapist will inextricably lead to change.

Freud's innovations provide several critical observations about the requirements for change. While creating change with believers may be relatively easy, creating belief is much of the battle. Freud introduced an important refinement for dealing with nonbelief and resistance to change. In systems previous to his, nonbelief could be countered only with more vigorous efforts to persuade. While Christianity can appeal to God's inexorable ways and the power of the Evil One to account for failure, Mesmer's system was helpless against disbelief and faltered and declined rapidly with the rise of skepticism. Freud introduced the notion that resistance proves the validity of his system. The person's resistance to insight and change is the evidence of defense mechanisms, of the ego's actions to protect itself from the id's unbearable attack and the danger posed by reality confrontation. Freud's innovation responded to growing resistance among clients to hypnosis and cathartic treatment, and it countered opposition to treatment. Certainly, skepticism is a common tool clients use to counter therapists' efforts to entice them into changing, and therapists must have ways of countering the client's resistance and to turn resistance into a force toward change. Erickson's (Haley, 1973) and Haley's (1963) emphasis on siding with the resistance are clear manifestations of this strategy, and the paradox of encouraging symptoms as a means of eliminating them is nearly universal in counseling and psychotherapy systems, a strategy described later as the negation paradox.

Freud's second innovation was his emphasis on transference. Freud was more interested in behavior changes than were his predecessors; although, like them, he focused on psychosomatic problems as well and did not differentiate between psychosomatic and behavioral problems. Freud noted that persons reported troubling relationships with others in their histories and would bring their troubled patterns into the interaction with the therapist. Freud saw that the resolution of transference was critical to the success of the therapy. He was the first "interactionist" and implicitly introduced the notion that the therapist's job was to encourage the client to act out his or her symptomatic interactional patterns with the therapist (i.e., to encourage transference). The therapist then frustrated the pattern through responding in most unorthodox ways such as silence, acceptance, interpretation, and reflection, frustrating the patient to the point of abandoning the symptom pattern and thus resolving the transference. This basic strategy is most clear in Gestalt therapy with its concept of frustration (Eshbaugh, 1976), but it is also apparent in all of the talking cures of today.

Finally, Freud's work points out the importance of a therapy system having an agent or entity responsible for the change that exerts a continuous action on the client, with the action extending indefinitely beyond treatment. Christian healers (and witches) have continuous action agents, as did Mesmer. The hypnotists who followed Mesmer did not, and they were discouraged to find their clients' symptoms returning in time. Freud reintroduced the continuous action agent, as have all subsequent systems. Most of the agents in current systems are growth processes inside the client. Some, such as in behaviorism, are external agents such as environmental and social reinforcement, which are themselves tied to the conditioning potentialities of the clients.

This brief look at the history of persuasion and healing suggests that the following principles are important for healing through interaction:

1. Client belief in a doctrine of how change occurs is essential to change.
2. Therapist belief in a doctrine of change is essential; the therapist's belief has effects through encouraging the client's belief.
3. The doctrine must have an agent of change that is released or enabled in the treatment process, has inevitable effects, works beyond the client's self-control in creating uncontrollable change, and has long-term carry through.
4. The course of treatment and change must have ritual so that the patient and therapist can know that the process is proceeding and can point to the expected events via the rapport phenomenon to assure themselves that the doctrine is true.
5. The doctrine must be able to overcome disbelief and resistance, perhaps by converting them into proof of the validity of the doctrine or making them the means of change. The doctrine needs a "catch 22" clause.
6. The doctrine must generate therapist behavior that encourages the patient to introduce symptomatic interactional behavior into the interchange with the therapist and discourages and eliminates the symptoms.

CHAPTER 2

Interaction Dynamics

Change is a consequence of the client's belief that change will occur operationalized through interaction with a helper. It seems not to matter what is believed as long as the system has a change or healing agent, and as long as the person believes in the inevitable progress of the agent. Theories of counseling and psychotherapy focus on how healing agents bring about change and how counselor verbal interventions facilitate the process. But why do counselors' remarks affect clients at all? Why clients accept, process, and integrate counselor remarks is seldom addressed in counseling theories because it is assumed.

Freud noted that in the relationship between counselor and client it took something special to make counselor remarks have their desired impact on clients. He labeled the special condition transference. Theorists since Freud have recognized the special requirements of the interaction between counselor and client for therapy to have its desired effect, and they have emphasized certain qualities of the relationship between counselor and client as necessary and, for some, sufficient for change. Among major theorists, Carl Rogers (1957) brought the greatest attention to the counseling relationship. He argued that a relationship of empathy, regard, and genuineness was critical to counseling success. The purpose of this chapter is to identify the aspects of relationship that are required for counselor remarks to affect client thinking, acting, and feeling.

A MODEL OF INTERACTION

People as Open Systems

People are open biological systems that act on their environments to maintain themselves and grow in the direction of increasing differentiation and complexity. Von Bertalanffy (1968) applied general systems theory to biological organisms and defined them as open systems as opposed to closed systems. The quantity of energy of a closed system is fixed, and the system's behavior is summarized in the laws of energy conservation and entropy. Freud's views of human behavior are based on these principles, which were newly discovered when he was a student with Brücke in Vienna. Closed systems experiencing energy diffusion to the lowest potential of organization over time. For example, heat in a sealed and insulated area will dissipate throughout the area rather than remain differentiated in hot and cold spots. In contrast, living open systems continually draw energy from their environments and increase and maintain their structural differentiation. Living organisms act on their environments to obtain needed inputs and avoid environmental conditions that threaten their integrity. Growth and differentiation are the result of intrinsic qualities of the organism that are just beginning to be understood.

Changes within the organism are responsible for its behavior. Internal changes may originate within or outside of the organism. Behavior is intricately tied to intrinsic processes described by concepts such as "steady states" and "equifinality." Internal elements of living organisms maintain relatively constant levels of interaction, or steady states. An easily identifiable behavioral consequence of steady states is periodic eating. Anyone who has gone beyond dinner time without eating knows the biological and psychological consequences that inexorably increase efforts to acquire dinner. Yet, living organisms are not simply maintainers of steady states, for the states constantly shift. Organisms increase in complexity and differentiation in time as if there were some ultimate pattern or state to be achieved. They strive to achieve the same end regardless of the current environmental state, a phenomenon captured in the label "equifinality." An organism will alter its behavior as required by a wide variety of circumstances to achieve a particular end or state. Behavior is a function of rhythmic and developmental processes intrinsic to the state of living. While it may be useful to conceptualize persons with separate biological, psychological, and spiritual frameworks, persons are unified beings who act on their environments to create the conditions necessary for their development and maintenance.

People as Social Beings

People behave to control their environments. Their abilities and skills are directed to that purpose. They are able to sense important aspects and variations in the environment, to act on the environment, and to remember relationships among events. Behavioral research has revealed orderly relationships between peoples' acts and environmental conditions that suggest the existence of these capabilities and capacities (Skinner, 1953). The research also suggests that the environment controls people rather than the other way around. It seems clear that if people strive to control their environment, their environment will exert control on them. For example, if a gunner is bent on hitting a moving target, the target will exert control on the gunner's behavior, but only because of the gunner's determination to hit the target. When the gunner develops other interests, the target is stripped of its ability to affect the gunner.

A complicating factor in understanding behavior is that people are social creatures who spend most of their time interacting with others. Most people do not draw their sustenance directly from interacting with the nonhuman environment, but from interacting with other people. The system of people in concert produces the sustenance for the individuals that make up the system. Individual existence and development depend on integration into the social system and on the system's success in generating resources and distributing them among its members. The critical task for everyone is to interact with others in ways that sustain the person and the system. Because their environment is essentially made up of others, people behave to control others and in turn are controlled by others. Human behavior is almost entirely social behavior. It is intended to influence others and is influenced by others in the social collective.

"Behavior" denotes the relationship between states or actions of an entity and states or actions of its environment (Klir & Valach, 1967). A person's social behavior is the relationship between the individual's actions and the actions of those with whom he or she interacts. Understanding a person's social behavior requires identifying the effects on another's actions that the person's actions achieve. An individual's social behavior can be understood only in the context of interaction with others.

Interaction

Interpersonal behavior seeks to control. Yet, because each person is independent, self-generating, and willful, to say that one person controls another is wrong if control is viewed as direct, mechanical, or inevitable. Rather, people create circumstances that invite others to act one way rather than another. People make certain responses more attractive and others less attractive and invite interactants to take advantage of the contingencies thus created. But others cannot be compelled to do anything. Others might feel they have no "reasonable" choice, but this is quite different from having no choice. Living creatures cannot be forced to do anything because they are self-determining. But they can be enticed into almost anything because they are vulnerable to their own needs and seek to control their environments for their benefit. Controlling another's actions is a matter of creating opportunities for the other that are too good to ignore, or making alternatives too bad to choose. Changing another's behavior, changing the relationship between his or her actions and the actions of the environment, is a matter of shifting the other's perceptions of the consequences of actions and events so that realignment among them is too advantageous to be ignored.

When two people interact, they form a system that is distinguishable as a unit. They are the elements of the system and are interrelated by their communications or behaviors with respect to one another. Their actions are partially controlled by the system they created. They form an open system in that outside events affect the interaction. Behavior in the system has characteristics that transcend the characteristics of either element. One such characteristic is *circular causality*. Each person's acts are at once a cause of the other's acts and an effect of the other's acts. Each act is a link in a continuous chain of interaction. To label one party's acts as the originating cause of an act of the other is to superimpose an arbitrary punctuation on the events (Watzlawick, Beavin, & Jackson, 1967). Each act is a cause of the events that follow and a consequence of the events that preceded. Each act carries the history of previous actions forward to the next event. In responding to the other's last act, each person is responding also to his or her previous act, the meaning of which is carried in the other's last act. In this sense, each person's actions are responses to his or her previous actions. Thus, a person's attempt to change the other's behavior is often an attempt to alter the impact of the person's previous attempts to change the other's behavior.

Circular causality and other associated effects are the consequences of each person's environment being another who is working to control the person. Neither person is strictly controlled by the other, but is acting on the other to exert control. Each person strives to entice the other to act in ways that will render the interaction to the person's purposes. Control of another can be achieved only by shaping the other's efforts to control. Efforts to control are based on a person's purposes in a relationship and the person's impressions of the characteristics and vulnerabilities of the other. Thus, managing other's impressions of one's characteristics and vulnerabilities is a vital part of relationship control. The other can be enticed into behaving as desired by giving the impression that such behavior will generate the relationship he or she desires.

Every action in an interaction simultaneously responds to the other's action and invites the other to seek to control the relationship by behaving as the person wishes. In contrast, interacting with a tree with the intent of chopping it down is simple (Minuchin, 1974). The woodsman need not worry about the tree's impression of his objectives in order to induce the tree to behave so as to render it vulnerable to being chopped down. In interaction with persons, however, guiding their impressions of our charcteristics and intentions is a major concern, for their behavior is guided by their perceptions of us and our intentions. Managing others' impressions is a vital part of attempts to encourage others to behave in a way that allows our communications to have intended effects on their behavior.

Figure 2 depicts the two-person interaction. In the diagram, each person's communications are his or her attempts to control the actions of the other. But for the other, the person's communications are feedback on the effects of the other's earlier attempts to control the person. Communications reflect (a) what the sender would like the other to do, (b) the sender's understanding of the other's purposes, (c) the sender's predictions of how the other needs to see the sender to encourage the other to behave as the sender desires, and (d) the sender's prediction of how to capitalize on the other's purposes and intentions to invite the other to seek to control the sender in a way consonant with the sender's objectives. Communications are complex.

Communications are not straightforward because persons are concerned about managing others' impressions and expectations in order to influence how others attempt to control them. The underlying principle is that another's responses to a person's attempt to control the other is the other's attempt to control the person. Thus, the person's task is to influence how the other predicts the person might best be controlled. The key to effective relationship control is to induce the other to try to control us as we wish to be controlled. The task of control is not to command the

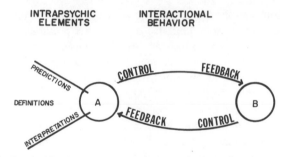

Figure 2   The interlocking interaction system of control and feedback between two people.

other to do as we wish but to present the other opportunities to control us with actions we wish them to perform. Impression management is a critical aspect of interpersonal relationships. The success of a person's attempts to control the other is indicated in the other's attempts to control the person, which is the feedback function of the other's communications.

Aspects of Communication

Every communications has content and relationship implications (Watzlawick, Beavin, & Jackson, 1967). The *content* of a communication is the manifest or symbolic message it carries. Thus, the content of the words you (the reader) are reading is interactional communication. Watzlawick, Beavin, and Jackson note that much of the content of a message is carried in the *digital* communication system, the sounds and letters that combine in a myriad of ways to convey precise meanings that are generally agreed upon and understood within a verbal community. The *relationship* implication of communications is the understanding of how communicator and communicatee should relate that is implied in the communication. For example, the letters and words you are reading are communicating a content to you, but they also propose a relationship between you, the reader, and us, the writers. We are proposing that we "talk" and you "listen." As you do so, you are accepting the relationship this communication proposes. Likewise, a teacher lecturing before a class is proposing a relationship in which he or she presents and the class members take notes and listen. As the class members file in and sit in their chairs with pens poised expectantly, they are proposing a relationship in which they listen and the lecturer talks. Anyone who has attempted to get class participation after a period of lecturing knows that the relationship is established by both parties and is very difficult to change unilaterally.

As people talk to one another, they are simultaneously presenting content and proposing relationships of a particular kind. Even the content aspects of communication carry the message, "Ours is a relationship that should include talking about these matters." Issues like who has overt control, when and how this control is to be exercised, how broad the relationship is to be, what behavior is to be included, when it is to occur—all must be dealt with in any relationship.

Usually, how people relate to each other is negotiated outside of their awareness, and attention is focused on the content aspect of communications. Sometimes the nature of a relationship is the content of communication. This usually occurs only when "automatic" relationship determination aspects of communications do not produce the outcomes the parties expected. Even then, however, conversation about relationship is itself an attempt to effect the relationship desired rather than objective analysis of the relationship. What persons say about a relationship is intended to change the relationship according to their desires rather than to objectively describe the interaction. Counselors focus on their relationships with clients as a means of changing clients' behaviors rather than to objectively describe the relationships.

Communication occurs on two channels, digital and analogical (Bateson, 1972). *Digital communication,* mentioned earlier, is that finite set of sounds and letters that can be combined in a multitude of ways to produce many meanings. *Analogical communication* is comprised of gestures, voice qualities, body movements, and facial movements; it is a good deal less flexible than the digital system. It is a more primitive communication system (Bateson, 1972). Digital and analogical communication media qualify one another so that a particular message can be congruent, where the two channels reinforce the same meaning, or incongruent, where they qualify one another to change the meaning of the message from what the digital communication proposes. For example, when a man digitally communicates that he loves a woman, but at the same time he grimaces, speaks in a low voice, and holds up his hand as if to fend her off, she may feel he is just saying that to fend off some unwanted threat, or as a joke, but she is unlikely to interpret the message as a straightforward statement of affection. Digital and analogical channels combine in the determination of both content and relationship aspects of communication.

Intrapsychic Components

An individual communicates content and relationship meanings on both digital and analogical channels to control another's content and relationship messages. Each communication is also feedback to the other about the impact of his or her previous messages exchanged in the system. Personal causes stem from the desires, previous experiences, and response capabilities of the interactants. Personal influences on communications are conceptualized as intrapsychic processes of interpretation, definition, and prediction as indicated in Figure 2. Another's communication is feedback about the effects of previous communications, the other's purposes, the impressions the other thinks the person will be vulnerable to, and the other's impressions of the person. People interpret the meanings of feedback according to their previous experiences. Interpretations of the meaning of feedback are limited by previous experience, and they tend to remain stable. Interpretive frameworks change as each new experience of feedback is processed, but dramatic change is unusual. People tend to construe new experiences in terms of their previous understandings and therefore tend to pick up that which fits their interpretive screens.

A second intrapsychic process is the comparison and evaluation of interpreted feedback in terms of the relationship definition the person hoped to achieve. Definitions of relationships are the positions or roles persons wish to have vis-à-vis others. Relationship definitions are derived from a person's past experiences in positions with others, especially in the primary family, as well as the person's notions of situational constraints on appropriate positions. In the primary family, persons learn a number of definitions or roles by living them and from the modeling of parents, siblings, and friends. The relationship definitions a person acquires, and the contexts they are tied to as appropriate, are relatively fixed but also change with experience. They are the templates against which the person compares interpreted feedback to determine if his or her previous efforts at control have created the appropriate responses from the other. If the obtained and desired behaviors diverge, the person may switch to another definition or may make further attempts to obtain appropriate behavior from the other.

The third intrapsychic process is the prediction of what behavior will stimulate desired feedback from the other. From past experiences, persons know about relationships among their own behaviors and feedback from others. Persons acquire through experience, modeling, and other sources knowledge of functional relationships that guide them on how desired changes in others' behaviors can be obtained through the impact of their own behaviors. The repertoire grows with experience. However, the basic patterning comes from experiences in the primary family system, and substantial change is unlikely without new relationships that have many of the same qualities that primary relationships had.

Repertoires of interpretations, definitions, and predictions are intimately tied to internal states and exist to serve the person's needs for maintenance and development. People use experiences to improve their ability to survive and to grow as entities. They are not controlled, but are guided by experience as they act on the environment for their own purposes. Concepts like learning, extinction, secondary reinforcement, and negative reinforcement capture many of the behavioral characteristics of persons, but they give the wrong impression of persons being controlled by environments rather than of persons using experiences to control their environments. Initiative and power of action reside with the person, not the environment.

Most of the processes of interpretation, definition comparison, and prediction are not available in consciousness. There is a gulf of difference between behaving and being self-conscious about behaving. Reflective, thoughtful behavior is the exception rather than the rule (Taylor & Fiske, 1978). Behavior has the purpose of gaining control of the environment, and it usually occurs without reflective thought. Bateson (1972) has referred to the concept of deep programming to capture the notion that persons process information with the products of previous experience but are not self-conscious about the processing. Bateson presents the analogy of television to illustrate the limitations of awareness. Awareness is like the picture on the video screen. We can self-consciously attend to and manipulate the objects and relationships on the screen. However, the screen does not reflect the many processes and decisions that occurred in placing the picture on the screen. Tremendous selection and interpretation has occurred before we become aware, and these processes are outside of our consciousness. Unconscious processes reflect our

e·   · have once been relationships and decisions we were aware of,
                                    ·ion they "sank" out of consciousness. Langer (1978)
                                          ·· ᵏᵉᵉᵖ items in consciousness is most
                                                    f repetitious, overlearned
                                                    essing matters while at the

)erson interacts with another
                                                    e new, highly critical, very
                                                    tention are in awareness. An
                                                    others or to themselves only
                                                    s. Consciousness is no doubt
)le to describe the contents of
                                                    community (Skinner, 1957); it
                                                    consciousness about conscious-

Laws o.

The model of interaction   persons act to control others and that
interaction behavior is a function o. ._ m and intrapsychic causes. A number of
relationships can be deduced from these assumptions about behavior in interaction.
These relationships were first suggested in the seminal work of Jackson, Bateson,
Haley, Watzlawick, and their collegues (Jackson, 1968a, 1968b) and are stated as
laws of interaction.

First Law: Past Interaction Patterns are Replicated in Present and Future Interactions

Because interpretations of events, relationship definitions, and predictions of how to
effect change are drawn from past experience, persons act on current relationships
to form them in the image of past relationships. Current behaviors are screened and
interpreted with frameworks from the past. Variations of current behavior from
relationship definitions from the past are taken as variance to be eliminated, and
strategies to change the other are based on understandings from the past. These
factors conspire to conform current interactions to the molds of the past. People act
as cybernetic feedback systems to conform and maintain interactions in familiar
patterns; they create equifinality. Not only will relationship definitions from the past
guide individuals to reestablish previous patterns, but their interpretations of events
will tend to inhibit observation of differences or new aspects in current relationships. Their predictions of how to effect change in the behavior of others will tend
to be self-fulfilling in that they will tend to generate the responses from others that
the individuals expect (Snyder & Swann, Jr., 1978). Change in interactional
behavior is obviously difficult and unusual.
    The effect is least apparent for persons who have a wide variety of past
relationship experiences to draw upon. The effect is most apparent for those with

restricted experiences. If people have few definitions to work from, their behavior will likely be inappropriate much of the time, and they are likely candidates for counseling and psychotherapy. People experience greatest difficulty when they enter new situations and relationships, perhaps as the consequences of growth, someone else's change, or other environmental change factors. Haley (1973) points out that personal problems occur at points of change in the life cycle.

The first law suggests that persons will select marriage partners who have important interactional commonalities with those of the persons' primary families. Also, persons marrying a second time will likely marry others who are interactionally similar to their first choices. Finally, persons' interaction patterns with their children are probably similar to their interactional experiences as children in their primary families of origin.

Second Law: Attempts to Change a Relationship Will Stimulate Efforts to Reestablish It

This law holds for relationships that are formed and have stablized into identifiable patterns. It is assumed that the patterns represent somewhat satisfactory fittings with participants' relationship definitions, and thus most changes would diminish rather than increase the fitting between relationship patterns and desired definitions. It seems reasonable to assume that, as a relationship stabilizes, the participants will have proposed and accepted patterns of interaction that were mutually acceptable, and that further changes either party might desire have not been made because they are not mutually acceptable. Thus, proposing change increases the discrepancy between observed and desired relationship pattern and will stimulate the other to act to correct the discrepancy introduced by the proposal to change. The law has important implications for persons in established relationships who are dissatisfied with each other's feedback. If feedback does not conform to desired definition, persons are stimulated to attempt to change the other's behavior. If both are dissatisfied, then both are attempting to change the other, and are thus working with each other's efforts to stimulate change. Further attempts to change the other will create even greater discrepancy between feedback and desired definition and will increase the vigor of the other's change attempts. The discrepancy for both thus increases and both further escalate efforts to create change. As the process escalates, each party makes more extreme efforts to change the other and each in turn is faced with increasingly extreme behavior to change. Much of the pathology seen in psychotherapy probably has been produced in such escalating cycles.

Watzlawick, Beavin, and Jackson (1967) noted that in the escalation process, solutions tried by the interacting parties are the causes of the problem. Attempts to change the other are the cause of the other's attempt to change the person and are the very behaviors both want to eliminate. Efforts to change the other create the problems to be solved, so that the harder each tries to reform the other's actions, the more extreme the other's acts to be reformed become. For example, suppose a wife predicts that the way to draw her husband closer to her is to act helpless and in need of his attention and care, and the husband attempts to stop her from being so

helpless by avoiding her. The stage thus is set for a runaway relationsh
the wife becomes more and more helpless and in need of attention and t
grows more and more distant, resentful, and absent from the home. Th
relationship can only lead to a cataclysmic breakdown of the interaction system,
leaving both parties with serious behavioral problems.

Problematic behaviors are often attempts to overcome efforts to stop the
problematic behaviors, and thus escalate in the face of efforts to stop them. The
utility of paradoxical injunctions in therapy is based on this dynamic. A paradoxical
injunction stimulates the client to diminish his or her symptoms by directing or
encouraging the client to perform them. Coming against the symptom escalates it,
while accepting and encouraging it diminishes it. Encouraging the symptom
undercuts its potential value to reform the other and eliminates or undercuts the
strategy for change by eliminating its stimulant. Palazzoli, Boscolo, Cecchin, and
Prata (1978) indicated that extreme symptomatic behavior by a member of a family
group is best seen as that member's attempt to hold the family together by
counteracting others' attempts to change the family. It is a homostatic measure
working for the maintenance of the family group. Reinforcing the stability of the
group by encouraging the extreme behavior removes the stimulus to the extreme
behavior, and the extreme behavior drops out. This phenomenon is a result of
circular causality in interaction and the cybernetic character of the participants in the
system. Diminishing efforts to counteract the others' efforts to change the system
removes the stimulus to the others' efforts to change, diminishes efforts to prevent
change, and thus allows the system to evolve and change. In counseling, reinforcing
the status quo often results in change. Reinforcing the continuance of a system
allows participants to stop trying to prevent the system's collapse. As their
interaction behavior is thus changed, the system changes.

Third Law: Control of Others is Gained through Yielding Control to Them

Each participant in an interaction seeks to control the relationship to attain his or her
desired definition. The desire to control relationships makes persons vulnerable to
opportunities to take control. Thus, another's behavior can be channeled by making
such opportunities available. Change in another's behavior can be achieved by
making it possible and inviting for the other to control the person through changing
his or her behavior. Because behavior is in the service of control, the other can be
induced to change in particular ways by creating an opportunity for more
advantageous control through behaving thusly and by yielding control to the other as
the other responds to the opportunity by changing. Both push and pull principles can
be applied. A person wishing to change another can refuse to be controlled in any
way but the way desired. The person can punish efforts to control by means of other
strategies and reward the desired strategy. Counselors invite clients to control them
by adopting the control strategies counselors want clients to use. In the earlier
example of husband and wife, the wife's helplessness invites the husband to assume
dominant, overt control over her. Unfortunately, her invitation is not successful

because she has incorrectly read the husband's desires, interpretations, and predictions. Probably, her invitation to dominate would be more effective if it were couched in the behavior of her independence and self-sufficiency.

Principles of Control

The concepts discussed so far suggest that control of another in interaction requires the following:

1. *A Guiding Definition of the Relationship.* Without some notion of what the relationship should be like, control has no meaning. While persons are never without a definition, they at times lack a definition that fits the situation.
2. *Accurate Interpretation of the Others' Definitions, Interpretations, and Predictions as They are Applied to This Relationship.* Reading feedback from the other to deduce the other's internal equipment is essential if a person is to use the other's system to guide the other to seek to control as the person wishes.
3. *Accurate Predictions of How Behaviors Will Affect the Other.* Accuracy is dependent on a good theory of how others will interpret behavior. When predictions are accurate, the other will deduce from the person's behavior characteristics of the person that will suggest that the person can be controlled using the tactic the person wants the other to use.
4. *Interpersonal Skills to Accurately Portray Intended Meanings.* Persons must have the interpersonal skills necessary to communicate intended messages.

All the above processes go on in day-to-day interactions more or less outside of conscious awareness. Interaction behavior is highly complex and would no doubt break down if it were not more or less automatic.

INTERACTION DYNAMICS

Relationship Incongruence

Feedback from interaction may or may not match a person's definition of what the relationship should be like. To the extent it does, behavior will intend to maintain the relationship. To the extent feedback does not match definitions, behavior will intend to change the other's behavior in the direction of the desired pattern.

When feedback is close to desired definition for both parties, a relationship is congruent. When one or both experience discrepancy, a relationship is incongruent. In incongruent relationships, efforts are ongoing to create change. The participants are attempting to influence each other to change control strategies. If only one party experiences discrepancy and tries to change the interaction, the other's actions intend to eliminate the person's attempts to initiate change. Many of the actions of participants in incongruent relationships are efforts to change the relationship, and

the most likely result is the termination of the relationship. The fi
interaction, that past patterns are replicated in present relationships, has
effect through the termination of relationships that do not meet (
Termination is initiated by a party no longer willing to put up with incessant
demands for change, or a party no longer hopeful of stimulating needed change in
the other.

Another possible outcome of incongruence is for one or both parties to accept the
relationship definition the other offers, change behavior, and alter intrapsychic
causes of behavior. Thus, incongruence can lead to relationship termination or to
behavior and intrapsychic changes of one or both parties. Incongruence does not
necessarily lead to these solutions, however. Relationships can remain incongruent
for some time as the parties maneuver for advantage. In stable incongruent
relationships, ploy and counterploy cycle in patterns in what Watzlawick called
games without end (Watzlawick, Beavin, & Jackson, 1967). Thus, the term
stability applies to the likely continuance or discontinuance of a relationship and is
conceptually independent of congruence.

The concepts of incongruence and stability suggest four types of relationships:
stable congruent, unstable congruent, stable incongruent, and unstable incongruent.
Stable congruent relationships are characterized by mutuality and maintenance.
Participants engage in mutually agreeable interaction patterns without the interrup-
tions of discrepancy or change. Unstable congruent relationships are characterized
by mutuality and change. While the interaction is mutually agreeable, it is also
prone to interruption, perhaps from the interference of external factors or from
variations in the participants' need for the relationship. Stable incongruent relationships are characterized by constant efforts to stimulate change and to resist the
other's efforts to stimulate change that reinforce each other in patterns that cycle
endlessly. Neither party will accept the other's proposals, and the relationship has
mutuality only in the sense of a tacit acceptance of repeating patterns of
disagreement and dogged determination to continue the relationship. Unstable
incongruent relationships are at risk, and either one or both parties will change or
the relationship will terminate. Runaway relationships that escalate to ever more
extreme efforts to control and that end cataclysmically are unstable incongruent
relationships.

Relationship types have special significance to the nature of psychological
symptoms and the treatment of symptoms. The term *chronic* is related to stable
incongruent interactions, and *acute* to unstable incongruent relationships. Jackson
(1968c) proposes that unstable incongruent relationships produce problems that are
quite amenable to crises-oriented short-term counseling, due to their instability.
Stable incongruent relationships produce resilient symptoms such as schizophrenia.
Persons with problems associated with stable incongruent relationships do not come
to treatment unless instability is introduced into their relationships, such as children
being born or growing up, death, new potential partners, physical breakdown,
retirement, and the like. Symptom patterns developed in stable incongruent
relationships are more intractable to treatment than those of unstable incongruent
relationships. Possibly a distinction between counseling and psychotherapy could

be made along the same lines, with counseling more attuned to unstable incongruent problems and psychotherapy to stable incongruent problems.

Unstable incongruent relationships are of particular interest because they can stimulate interactants to change if the participants can be prevented from terminating the relationship. Because the objective of psychological helping is to change client behaviors, means of preventing termination of unstable incongruent relationships are of particular importance to psychological helpers. Also of interest is how to guide change to focus on the client rather than the counselor and on therapeutic rather than pathological change. To be a change process, counseling and therapy must avoid stability. When counselor and client achieve congruence in their relationship on grounds other than client improvement, it is not counseling but friendship or some other stable nontherapeutic relationship. When counseling stabilizes in an incongruent pattern, the counselor has failed to stimulate change and instead has become part of the process of producing psychological symptoms, either for the client or for the counselor. Thus, the following are key questions about the therapeutic process:

1. What factors work against the termination of a relationship in the face of incongruence?
2. What factors yield one person vulnerable to change rather than the other in an incongruent relationship?
3. What factors influence what behavior a person will change in response to incongruence?
4. How can psychological helping be prevented from achieving congruence on some basis other than the client's health?
5. What factors work against counseling degenerating from unstable incongruence to stable incongruence rather than achieving congruence based on the client's health?

The rest of this chapter is a brief presentation of the relationship factors necessary for successful counseling and psychotherapy. Chapters 3-9 focus in depth on aspects of the change process, review research bearing on the processes, and identify hypotheses for further research.

Dependence and Social Power

The most important determinant of change in a relationship is the dependence of the parties on one another. Dependence determines the vulnerability of a person to another's proposals for the definition of relationship. *Dependence* is a joint function of need and resources, as is depicted in Figure 3. A *need* is conceptualized as a

$$D = SP = f(N \cong R)$$

Figure 3 Dependence and social power. Dependence (D) of a person on another and the social power *(SP) of another on the person* are a function *(f)* of the correspondence ($\cong$) of the person's perceived needs (N) and the person's perception of the other's resources *(R)*.

perceived lack of a physical or psychological quality, such as affection, information, experience, food, safety, and so on. A *resource* is a perceived ability to provide such a quality. When a person perceives himself or herself to have a need and another to have the ability to deliver a resource to meet the need, the person is dependent on the other. The amount of dependence depends on the magnitude of the need and the magnitude of the resource that corresponds to the need (Strong & Matross, 1973). Dependence is based on perceived needs and the resources the person perceives another to have rather than on needs and resources estimated in some other way. Dependence is a function of perception. Dependence is not a function of the other's notions of his or her resources, but only of the person's perceptions of the other's resources.

Because of the dependent person's need for the other's resources, the person is willing or vulnerable to change to establish or maintain the relationship and will change if necessary to maintain the relationship. Dependency has magnitude. A person can be more or less dependent, more or less vulnerable to the other's demands for change. The other side of dependence is social power. *Social power* is a person's ability to influence another. Social power is rooted in the other's dependence and therefore has magnitude. The constructs of dependence and social power are tied operationally to the observation of one person changing actions as a result of another's request. That is, when one person changes behavior as a result of another's request that the person do so, dependence and power are inferred. Dependence and social power also can be inferred from the impact of changing perceptions of needs and resources on the outcome of influence.

Interdependence and Relationship Formation

The functioning of dependence and change in interaction is complicated by the dependence of the parties in interaction on each other. It is never the case that one party is dependent and the other is not, because a person without dependence would not interact with another at all. But a living organism is never without needs. It is doubtful that anyone is ever without needs that could be met by the resources of others. People are social creatures and have some level of need for the presence of others throughout life.

The absolute levels and relative balance of dependency perceived by the parties on each other largely determine the outcome of interaction. Table 1 presents several different relative levels of dependence between person A and person B. For each interdependence balance, B's response to A's proposal that B change is indicated in the third column. When A is much more dependent on B than B is on A, B is likely to reject A's proposal (assuming that A's proposal for relationship definition is at odds with B's desired definition). Contrariwise, when B's dependence is greater than A's, B is likely to comply. However, consider the situation where the two are not equal in dependence, but both are substantially dependent on the other. Then, simple compliance or rejection to discrepant proposals is not the predicted outcome. When a person is only slightly dependent on another, he or she has a strong hand in determining the fate of the other. If the other does not do as the person wishes, he or

Table 1. B's Response to A's Proposal at Different Social Power Interdependencies (Cost of Compliance = 4)

Social Power Interdependency Type	A	B	B's Response
Balanced-low	1	1	Reject
Unbalanced-low	1	5	Reject
	5	1	Comply
Unbalanced-high	3	5	Negotiate/reject
	5	3	Negotiate/comply
Balanced-high	5	5	Negotiate

she simply terminates the relationship. The other has little power to work with, and is relatively helpless. On the other hand, when both parties are strongly dependent on each other, both are reluctant to terminate the relationship and lose the possibility of obtaining the valuable resources controlled by the other. Thus, even the person in the high power position is significantly vulnerable to the other's counterproposals. The other, taking advantage of the person's dependence, is seldom in the position of complete compliance with the proposals of the more powerful person because the more powerful person is reluctant to reject completely the counterproposals of the more dependent other. Both parties can threaten to terminate the relationship to good advantage, but neither party is likely to carry out the threat. Therefore, the likely process of relationship formation is give and take on both sides, of negotiation, with the more dependent person giving more, and the more powerful person giving less. When the two interactants are equally and highly dependent, there is little alternative for either but to negotiate for relationship definition, with both giving and taking.

Termination of a relationship is partially a function of the magnitude of the parties dependence on each other. The more the dependence, the more robust the relationship and the more likely incongruence is to result in behavioral change of one or both parties rather than termination. A relationship may be only as robust as the least dependent party, for the level of dependence sets a ceiling on the amount of discrepancy tolerated by that party. On the other hand, the other's level of dependency can increase the relationship's robustness in the sense that a very dependent party will potentially make massive concessions to the low dependent party, and thus enable their relationship to survive considerable incongruence. Within the context of some minimum level of dependence for each, the robustness of a relationship is the total absolute magnitude of dependence of the parties in the relationship.

The effects of power balance discussed here hold when everything else is held constant or equal. Everything else is never constant in the dynamic world of interpersonal relationships.

Impression Management

Obtaining desired relationship definitions is a consequence of social power, which in turn is a function of the other's perception of needs and resources. Thus, managing others' impressions of one's needs and resources is crucial to the control of relationships. In two-way interaction, each person's predictions of the other's perceived dependence is a critical factor. If a person believes that the other and the person are equally dependent in a relationship, and the other perceives that he or she is less dependent than the person is, the other is likely to concede less than the person asks. Differences in perception produce unexpected outcomes and increase the probability of termination as the outcome of relationship incongruence. Each party's behavior is based on his or her perception of the situation, and each party will usually do all he or she can to maximize the other's perception of personal dependence. On the other hand, a reverse strategy could have the effect of inviting the other to take the upper hand in the relationship, which could be the person's desired definition of the relationship.

An important concept in the dynamics of social power balance and its effects on the negotiation of relationship definition is Thibaut and Kelley's (1959) comparison level of alternatives. If a party knows of an alternative source of needed resources, his or her dependence on the interactant is much reduced, and the other's ability to gain compliance and even negotiation is undercut. Thus, another strategy in the management of another's perception of the power balance in interaction is to give the impression of the ready availability of yet others with resources equivalent to the other.

Change as a Power Enhancement Tactic

Who changes in an unstable incongruent relationship that does not terminate, and what is changed, depend on the relative power of the interactants and on the nature of their dependencies on each other. Speaking generally, the most dependent person will do the most changing when incongruence is introduced into a relationship. What specific behaviors change is a function of the needs of the individual who does not change and the resources of the person who does. Change is a strategy for obtaining power in a relationship, for the change provides resources for the needs of the more powerful person. For example, Jones (1964) found that, in two hierarchical organizations, subordinates gained power on their superiors by complying with organizational requirements. Persons in high power positions need to have others do as they wish, or their power is nonexistent. Also, Cialdini and his colleagues (Cialdini, Braver, & Lewis, 1974; Cialdini & Mirels, 1976) have found that conformity results in the persuader perceiving the conformer to have higher intelligence and attractiveness than nonconformers. One of the most potent weapons a low power person has is conformity to the needs of the high power party.

Needs are intimately tied to relationship definitions, since the function of definitions is to establish relationships that persons believe are instrumental to meeting their needs. Proposals to change definitions of relationships are closely tied to the needs of the proposer, who strives to establish relationships that will satisfy his or her needs. To obtain compliance, persons attempt to make it to the other's advantage to change behavior to better conform to the person's needs. People's vulnerabilities to others' control reside in the relationship patterns they propose because their proposals are based on their needs. By changing as the other proposes, the person enhances the resources the other perceives the person to have that relate to the other's needs. Change increases the dependence of the influencer and the power of the changer. Change is a strategy to gain power in relationship and to increase the dependence of a more powerful person. Accepting another's invitation to control in a particular way (changing) neutralizes the other's power advantage by increasing the other's perception of the resources we can supply. The direction of change in a relationship is towards the needs of the more powerful member and is an adjustment by the less powerful person to neutralize the power advantage of the other.

Needs and the Nature of Change

The needs and resources of clients and counselors are critical to the course and outcome of the counseling process. Client needs in the relationship are rather more easily specified than are the counselor's. The next chapter reviews research on client needs and the resources of counselors that meet these needs. Client needs relate to their difficulties in living. Perhaps a client is suffering physical and psychological discomfort that is a consequence of strategies for controlling others. Perhaps a client is failing to control others or is having difficulty maintaining necessary relationships. Perhaps a client faces an uncertain future or difficult decisions in his or her educational, vocational, or personal life. For these needs, the counselor's greatest resource is expertise in the areas of interpersonal relations, education, vocations, life planning, and so on. People need to be liked and listened to and the counselor is as adept at providing these resources as anyone else.

The helping professions have not been attuned to the need of satisfaction counselors derive from counseling. This is a grave oversight. While client behavior change is a function of the counselor's power in the relationship, the nature of the client's change represents the nature of the counselor's needs in the relationship. Enumerating counselor needs is difficult. Counselors seem to be self-selected from persons with high interests in social welfare and in helping others, and with strong needs to control others. The strongest counselor need operating in counseling is probably the need to convert others to the truth. Such a need is reflected in the counselor's dependence on some framework of meaning and existence, and in the proselytizing counselors do, perhaps to maintain and validate their faiths (Festinger, Riecken, & Schachter, 1956). Counselors and therapists have strong commitments to views of ultimate truth and the ''good life'' and are strongly motivated to enlighten others. Such needs provide clients means for controlling counselors by exploiting the counselors' needs through adoption of the counselors' notions of truth, a resource available to most clients.

The counselor's consistent proposal for the definition of the counseling relationship entails the client's behaving in accord with the counselor's notions of the good life. The counseling relationship can obtain congruence on the basis of the client behaving in a healthy way as defined by the counselor. This analysis is consistent with the belief and faith effects and the effects of the changing zeitgeist on counseling philosophies noted in the first chapter, and with the phenomena of client convergence to counselor attitudes and beliefs reviewed in Chapter 3.

Other counselor needs probably include needs to be helpful, to be accepted as an authority, and common human needs for affection, confirmation, sex, and so on. Some of these needs are potential explanations for failure in counseling, since the client can exploit these counselor vulnerabilities through providing correspondent resources, and thus achieve congruence and power equity with the counselor on some basis other than positive change. The exchange of sexual favors between counselor and client as an outcome of counseling has received increasing attention, and an American Psychological Association statement of ethics has been written to control this source of counseling failure. Kell and Mueller (1966) document how the counselor need to be seen as competent can be exploited by clients, degenerating the relationship to stable incongruency and symptom generation.

Discrepancy and Change

Obtaining desired change is not dependent solely on the power advantage of the persuader, but also on the difference between what the persuader proposes and the recipient's desired definition, a difference labeled psychological discrepancy. Psychological discrepancy is a central concept in attitude change research and is the same as the depth concept of interpretations. Discrepancy is the person's perception of the psychological distance between a relationship definition proposed by another and the person's preferred relationship definition. It is the psychological cost of compliance incurred by the recipient of discrepant relationship proposals. Changing behavior and related intrapsychic equipment is costly. Small adjustments are perhaps not too costly, but changes of major proportions cost the person a great deal in terms of perceptions of self and relationships with others, to say nothing of the need to readjust all other cognitive and behavioral components as demanded by consistency and impression management with interactants.

Figure 4 is a diagram of the relationship of the cost of compliance to a proposed change and the social power of the proposer. When the cost of compliance is greater than the social power of the other, the person can be expected to reject the proposal. Conversely, when the cost is less than the power of the proposer, and all other things are equal, the person will comply. Both cost and power (dependence) are as perceived by the person deciding to reject or comply with the proposal. Because alternative interactants with nearly equivalent resources are often available, and because of interdependency, an interactant cannot usually be expected to accept a proposal or comply if the cost of compliance is high. In psychological helping, as well as in other change processes where change is desired more than self-selection of interactants already suited for one's purposes, it is essential to avoid proposing

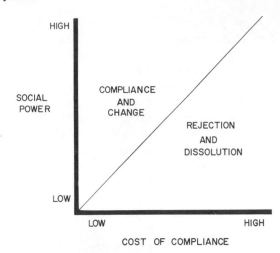

Figure 4   Change or dissolution of relationship as a joint function of social power and cost or compliance.

more change than the person will tolerate. Rejection of a proposal results in a test of the persuader's toleration of the relationship without the desired qualities. Continued persistence about a desired change will likely lead the person to terminate the relationship and thus remove any opportunity to obtain change.

Effective management of change requires the persuader to assess the other's desired relationship, the discrepancy the other will likely perceive with various proposed changes, and the amount of dependence the other perceives himself or herself to have on the persuader. An effective persuader tailors successive proposals to never exceed the other's toleration for discrepancy, but moves incessantly toward the ultimate desired relationship definition. Essentially, the successful influencer takes whatever change is obtained at any given moment and persists until the full change is obtained. The influencer must work at affecting the other's perceptions of relative dependence and proposal discrepancy while managing proposals for change to obtain compliance rather than rejection. These considerations lead to the following notions of how to maximize influence:

1.   Maximize the other's perception of the power imbalance in the relationship by (a) accenting the other's perception of the other's needs and the appropriateness of one's resources to the needs; (b) diminishing the other's perception of one's dependency on the other, except for the need one wishes the other to capitalize on; (c) enhancing the other's perception of the relative lack of alternative sources of needed resources; and (d) enhancing the other's perception of the existence of alternative sources of resources for the influencer.

2.   Diminish the other's perception of the costs of compliance with one's proposals while emphasizing the costs of continued noncompliance.

3. Carefully pace the costs of proposals with the amount of dependence operational for each proposal and avoid overshooting persuasion power and causing rejection and possibly relationship termination. When in doubt, go for less change rather than more. Use the other's reactions to proposals to diagnose his or her perceptions of costs and dependence. Be quick to accept rejections rather than risk termination.

The above considerations lead to a three-phase conception of counseling and therapy as depicted in Figure 5. In the diagram, the counselor and the client are seen as having discrepant relationship definitions. The persons are depicted as arrows traveling down their respective avenues of meaning. In the first phase of counseling, the counselor traverses into the client's avenue of meaning, accepting the client's definitions in order to learn what they are. The counselor thus builds the client's dependence in preparation for the second phase. In the second phase, the counselor begins to move back to his or her own avenue of meaning, proposing changes to the client in ways that make the relationship incongruent and bring the client into discrepancy, but only as much as the client's dependency can tolerate. The second phase may be long or short, depending on the vicissitudes of the power struggle between counselor and client, the counselor's skills in assessing discrepancy and dependency, and the counselor's ability to counter the client's counter strategies that do not entail compliance to the counselor's proposals as the major method of power equalization. As the counselor is successful in encouraging the client to change, the discrepancies experienced by the client decrease and the relationship enters the third phase and becomes increasingly congruent. As the relationship becomes congruent within the counselor's meanings and definitions, the needs that attached the client to the counselor (symptom pain, uncertainty about the future, etc.) disappear, and the congruent but unstable relationship terminates.

Tactics to Counter Power

Other tactics besides compliance and change are available to a low power party for gaining control of a higher power interactant. These methods operate on the perception of the source of behavior to affect the interactant's view of one's ability to change. A most important strategy is to place compliance or noncompliance outside voluntary control. For example, if a friend wants help to move his furniture, we can avoid compliance without damaging our ability to call on the friend for similar tasks by finding ourselves to be ill, or by noting that our mothers-in-law require our help at the same time, or by exclaiming about the load of work at the office that we must do. Appeal to uncontrollable causes eliminates our ability to comply or not comply. If a teacher insists that a student continue working on problems, the student can counter her demand by pointing out that he or she does not have the ability to do them. Perhaps a wife wants her husband to assume the shopping, but the husband finds that he is overcome with nausea whenever he approaches a food store. Perhaps a husband wants his wife to accept a less intense

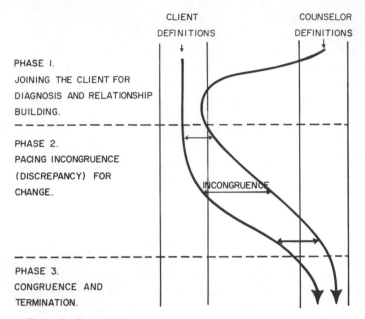

CLIENT
DEFINITIONS

COUNSELOR
DEFINITIONS

PHASE I.
JOINING THE CLIENT FOR
DIAGNOSIS AND RELATIONSHIP
BUILDING.

PHASE 2.
PACING INCONGRUENCE
(DISCREPANCY) FOR
CHANGE.

INCONGRUENCE

PHASE 3.
CONGRUENCE AND
TERMINATION.

Figure 5 Phases of the change process in counseling and psychotherapy.

relationship, but the wife's "illness" prevents her from being able to comply. Perhaps a counselor wishes a client to cease being depressed, but when the counselor asks the client to do so, the client is unable to prevent the onset of the depression in spite of efforts to comply. Most symptoms in personal counseling and therapy are uncontrollable. This reflects the nature of the incongruent relationships in which the symptoms were developed. Uncontrollability is a powerful strategy for overcoming more powerful interactants. In extreme forms, the uncontrollability tactic is undesirable, for uncontrollable behavior includes personally damaging aspects such as paralysis, depression, anxiety, helplessness, loss of contact with reality, and impulsiveness. Also, the strategy may drive the interactant out of the relationship.

The client's uncontrollable control strategies must be countered in counseling and therapy or the relationship will degenerate into stable incongruence. Countering the tactic is difficult because direct attempts to change the interactant will elicit increased helplessness in accord with the second law of interaction. Controlling uncontrollable behavior requires the *opposite* tactic. When an interactant encourages uncontrollable behavior, he or she is no longer controlled or nullified by it, but rather controls the other through the other's uncontrollable behavior. Encouraging uncontrollable behavior reverses the dynamics of relationship control because of the circular causality in interaction, and the other will likely abandon the tactic as unsuccessful. Freud introduced the notion of not requiring clients to give up symptoms directly, but rather being permissive and using symptoms to control the

client. The process of removing uncontrollable relationship tactics by encouragi
them is called the *negation paradox* and is discussed in Chapter 5.

Counselors and therapists rely on the uncontrollable strategy to overcome client
attempts to counter change. Most counseling systems posit some uncontrollable
force to account for the client's inevitable change. The uncontrollableness of the
''cause'' of the client's change renders client compliance with the counselor's
proposals difficult to counteract. Also, attributing change to an uncontrollable agent
inside the client such as actualization potential, ego energy, rationality, reinforcement, magnetism, or the Holy Spirit allows the client to conform to the counselor's
proposed definition and at the same time claim that the change had nothing to do
with the counselor. Using the uncontrollable tactic, the counselor enables the client
to undercut the counselor's power differential by changing as the counselor wishes.
Attribution of therapeutic change to uncontrollable sources allows clients to gain the
benefits of compliance without the disadvantages, and it thus increases the
likelihood of therapeutic change as the outcome of counseling and therapy.

the client, the relationship, and the process of change, and a language to communicate such understanding. These frameworks include explanations of change, but such explanations serve less the goal of scientific understanding of change than that of client improvement. For example, some theoretical postions place the locus of change "in" the client and deny that influence plays a direct role in producing it. Change is seen as the client's responsibility. Yet, radically different theoretical orientations not only effect comparable changes in clients, but may effect them through similar processes. What the therapist says and does—that which distinguishes therapists working from different orientations—may have less to do with change than features of the interaction that contribute to the possibility of social influence.

The idea that therapist interventions should be examined in terms of their functioning and independent of their specific content has made attitude change theory and research especially relevant to understanding basic therapeutic processes. Since Jerome Frank's publication of *Persuasion and Healing* in 1961, a number of writers have adapted social psychological concepts of attitude, influence, and change in studying counseling and psychotherapy. Frank compiled data from anthropology, sociology, and social psychology to support the thesis that psychotherapy, as well as less scientific healing practices, could be considered an influence process. Strong (1968) made a similar case regarding counseling, and he drew upon specific laboratory studies of attitude change to support the idea. Levy (1963) developed a theory of psychological interpretation which concentrated not on the theoretical value of interpretive interventions, but on their ability to change the client's perceptual-cognitive structure, change he explained using Festinger's (1957) theory of cognitive dissonance. Goldstein, Heller, and Sechrest (1966) stressed the importance of considering therapeutic change as continuous with nontherapeutic change, focusing on basic similarities among change processes in a way that would make psychotherapy more easily researchable and less tied to unsupportable theoretical assertions. Such a focus on the *how* of change has the advantage of being equally applicable to a variety of therapeutic orientations, construing change in ways that may be studied outside the frameworks offered by the orientations. These writings have stimulated what Goldstein (1966) called "extrapolatory research," which applied influence phenomena investigated by social psychologists to counseling and psychotherapy settings.

Social Influence

Attitude change research concerns the conditions under which receiving information that differs from one's present attitudes leads to changes in the attitudes. Social influence refers to attitude change in an interpersonal setting, where the discrepant information is communicated, or awareness of it elicited, by another person. The focus of the social influence paradigm is on two sets of variables, the communicator's characteristics and the nature of the presentation; both affect the extent to which influence occurs in an interaction. In counseling and psychotherapy, these variables correspond to the therapist's social power, or ability to influence the client in the relationship, and the nature of the therapist's interventions. Influence is not always effected through the communication of discrepant information, as in the case of a therapist's interpretation, but it may result from interventions that increase client involvement in an issue, manipulate client commitment to a position, or prompt the client to note previously unnoticed relationships among attitudes. Many of the therapist's interventions do not seem to the client like influence at all, because the counselor may simply help the client focus on his or her own behavior, and the client is led to attribute changes to intrapsychic rather than interpersonal processes. Attitude change in counseling and psychotherapy is seldom the consequence of overt persuasion; it results from the therapist's creating the conditions for change which, in turn, appears spontaneous to the client.

Construing counseling and psychotherapy as social influence does not imply that the therapist is underhanded or deceitful. A therapist may be so, as might anyone engaged in human discourse. To communicate is to influence. Asserting that the therapist influences the client is simply to emphasize that the therapist's behavior deliberately affects how the client thinks, feels, and acts. It has nothing to do with the therapist's motives, which may be humane or cruel, but with the function of the therapist's behavior.

The social influence model, with its focus on attitude change, has a strong cognitive flavor. The primarily cognitive nature of attitude change concepts does not diminish the relevance of social influence to emotional and overt behavior change. These may also be linked to basic influence processes. Thus, social influence need not be applied only to existing congitive approaches, but to relationship, humanistic, existential, and behavioral approaches as well. Indeed, the model should not be considered a theoretical orientation on par with these approaches. It offers little in the way of communication skills, relationship-building techniques, or other interventions. Social influence is a metatheory, a conceptual framework intended to account for the effectiveness of existing strategies across a range of theoretical orientations. Its value rests in its potential for allowing practitioners to enhance the effectiveness of their work through understanding and maximizing the critical variables for effecting change, regardless of theoretical orientation.

Attitudes

Social psychologists (e.g., Zimbardo, Ebbesen, & Maslach, 1977) and psychotherapists (e.g., Frank, 1973) have conceptualized attitudes as constructs mediating perceptions, thoughts, feelings, and actions. Attitudes are hypothetical constructs that are seen to predispose people to respond in certain ways to their environment, and such responses therefore serve as indicators of attitudes. Attitudes have cognitive, affective, and conative components. The cognitive component affects how a person construes the environment; it may be inferred from measures of the person's verbal behavior, including performance on surveys, tests, and other psychological measures. Cognitions are people's beliefs about the world, ranging from inarticulable assumptions to fully verbalized positions. They determine not only how people think about their experience, but to some extent they experience itself, since they include conceptual categories used in objects, events, and relationships. Attitudes in this sense are not discernable truths, but what is believed to be true (Kruglanski, 1980). Kelly's (1955) constructs, implicit personality theories (Schneider, Hastorf, & Ellsworth, 1979), and causal attributions (Kelley, 1967) are examples of the cognitive component of attitudes.

The affective component of attitudes is most apparent in the emotional associations people have with objects or events, and it may be assessed by verbal or physiological measures. The affective component is generally related to evaluation, experienced as positive or negative feelings toward the object of the attitude. Some researchers (e.g., Rosenberg, 1960) have hypothesized that cognitive and affective components of attitudes tend toward congruence and have found changes in one component to be accompanied by changes in the other. The conative component of attitudes refers to the tendency to behave. Besides self-report of how people would behave toward a particular object, the conative component may be assessed by observing people's actions toward the object.

The three components of attitudes are inextricably related and, however assessed, represent inferred tendencies to respond in three different ways. McGuire (1969), noting the typically high correlations among the cognitive, affective, and conative components, has suggested that they reflect different, imperfect ways of measuring attitudes, rather than distinct components. The components of attitudes seem to be causally interactive. Overt behavior change can lead to or result from changes in belief, for example. Stable attitude change probably results from an ongoing interplay of minimal shifts in feeling, thinking, and acting; each shift, however slight, contributes to alterations in the three components.

McGuire has described four functions of attitudes. First, attitudes are utilitarian, promoting adaptive or goal-directed behavior. Second, attitudes serve to simplify and organize experience and to allow the individual to comprehend events and relationships without being overwhelmed by their complexity. Third, attitudes are expressive and reflect the individual's evaluative, emotionally based reactions to persons, objects, or events. Fourth, attitudes perform a defensive function. They protect the individual from intense negative feelings and enable adaptive behavior in situations that might otherwise be debilitating. All of these functions are important in counseling and psychotherapy. The therapist–client interaction focuses on the adaptive and maladaptive behavior of the client. Attitudes that interfere with adaptive behavior, such as unrealistic or ill-defined goals, distorted perceptions, intense or unclear feelings, and faulty, unexamined assumptions, become the focus of the therapist's and client's attention. The therapist's interventions promote changes in the substance of the client's attitudes, thus altering the way they function for the client.

Attitudes determine organized, meaningful experience of the world for the individual, and they mediate his or her adaptive responding to that experience. Changes in attitudes are changes in the way one sees the world and reacts to it. An individual's attitudes comprise a perceptual-cognitive system that is relatively stable, but also changeable, since it is the product of learning. This organized collection of attitudes is the primary locus of change in counseling and psychotherapy. Frank (1973) called it the "assumptive world":

> This is a short-hand expression for a highly structured, complex, interacting set of values, expectations, and images of oneself and others, which guide and in turn are guided by a person's perceptions and behavior and which are closely related to his emotional states and . . . feelings of well being. (p. 27)

The therapist's responses to the client bring aspects of the client's assumptive world into awareness, making verbally explicit such things as the mixed feelings of the client toward her husband, interpretations the client has been placing upon the actions of his co-workers, interactional behavior that contradicts the client's strongly held values, and so on. Such attitudes, verbalized by the client in the session, become the target of the therapist's interventions, which present (however subtly) alternative ways of construing experience. Therapeutic outcomes thus begin with, and are maintained by, alterations in the client's assumptive world.

The idea that the therapist's interventions primarily affect the client's perceptual-cognitive system, thereby mediating other changes, was elaborated by Levy (1963), who conceptualized psychotherapy as an interpretive process. Considering interpretation broadly to include a variety of interventions, he noted that its essential function is to alter meanings that the client attaches to events. The therapist's remarks to the client bring a new frame of reference to bear on events in the client's life, so as to create possibilities for change where formerly the client has seen none. The therapist's language restructures the experience of the client by influencing the client to employ new labels for events, to see events in a different relationship to one another, and to alter the evaluative associations with events. Hence, interpretations change attitudes. For example, the therapist may first use interpretation to suggest that the client is reluctant to express anger because it would be impolite, thus labeling the client's experience ("reluctant") and drawing a causal relationship between two events ("because it would be impolite"). Over time, the client is persuaded to view some circumstances as appropriate for expressing anger. In a therapy group, the client may see (if directed where to look) that his or her anger is not considered impolite by others; the client may come to believe (if the therapist brings attention to and labels certain interactions) that awareness and expression of anger is normal and potentially facilitative in social relationships. The specific content of the therapist's interventions—in this case, the labels and rationale attached to the expression of anger—is important only insofar as it creates possibilities for change. The effectiveness, not the truth, of the intervention is the key issue. Interpretation, as Levy has described it, may range from selective responding to the client's behavior to direct statements that are at variance with the client's attitudes, including the client's awareness of events and beliefs about events. Client change is rooted in the relabeling and reconceptualization that is stimulated and solidified by the interpretational process of therapy.

Cognitive Consistency

Theories of cognitive consistency postulate that related attitudes held by an individual tend toward internal consistency (Abelson et al., 1968). If new information is introduced producing an inconsistency among attitudes, then one or more of them will change so that greater consistency is achieved. The communicator's credibility, the recipient's involvement in an issue, and the discrepancy of the new information from the recipient's current attitudes are some of the circumstances affecting which attitudes will change, and how much they will change, in efforts to reestablish consistency. Festinger's (1957) theory of cognitive dissonance is the most prominent and elaborate example of the use of cognitive consistency. Rosenberg (1960) applied the consistency notion to cognitive and affective change; Rokeach (1973) to changes based on values and self-perceptions; and Goethals (1976) to changes based on perceptions of the communicator.

Cognitive consistency is an appealing concept in counseling any psychotherapy because so many of the changes clients make include, first, the realization of disparate, seemingly incongruent elements in their thoughts, feelings, actions, values, and perceptions, and second, an integration of these into a coherent understanding, implying or even necessitating change in behavior. In describing cognitive inconsistency, Aronson (1969) pointed out that attitudes that are inconsistent *psychologically* stimulate the individual to seek some resolution; the attitudes need not be logically contradictory. Attitudes or components of attitudes are psychologically inconsistent if, taken together, they make no sense to the individual, if he or she would have difficulty holding both at the same time. For example, often a therapist's interpretation draws the client's behavior in sharp contrast to basic and positive values held by the client. The therapist may translate crying into manipulation, anger into hurt, boasting into insecurity. The negative label creates a psychological inconsistency between the client's overall self-perception and estimation of that behavior. It is also common for the client to observe that his or her behavior does not have the same effect on the therapist as on family members and friends. The interested concern of the therapist in response to the client's disclosure of disgusting behavior, the therapist's angry reaction to the client's niceness, the encouragement the therapist gives to the client's attacks—all promote psychological inconsistency by contrasting what the client believes will occur with what the client observes to occur.

Psychological inconsistency seems typically to arise from the "violation of an expectancy" (Aronson, 1969, p. 7). Expectancies based on personal experience, beliefs about oneself and others, knowledge of the world, and cultural norms contribute to psychological inconsistency when the individual encounters information that does not follow from them. Attitudes about the world and oneself are supported by direct and indirect observations of the world. Since attitudes are vital to the individual's interaction with and adaptation to the world, observations that contradict those attitudes can have important implications for his or her functioning. Psychological inconsistency is a press for change to establish greater cognitive consistency. The nature of psychological inconsistency and the extent of the press are variable. Inconsistencies may be tolerated, even preferred to resolution, or they may be quite troubling—it depends on the importance of the expectancy violated and on the characteristics of the information that violates it. Aronson (1969) suggested that since some of the firmest expectancies are based on self-concept, the clearest instances of psychological inconsistency occur when the individual perceives his or her behavior to be discrepant from more stable self-perceptions. Many of the therapist's interventions identify discrepancies between the client's behavior and deeply held values or beliefs; the importance of the resulting psychological inconsistencies to the client provides considerable leverage for the therapist to use in promoting change.

Tannenbaum (1968b) has held that there is a need for cognitive consistency because it is adaptive for the individual to have a "stable predictive view of his environment" (p. 344). Kelman and Baron (1968) described cognitive inconsistency as a signal to the individual which:

> sets into motion active (though not necessarily conscious) searching behavior, designed to assess the functional implications of the inconsistency. That is, the individual surveys those regions of his life space that are marked by the inconsistency in order to determine whether indeed it indicates a threat to the achievement of some of his goals or a possibility of a more effective utilization of his resources for the achievement of those goals. The discovery of such implications provides a challenge to the individual to re-examine his attitudes, his actions, and his social relationships, with an eye to improving his ability to cope with his environment. (pp. 331–332).

Cognitive inconsistency stimulates a search to discern the threat posed to the individual's coping mechanisms and coherent sense of self and the environment. The goal of inconsistency resolution is the reestablishment of effective coping ability. If the cognitive inconsistency obstructs adaptation, efforts will be made to reduce it. This conceptualization accounts for situations in which inconsistencies are tolerated or even ignored by the person: they pose no threat to adaptive functioning. Thus, the motivational properties of cognitive inconsistency are corrected to the functions served by attitudes.

Emotional arousal does not seem to be a necessary component of attitude change via cognitive inconsistency, though it may be an important factor. Though it makes intuitive sense to view cognitive inconsistency as stressful and its resolution as stress reducing, there are numerous instances where stress is not apparent and change occurs anyway. Bem (1972), in fact, has argued that cognitive consistency may not motivate attitude change at all. Rather, change may be the consequence of self-perception. When individuals perceive themselves to behave in counterattitudinal ways, they simply alter their attitudes accordingly. Tannenbaum (1968a) has explained that even when stress is present in the attitude change process, its exact role is unclear. It may mediate responses to inconsistency, serving to motivate efforts to achieve consistency. Stress may be incidental to the attitude change process, resulting from cognitive inconsistency but independent of other responses which also result directly from inconsistency. Or stress might be the result, not of cognitive inconsistency directly, but of the coping activity which responds to the inconsistency. The realization that one has changed attitudes because of a prior inconsistency can be discomforting, as data reported by Tannenbaum indicate.

The role of emotional arousal in counseling and psychotherapy is equally unclear, beyond the observation that it is frequently present when change occurs. The possibilities offered by Tannenbaum are all plausible in the therapeutic setting. Attitudes that are the target of change in therapy typically have strong affective components, and arousal might be expected as they are disclosed, scrutinized, and altered. Emotional arousal is also an expression of client need, contributing to therapist social power, which in turn is partly a function of need. The emotional involvement of the client thus may enhance influenceability. This notion and supporting evidence are discussed in the section on "Social Power."

Attitude Change

The therapist and client engage in an ongoing process of creating and resolving cognitive inconsistencies. The therapist, using anything from a word with a slightly different meaning to a full-blown interpretation, from a suggestion to pursue a topic further to explicit homework assignments, brings into focus feelings, thoughts, and actions that are psychologically inconsistent and demand resolution. The therapist's interventions also close off alternative avenues of resolution in favor of that which promotes client change. One of the contributions of dissonance theory has been to bring into a single framework the several possible responses to cognitive inconsistency. Dissonance that has been aroused by receiving discrepant information may be reduced by (a) changing attitudes in the direction of the discrepancy, (b) persuading the communicator to one's own point of view (thereby changing the belief that the communicator disagrees), (c) strengthening one's own position with supporting attitudes, (d) discrediting the communication (thereby reducing his or her social power), and (e) minimizing the importance of the issue that the attitude concerns. All of these change attitudes: the attitude in question, attitudes concerning the communicator and his or her position, attitudes about the issue and support for it. As Aronson (1969) pointed out, dissonance experiments are arranged so that all of the avenues of dissonance reduction—except change in the target attitude—are rendered inaccessible to subjects. Similarly, Strong (1968) proposed that therapists promote influence by arranging conditions in the interview so that the client will not choose alternatives to attitude change in responding to the cognitive inconsistencies that the therapist helps to create.

Laboratory and therapeutic settings differ in ways that make therapeutic change both easier and more difficult to effect than experimental attitude change. On the difficult side, the therapist does not have the control of the experimenter, who can determine the particular attitude to be changed, what information the subject receives about it, and how the subject perceives the source of the information. In experiments, statements intended to influence and information about the source are frequently presented on paper. The subject does not interact with the source. In counseling and psychotherapy, changes are effected through the medium of conversation, with many attitudes at varying degrees of clarity coming into play at once. The therapist, however, has the advantage of working with attitudes that are intimately important to the client, in a relationship in which the therapist can develop considerable social power, and in face-to-face interaction with the client over time. Under these conditions, the client cannot easily discount the importance of inconsistencies between old attitudes and new points of view, nor derogate source. Opposing the content of the therapist's statements by strengthening or defending one's own viewpoint, and resisting the therapist's interventions by derogating the source or devaluing the issue, do occur (Strong & Matross, 1973), for the client is not a passive interactant; but the therapist's social power provides him or her with the ability to counter these attempts not to change.

VARIABLES AFFECTING ATTITUDE CHANGE

Therapist communications are the instrument of change, and a number of variables contribute to their efficacy. *Discrepancy* between communicated information and the client's attitudes determines the extent of change. *Involvement,* the importance of the issue to the client; therapist *social power,* the ability to influence; and the *commitment* of the client to particular attitudes and behaviors interact to affect how information is processed and what changes are made. The social context of influence is the simultaneous operation of these variables.

Discrepancy, Involvement, and Credibility

Cognitive inconsistency results when an individual becomes aware of information discrepant from present beliefs. This discrepant information may be communicated by another or may arise from performing behavior that is incompatible with attitudes. Both means of creating discrepancy are common experimental paradigms in social psychology and are representative of events in counseling and psychotherapy. Therapists' interpretations and interpersonal feedback in the therapy group are samples of inducing inconsistency via communication. Leading the client to express and label feelings, to ''own'' statements, and to take alternative approaches in a role play are examples of inducing inconsistency behaviorally. Attitude change can also follow the reception of or commitment to positions *consonant* with attitudes. This has the effect of strengthening attitudes and increasing resistance to change. Such strengthening is a frequent and important part of therapeutic change. Communications that express discrepant and consonant attitudes are discussed below. Behavioral compliance with discrepant and consonant positions is discussed in the section on ''Commitment.''

The relationship between the amount of change advocated (i.e., the size of the discrepancy) and that obtained is generally positive and linear (McGuire, 1969). This relationship seems to hold up to very large discrepancies, where it becomes curvilinear, and increasing discrepancies lead to less attitude change. Ego involvement and source credibility interact with discrepancy to affect its relationship to attitude change. Zimbardo (1960) operationalized involvement as the perceived importance of an issue to the individual independent of his or her taking a position on it. His subjects were told that their opinions about a case study would either "be a good indicator of their basic social value, . . . personalities, . . . and outlook on important life problems" (p. 88), or of no informational value whatsoever. Greater involvement led to greater attitude change, though change was a positive function of discrepancy at both levels of involvement. Rhine and Severance (1970) equated ego involvement with the importance of an issue, as rated by control subjects, and found it to interact with discrepancy. For the low involvement issue, attitude change increased with discrepancy, but for the high involvement issue, attitude change did not vary with discrepancy.

Involvement has also been operationalized as commitment to a position on an issue, as opposed to issue importance. Freedman (1964) and Greenwald (1964) manipulated involvement by stressing the personal importance of subjects' taking the position they did. They found high involvement to result in less attitude change at high levels of discrepancy; greater change occurred with low involvement and low to moderate discrepancy. Ostrom and Brock (1968) defined involvement in terms of a "value-bonding" process, whereby it varies with the relevance of an attitude to the individual's values, particularly those that are centrally important to his or her self-definition. Involvement manipulations that explicitly or implicitly draw such a relationship are expected to arouse commitment to a position and resistance to change. Like Freedman and Greenwald, Ostrom and Brock (1968), who had subjects specifically relate positions on an issue to their personal values, obtained greater resistance to change with high involvement upon presenting them with highly discrepant information.

Credibility of the source of information affects the relationship between discrepancy and attitude change. Credibility in social influence depends upon the communicator being perceived by the recipient as expert and trustworthy, that is, able and willing to communicate valid information (Hovland, Janis, & Kelley, 1953). According to dissonance theory, high credibility limits the extent to which one can discredit the communicator of a discrepant message, thus increasing the likelihood of attitude change in the direction of the discrepancy as the mode of reducing dissonance. Aronson, Turner, and Carlsmith (1963) compared highly and moderately credible sources for their persuasiveness in delivering messages at three levels of discrepancy. For the highly credible source, they found that the amount of change obtained was a positive linear function of the amount advocated. For the moderately credible source, the relationship was curvilinear, with the greatest change occurring at moderate discrepancy. Derogation of the communication (message and source) was also measured, but contrary to the prediction of dissonance theory, it was not found to vary with level of discrepancy, even in the moderate credibility condition. Bergin (1962), however, did obtain such an effect. In addition to replicating Aronson, Turner, and Carlsmith's finding of a linear relationship between discrepancy and attitude change in the high credibility condition, he found derogation of the low (*not* moderate) credibility source to increase with increasing discrepancy. Bochner and Insko (1966) investigated source credibility and eight levels of discrepancy, measuring source and message disparagement separately. They found that even with a wide range of discrepant messages, the relationship between discrepancy and attitude change was linear in the high credibility condition and curvilinear in the moderate credibility condition. In addition, the highly credible source was less persuasive than the moderately credible source when discrepancies were small. Disparagement of source— lowering estimates of source credibility—increased with increasing discrepancy for the moderately credible source. Disparagement of the message increased with discrepancy regardless of source credibility. The results supported the dissonance theory prediction that as the amount of change advocated (and thus dissonance) increases, disparagement of the message and, if possible, the source of the message is increasingly chosen as a mode of reducing dissonance. Rhine and Severance (1970) varied source credibility, along with the ego involvement and discrepancy variables described earlier. In this study, not only did source derogation *not* occur in the low involvement condition, but subjects actually became more positive toward the source. In the high involvement condition, there was no change in attitude toward the source. In addition, source credibility in this study did not differentially affect attitude change. The authors hypothesized that source credibility may be important only in instances of low ego involvement.

When discrepancy is very low or even absent, attitude change might not be expected. However, receiving information consonant with one's own position can have important effects on attitudes. Goethals and his colleagues (Goethals, 1972; Goethals & Nelson, 1973) have shown that the effects of receiving consonant information depended on the nature of the message and information about the source. In their analysis, the influence process includes judgments concerning what the content of the message—the position advocated—may be attributed to. Subjects in a study by Goethals (1972) were required to judge an ambiguous situation and to indicate their confidence in the judgment. Then the subjects received a communicator's judgment, along with information about the communicator that led them to believe that the communicator was either similar or dissimilar in interpersonal orientation (a quality relevant to the judgment task) and had received either the same or different data as a basis for the judgment. Subjects receiving an agreeing judgment increased confidence in their judgment if the communicator was dissimilar but had the same data, or was similar but had different data. In the former case, Goethals (1972) argued, subjects' confidence increased because someone with a very different viewpoint arrived at the same conclusion as the subject, thus lending *consensus* to the subject's judgment and reducing the possibility that the subject's judgment reflected personal bias. In the latter case, the subject's confidence increased when there was consensus across individuals with different interpersonal orientations but the same data or *consistency* across modalities, that is, different data as viewed by similar individuals. Consensus and consistency are common dimensions used by individuals to make causal attributions about an entity, in this case, a judgment (Kelley, 1967). A later study (Goethals & Nelson, 1973) showed that these effects occur when the attitudes in question are beliefs that may be verified by evidence, but not when they are value judgments. When the judgment task in this study concerned the academic success of college students (a belief), an agreeing judgment by a dissimilar communicator increased subjects' confidence more than one by a similar communicator. However, when the task involved rating which students they liked more (a value), agreement from a similar communicator raised confidence more. These findings have clear implications not only about how to strengthen attitudes, but also for source characteristics contributing to the communicator's social power.

Discrepancy is at the core of the influence process in counseling and psychotherapy. Strong (1978) argued that change is a response to cognitive inconsistencies created by making clients aware of discrepancies in their thoughts, feelings, and actions. Levy (1963) included cognitive discrepancies among the key ''differentials'' operating in the therapeutic situation. A second differential, also a source of discrepancy, is between the therapist's and client's emotional reactions to events. These, too, stimulate change by drawing into contrast how the client does respond and how the client might alternatively respond. The mechanism of cognitive consistency applies equally well to affective events, since attitudes have a strong affective component.

Attitude change via induced discrepancy in counseling and psychotherapy is indirectly documented in studies of convergence. In such studies, measures of client and therapist attitudes indicate that the clients become increasingly like the therapists over the course of therapy. According to Pepinsky and Karst's (1964) review, manifestations of convergence are present in the client's language, values, and personality. Persons and Pepinsky (1966) found convergence among incarcerated delinquents toward their therapists' personality traits, values, and overt behavior, but only when therapists were perceived as warm and understanding. Convergence in values has also been reported by Rosenthal (1955) and Petoney (1966). Other studies have shown convergence of cognitive variables. Edwards and Edgerly (1970) found low congruence in the evaluative meanings attached to concepts to be most associated with change, and Cook (1966) found greatest change with medium congruence between therapist and client evaluative meanings. Beutler, Johnson, Neville, Elkins, and Jobe (1975) found low initial congruence between client and therapist attitudes to be associated with greater therapist influence. Beutler (1971) reported a nonsignificant trend for therapist–client convergence in marital therapy that was unrelated to improvement; improvement instead was associated with convergence between husband and wife. Beutler, Jobe, and Elkins (1976) also found client attitude change to be greater where therapist and client attitudes initially differed, but found improvement to be related to therapist–client similarity. Landfield (1971) found that initial therapist–client incongruence in the organization of personal constructs (dimensions for viewing and interpreting the world) facilitated client improvement and that improvement was associated with convergence toward the therapist's organization of personal constructs. Initial incongruence in the content of the constructs, however, led to premature termination, indicating the importance of ''shared meaningfulness'' (p. 79) in an endeavor that depends on discrepancies to effect change.

See next page

Although the studies of convergence reviewed above suggest that cognitive consistency is a key mechanism of change, they do not directly assess how change occurs. While the particulars of counseling and psychotherapy differ from those of the social psychology laboratory, extrapolations may nevertheless shed light on how therapists might employ discrepancy to promote change. To begin with, the relationship between discrepancy and attitude change appears not to be positive and linear in the therapeutic setting. Browning (1966) found interpretations of lower discrepancy to produce greater insight and client agreement, although they did not necessarily result in greater change. Claiborn, Ward, and Strong (1981) found congruence between the counselor's interpretations and the client's beliefs to be more facilitative of change than large discrepancies in content. In analogue interview studies, both Bergin (1962) and Strong and Dixon (1971) obtained greater change with influence attempts of medium discrepancy. These findings may reflect high ego involvement of the subjects in the issues, the impact of an intimate relationship, or the nature of the change advocated. For instance, in the Claiborn, Ward, and Strong (1981) study, clients were influenced to change causal attributions regarding their problem, and the counselor's interpretations necessarily included a complex set of attitudes. Such a situation, typical of psychotherapy, differs considerably from experiments in which subjects are influenced to shift positions with regard to a single issue. The implications of these factors have not yet been explored.

It may be safe to say that therapist interventions—particularly those performing the interpretational function of changing client conceptualizations—generally effect change in small increments. They certainly need to be large enough, however, to promote cognitive inconsistency and its press for change. If the issue is important to the client, and at the same time confusing or otherwise disturbing, the client's ego involvement will facilitate change in the direction offered by the therapist, and the therapist's interventions may be more discrepant. If the client is committed to a position on an issue, interventions of small discrepancy are warranted since larger discrepancies are likely to produce resistance.

Research on consonant communication suggests that interventions of very low discrepancy may strengthen the client's confidence in his or her position, depending especially on how the therapist is perceived. If such strengthening is the desired outcome, the therapist should attend to providing consensual data, a common technique in group work. If strengthening is not desired, the therapist may choose to influence the client with discrepancies small enough to appear acceptable to the client (Strong & Matross, 1973). According to Sherif and Hovland's (1961) social judgment theory, such communications fall within the "latitude of acceptance," and the individual will be influenced to adopt the position by perceiving it to be more similar to his or her original position than it is. The process of influence by perceptual distortion is called *assimilation*, and it is evident in therapeutic interventions that employ subtle shifts in meaning or construction, as in the restatements and reflections of the client-centered approach.

Social Power

If discrepancy is the internal mechanism of change, then social power provides the interpersonal leverage. Social power, a field theory concept, is "the maximum 'resultant' force A can bring to bear on B with respect to a particular region of B's life space" (Schopler, 1965, p. 197). In the therapeutic relationship, the therapist's social power corresponds to his or her ability to induce client compliance with suggested behaviors and acceptance of communicated ideas. "Resultant" is an important part of the definition, because therapist power is not absolute, nor does influence go unimpeded. The nature and degree of the therapist's social power set limits on the types of interventions he or she may use effectively and on the amount of discrepancy they can advocate. Moreover, the therapist's efforts to gain compliance are invariably met with client attempts to counter those efforts. Social power, then, represents forces available to the therapist over and above anticompliance forces manifest in the client's communication.

Strong and Matross (1973) outlined how social power may operate in therapeutic settings. In their field theory analysis, three forces function simultaneously in the therapist–client interaction to determine change. The therapist's social power is a force promoting change in thoughts, feelings, and actions. Working against change are the client's opposition to the content of the therapist's interventions and resistance to the act of intervention. Opposition is disagreement with the therapist's viewpoint. Opposition forces are linked to discrepancy, as client opposition is stimulated by advocacy of too great a change. Resistance forces, on the other hand, concern not what the therapist says but how the therapist presents it. Resistance is stimulated by therapist activities that the client considers illegitimate. Overcoming client opposition entails reducing support for the client's position, advocating a position that is not too discrepant, and closing off alternative paths of reducing cognitive inconsistency. Overcoming client resistance is an interpersonal matter; it involves the maintenance of a social power base appropriate to change strategies employed by the therapist.

French and Raven (1959) have cited five sources of social power: ability to reward or to punish others (reward and coercive power); social sanction to induce compliance (legitimate power); characteristics that promote identification by others (referent power); and special knowledge (expert power). All of these obtain, to some extent, in counseling and psychotherapy, though for the therapist reward and coercive power are secondary functions of expert, referent, and legitimate power. Each social power base relies on the client's perceiving that the therapist has the necessary qualities and resources to meet the client's needs. Strong and Matross (1973) expressed this in the symobolic formula, $P = f(R \cong N)$, indicating that therapist social power is a function of correspondence ($\cong$) between the therapist's resources and the client's needs, both as perceived by the client. To the extent that such a correspondences exists, the therapist is socially powerful vis-à-vis the client and, conversely, the client is dependent on the therapist. Client dependency is both essential to change and "self-canceling" (Strong, 1978, p. 106). Successful therapy, by reducing the needs of the client for the therapist's resources, reduces the dependency based on those needs as well as the therapist's ability to induce compliance. The forces holding the relationship together are eliminated by its success, and the relationship dissolves.

The legitimate power of the therapist derives from his or her acknowledged role as a helper. A therapist need not be a professional to be legitimate, but must be seen by the client as an appropriate person to deliver the required services. The therapist's legitimacy depends partly on whom the client's social group considers an appropriate helper for the problem in question, partly on the client's own preference, and partly on information provided by the helper or helping agency. In counseling and psychotherapy, the legitimate power base contributes to the "status differential" (Levy, 1963) between therapist and client; it places the therapist "one-up" in the relationship. The voluntary and contractual nature of their work together adds to the therapist's legitimacy and corresponding status. The knowledge, training, and reputation of the therapist affects legitimacy by contributing to the client's confidence in the correctness and appropriateness of the therapist's activities. Without legitimacy, aspects of the therapeutic process such as intimate self-disclosure and the outward peculiarities of the therapist's techniques would arouse insurmountable threat and resistance. Legitimacy is requisite for the development of trust in the relationship.

Expert power derives from client perceptions of the therapist's knowledge and skills to bring about change. The corresponding need is the client's awareness of difficulties and desire to change. According to Hovland, Janis, and Kelley (1953), expertness is the communicator's being "perceived to be the source of valid assertions" (.p. 21), and it contributes to communicator credibility, along with trustworthiness. Communicator credibility promotes attitude change by making it unlikely that the recipient will derogate the communicator or discount the communication. Thus, to the extent that the therapist is seen as an expert in dealing with the client's problems, client opposition to the therapist's discrepant viewpoint is diminished.

Client attraction to the therapist is the source of the therapist's social power as a referent. Interpersonal attraction to an individual depends on perceptions of similarity or liking (Berscheid & Walster, 1978). To the extent that the client perceives the therapist to have qualities or experiences similar to the client's, or to like the client, the therapist may occupy the influential role of a referent. As one who shares basic values, styles of behaving, or past experiences, the therapist has the credibility of an esteemed peer whose world view is essentially the same as the client's but whose adaptation to the world is more effective. Given their basic similarity and important differences, the therapist as referent represents discrepancy itself to the client. Interpersonal attraction provides the therapist with the influence potential to bring about resolution.

The combination of legitimacy, expertness, and attractiveness that comprises a therapist's social power depends on client needs and perceptions. Particular therapists and therapeutic orientations may emphasize one social power base more than the others. However, a therapist could not work without basic legitimacy, some perceived expertise, and even common understandings based on personal experience or shared values. Beyond this, it is important for the therapist to be aware of the power bases from which he or she operates, since there is evidence that incongruous shifts from one to the other can violate client expectations and arouse resistance (Dell, 1973).

Credibility

Communicator credibility interacts with message discrepancy and recipient involvement to affect attitude change. Credibility—expertness and trustworthiness—is unquestionably a powerful variable in the influence process. A communicator is perceived as credible on the basis of behavior, reputation, and a variety of objective cues, such as title and position (Strong, 1968). Credibility and attitude change have been studied by Aronson, Turner, and Carlsmith (1963), who manipulated reputation and used a written influence attempt; Bochner and Insko (1966), using a similar methodology but with eight levels of discrepancy; and Bergin (1962), who presented the influence in an interview context, varying objective cues to produce levels of credibility. In each case, the highly credible source produced greater attitude change than less credible sources in interaction with discrepancy; greater credibility was required to obtain change as the amount of change advocated increased. Rhine and Severance (1970) have suggested, however, that this relationship may not obtain with an issue that is highly involving. When their subjects were personally involved in an issue, communicator credibility did not affect influence.

Mills and Harvey (1972) reported that the expert's ability to influence is greater when the recipient knows beforehand of the communicator's credentials. Norman (1976) found the expert to be more influential, depending on the use of supportive arguments. In both studies, the attractive communicator's influence was unaffected by these variables. The last finding fits Strong's (1968) description of an expert communicator as presenting "rational and knowledgeable arguments" (p. 216) and McGuire's (1969) linking the persuasive impact of credibility to a "rational, problem-solving . . . [recipient] trying to adjust his belief system as closely as possible to external reality" (p. 182).

A number of studies have provided evidence on the importance of expertness in therapy or therapylike settings. In a counseling analogue study, Strong and Schmidt (1970a) manipulated interviewer expertness by varying title and behavior. Both manipulations were perceived as relevant to the interviewer's expertness and jointly affected attitude change. The behavioral manipulation of expertness was rather all-encompassing, based on roles developed by Schmidt and Strong (1970):

> The *expert* was attentive and interested in the subject. He looked at the subject; he leaned toward him and was responsive to the subject by his facial expressions, head nods, posture, and so on. He used hand gestures to emphasize his points. The *inexpert* was inattentive to the subject. He either did not look at

the subject, or gave him a deadpan stare and was not reactive to him. He either did not use gestures, or his gestures were stiff, formal, and overdone. While the *expert* performed with an air of confidence, the *inexpert* was unsure, nervous, and lacked confidence.

The *expert* was organized and knew what he was doing. He structured the interview by suggesting possible topics and where the subject might begin. He described the task to the subject, and he explained that his own role in the interview was to facilitate the subject's discussions. The *inexpert* was confused and unsure of where to begin. He offered only minimal help to the subject and did not clarify his role in the interview. (p. 87)

Greenberg (1969) manipulated presession information given to subjects concerning the therapist's amount of experience and found it affected their receptivity to his influence. Guttman and Haase (1972) also varied presession information regarding expertness given to subjects who were then interviewed about the results of psychological tests. Although subjects reported learning more from the "nonexpert" (*not* an inexpert, as in other studies), an objective measure indicated that they actually learned more from the expert. This contrasts with social psychological findings reported by McGuire (1969) of greater influence but less message learning from a highly credible source. Binderman, Fretz, Scott, and Abrams, (1972) found that a counselor introduced as a Ph.D. produced greater change through interpreting psychological test results than the same individual introduced as a practicum student. Higher credibility was especially important with large discrepancies between test results and subjects' self-assessments. In the study most resembling therapy, Browning (1966) varied the prestige by which the therapist was introduced prior to subjects meeting with him for several interviews. Results indicated that the therapist, who made interpretations of varying discrepancy, was more influential with subjects when they had received the high prestige introduction.

Therapists may establish their expertness by objective evidence of status and credentials, reputation as an expert, and behavior in the interview. The therapist's title indicates status relative to the client and professional training. Introductions as "Dr. ____," a psychologist, or a Ph.D. influence perceived expertness (e.g., Guttman & Haase, 1972; Hartley, 1969). Other evidence of expertise may stem from the therapist's reputation for having needed resources or from contextual cues. Willingness to help (Savitsky, Zarle, & Keedy, 1976), evidence of prior accomplishments (Claiborn & Schmidt, 1977; Spiegel, 1976), and diplomas and awards (Heppner & Pew, 1977; Siegel & Sell, 1978) have been found to affect perceived expertness. Casual and professional attire is associated with greater expertness when congruent with behavioral manner in the interview than when incongruent (Kerr & Dell, 1976), suggesting that consistency among cues may be important in attributions of expertise. Violation of expectancies can also enhance expertness, however, as in the case of peer helpers who are particularly accomplished in their work (Claiborn & Schmidt, 1977).

Behavioral evidence of expertness includes a wide range of cues, some stylistic and some based in the sort of interventions used. Therapists who are warm, responsive, confident, and verbally and nonverbally active are seen as more expert than those who are not (Dell & Schmidt, 1976; Greenwood, 1973; Scheid, 1976; Schmidt & Strong, 1970). The use of professional jargon (Atkinson & Carskaddon, 1975), psychological interpretations (Claiborn, 1979), and statements of personal reaction to the client's disclosure (McCarthy & Betz, 1978) have also been found to increase perceived expertness. Generally, behavior that indicates therapist knowledge and confidence increases expertness perceptions. To the extent the therapist offers the client new content, the client can make attributions regarding the therapist's superior resources. To the extent that the therapist offers it assuredly, the client obtains data supporting these attributions.

Trustworthiness as a separate variable has been less explored in social influence research, though there is some indication that it is an important component of source credibility (e.g., Walster, Aronson, & Abrahams, 1966; Zagona & Harter, 1966). Strong and Schmidt (1970b), in a one-interview counseling analogue, were not able to produce attitude change differences by varying the interviewer's trustworthiness behaviorally. Rothmeier and Dixon (1980) manipulated untrustworthiness with interviewer inaccuracies, inconsistent behavior, and violations of confidentiality. Trustworthy interviewers were characterized by competent interviewing. Greater influence was obtained in the trustworthy condition after two interviews. The trustworthy and untrustworthy roles were nonverbally as well as verbally distinguished, however, and the differences may have been due to the nonverbal behavior of the interviewers. Kaul and Schmidt (1971) and Roll, Schmidt, and Kaul (1972) have reported nonverbal manner to be a more potent factor than verbal content in effecting trustworthiness perceptions. Merluzzi, Banikiotes, and Missbach (1978), on the other hand, did find that female interviewers who self-disclosed less were perceived as more trustworthy, an effect not observed for males. Trustworthiness seems the *sine qua non* of therapy: it is not as difficult to achieve as expertness and attractiveness, but the therapist is lost without it. It is the necessary foundation upon which social power is established.

Attractiveness

Ability to influence is enhanced as the recipient perceives the communicator to be similar or compatible, or feels the communicator likes him or her. Back (1951) found that subjects in pairs who believed themselves to be well matched, according to descriptions of self and preferred other, influenced each other more than those who believed they were not well matched. In a verbal conditioning task, Sapolsky (1960) found that subjects believing themselves to be poorly matched with the experimenter were less willing to be influenced than subjects who believed they were well matched. The effects were the same for perceived matching based on bogus preexperimental instructions as for matching on the FIRO-B, though in the former case the effect was more immediate. Berscheid (1966) found that when perceived similarity was relevant to the issue, greater change occurred than when it was irrelevant. Clearly perceived similarities are the keys to influence from a referent base, though actual similarities may contribute to these perceptions. Simons, Berkowitz, and Moyer (1970) distinguished between similarity in the attitudes people hold and similarity in the social group to which they belong. On the basis of their review of research, they drew the following conclusions regarding similarity and influence:

> 1. Relevant attitudinal similarities have positive effects on attitude change; equivalent dissimilarities have negative effects; irrelevant attitudinal similarities have insignificant effects. (p. 9)
> 2. The relationship between relevant membership-group similarities and attitude change is a function of the perceived status of the receiver relative to the source. Irrelevant membership-group similarities have little or no effect on attitude change. (p. 10)
> 3. Attitude change toward the position advocated by the source depends on the extent to which interpersonal similarities or dissimilarities are perceived as having instrumental value for the receiver. (p. 12)

This last assertion is equivalent to the concept of social power as need—resource correspondence (Strong & Matross, 1973) and points to the mechanism underlying influence from a referent base.

Perceived liking is also a source of communicator attractiveness. Mills and Harvey (1972) and Norman (1976) operationalized attractiveness as membership in the subject's peer group, popularity, and attractive physical appearance (in a photograph); they found the attractive communicator to be more consistently influential than the unattractive expert communicator. The expert required supportive arguments or subject's prior knowledge of his expertise in order to be influential. McGuire (1969), however, has noted theoretical and empirical instances of greater attitude change from disliked sources. Such change can occur as the recipient attempts to justify listening to or complying with a disliked communicator. Goethals (1976) has also demonstrated that dissimilar communicators are more effective, particularly when they provide consensus by agreeing with the recipient. The relationship between attraction and influence is obviously complex.

Research relevant to counseling and psychotherapy has examined attraction separately and in interaction with credibility. Greenberg (1969) found that subjects were more open to influence when a therapist they listened to on tape was introduced as a warm person than when he was introduced as a cold person. In similar studies, Goldstein (1971) reported that presession information regarding therapist warmth and background similarity led to differential attraction, but not always receptivity to influence. However, in studies with clients in a clinic, Goldstein found that presession information regarding similarity had no effect on subjects' attraction to the interviewer. He suggested that impressions gained during interaction are much more powerful determinants of attraction than is presession information. Goldstein has also reported that similarity in issues of concern can be more significant than positions on those issues in determining attraction. In one of his studies, alcoholic clients were more attracted to the therapist when presession information regarded attitudes that were relevant to the problem area of alcoholism than when they were irrelevant to the issue. Goldstein speculated that people seeking change may be more attracted to help givers who do *not* share their attitudes, at least in some respects. The literature on convergence and the theory of discrepancy presented above lends support to this viewpoint.

Perceived attractiveness is largely affected by therapist behavior, and nonverbal cues are among the most potent. Cash and his colleagues (Cash, Begley, McCown, & Weise, 1976; Cash & Kehr, 1978) have found physical attractiveness to contribute to positive reactions to counselors, although counselor self-disclosure was a stronger variable affecting such reactions (Cash & Salzbach, 1978). Affiliative and active nonverbal behaviors have been shown to enhance attractiveness perceptions (Claiborn, 1979; LaCrosse, 1975; Strong, Taylor, Bratten, & Loper, 1971). These include smiling, responsive head nodding, gestures, high eye contact, and forward posture, which indicate liking for the client or involvement in the interview. Verbal statements of liking (Bayes, 1972) can increase attractiveness, but it is improbable that they can do so in the absence of validating nonverbal cues. Statements of similarity to the client can also contribute to the therapist's attractiveness, especially if they imply an understanding of the client's experience (Hoffman-Graff, 1977).

While many analogue studes have shown that therapist attractiveness can be affected by introductions and interview behavior, the majority of studies have not demonstrated an influence effect (Dell, 1973; Schmidt & Strong, 1971; Sell, 1974). Patton (1969), however, manipulated presession information concerning liking and liking behavior in the interview and found attractive interviewers to be more influential than unattractive ones. Strong and Dixon (1971) varied expertness in presession information and attractiveness in interviewer behavior and found that attractive behavior rendered inexpert interviewers influential, though if the interviewers were expert, they were influential regardless of their attractiveness.

Ample literature suggests that therapists who behave positively toward the client facilitate change, yet a variety of interventions provide exceptions to this generalization. Attraction based on similarities is a still greater problem and revolves around the question, "Similar in what way?" It has been shown that client perceptions of therapist similarity in attitudes, background, and group membership do not necessarily enhance attraction to the therapist let alone reliably increase receptivity to the therapist's influence. The "status differential" that is unavoidably present in the therapeutic relationship and the heavy reliance on discrepancy to produce change complicate relationships among perceived similarity, attraction, and change. On the other hand, the importance to therapy of shared meanings, interpersonal rapport, and a referent viewpoint against which to assess reality cannot be discounted. Further research on similarity and discrepancy, topic relevance, group versus attitude similarity, value similarity versus interpersonal compatibility, and interactions among similarity, status, and expertness will clarify this confusing picture.

Need

The client's need for the therapist's resources helps to establish and maintain the social power balance for the duration of the relationship. Need creates client dependence on the therapist and increases the extent to which the therapist may influence the client. Need is a difficult concept to generalize and study. Hoehn-Saric, Frank, and Gurland (1968) induced emotional arousal with ether to study influence in psychotherapy. They found arousal to increase susceptibility to the therapist's influence regarding concepts important in the patients' lives. Susceptibility was greater, in fact, after arousal had subsided somewhat:

> After the acute phase wore off, . . . [the patients] seemed more dependent, eager to talk about themselves and very receptive to the therapist's comments. Repeated exposure to sessions in which suggestion was given seems to have made patients more susceptible to it. (p. 130)

The authors offered a number of explanations for this effect, including heightened expectation, therapist credibility, and message repetition. The most compelling was that the emotional arousal was accompanied by increased cognitive disorganization and dependency of the patient on the therapist to provide "a strongly structured cognitive framework" (p. 131) to counteract the confusion. This was supported in part by the observation that suggestions were more likely to be accepted if accompanied by a rationale. Such an explanation fits well with the formula presented by Strong and Matross (1973), linking the therapist's social power to a perceived need—resource correspondence. A second study (Hoehn-Saric, Liberman, Imber, Stone, Pande, & Frank, 1972) tightened controls to eliminate competing explanations; the factors of therapist credibility and prior patient expectations were made constant by the use of elaborate drug administration procedures in the two treatments. Again, under high arousal, patients exhibited greater susceptibility to the therapist's influence, confirming the explanation that arousal itself accounted for the effect.

Heppner and Dixon (1978) explicitly tested the Strong and Matross formula in a counseling analogue, defining need as client's self-perceived dissatisfaction with current behavior and found that need has no effect on influence. Dixon and Claiborn (1980) studied need as a request for help with dissatisfying behavior and as commitment to change behavior in career counseling. High levels of both variables were associated with greater influence. Clients complied with the counselor's behavioral directives primarily if they had committed themselves to change by contracting, but were also more likely to comply if they had defined themselves as needing help at the outset of counseling.

Commitment

When influence is effected through communication, the communicator who possesses social power presents the recipient with discrepant messages, and attitude change results from the recipient's efforts to resolve the cognitive inconsistencies the messages create. However, not all cognitive inconsistencies are the product of discrepant communications. They may result from the individual's commitment to counterattitudinal behavior. In this case, discrepancy is directly attributable to a single individual, who is both the source of the discrepant behavior and the recipient of its implications in the form of cognitive inconsistency. A second individual, however, may stimulate cognitive inconsistency by indirectly inducing compliance with counterattitudinal behavior. This is the role of the experimenter in social psychological studies and of the therapist in counseling and psychotherapy.

Brehm and Cohen (1962) stressed the importance of commitment as a condition for the arousal of cognitive inconsistency. Commitment concerns cognitive or overt acts that have definite behavioral implications for the individual in the future, the awareness of which is accompanied by a sense of irrevocability (Gerard, 1968). The very nature of commitment renders corresponding cognitions resistant to change and places restrictions on how cognitive inconsistencies are resolved.

Commitment to behavior discrepant from attitudes the individual holds generates cognitive inconsistency. This is especially true if commitment is public—observed by others—and if the individual perceives the act to have been freely chosen. These conditions make the position expressed difficult to discount or revoke and lead to attitude change in the direction of the commitment. Brock (1962), for example, was able to change non-Catholic students' attitudes toward Catholicism by having them write essays on "Why I Would Like to Become a Catholic." Subjects in a study by Cohen and Latané (1962) changed their attitudes on the issue of a compulsory religion course as a result of verbally expressing a position discrepant from their own. In both of these studies, choice contributed to the effects of commitment: subjects who perceived themselves to have a high degree of choice about whether to express the counterattitudinal position showed more change than subjects who felt they had little choice but to comply. Similarly, the lack of incentive enhances behavioral commitment. Cohen (1962) found that when subjects wrote an essay counter to their opinion, the less the incentive, the greater the subsequent attitude change. Change occurred to justify the behavior. Public commitment to a position, in contrast to an anonymous expression, has been found to interact with the effects of incentive. Carlsmith, Collins, and Helmreich (1966) found that interpersonal expression of a discrepant attitude produced greater attitude change under the low incentive condition, but when subjects anonymously advocated the discrepant position, greater attitude change occurred in the high incentive condition. In judgment experiments, commitment has been manipulated by varying the future implications of the subjects' behavior. To produce high commitment, Brehm and Leventhal(1962) informed subjects that one particular judgment in an unfinished series of weight estimates would be considered the final estimate of the average weight of the whole series. The low commitment condition did not include this information. Discrepancy was then introduced by making the next weight in the series unexpectedly heavy. Committed subjects did not revise their average estimate based on incoming discrepant information as uncommitted subjects did, but instead distorted the new information. Commitment in the form of expectation of a certain outcome similarly has been found to affect perceptual judgments leading to that outcome (Thibaut & Ross, 1969). Commitment to certain outcomes affects how individuals process discrepant information (Wicklund & Brehm, 1976). Commitment increases resistance of attitudes to change by distorting perception of information discrepant with those attitudes.

Commitment to consonant behavior, publicly expressing an attitude that one *does* hold, renders the attitude more resistant to change. Evidence for this was reported by Kiesler and Sakumura (1966). They induced subjects to express verbally a position with which the subjects agreed, for either a high or low monetary reward. Then subjects received a communication discrepant with that position. Subjects who received the lower incentive and were consequently more committed showed less attitude change (greater resistance to change). In a similar study, Kiesler, Pallak, and Kanouse (1968) varied the degree of commitment to consonant behavior by having subjects communicate their position publicly (high commitment) or anonymously (low commitment). Then subjects wrote essays containing a discrepant position. High commitment subjects displayed greater resistance to attitude change than did low commitment subjects. Low commitment subjects displayed a comparably high resistance to change only if they perceived themselves to have little choice but to write the essay. Low commitment subjects who felt free to choose changed their attitudes the most. Halverson and Pallak (1978) studied commitment in subjects who held moderate and extreme positions. Perhaps due to a ceiling effect, degree of commitment had no effect on resistance to change in subjects holding extreme positions. For subjects holding moderate positions, however, high commitment via public expression produced greater resistance to change when subjects were met with discrepant communication. The authors suggested that such commitment may increase ego involvement with an issue.

Commitment to interaction with others in the future has been shown to affect the influence others have over the individual's attitudes. Kiesler, and his colleagues (e.g., Kiesler & Corbin, 1965; Kiesler, Zanna, & DeSalvo, 1966) found that commitment to future interaction with a group altered the often demonstrated relationship between a group's attractiveness and its influence. In their experiments, subjects interacted in a small group performing an evaluative task and then received feedback about how well they were accepted by group members (the attraction manipulation). Subjects were then shown ratings from the other group members on the evaluative task that were discrepant from their own and were given an opportunity to change their ratings. Subjects in the low attraction condition exhibited less attitude change than subjects in the high attraction condition, but only when the subjects did not expect to meet again with the group. When the subjects were committed to future interaction with the group, the effect was reversed with greater influence occurring in the low attraction condition. The authors concluded that when an individual is committed to further contact with others who are not accepting, the cognitive inconsistency may be resolved by attitude change in the direction of agreement with the group. If one is not so committed, other modes establishing consistency, such as rejection of the group, are available.

Perceived choice and commitment to a particular course of action have been shown to alter the effects of other variables on behavior. In studies on physiological drives, subjects in a state of deprivation, such as hunger or thirst, are asked to commit themselves to more deprivation for either high or low justification, creating conditions of low and high cognitive inconsistency, respectively. Results have generally shown that subjects who chose continued deprivation for little justifcation experienced less deprivation (e.g., Brehm & Crocker, 1962) and exhibited less consummatory behavior (e.g., Mansson, 1969) than subjects who felt justified in continuing deprivation. The arousal of cognitive inconsistency altered the motivational effects of physiological deprivation; to resolve the inconsistency subjects changed cognitions and behavior relevant to their hunger or thirst. Similar results have been obtained in studies of social deprivation. In a verbal conditioning study with social approval as the reinforcer, Cohen, Greenbaum, and Mansson (1963) deprived subjects of reinforcement for the final 10 minutes of a 15-minute interview. Subjects were then asked to volunteer for a second interview with a disapproving interviewer and offered either a sufficient or insufficient incentive to do so. Results indicated that the social approval in the second interview was an effective reinforcer only for subjects offered the sufficient incentive. Subjects without sufficient incentive for being interviewed minimized the social deprivation, which they had chosen with little justification, as a response to cognitive inconsistency. Since the strength of social approval was dependent on the need for it (deprivation), the reinforcer was relatively impotent for these subjects. As Wicklund and Brehm (1976) summed up the effects of cognitive inconsistency, or dissonance, on deprivation and subsequent reinforcement:

> Whenever a reinforcer has an impact on learning, the effectiveness of that reinforcer can be curtailed if the individual commits himself, under dissonance-arousing circumstances, to doing without that reinforcer. Cognitive dissonance has the effect of bringing forth derogation of that reinforcer, and it appears that the behavior of a person who convinces himself he has no need for reinforcement is then less subject to being "shaped up" by such reinforcement. (pp. 195–196)

Behavior contrary to firmly held beliefs is productive of cognitive inconsistency when freely choosing the behavior removes the possibility of justifying it with the belief that one was not responsible. Glass (1964) varied both the self-esteem of subjects by false feedback and the degree of choice they had to aggress against a confederate. Subjects in the high self-esteem (high choice) group liked the confederate least; they responded to self-inconsistent behavior with cognitions rendering the confederate more deserving of the aggression. Brock and Buss (1962) studied the same aggressive behavior, not as inconsistent with self-concept, but with the attitude that it is wrong to use electric shock in scientific research with human subjects. Subjects in the high choice condition responded to their own counterattitudinal behavior by minimizing the painfulness of the shock, as well as by disparaging the recipient of the shock. These responses served to make the unethical behavior less real and the recipient of aggression more deserving; thus the behavior was less of a violation of the subjects' ethics. Firestone (1969) placed subjects in the position of receiving aggression and studied their responses when they were given an opportunity to retaliate. He found that subjects who had been verbally attacked by a confederate rated the confederate more positively if they chose to meet with him again than if they were given no choice. When the confederate continued to provoke subjects with an electric shock during a task, those who had chosen to participate with the confederate retaliated least when given an opportunity to shock him. Cognitive inconsistency aroused by choosing to receive aggression led not to frustration and strong retaliation, but to a "turn-the-other-cheek" phenomenon (Zimbardo, 1968).

Commitment and choice are critical concepts in counseling and psychotherapy. Part of the lore of many theoretical orientations is the assertion that the client must be "committed" to change, which is perhaps true, but this is something like saying a student must be motivated to learn. The client's commitment to specific attitudes and actions must be shaped in the social influence process, and this is the therapist's responsibility. Commitment under conditions of perceived choice and public expression affects attitude change and resistance to change. The role of the therapist is to promote both, and a number of therapeutic interventions manipulate client commitment to yield these effects. Clients are induced to commit themselves to attitudes and behavior discrepant from what they believe through role playing, restatements suggested by the therapist, and otherwise behaving "as if" something about themselves or the world were true. Therapists frequently elicit feelings, ideas, and actions discrepant from the client's established self-concept, and promoting the client's commitment to that aspect of his or her behavior is one way of altering self-concept to incorporate the new behavior. For the therapist it is a foothold for influencing the client. Research on commitment to consonant positions is also relevant to therapeutic interventions. Commitment strengthens attitudes, even in the face of counterarguments. Interventions that elicit verbal commitment or shape behavioral commitment to desired attitudes, in light of the changes the client is making, might appropriately enhance their robustness.

Choice, too, is an important element in the philosophy and language of therapeutic approaches. It is important for the client to attribute change not to the therapist's influence but to his or her own self. Winett (1970) has noted the relevance of dissonance research to the therapist's "creating an illusion of choice" (p. 22) when advocating discrepant behavior for the client. Commitment and subsequent attitude change are greater and more permanent if the client is able to attribute actions to internal causes. Actual choice is not the issue; perceived or inferred choice is.

ATTITUDE CHANGE STRATEGIES

The therapeutic process is an ongoing series of attitude changes. The therapist manages the attitudes that the client has of him or her as a communicator, thereby establishing a base of social power in the relationship. The shaping of these attitudes often begins before therapy, as the therapist's reputation and client expectations and needs promote beliefs about how the therapist can help the client. Based on attitudes about the therapist's credibility, willingness to help, and ability to comprehend the unique situation of the client, the client acquires hope that the therapist will succeed in helping the client achieve goals. The importance of hope cannot be overstressed, since it contributes substantially to the effectiveness of therapy (Frank, 1973). Once established, the therapist's social power must be maintained in the relationship. Client attitudes toward the therapist necessarily vary with the experience of therapy. This has been documented by Hartley's (1969) data on the variability of counselor credibility over the course of group counseling. The client's expectation and motivation to change should also vary. Attitudes are shaped by experience, and attitudinal components of social power are no exception. Some of the influence strategies of the therapist function to maintain the social power balance between therapist and client and to alter the nature of that balance as the relationship requires. An example of such alteration is the expert therapist's evolution of a referent base to shape a client's belief that the therapist is helping out of a basic compatibility with the client, rather than a sense of professional duty. The therapist may also maintain social power by manipulating client commitment to the relationship and belief about the need for therapy. Strong, Wambach, Lopez, and Cooper (1979) found that interpretations labeling client behavior more negatively than the clients had labeled it increased clients' perceptions of the severity of the problem and, one might hypothesize, increased their need to change. The clinical literature abounds with examples of using homework (Haley, 1976), paradoxical directives (Jackson 1968c), and emotional arousal (Perls, 1969) to shape the client's commitment to working or to enhance the client's perceived needs.

The central task in therapy is to effect change relevant to client needs and goals. The attitude change model presented in this chapter considers the underlying mechanism of change to be the creation and resolution of cognitive inconsistencies. Efforts to effect attitude change face what Aronson (1969) called the "multiple mode problem" (p. 16), namely, that there are a variety of responses to cognitive inconsistency, and the individual's choice among them is not always easy to predict. What changes will occur in response to a therapist's influence attempts depend on how the variables discussed in this chapter are brought to bear in the therapeutic situation.

Attitude change experiments and counseling and psychotherapy typically promote efforts to resolve cognitive inconsistencies by generating them and blocking the recipient's attempts to avoid facing them. Change occurs to the extent that the source of discrepant information is difficult to derogate and inconsistencies are unavoidable. The importance of attitudes to the individual's functioning, the nature of the discrepancy, and the individual's commitment to particular beliefs all contribute to the unavoidability of inconsistencies and thus to the individual's response to them. Kelman and Baron (1968) have noted that the importance of cognitions involved in an inconsistency determines whether the individual will seek to resolve or maintain it. If the cognitions are associated with different goals, and are therefore independently useful, the individual will maintain the inconsistencies.

If the inconsistent cognitions concern the achievement of a single goal, resolution and attitude change are more probably responses. The communication of small discrepancies and the lack of public commitment to a position on an issue also make avoidance of inconsistencies more likely than attitude change. In addition, research has shown that responses to cognitive inconsistency are affected by the availability of plausible cognitions to employ in resolution (Brock & Buss, 1962; Walster, Berscheid, & Barclay, 1967).

As an influence agent, the therapist works on several fronts at once, recognizing attitudes that require change, anticipating obstacles to change, and formulating discrepancies that will lead to change, in the desired direction. The strategies employed by the therapist contribute variously to the creation and resolution of cognitive inconsistencies with the result that the client's thoughts, feelings, and actions change over time in ways relevant to the relief of pain and the achievement of goals.

Many of the therapist's statements directly serve an interpretational function by offering the client information discrepant with the client's own viewpoint. Levy (1963) noted the dual nature of interpretation: the semantic aspect alters the meanings attached to objects, persons, and events in the client's life. The propositional aspect draws relationships among events important to the client. The therapist performs a semantic function in statements that relabel the experiences of the client by bringing a new vocabulary to bear on them. The vocabulary is determined partly by the therapist's theoretical orientation and partly by the terminology shared among orientations; it is not strictly theory-based. By influencing the client to apply new language to old phenomena and to organize phenomena is new ways, the therapist changes the perceptual-cognitive tools with which the client construes and responds to experience. The use of relabeling is implicitly documented in some convergence studies (e.g., Pepinsky & Karst, 1964) in which the therapist's conceptual language is adopted by the client in referring to significant aspects of the client's life. The effects of relabeling are illustrated in research on dispositional attributions (e.g., Dweck, 1975; Snyder & Swan, 1978). When a quality or disposition is attributed to individuals, they tend to behave in accordance with the attribution. Strong (1978) has suggested that the same mechanism occurs in therapy when the therapist, for example, attributes worth to the client. Over time, the client acquires a belief in his or her basic worth. On a more particular level, relabeling the client's emotional states is also a powerful source of change. Research indicates that emotional experience is heavily dependent on cognitive labeling, that is, to what the individual attributes physiological arousal (Schachter & Singer, 1962; Valins, 1966). In therapy, states of arousal and confusion are the targets for the therapist's influence. The labels attached to the client's emotional states in the form of reflections and interpretations affect the way the client views his or her reactivity to the environment. To convince the client that "in addition to being upset, you're also angry" alters a self-perception, substitutes greater clarity for what had been vague, and places the client in a different relationship to stimulus events.

The propositional function of interpretation is carried out by therapist statements that offer the client an alternative conceptualization of events. This conceptualization follows from the therapist's theoretical orientation. The relationships expressed by interpretations are particular forms of relationships embodied in the postulates of the theory. Most relationships are causal, as problematic behaviors of the client are linked to antecedent or consequent conditions in the client's life. Causal attributions are not an end in themselves, but prepare the client for change by supplying a coherent rationale for other change strategies. Relating a client's nervous tic to situations in which the client feels angry but does not express it might lay the groundwork for learning effective ways to cope with anger. Relating the client's poor self-concept to its manipulative, guilt-inducing effects on others might be a first step in altering the client's interpersonal behavior. These examples represent two forms of interpretation. The first connects behavior with its cause; the second considers behavior in terms of its pragmatic effects. The theoretical content of interpretation is secondary to the effects of interpretation in preparing the client to change. The outcome of the therapist's influence is not insight, but attitude change toward a way of considering experience that is compatible with behaving differently. Research on interpretation as causal attribution has demonstrated this point (Claiborn, Ward, & Strong, 1981; Strong, Wambach, Lopez, & Cooper, 1979). In these studies, two attributional frameworks representing different theoretical approaches to a problem were constructed. One linked the client's problem behavior to immediate environmental antecedents as a rationale for emphasizing the importance of self-control, discipline, and effort. The other treated the same behavior as an expression of unresolved conflicts and unexpressed feelings from the client's remote past and used this as a rationale for deemphasizing self-control and promoting self-awareness. The use of both frameworks persuaded clients to conceptualize their problems differently and led to behavior change. Differences between them were obtained in the patterns of change they produced (Strong, Wambach, Lopez & Cooper) and depended on the discrepancy between the interpretations and the client's prior beliefs (Claiborn, Ward, & Strong). Small discrepancies were associated with more positive change, suggesting that though discrepancy produces change, it does so in small increments. Interpretive interventions that are optionally discrepant from the client's own viewpoint can, over time, create a new viewpoint facilitative of change. The content of interventions is not the issue, as long as it is not too discrepant. What is important is the coherence interventions bring to clients' beliefs about their problems, themselves, and their environments, and the rationale for change that the new understandings provide.

Not all of the discrepancies of therapy are communicated directly by the therapist; some are elicited from the client. By probing, restating, and otherwise selectively responding to the client's disclosure, the therapist brings into focus discrepancies among aspects of the information disclosed. The client is thus pressed to resolve the exposed inconsistencies. McGuire (1960) and Rosen and Wyer (1972) demonstrated indirect influence in a technique called the Socratic method. It included:

eliciting the persuasive material from the person's own cognitive repertory, rather than presenting it from outside. Specifically, . . . asking the person his opinions on logically related issues, thus sensitizing him to any inconsistencies that exist among . . . stands on these issues and producing a change toward greater mutual consistency. (McGuire, 1960, p. 345)

This procedure is analogous to the therapist drawing out rather than putting forth discrepant material, and thus making the client the source of his or her own influence in counseling and psychotherapy. Cognitive inconsistency is produced by the temporal contiguity of discrepant information that the client discloses. Matross (1974) has applied the Socratic method to therapeutic situations as a way of altering clients' self-perceptions. His procedure is the following:

1. Identify the self-perception which needs to be changed, e.g., a belief that one is incompetent and unable to achieve. Then think of actions which would be inconsistent with the target attitude. In our example, actions involving hard work, extra effort, and unusual striving are likely to have resulted in genuine achievement and would be inconsistent with a perception of incompetence.

2. Start questioning the person about specific behaviors relating to the target attitude. Start with a general lead, such as, "Let's talk about your achievement. Can you think of some examples which illustrate the ways you try to achieve?"

3. Continue the questioning, asking for exactly what you want. Initially a person may give you an example which you don't want (e.g., "I goofed off and flunked biology"). Acknowledge such nontarget examples with the briefest of summaries (e.g., "So biology was bad news") and move on to a question explicitly requesting a target example, "Can you think of a time when you really put out a lot of effort and came through when you had to?"

4. Ask detailed questions about the effects of the target behavior and the effects of nontarget actions the person could have taken, e.g., "What were the results of putting out that effort on the psychology paper? Did you get a better grade? Did your teacher think it was pretty good? Did you get a sense of personal satisfaction?" Summarize the answers to these questions and then ask questions about the effects of nontarget alternatives, e.g., "Suppose you hadn't re-searched that paper so well. Suppose you had only read a few pages and not put out much effort at all. Do you think you would have done poorly?" Give a final summary of the example, contrasting what the person did with the things he did not do, e.g., "You could have sloughed off, spent only a couple of hours in the library, and copied a lot of that paper. If you had done that, you would have gotten a low grade, disappointed your teacher and yourself. Instead you chose to push hard, studying many hours, reading several books and giving them a lot of thought. As a consequence of this effort, you got a good grade, pleased the teacher and gained self-respect."

5. Continue asking for examples of target behaviors and going through the question sequence above. When the conversation comes to a logical conclusion, offer a final summary. Take your three or four best examples of target behaviors and emphasize how these form a consistent pattern, with only a brief nonspecific acknowledgment of contrary behavior, e.g., "On the one hand, there are times when you don't exert much effort and don't achieve. On the

other hand, there are several times when you do exert a lot of effort and do very well. For example, ..."[1] (Johnson, 1980, pp. 81–82).

Changes effected in one attitude may result in changes in related attitudes that are not the target of influence. One pair of studies demonstrated that changes in the cognitive or affective component of attitudes led to changes in the other component. Carlson (1956) found alterations in cognitive structure, including attitudes toward particular issues, to result in affective changes. Rosenberg (1960) showed the reverse effect; by hypnotically inducing feeling states associated with issues, he obtained greater cognitive restructuring regarding those issues. McGuire (1960) produced a similar effect with logically related attitudes. After effecting change in an attitude on an explicit issue, he discovered changes in related attitudes that had not been explicitly mentioned in the influence. Indirect influence has the benefit of producing changes that are internally caused, thus confirming the assertion put forth by many therapists to their clients that the changes are coming from the client's internal processes and not from the therapist's influence.

Changes that clients see as chosen or internally caused might be expected to be easier to effect and more enduring. This has less to do with reality than with attributions the client makes. Methods of indirect influence base client change in the client, who is the source of the discrepant information. The press of cognitive consistency is strongest when the consistency concerns elements of the client's self-concept (Aronson, 1969). Interventions that contrast client behavior with deeply held values, that label the client's prior behavior as an expression of commitment to a position, or that elicit inconsistencies among attitudes that have clear adaptive significance for the client all employ indirect influence. These methods are more popular in the humanistic or "nondirective" therapies, since they are more compatible with the philosophical underpinnings of such orientations. But they should not be taken to be the absence of influence or a superior path to change.

[1] Reprinted with permission from *Helping People Change*, 2nd ed., F. H. Kanfer and A. P. Goldstein (Eds.) New York: Pergamon Press, Inc. © 1980.

CHAPTER 4

Interdependence and Change

Controlling and changing other people is continuously complicated by the efforts of others to control and change us. We tend to think about change in terms of unidirectional cause and effect relationships. Yet social interaction never conforms to the unidirectional model of causation. Social interaction is circular, and each event is both cause and effect. Social power and dependence are crucial to the process and outcome of social interaction, and interactants constantly operate on the other's perceptions of needs and resources in addition to using their power to establish the relationships they desire. The processes of affecting perceptions and influencing actions are conceptually separable, but they are not separable in the behavior of interactants. All behavior affects power and influence simultaneously. An attempt to influence another also affects the other's perceptions of power and dependence (Claiborn, 1979), and an attempt to affect another's impressions also proposes that the other change or not change (Hoffman & Spencer, 1977).

Most social psychological research on how people manage interdependence was not conceived to address the question of interdependence. The experiments were conceived as unidirectional events, with experimenters manipulating significant aspects of subjects' environments, and subjects accommodating to the social situation in which they found themselves. From the interactional point of view, experiments are understood differently. Subject responses to the machinations of experimenters are active attempts to control experimenters. Subjects' behaviors in experiments are their efforts to present themselves to experimenters in the best possible light, not only as willing to contribute to the advancement of science, but also as individuals of integrity, capability, fairness, and modesty. The mark of their success is the experimenters' ignorance of the control subjects' exercise. Insufficient appreciation of the interactional nature of the experiment has led to the development of theories in social psychology that assume that subjects' behavior in the laboratory is an expression of internal processes rather than of counterstrategies to control experimenters, a situation analogous to the focus in psychotherapy on internal dynamics of clients rather than on interaction dynamics between therapists and clients.

The interactive nature of the social psychological experiment has not been overlooked. Orne (1959, 1962, 1969, & 1970) argued 20 years ago that subjects try to figure out what the purpose of an experiment is and what is expected of them by evaluating all the cues provided to them in an experiment, cues he labeled the *demand characteristics* of the experiment. Rosenberg (1965, 1969) argued that not only are subjects actively construing the experimenter's intentions for them, but they are also trying to look good to the experimenter and are on their guard for hidden meanings. In a series of studies on on a variety of experimental paradigms and tasks, Page has shown most convincingly that the results of studies on verbal conditioning (Page, 1974; Page & Kahle, 1976; and Patty & Page, 1973), conditioning of attitudes (Page, 1976), and aggression (Page & Scheidt, 1971) are better accounted for by students' inferences about experimenters' intentions and students' desires to look good than by notions of conditioning and social learning. In the same vein, Aronson and Carlsmith (1968) argued that an essential aspect of a valid experiment is to guide subjects' inferences of what an experiment is about to a particular conclusion rather than to leave their perceptions to chance.

Most psychologists concerned about the social psychology of experiments view subjects' concerns of how the experimenter views them as a source of error in experiments. But it could be argued that subjects' machinations in experiments should be the object of interest in experiments. Naiveté about subjects' efforts to manage and control experimenters can only yield false conclusions and misleading theories. Surely, how subjects manage experimenters is the most important subject for theory and research in social and therapeutic psychology, for how people manage others is what behavior and behavior change are all about. For this reason, social psychological research is reviewed in this chapter from the perspective of what it can tell us about how people control others.

The view of persons seeking to control others is as old as interaction itself. Erving Goffman has had the most influence in bringing the view to the attention of social scientists through his work on the social self in interaction (1956, 1959, & 1961). He has written extensively on how individuals present themselves to control others and how they signal the kind of interaction they expect. He describes social behavior as learned and norm-controlled such that much of behavior is ritualistic and stereotyped. For him, social control is the objective of interaction.

> Regardless of the particular objective which the individual has in mind, and of his motive for having this objective, it will be in his interests to control the conduct of others, especially their responsive treatment of him. This control is achieved largely by influencing the definition of the situation which the others come to formulate, and he can influence this definition by expressing himself in such a way as to give them the kind of impression that will lead them to act voluntarily in accordance with his own plan. (1959, pp. 3−4)

Goffman's conception of social interaction as ritualized and normatively controlled seems to have resulted in the view that social behaviors that deviate from some notion of the norm are biased and represent errors in the social interaction process. For example, E. E. Jones (1964) treated ingratiation as a source of error in interaction, as a deviation from the social norm, a deviation in which people unfairly attempt to better themselves at the other's expense. Many writers on attribution processes identify as errors behaviors that are different from the expectancies of the experimenter or that violate rules of rational information processing (Kelley, 1967; Ross, 1977; Snyder, 1976). If we see the individual as working for social control through presenting himself and others in particular lights (i.e., managing impressions), these exceptions to rationality and expected behavior are not errors but are clear expressions of the underlying functions of interaction. In social interaction, persons' statements of causality and of their own characteristics are not intended to be accurate, but are intended to manage the perceptions and behaviors of others (Orvis, Kelley, & Butler, 1976; Palazzoli, Boscolo, Cecchin, & Prata, 1978).

In a series of provocative papers, Tedeschi and his colleagues (Gaes & Tedeschi, 1978; Gaes, Kalle, & Tedeschi, 1978; Kane, Joseph, & Tedeschi, 1976; Rivera & Tedeschi, 1976; Tedeschi, Horai, Lindskold, & Faley, 1970; Tedeschi, Schlenker, & Bonoma, 1971) have reexamined laboratory phenomena supporting theories of cognitive consistency, self-perception, perceived freedom, equity, reactance, and aggression and have shown that the data better support impression management theory as the explanation of behavior than the alternative theories. Viewing persons as trying to control their interactants and, therefore, as trying to manage the impressions others form through managing their own public behavior provides a motivational basis for the phenomena underlying the alternative theories. For example, cognitive consistency theories document persons' reluctance to appear inconsistent. Why this is so and when consistency management occurs are not well addressed. Are persons born with an intolerance for incongruity and a means for detecting it? Do they acquire this intolerance through their induction into the social community? Why is inconsistency intolerable sometimes and at other times tolerable and even desirable? Recent research focused on identifying when a person is concerned with inconsistency suggests that consistency is a concern only when persons think another is observing them (Tedeschi, Schlenker, & Bonoma, 1976, p. 687). This research, reviewed below, suggests that appearing consistent is an important strategy of impression management.

When persons are concerned with managing their impressions of themselves to facilitate their ability to control others, what impressions might we expect them to seek to establish? The analysis of social power in Chapters 2 and 3 suggests that persons will attempt to present a view to others of capability, independence, social responsiveness, integrity, attractiveness, reliability, fairness, humility, and other socially desirable characteristics. However, the answer to what is a good impression is necessarily culturally relative. What is valued in persons in one group may not be valued in another, or may not be valued in the same group at a different time. Tedeschi, Schlenker, and Bonoma (1971) argue that psychological research has identified several valued qualities, including consistency, fairness, and freedom from constraint. These characteristics enhance people's credibility and enable them to be more successful in influencing others now and in the future. Research in social psychology can be seen as a catalog of qualities that the college sophomore culture in 1970–1980 America finds important for maintaining credibility with psychologists. Probably the results can be generalized to the broader American culture, but we must keep in mind that the results are culturally relative. This chapter looks at the evidence of how people manage interdependence in terms of how they manage others' impressions of their integrity and capability, affect others' behavior, and discern liking, personal causes, and others' impressions of them. The final section explores applications of the findings to helping people change in counseling and psychotherapy.

MANAGING THREATS TO INTEGRITY

Perceptions of resources and needs are the most crucial impressions to be managed in interactions with others. When a person gives the impression of being deficient—such as being out of emotional control, insincere, socially insensitive, ignorant, or dumb—others perceive the person to have needs for their resources and act to influence or change the person so that the person conforms more closely to the others' desires. Inversely, if a person gives the impression of being capable, socially sensitive, sincere, and having integrity, he or she will be able to influence others to meet his or her needs due to others' perception of the person's ample resources. A person's ability to influence others and to fend off influence from others is his or her credibility.

Credibility can be divided into two components, capability and integrity. Capability is the person's abilities and skills to solve problems and cope success-fully with difficult circumstances. Integrity is the person's manner of dealing with others. From the other's point of view, integrity answers the question of whether the person can be expected to act narrowly for his or her own short-term benefit with disregard for others or to take a longer-range view and to act for the collective good. Integrity subsumes such concepts as morality, fairness, self-sacrifice, reliability, humility, honesty, and trustworthiness.

Rokeach (1973) has argued that the core values for everyone are capability and integrity. In a series of studies, Rokeach and his colleagues have shown that, when another presents compelling data that a person's current position lacks integrity or implies inability, the person will make rapid and far-reaching changes to restore his or her image. Rokeach views the phenomenon from the standpoint of self-concept rather than public image, but the observed results fit either view. For example, Rokeach and McLellan (1972) presented college students with data showing that persons concerned with civil rights valued both freedom and equality, while those against civil rights valued only freedom and "evidently care a great deal about their own freedom but are indifferent to others' freedom." This simple educational effort resulted in dramatic increases in the students' self-ratings of valuing equality and freedom and in higher levels of involvement in civil rights efforts up to four months after the experiment. Other studies have shown changes in relation to racism (Rokeach & Cochrane, 1972), environmental issues (Hollen, 1972), locus of control (Hamid & Flay, 1974), and in values and effectiveness in teaching (Greenstein, 1976).

Malevolence

Aronson (1969) argued that much of the evidence supporting dissonance theory does not speak of the person's concern for the consistency of surface cognitions, but of the person's concern for integrity. In experiments where a person tells another that some task is enjoyable when it is in fact boring, the person's attitude change does not reflect the person's concern for the inconsistency between the surface cognitions "the task is boring" and "I told that student the task is enjoyable," but rather is a consequence of the implications of the two cognitions: "I am a liar." The attitude change is an attempt to fend off the experimenter's and other observers' inference that the person is a liar and is motivated to harm others. Being perceived as a liar and malevolent would seriously damage the person's credibility.

A frequently used method of studying cognitive consistency has been to induce college students to carry out negative social acts that contradict the students' previously stated values and opinions. For example, Hoyt, Henley, and Collins (1972) induced college students to write essays proposing that tooth brushing was unhelpful and even damaging to the health. The experimenter told students in a "high choice" condition that, while they were free to write essays either pro or anti-tooth brushing, the experimenter had many pro statements and needed more "don't brush" arguments. The experimenter stressed the students' involvement in deciding to write the essays, their decision to help, and their choosing to help. In "low choice" conditions, the experimenter did not mention choice or decision. Instead, the experimenter said, "What you are going to do is. . . ." Hoyt and colleagues found that students in the high choice condition that thought the essays would lead young people to more tooth decay rated themselves more anti-tooth brushing than those in the low choice conditions.

In another common experimental paradigm, Calder, Ross, and Insko (1973) led students to tell other students that an experiment was interesting when it was terribly dull. They found that students who were led to believe that they had a choice in the matter and whose action had high consequences (they succeeded in convincing the next subject) rated their enjoyment of the experiment significantly higher than those who had no choice or low consequences. In the original study of this type, Festinger and Carlsmith (1959) found that students paid $1 increased their rated liking for the experimental task more than students paid $20 for "misinforming" their fellow students.

In experiments where students are induced to make statements contrary to their previous opinions and contrary to social desirability, change in attitudes or opinions has been found only when: (a) the experimenters' emphasized the subject's freedom to choose; (b) serious consequences were likely to befall the person to whom the false statement was made; (c) compensation was not provided to the recipient of the false message for the negative effects incurred because of the message; (d) students were inadequately compensated for making the statement; (e) the students had not been previously mistreated by the message recipients; and (f) observers attributed high decision freedom to the student making the statement (Goethals & Cooper, 1972; Harvey & Mills, 1971; Heslin & Amo, 1972; Holmes & Strickland, 1970;

Pallak, Sogin, & Van Zante, 1974; Riess & Schlenker, 1977; Sherman, 1970; Verhaeghe, 1976).

Theories of cognitive consistency, self-esteem protection, and perceived freedom have been proposed to account for the diversity of conditions in which students do not resort to opinion change in response to behaving in a manner that has negative consequences for another. The phenomena can best be accounted for by the hypotheses that persons change in order to protect their credibility with others, including experimenters and students who receive the messages. Gaes, Kalle, and Tedeschi (1978) point out that when students resort to changing their ratings as a resolution to counterattitudinal behavior that has negative consequences, they do not change their ratings from like to dislike, but only from like to neutral, a position that can accommodate their pretrial behavior as well as their posttrial behavior. It is apparent that a change of self-rating is not the preferred way of resolving the dilemma. The factors listed above block an appeal to external circumstances to account for or diminish the importance of the behavior. If the person can point to a lack of choice, a lack of effect on the other, compensation to the victim, financial inducement, revenge, or some other extenuating circumstance, the negative act is accounted for and does not require further rationalization. Kelley (1971) and Quattrone and Jones (1978) refer to a discounting principle as a basic factor in persons' efforts to account for their behavior to others. Essentially, the discounting principle is that if some extenuating circumstance can be found, the person's acts can be attributed to the circumstance as sufficient cause. Another means of discounting negative acts is to find that they had no negative effects on others. Thus when victims are compensated for their suffering, when the intended victims did not believe the student, or when no one hears the person's statement, the person does not change his or her attitudes. Such factors removed the necessity for resorting to opinion change to maintain credibility.

Gaes, Kalle, and Tedeschi (1978) directly assessed whether self-rating change as a consequence of counterattitudinal behavior that has negative consequences for a victim is a result of the subject's concern for his or her public image or for personal consistency. Using the anti-tooth brushing approach of Hoyt, Henley, and Collins, Gaes and colleagues explored the effects of anonymous versus public participation in an experiment, and self-ratings under conditions where dissimulation or lying could or could not be detected. Students wrote anti-brushing essays under high choice and high consequence conditions. High consequences were created by telling subjects that the pro- and anti-brushing essays would be used in junior high classes with the expectation that high school students who believed the anti-brushing essays would brush less and experience more decay than those who kept on brushing or brushed more. The experiment replicated the Hoyt, Henley, and Collins conditions where students changed their ratings toward the anti-brushing pole on posttreatment self-ratings.

The independent variables were subjects' belief that their self-ratings could be identified with them, and the verifiability of the truthfulness of their answers. In an anonymity condition, students signed up for the experiment with false names that they used throughout the study, and the experimenter identified himself as a technician from a nearby manufacturing plant with no connection to the psychology department. In the comparison conditions, students used their own names and the experimenter introduced himself as a representative of the psychology department. The verifiability of the truthfulness of self-ratings was manipulated by attaching half of the subjects to an elaborate mechanism presented as a foolproof detector of the truthfulness of responses. The subjects were put through a "calibration sequence" on the first few postexperiment questions for which the experimenter knew the subjects' previous answers; the experimenter was thus able to demonstrate the inerrant ability of the apparatus. The other half of the students completed paper and pencil self-rating forms.

Gaes, Kalle, and Tedeschi found that under conditions of anonymity and/or "verifiability" of ratings, the students did not change their ratings of their opinions about the value of tooth brushing. Students in the public and "nonverifiable" condition did change, just as they had in the earlier Hoyt, Henley, and Collins study. Consistent with the impression management point of view, subjects in the verifiable conditions rated themselves as less consistent but more legitimate, constrained, and benevolent than did subjects who rated themselves with the paper and pencil procedure. Conversely, in the paper and pencil conditions, students rated the experimenter as more manipulated and constrained than did students not free to attempt to manage the experimenter's perception of them. Gaes, Kalle, and Tedeschi concluded:

> From the impression management point of view, the purpose of attitude moderation is to deny malevolence in writing the counter-attitudinal essay. If tooth brushing were not actually beneficial to one's health, it would not be so bad to say it is harmful. The intended effect of moderation is to deny responsibility for the negative action when it is ambiguous whether or not the observer (experimenter) will impute responsibility and blame. This interpretation accounts for why free choice and negative consequences are necessary conditions for obtaining the moderation effect in the forced compliance situation. The use of attitudes for purposes of interpersonal politics has also been documented in studies of anticipatory belief change [Cialdini, Levy, Herman, & Evenbeck, 1973; Hass & Mann, 1976]. (p. 802)

People's tactics of shifting their public opinions to a neutral position so that negative public behavior takes on the appearance of being possibly uninformed, but not malevolent, diminishes loss of perceived integrity, but also is a secondary option, as it is resorted to only when the act cannot be discounted. The tactic has the potential of undoing the person, for if the change is detected, the person could be labeled insincere and manipulative. In a second experiment, Gaes, Kalle, and Tedeschi (1978) measured students' attitudes towards tooth brushing twice after they wrote the anti-brushing essays. One half of the subjects first recorded their opinion on a paper and pencil questionnaire; the other half used the verifiable procedure. The second rating for each group was with the other procedure. They found, as before, that subjects using the paper and pencil procedure demonstrated the moderation effect, while the verifiable-procedure-first subjects did not moderate their pro-brushing stand. On the second measures, the subjects' ratings were consistent with their ratings on the first procedure. Self-descriptive adjectives indicated that those who moderated their opinions and then maintained consistency in the verifiable procedure, as compared to those who did not moderate their ratings (verifiable procedure followed by the paper and pencil procedure), described themselves as less consistent, more guilty, and more embarrassed, and rated the experimenter as seeing them as more guilty. In explaining these results, Gaes, Kalle, and Tedeschi comment:

> In the [paper and pencil first] condition, the subject faced a choice either to change her attitude on a second attitude assessment and reveal the deliberateness with which she lied on a prior measure or to maintain consistency and thus lie in the hope that she would not be detected. The lack of change indicated that the latter choice was the preferred one. (p. 507)

The self-descriptive adjective results support the inference that students feared being detected as lying. They were embarrassed, felt guilty, and admitted inconsistency. Yet, this discomfort was preferable to eschewing the moderation effect and appearing as a blatant liar to the experimenter. Under circumstances such as these, the threatened loss of credibility created by being inconsistent, and thus admitting insincerity, dissimulation, and deceptiveness, creates pressure to maintain the lie in the hope of not being detected.

Given the emotionally charged nature of the counterattitudinal effect in forced compliance experiments with negative social behavior, there is little wonder that negative affect is often found and reported in such studies. A number of studies have found that accenting the negative affect increases the moderation effect, while diminishing affect diminishes the effect (Cooper, Fazio, & Rhodewalt, 1978; Cooper, Zanna, & Taves, 1978; Rhodewalt & Comer, 1979; Zanna, Higgins, & Taves, 1976). The phenomena is probably related to the development of moral behavior. Dienstbier (1978) has found that negative affect cues the person to the danger of being unmasked in immoral behavior, and thus is correlated with the person's efforts to maintain his or her perception of being credible.

Persons are most reluctant to give the impression of willfully performing acts others see as harmful. Being seen as malevolent, of desiring to do harm, seems to have a profoundly negative impact on a person's credibility with others. Research suggests that persons will adopt several strategies to avoid the label of malevolence. The strategies can be ordered in terms of their cost to the person as inferred from the order in which persons resort to the various strategies. The least costly strategy for avoiding the impression of malevolence is to discount the act as being caused by external forces or being of no consequence. When possible, students claim that they had no choice in performing the act—they were following orders. In the same vein, they are quick to claim that the act had no negative consequences. For example, writing an anti-tooth brushing essay has no effect unless the experimenter points out that people will suffer as a result of it. Lying to another student about how enjoyable a task is has no consequence if the other student is well compensated for his efforts. Lying is discounted if the liar is well compensated. Another form of discounting is to find that the victim deserved the negative consequences. When students have been mistreated by the victim earlier in an experiment, lying to the victim later has no attitudinal consequences (Verhaeghe, 1976). Walster, Berscheid, and Walster (1973) point out that doing harm often leads to justification on the basis that the victim needed or deserved the harm.

The second least costly strategy is attitude moderation, lying about one's opinion of the potential harm of the act or of one's honest evaluation of the task. The "attitude change" strategy denies malevolence by claiming not to believe the act was, in fact, negative. Students seem to say, "I actually thought the act was OK, so I didn't really lie," and, "I'm not really sure that tooth brushing actually helps anyway, so my essay isn't much of a distortion of my views. After all, if harm did come of my actions, it was unintentional. I did not personally foresee such a result." The power of the charge of malevolence can be seen in the person's desperate efforts to head it off by lying, dissimulating, rationalizing, or shifting ground. This seems to begin at an early age. Often children's response when they have been caught doing something they should not do and their attempts to discount the act are cut off, is that they "didn't know [the act had negative consequences]". Resort to the moderation effect is a judgment based on considerations of the probability of getting caught. If a person knows fully well that the potential accuser knows his or her prior position, moderation is cut off. For example, Wixon and Laird (1976) found that when persons were reminded of their previous attitudes after they engaged in the counterattitudinal behavior, but before they were asked to draw conclusions about it, they did not resort to moderation. Gaes, Kalle, and Tedeschi (1978) found that students did not resort to moderation when they were sure they would be detected. However, once a person is committed to the lie, backing off of it exposes the lie for what it is and the person must then stand for the consequences. On the other hand, a person might escape detection by being tenacious. It is surely easier to rationalize a small opinion change than to admit a baldfaced lie.

Subjects' reactions to the second measurement with the verifiable procedure in Gaes, Kalle, and Tedeschi's study suggest the next least costly means of escaping the label of malevolence. Subjects described themselves as embarrassed, guilty, and inconsistent when they maintained the opinion moderation position established on the paper and pencil procedure in the verifiable procedure. The subjects presented themselves as personally upset by what they had done and that they found themselves to be inconsistent. They seem to be proposing that it is not that they were malevolent, but rather that they were helpless creatures and not able to maintain consistency. It was not their will, but more basic abilities that they could not control that were to blame. "I could not help it," is not an appeal to the discounting principle, but to uncontrollable elements inside the individual. Studies on persons' attempts to rationalize failure suggest that under certain circumstances people are more inclined to attribute failure to ability rather than to willful intentions. Passer, Kelley, and Michela (1978) found that people think better of those who cannot help negative actions because of their poor abilities than they do of those who willfully damage and frustrate others.

The sequence of strategies for dealing with the commission of socially undesirable acts is related to psychological symptoms and therapeutic treatment. Persons coming for therapeutic help usually claim to be unable to control what they are doing, the most costly strategy enumerated above. Also, research on outcomes of counseling and psychotherapy has repeatedly found that those who blame others and circumstances for their troubles are not likely to be helped in therapy (Stieper & Wiener, 1965; Bulman & Wortman, 1977). Psychotherapy and counseling seek to lead people to see their problems as due to their internal characteristics. Is the basic change strategy of treatment to escalate the negative personal implications of the client's behavior to the point of mobilizing his or her efforts to change? Later in this chapter, we will discuss how people try to change others, and we will argue that this is the most common strategy for changing others.

Unfairness

Fairness in relationships is a major concern for members of any group, though groups differ in what they understand to be fair. A basic assumption of equity theory is that, "Groups will generally reward members who treat others equitably and generally punish (increase the costs for) members who treat other inequitably" (Walster, Berscheid, & Walster, 1973, p. 151). Adams (1965) sees the concern for equity as an internal drive akin to dissonance such that people become discomforted when confronted by their own or other's inequity and are thus motivated to redress it. In impression management terms, individuals are anxious to appear equitable to others and thus, for the benefit of observers, appear unhappy when they experience positive inequity. Privately, they are quite content with self-enhancing outcomes.

> An individual who is overpaid relative to others who have done essentially the same amount and quality of work privately experiences no guilt or distress, but feels he or she needs to express such negative feelings in order to show strong support for the important social norm of equity. (Rivera & Tedeschi, 1976, p. 896)

Many studies show that people rate themselves as uncomfortable, rate tasks harder, and work harder when they feel they have been overpaid (Walster, Berscheid, & Walster, 1973). Using an experimental design typical for studies of positive inequity, Morse, Gruzen, and Reis (1976) asked students to proofread a printed text in a study of "urban stress." Subjects proofread while listening to urban noises such as street noise and ratio static. Half of the students were paid what they had indicated would be fair; the other half were paid twice that amount. As usual, overpaid students rated the task as harder and detected more errors in the text than did students paid what they thought was fair. However, overpaid subjects' task ratings and task performances varied depending on what the students believed the experimenter would see. Subjects in an "unaware" condition who believed the experimenter would see only their task performance, rated the task to be less difficult and performed significantly better than those in an "aware" condition who thought the experimenter would see both task rating and task performance. Apparently, when the experimenter would see both, the greater rated difficulty of the task rationalized higher payment and allowed less effortful performance. When the experimenter would see only the performance, greater effort was needed to justify higher payment. Morse, Gruzen, and Reis concluded:

> Our results imply that self-presentational concerns are an important considera-
> tion in an individual's response to inequity. If we recall that the experimenter
> would grade the performance of all subjects (i.e., all *could* have presented
> themselves favorably by performing well) but see the ratings of *only* those in the
> aware condition, it indicates that, when feasible, subjects will prefer the less
> difficult alternative of changing their congnitions about the task to working
> harder. (1976)

To test the impression management hypothesis further, Reis and Gruzen (1976) made subjects responsible for allocating a $5 payment among themselves and three partners in a laboratory production task. When the subjects were to report their allocation to the experimenter, they allocated the payment according to the principle of matching payment to relative contributions to production (equity). When only the other subjects were aware of the payments, the subjects distributed the payment equally, disregarding their different contributions to group productivity. When neither experimenter nor other subjects were aware of the distribution (i.e., it was completely private), the subjects distributed more of the payment to themselves. Likewise, deCarufel and Schopler (1979) found that when subjects had delivered a message to an allocator demanding equity in the distribution of funds in a laboratory experiment, they reported most satisfaction when the succeeding distribution was equitable, and dissatisfaction when the succeeding distributions were inequitable in a way favoring them. Other subjects who had demanded a change favorable to them, but had not specified equity, were increasingly pleased the more the change favored them, equitable or not. It would appear that to demand equity creates a credibility problem when rewards are inequitable in one's favor, and public face requires protest. Privately, the protest rings false.

The results of the above experiments suggest that when not constrained by the necessity to manage others' impressions to protect credibility, persons are inclined to look out for themselves. People's private and public reactions to positive inequity are vastly different. Privately, overpaid persons are pleased. Publicly, they look uncomfortable, concerned about others, and inclined to manage their ratings and other public behavior to remove the appearance of unfairness. To test this hypothesis, Rivera and Tedeschi (1976) asked subjects in groups of three to carry out a laboratory task in which one (a confederate) was assigned the role of supervisor, and the other two worker's roles. The two workers completed different laboratory tasks in private and returned to the common room. The supervisor then distributed the $1.00 payment for the tasks. The workers were told they did equally well, but one subject was given $.50, $.75, or $.90 of the $1.00. Subjects' reactions were measured on a paper and pencil questionnaire or on the verifiable procedure (described earlier) that was presented to the subjects as able to deduce the validity of their responses. As expected, on the paper and pencil questionnaire the more inequitable the payment received, the more subjects presented themselves as guilty, less happy, liking the supervisor less, and less desirous to work with the supervisor again. With the verifiable procedure, subjects rated themselves at a low level of guilt at all payment levels; but the more they were paid (thus the more they suffered positive inequity), the more happy they rated themselves, the more they liked the supervisor, and the greater the desire they had to work with the supervisor again. Rivera and Tedeschi concluded that:

> The pattern of results obtained in the present study supports an impression-management interpretation of public responses to experiencing positive inequity, and is contrary to the postulated intraphysic processes that have been proposed as mediating post allocation responses. (1976, p. 899)

They also point out that:

> As we have seen, impression-management strategies, which include feigning of guilt and dislike for an unfair allocator, are unmasked and the opposite feelings are found when persons believe their lies can be detected. (p. 900)

These studies show that people attempt to appear fair to others. People are sensitive to what those observing them believe is fair and vary their behavior accordingly (Reis & Gruzen, 1976). The studies also suggest a division between what people "really" feel (perhaps better, what people privately feel and think), and the behavior they display publicly. Possibly, people's private evaluations of circumstances follow hedonistic principles, but their public behavior is in the service of impression management. In counseling and psychotherapy, moving from the public to the private level is an important objective. But is there a private level? Perhaps the private level is but another more devious impression presented to meet a more demanding and skeptical audience. In Rivera and Tedeschi's experiment, were subjects in these verifiable procedures presenting their real attitudes, or only those attitudes appropriate for the demand to "level"? Perhaps the issue of what is real and what is for impression only cannot be unraveled. Or perhaps we will have a deeper understanding of people if we view every face they put on as intended to manage our impression of them, deftly suited to the demands of the audience and situation. Thus, Rivera and Tedeschi's "private" ratings, obtained under the perception that lies could be detected, are what 1976 college sophomores deem best suited to maintain credibility in these circumstances. This extreme view of people's unrelenting efforts to manage others' views of them flows from the interactional view of the constant need for control, and echos the findings of Palazzoli, Boscolo, Cecchin, and Prata (1978) in recent work with schizophrenics. They were able to make therapeutic progress in working with troubled families only when they abandoned the hypothesis that people are—at least sometimes—what they do, and adopted without reservation the hypothesis that people behave for effect: the significance of behavior is the effect it achieves.

Research on intrinsic motivation, like the studies of positive inequity, has found that persons decrease their ratings of liking for tasks when they receive positive external rewards for performing them. For example, Benware and Deci (1975) asked college students to read essays expressing an attitude that the students strongly endorsed (student control of university course offerings) to other students. One group of readers were paid $7.50 for their efforts; no mention of money was made to the other readers. Students who received payment for advocating their own personal views significantly decreased their allegiance to the views compared to unpaid students. The negative impact of external justification on intrinsic motivation and performance has been demonstrated in laboratory and field settings (Deci, 1971, 1972; Smith & Pittman, 1978; Uranowitz, 1975) and with children's liking for play objects (Dollinger & Thelen, 1978; Lepper & Green, 1975) and for games (Kruglanski, Alon, & Lewis, 1972). In impression management terms, if others know that a person received a reward for performing a task, they will account for the performance with the reward and discount the behavior as expressing something about the person. To claim personal commitment to an issue when one has gained substantial payment for proclaiming it sounds hypocritical and insincere. A better impression can be obtained by down-playing intrinsic interest in the issue. Thus, as in the positive inequity circumstance, increasing external payment leads to public displays of decreased commitment, decreased pleasure, greater difficulty, and so on.

The research on intrinsic motivation (or the "overjustification effect," Smith & Pittman, 1978) suggests that persons are quite sensitive to the discounting principle and are reluctant to claim intrinsic reasons for behavior when external justifications are readily apparent to observers. Quattrone and Jones (1978) and Baumeister and Jones (1978) demonstrated that people do indeed intuitively and/or rationally use discounting and augmenting principles in self-presentation in the service of guiding others to impressions desired by the presenter. Quattrone and Jones asked students to imagine that they were actors who wanted a particular part in a play. They asked them to indicate what information they would present to the casting director, given that they had performed well in tryouts or had not had the opportunity to try out. When the students presented themselves with the aid of the behavioral evidence of their ability to do the part, they chose to reveal impediments to their performance, thus augmenting the impression of their overwhelming talent. When they had not yet had the opportunity to perform, they emphasized factors that should facilitate a good performance such as training, experience, and recent practice. Baumeister and Jones asked students to gain a favorable impression from another who had favorable or unfavorable prior information about them. The students' self-presentations clearly discounted and compensated for negative information and modestly augmented positive information.

The effect of an act's positive external consequence to the actor depends on what the actor believes the observer believes is the relationship between task performance and the consequence. For example, if a person believes the observer believes the person freely chose to perform the act with full knowledge of the external consequences,then the person discounts intrinsic motivation as a cause of his or her action if the external consequences are substantial. On the other hand, if the person believes the observer believes the person had no choice but to carry out the act, the person is free to express his pleasure or disappointment in a large or small external consequence without appearing to be hypocritical. For example, Folger, Rosenfield, and Hays (1978) found that when college students agreed to work at an experiment beyond the time they initially signed up for, if the experimenter emphasized choice, high payment for the extra time was associated with lower self-rated interest in the task (assembling a rather challenging crossword game), while low (no) payment led to higher ratings of intrinsic interest. However, when the subjects were freed from the appearance of having choice (the experimenter, after explaining the payment options, said, "Well, anyway, here's what you have to do"), they rated themselves more interested in the task the more the experimenter paid them. The result is reminiscent of Rivera and Tedeschi's (1976) public and private conditions: freed from the constraints of appearing fair and reasonable, students appeared appreciative of the advantage they had gained.

Enzle and Ross (1978) further revealed the subtlety of actors' impression management efforts. They told subjects that a high (or low) payment was contingent on completion of a task, or on the level of competence with which they completed the task. As usual, when the payment was contingent on completion of the task, low payment led to high intrinsic interest in the task and high payment led to low intrinsic interest ratings. However, when the payment was presented as based on the competence with which students performed the task, higher payment was associated with higher interest, and lower with lower interest. Enzle and Ross explained their findings in terms of Deci's (1975) theory of the different cognitive meanings of the contingencies. Payments for task completion signify external control over the person's behavior, while criterion contingent payment provides the individual with feedback about other views of their competence. The impression management point of view would add the subject's need to appear fair and reasonable in the light of others discounting their interest in a task they "chose" for high external gain.

Darley and Cooper (1972) demonstrated the augmenting effect of external impediments on intrinsic beliefs. They offered students high or low financial inducements to make public statements in favor of a strict dress code in high school, a stand the students opposed. While the experimenter emphasized the subjects' freedom in deciding to write the essay, he also went to considerable pains to point out that the essays were being collected for another organization and that the psychology department's only obligation was to solicit essays; whether the students wrote them did not matter to the department. Under these conditions, all students refused to write the essays. Later, students who had turned down the high incentive to write the essays rated themselves as much more against dress codes than did those in low incentive and control conditions. The external enticement rejected by the students served to augment their opinions: the stronger stand against dress codes served as the rationale for refusing the significant incentive, and the value of the incentive turned down revealed the depth of their conviction about dress codes.

People's concerns for appearing fair are heavily invoked in situations in which one person does a favor for another, self-discloses to another, or does harm to another. When another intentionally does a favor for a person, the person is expected to reciprocate. Nonreciprocation implies unfairness, self-centeredness, and so on. In another sense, receiving a favor severely limits the individual's future actions, and makes him or her vulnerable to the other's whims because of the pressure to reciprocate the favor to appear fair. Receiving a favor is another situation like the several above where the person's public reaction to receiving a favor is positive and includes liking for the favor doer. Privately, recipients of favors may well be displeased to be put into a one-down, vulnerable position, and resent the favor doer.

Several studies have shown the norm of reciprocity (Gouldner, 1960) in favor-doing circumstances. For example, Greenberg and Frisch (1972) found that students receiving considerable help from another student were more responsive to that student's later request for help than were students who received less help earlier, a relationship also documented by Kahn and Tice (1973) and Regan (1971). While favors have been shown to enhance public ratings of liking for the favor doer, reciprocity is much diminished if the recipient of the favor is able to identify other causes of the favor than the favor doer's desire to benefit him. Greenberg and Frisch and Leventhal, Weiss, and Long (1969) found that when students perceived the favor to be accidental, they were much less inclined to reciprocate than when the favor was clearly intentional. Likewise, reciprocity is diminished if the favor appears to the recipient to be motivated by ulterior motives (Lerner & Lichtman, 1968; Schopler & Thompson, 1968) or outside forces such that the benefactor does not intend the favor (Goranson & Berkowitz, 1966). Again, the powerful role of discounting in interaction is demonstrated.

Self-disclosure is a controversial topic in counseling and will be discussed at some length in Chapter 6. Research on self-disclosure in the laboratory conforms to one law: reciprocity. Subjects disclose at roughly the same level of intimacy and on the same topics as do their partners in experiments. Most of the research documents self-disclosure as a function of social equity, where reciprocal disclosure is nearly always obtained (Davis & Skinner, 1974; Ehrlich & Graeven, 1971; Lynn, 1978). Self-disclosure is an especially dramatic theatre of impression management because it involves telling interactants directly about one's characteristics. Revealing good things about one's self, as well as bad, has dramatic impact, and requires careful handling. Quattrone and Jones (1978) and Baumeister and Jones (1978), referred to earlier, have shown that people are fully aware of the effects of discounting and augmenting, and of appearing too egotistical or too self-deprecatory. In terms of fairness, self-disclosure places the person at an advantage or disadvantage, depending on what is revealed. The bulk of the research shows that recipients of self-disclosure in laboratory experiments tend to match the interactant's productions to neither exploit nor be exploited by their interactants. Most of these studies have given subjects explicit instructions to disclose about themselves in the experiment. Thus, the studies do not inform about the functioning of self-disclosure in more unrestrained situations. Perhaps what the studies show us is that people are cautious and maintain absolute equality when so restrained. The fact that much more than simple reciprocity is occurring has been shown in a few studies. Derlega, Harris, and Chaikin (1973) found that while subjects tended to reciprocate high and low levels of intimacy with interactants, they reported not liking high intimacy interactants who revealed deviant behavior. Archer and Berg (1978), studying reciprocity in an airport, found that people tended to reciprocate intimacy level, but at high intimacy levels several people offered help to the experimenter rather than reciprocated. Nelson-Jones and Strong (1976a) found that while students reciprocated to a fellow student's statements of how good he was, they indicated in ratings that they thoroughly disliked him. Nelson-Jones and Strong also found that disclosures of negative feelings about self led students to offer help to the discloser and to like him. These studies suggest that under some conditions, self-disclosure requires in-kind responses to maintain the appearance of fairness. Under other circumstances, accepting disclosure without reciprocity conveys the impression of concern and caring much more than does reciprocity, but also establishes the nonreciprocating person in the one-up position of help-giving. In other situations, not reciprocating may be accepting a one-down position, as when another's statements of prowess and ability are met with acclaim and flattery.

Weakness and Malevolence

When a person is harmed or threatened by another, not reciprocating harm or threat can be construed as weakness, and may encourage further threats. Worchel, Arnold, and Harrison (1978) argued that counteraggression is a power restoration tactic. In their study, students were insulted by another student (a confederate), and in a later learning situation the students were able to shock the confederate for giving wrong answers. Students shocked the confederate more when they believed the confederate knew they were responsible for the shocks. Thus, it appears that the students "counteraggression" had the purpose of affecting the other's impressions of the students.

Behaving aggressively to another without provocation can result in others attributing malevolence to the person, a perception that severely damages the person's credibility. Aggression is similar to the harm-doing underlying the forced compliance literature discussed earlier, with the exception that the studies discussed here entail the notion that the other is also doing harm. It is well to recall that one of the ways people resolved the personal threat posed by their harming others in the forced compliance studies was to discover that the victims harmed them first. Under these conditions, harm-doing had no effect on the individual's self-presentation (Verhaeghe, 1976).

Kimble, Fitz, and Onorad (1977) demonstrated the reciprocal nature of counteraggression in a study where students competed against each other in a complex reaction time task. On each trial, the winner was to punish the loser with a disagreeable buzzer. In actuality, the students did not compete against each other, but interacted with a preprogrammed apparatus on which the number of trials they would win, and the extent the "other" would punish them, was preset. The preprogrammed counteraggression strategies were set so that the extent of punishment to each student was a fixed percentage of the punishment the student meted out on the just-previous trial. Kimble, Fitz, and Onorad found that students responded to punishment in kind at all percentages of counteraggression. When the other responded to the subject with less punishment than the subject had previously used, the subject responded with less the next time. Likewise, when the other responded with more punishment, subjects also escalated. On a posttest questionnaire, students rated themselves as more fair than their opponents when the other responded with higher punishments, and less fair when the other responded with diminished aggression. When the subject aggressed less than the other, the inequity augmented the perception of fairness. When the subject aggressed more than the other, the undiscounted aggression resulted in a perception of unfairness. It should be noted that the close reciprocity of aggression to counteraggression in this study occurred under circumstances where the interactants had no previous history to color their judgments of what was fair or necessary to restore their credibility. The experiment was set up so that subjects believed that the others' behavior could only be seen as intentional and in response to the subjects' behavior. The students' concern about appearing fair resulted in the close reciprocity of their behaviors. Green, Stonner, and Shope (1975) report similar results.

Outside of the laboratory, Hart (1978) has shown that aggression and counteraggression have more of a biting edge. In studying discipline in the U.S. Army, he found escalation cycles in the relationship between discipline and misconduct. Officers punished enlisted men to the degree they felt was fair for the men's crimes. The enlisted men responded with increased lawlessness in the face of what they felt was unjust treatment. Officers then increased punishment for the increased lawlessness, and the enlisted men responded in turn to the ever-increasing injustices. In interaction, people often have differing perceptions of fairness and equity that lead to cycles of escalation. Certainly, difficulties in marriage follow such a course all too easily.

The reciprocation of aggression depends upon the aggression being seen as intentional and willful. In people's attempts to appear fair and nonmalevolent to experimenters and others, retaliation is tempered by the discounting principle. For example, in an experiment similar to Kimble, Fitz, and Onorad (1977), Dyck and Rule (1978) found that subjects retaliated much less when they believed the other did not know the intensity of punishment the other administered and thus could not intentionally have given high intensity punishment. Likewise, when the experimenter presented information about the punishment intensities used by most students, students retaliated less for high intensities when these were "what most students do." Students also retaliated less when they won most of the time or seldom, than when they won half of the time. Apparently, stronger shocks can be expected from an opponent who is on the losing side most of the time, as well as from an opponent who is winning most of the time. The loser might be expected to be frustrated with losing, and the winner frustrated with an opponent who apparently is not trying hard enough and could use some "encouragement." In both cases, the students' attributions for the others' stronger punishments identify situational causes and diminish the perceived intentionality of harm-doing.

Zillman and Cantor (1976) found, as would be expected with the discounting principle, that subjects lodged complaints about an experimenter who insulted them only when they did not have information that justified the behavior. Likewise, Kulik and Brown (1979) found that "anger, other-directed attributions of blame, and other-directed aggression were greatest in response to unjustified (illegitimate) thwartings. Justified (legitimate) thwartings produced intermediate anger and intermediate levels of blame and aggression internally and externally" (p. 183).

The above studies show that retaliation is a function of aggression that cannot be discounted (justified), a relationship that holds when the persons desire to avoid appearing unfair and malevolent to some observer. Legant and Mettee (1973) describe an interesting extension of the view that retaliation reflects a lack of justification (discount) and nonretaliation reflects sufficient justification (discount). They asked students to help one another learn concept formation problems by providing the other feedback in the form of electric shock. After the learner (a confederate) went into another room for the learning trials, the experimenter gave the student a choice of whether she wished to carry out the study. After the concept learning task was complete, the experimenter manipulated the subject's perception of the learner's view of her behavior. For half of the students, the learner was said to have been given a choice of being the learner or the teacher in the next round, while the other half of the subjects were told that the experimenter assigned roles for the next problem. After role assignments were decided, students rated their liking for the learner as very high when the learner chose to continue as the learner, and very low if the learner chose to be the teacher in the second round. Ratings were less extreme and reversed when the experimenter assigned roles for the second round of problems.

In considering the meaning of the results, it is well to remember that the student knew that the experimenter knew that she had chosen to shock the learner, but the learner had not seen the transaction. Thus, the subject could not know whether the learner saw the student's harm-doing as a function of the experimenter's orders or of chosen and expressed intentions. The experiments reviewed above suggest that the learner would be motivated to retaliate only if she believed the subject had intentionally chosen to harm her. Thus, choosing to continue to be the learner (and not retaliate) was to exonerate the subject from responsibility for the harm-doing, an act revealing a high sense of fairness and positive-mindedness in the learner, good grounds for liking. On the other hand, the learner's choice to become the teacher suggested that the learner held the student personally responsible for her harm-doing, was suspicious, untrusting, and negatively oriented, good grounds for dislike. Reinforcing this interpretation of results was the additional finding that the subjects who believed the learner had chosen to retaliate and thus held the subject responsible for the harm, rated themselves as having less freedom in the study and derogated the learner more than those on whom the learner chose not to retaliate. It would seem that the subject turned to other means of denying purposive harm-doing when the learner did not exonerate her, such as claiming to have had less freedom from external constraints and implying that the learner needed or deserved the punishment.

The results of the above studies suggest that the way to decrease another's aggressive behavior is to not retaliate. Of course, we must keep in mind that this is true under conditions in which persons wish to be seen as fair and when they lack prior histories on interaction. We do not know how far the results can be generalized. Whatever, the Legant and Mettee study suggests some of the mechanisms of how nonretaliation decreases aggression, beyond the reciprocity principle. Nonreciprocity implies that the nonreciprocator does not hold the harm-doer personally and willfully responsible for the harm. The "forgiving" interactant appears to attribute the harm to circumstances, external forces, unintentional personal factors, or other justifying factors. The forgiver has faith in the goodness of the harm-doer in the sense of not assuming that he or she purposely and intentionally was injurious. The harm-doer is thus spared the need to justify him- or herself and the resulting behavior. Also, future harm-doing has lost its greatest justification, the harm done by the other as the other seeks to restore equity (credibility) as he or she perceives it. These considerations have many implications for counseling, as well as for interpersonal relationships more generally. The consistent finding that counselors and therapists respond less to client hostility as they obtain more training and experience is probably related to this phenomenon (Haccoun & Lavigueur, 1979; Bohn, 1967).

Egotism

Persons are motivated to look good, and the research reviewed in this chapter identifies strong efforts in a person's presentation of self to this purpose. However, unrelenting emphasis on fine qualities and high capabilities has a boomerang effect on other's impressions of the discloser's integrity. Terms like "braggart," "full of himself," big-headed," and "egotistical" identify interactants' negative sanctions against unrelenting self-praise. The maintenance of integrity requires modesty about accomplishments. Yet, modesty would not seem to be an issue unless the audience clearly perceives the person as credible. Only after another has perceived a person's high level of abilities or excellent traits is modesty relevant. Depreciating abilities or traits, or identifying discounting factors for successes, would not seem a desirable tactic unless a strong, positive impression is secure.

An effect parallel to modesty is modertation of the discounting of poor performance. If possible, persons tend to attribute poor performance and negative acts to external circumstances. However, others react negatively to extreme use of discounting, since the person is seen as trying to "weasel out" of the implications of his or her behavior. Thus, people often evince a moderating effect for both good and poor performances. People often modestly play down the positive personal implications of positive performances and moderate their tendency to deny responsibility for poor performances when others are observing them.

Frey (1978) demonstrated the moderation effects of being observed in a study in which students took an intelligence test and evaluated the validity of the test under a variety of perceived public and private conditions. In "public" conditions, students were led to believe that the other members of the class and the experimenter would see their test results and/or their ratings of the test. In "confidential" conditions, students received their test scores in private envelopes and/or placed their ratings in envelopes that would not be available to the other class members or to the experimenter. The intelligence test results reported that students were either above or below what was described as average. When the results and ratings were confidential, students' ratings of the validity of the test were about the same whether they "scored" well or poorly on the instrument. When their results but not their ratings of the test were to be made public, their ratings of the validity of the test were very high if they scored well and very low if they scored poorly. However, when both the results and the ratings were to be made public, these differences did not appear. In fact, those obtaining positive results on the test rated it as slightly less valid than did those who did poorly. Both ratings were moderate. When the students' ratings of the test but not their scores were to be public, students receiving both positive and negative results rated the test as quite valid.

In Frey's study, students' strategies of impression management depended on the opportunities available to them to affect others' impressions. When neither results nor ratings were public, there was no impression to manage. When the results were to be public, but the ratings were not, the students' affective reactions to the good or poor images that resulted from the scores took full account on their ratings of the test. However, when results and ratings were public, the students responded modestly when they had high scores by rating the test lower than the private ratings suggested they "really" felt, and when they had low socres they moderated their negative feelings to appear fair in their evaluations of the test. These results are reminiscent of Rivera and Tedeschi's (1976) subjects' private and public reactions to positive inequity described earlier. Those for whom only ratings were to be public rated the validity of the test rather high. Frey suggested that the higher ratings were intended to convey the impression that they scored high, as all students "intuitively" recognized the tendency for those who did well to respond positively to the test.

Baumeister and Jones (1978), briefly described earlier, found strong evidence of modesty in an experiment on how students presented themselves to others who had prior positive or negative impressions of them. Baumeister and Jones told students that they would interact with one another in a game after they had an opportunity to become acquainted with one another through an exchange of information. First, the experimenters told the subjects that the other student would be given a report of a personality test they had take earlier. The reports were either positive or negative in cast and were "Barntum" reports rather than true reports of results; that is, the results were written to be generally applicable to most persons, half were generally negative, and the other half were positive. The students were shown their own reports first and were told the other would receive a copy of the report. Students were then asked to complete a questionnaire to be given to the other as a second source of information. Some of the items on the questionnaire were related to the characteristics reported on the test profile, while others were not. On the questionnaires, students who received the positive test reports tended to rate themselves neutrally to slightly negatively on all items of the questionnaire. On the other hand, students who had received negative test reports rated themselves negatively on items related to the content of the report (thus maintaining consistency) but positively on items not related to the report, an apparent effort to compensate for the negative cast of the prior report. Thus, students who believed others saw them in a positive light were modest, while students believing they were seen negatively tried to compensate and thus change that perception without being inconsistent.

Several other studies have obtained effects suggesting modesty. Jones (1964) found that those in positions of power in an organization revealed more failings (but failings unrelated to their positions and responsibilities) than did those with less power in the organization. Quattrone and Jones (1978) found that students in a role-taking study revealed more of their failings when they had previously performed a highly successful act than when they had not.

Modesty strategies have a hidden twist. While the persons are being modest by being somewhat negative about themselves, they are also augmenting the positiveness of their behavior. In spite of handicapping factors, they have managed to perform admirably. The effect of such a self-presentation strategy is increased credibility due to the augmenting principle. For example, Jones found that the self-derogating (modesty) behavior of leaders of an organization increased their followers' attraction to and liking of them and did not diminish their authority. Studies have demonstrated a "prat-fall" effect in which highly credible sources gain even more credibility through inadvertently revealing trivial faults (Helmereich, Aronson, & LeFan, 1970). When counselors present themselves as modest persons with faults, they no doubt enhance their credibility and do not undermine their perceived expertness.

Logically, if modesty enhances the integrity and thus the credibility of a capable person, behaving modestly should lead others to infer high capability. Modesty can be an ingratiation strategy as recognized in everyday interaction by such terms as "false modesty" and "bigotry." The strategy is carried to its final extreme in Moliere's *Tartuffe*.

MANAGING THREATS TO CAPABILITY

A key aspect of credibility is perceived ability to accomplish difficult tasks. Skills and abilities to accomplish interpersonal and impersonal objectives are closely linked to a person's worth to others in the sense of what the person can accomplish of value to others. Capability is thus a key component of a person's ability to influence others. People are very sensitive to other's evaluations of their capabilities and lose few opportunities to impress others with their capabilities or to defend against circumstances that could tarnish their image of capability. Yet, concerns for integrity constantly check the management of impressions of capability. Concern for modesty and rationality overrides extreme displays of capabilities. Thus, while evidence of a person's management of impressions of capabilities is abundant, the effect is at times attenuated and even sacrificed for the appearance of integrity.

Failure

Public behavioral evidence of incapability should provide vivid demonstrations of a person's concern for appearing capable, especially among college students. Failure at intellectual tasks strikes at the heart of a student's public image. Heider (1958) proposed that people account for outcomes on skill tasks with the factors of capability, effort, difficulty, and luck. The first two factors are characteristics of individuals. Capability has two components: *abilities* (fixed intrinsic aspects of a person) and *skills* (what the person has learned about accomplishing tasks in the past). A person's skills are limited by experience and ability, while abilities are limited in an absolute sense. *Effort* is the variable of the extent of application of skills and abilities to a task. Effort is controlled by will and by mood states, and thus can explain variations in task performance from moment to moment. Skills explain performance variations in a longer term, while ability explains long-range consistency in performance.

Difficulty and luck are causes of task performance that lie outside the person; they are attributes of tasks and environments. Task difficulty explains variations in the percentage of persons who succeed or fail at different tasks. A task on which many fail is difficult; a task on which many succeed is easy. On the other hand, variations in performances can be due to luck, a fortuitous circumstance of the situation that has nothing to do with the individual.

Capability, effort, difficulty, and luck provide a rich framework for accounting for task performance. External causes are closely linked to internal factors and can be applied only by subjective judgment and rules of thumb. Tasks that many fail are difficult, and a person who succeeds at difficult tasks is said to have high ability. Alternatively, when only one or a few performances are observed, the effective causal factor could be luck. A person can clearly establish his capability only by performing a number of difficult tasks well. As luck can only account for isolated instances, replications of success in face of difficulty will lead observers to attribute high capability to the succeeder.

Most people succeed at easy tasks, and a person's success on an easy task tells an observer very little about the person. Failure at an easy task, however, invokes a judgment of low capability. To avoid the odious implications of failure, a person must find a way of channeling the observer's attention to alternative interpretations of poor performance. If, after failure, a person succeeds on a more difficult task, the earlier failure becomes attributable to luck or effort and no longer clearly implies low capability. Poor performance, especially on easy tasks, implies a lack of effort to observers. Succeeding at more difficult tasks, or obviously not trying, tends to distract observers from the ability implications of initial failure and guides their attributions to luck or effort as more likely causes of the failing performance.

The strategy of performing better on subsequent trials carries with it the danger of continual failure, which would convince the observer that the person is incapable. This danger is especially paramount when the observer believes the subsequent tasks are of the same difficulty or of less difficulty than the first task. A second failure implies even lower capability than the first when the second task is believed easier than the first. A success on an easier task does not repair the damage of previous failure. On the other hand, if the observer believes that the second task is more difficult, failure on it does not imply less capability than the first failure, and success implies greater capability, thus removing the tarnish of the earlier failure from the image of capability.

To impress others as not trying to do well preserves the person's capability from judgment, and thus would appear to be a good strategy for avoiding attributions of poor capability when the person encounters failure. Yet, in a society that values working to full capability, a consistent image of "not trying" leads to moral castigation and derogation, and is thus potentially damaging to a person's integrity. For example, Leventhal and Whiteside (1973) found that students enforced the standard of full effort and full use of capability by awarding higher grades to persons of lower capability than to those of higher capability when both groups performed equally well. Not trying in circumstances of group interdependence for positive outcomes is also punished. Jones and DeCharms (1957) found in a laboratory task that persons whose performance jeopardized the group's success were derogated when the others perceived the failing members as not trying, but they were not derogated when the others attributed the failure to low capability. Thus, faced with failure, a person is no doubt reluctant to feign low effort, and probably will do so only when castigation of integrity seems unlikely and successful performance on subsequent tasks can repair the damaged image.

Research on the concept of learned helplessness (Wortman & Brehm, 1975; Seligman, 1974) bears directly on how persons manage their image of capability in the face of failure. Seligman found that laboratory animals experiencing unavoidable shock ceased trying to escape the shock after a while and instead huddled up to endure the aversive situation. He found that the animals were subsequently very slow to learn to avoid shock when avoidance was made possible and that the decrement in performance generalized to other situations. Seligman (1975) proposed that "learned helplessness" in animals was similar to the behavior of persons who suffer from depression: they acquire their difficulties in circumstances where they experience noncontingency between their actions and environmental events, and they inappropriately generalize the learned helplessness to other circumstances.

Researchers have attempted to demonstrate that repeated exposure to aversive circumstances from which persons cannot extract themselves produces learned helplessness and that learned helplessness generalizes to different situations. According to Seligman, the helpless reaction is a result of people learning that there is no relationship between their behavior and the difficult circumstances they experience, and thus they stop trying to control the circumstances. Research on this topic has typically asked students to perform challenging intellectual tasks and has visited the students efforts with feedback indicating failure. Helplessness "training" typically is followed by one or more "test" trials on which subjects are asked to perform different complex tasks. The test trials assess the generalization of the helplessness training effects to other situations.

From the point of view of impression management, subjects' reactions to failure in these experiments depend on who subjects think observed their failure, what they think these observers think about the causes of their failure, and what opportunities they have to influence the observers' impressions.

In one of the more carefully done studies on the effects of failure, Wortman, Panciera, Shusterman, and Hibscher (1976) recruited female college students for two studies—one on the effects of urban noise on task performance, and the other on concept formation. For each subject, the two studies were scheduled at adjoining times, but different persons called the subjects for each study in an attempt to make the subjects think the studies were independent. In the first session, the experimenter explained to the subject and to a confederate posing as a subject that they were to work 12 concealed figure problems within tight time limits. They would work separately and out of the sight of each other. They would hear occasional noise blasts on headphones. If they got the problems right, the number of noise blasts would be reduced.

In two conditions, subjects were given information about their own performance. In one condition, subjects were told that they got all 12 problems wrong. In another, they were told that they got 10 of the 12 problems right. In two other conditions, they were given information about their own performance and about the other's performance. In these conditions, buttons the experimenter said she would push to offset the noise when a problem was solved correctly were visible to the subject, thus allowing the subject to gather information about her performance compared to the other. All subjects in the ''button'' conditions were given feedback that they got all the problems wrong. In one of the conditions, the subject was able to observe that the other's button was pushed for 10 of the 12 problems. During a break in this condition, the experimenter remarked to the subject that she ''seemed to be having trouble with the problems.'' The experimenter then picked out a couple of problems that the subject had missed and proceeded to work them in front of the subject (p. 306). In the other condition, the subject was able to observe that the experimenter pushed neither hers nor the other's button. ''At the end of the session, the confederate remarked that she had had great difficulty solving the problems. The experimenter then pointed out that most participants had such difficulties'' (p. 307). After the training condition, subjects were given a stack of the similar problems and were told to work at their own pace for four minutes without the headphones. Subjects then reported to the second experiment down the hall and did nine puzzles.

From the impression management point of view, subjects who received the feedback that they missed all the problems without any information about others' performances probably concluded that they had looked incapable to the experimenter, since students would likely assume that the experimenter would not use a task on which no one succeeded. On the other hand, the subject that succeeded on 10 of 12 problems probably concluded that she had done all right in the eyes of the experimenter. In the other two conditions, subjects clearly failed. Yet, in one condition, most other students also failed, and students probably concluded that the significance of their failure was discounted by the difficulty of the task. In the other condition, however, students received information that the experimenter was dismayed at their poor performance.

The ''test'' items at the end of the first experiment provided an ideal opportunity for subjects to cast off the impression that their failure was due to their ability. A strong performance on the test items would suggest that previous poor performance was a function of the noise rather than of their ability to do the items. On the other hand, those who succeeded or whose failure was already discounted would have no special effects to manage, since their image was intact.

In the results of the study, those who failed and had no discounting factor made significantly fewer errors on the test items than the other subjects, and they completed more puzzles in the second experiment than did the others. Thus, those who failed provided evidence to observers that their failure was due to some special effect of noise on their performance, certainly not their ability. The fact that the students who failed performed better on the second experiment suggests that the students saw a connection between the studies. Perhaps because the studies were on the same floor of the psychology building and were scheduled together tipped the students off. As Gaes, Kalle, and Tedeschi (1978) showed in the forced compliance studies, if the two studies could be totally divorced in the students' minds, there would be no reason to suspect that helplessness training in one study would have any effect on performance in a second study. If a person's reactions to failure are focused on the management of observer's impressions, totally independent observers should attenuate the subjects' efforts to offset their tarnished images of capability. The Wortman et al. study, of all the studies on helplessness, comes closest to separating the training and test stages. But, obviously, even they failed.

Hanusa and Schulz (1977), in a study similar to Wortman, Panciera, and Shusterman (1976), led subjects in several conditions to believe thay they had not managed to solve any problems correctly. In an "ability" condition, the experimenter told students that "only 2 of 89 others who had taken the test solved zero problems" (p. 605). The experimenter later said, "I don't know what to say, everyone else did so well. I guess you weren't able to use information that was given to you" (p. 605). Subjects were tested in a second experiment presented to them as "intended to evaluate the effects of participation in previous experiments on maze performance." Unsurprisingly, subjects to whom the experimenter indicated that they had failed where others had succeeded performed significantly better on the test task than the subjects in other conditions. On the other hand, subjects to whom the experimenter indicated failure was due to a lack of effort tended to do less well on the test task than those for whom the experimenter indicated he believed failure was due to task difficulty. Thus, those who believed observers believed their failure reflected on their abilities provided the observers with contradictory evidence. Those who believed observers saw their failures as showing a lack of effort provided more evidence of low effort.

Frankel and Snyder (1978) tested the hypothesis that after failure persons would work harder on more difficult tasks than on moderately difficult or easy tasks. Using the two-part experiment, subjects were first informed that they had failed a task described to them as "a good predictor of intelligence." The second task was described either as a moderately difficult task on which most students had done well, or as an extremely difficult task on which students had done poorly. As predicted, subjects receiving the "difficult" description solved more anagrams more quickly than did subjects who received the "moderately difficult" task description. In contrast, subjects who "succeeded" in the training task performed better in "moderately difficult" and less well in the "difficult" conditions. Tennen and Eller (1977) found the same preference for difficult tasks following failure. They asked subjects to endure three sets of 48 trial discrimination tasks on which they received failure feedback. For half of the subjects, successive sets were presented as harder than the previous set. For the other half, successive sets were presented as easier than the previous set. On anagrams comprising the test tasks, subjects receiving the "successively easier" sets performed significantly more poorly and took considerably longer in finding the solutions than subjects in any of the other conditions. Subjects in the "successively harder" condition performed better and more rapidly than did subjects in all but one of the other conditions. Subjects also performed well in a condition where they experienced only one set of discrimination problems on which they failed. Subjects in this single task training group showed the facilitative effect of failure found also by Wortman, Panciera, Shusterman, and Hibscher (1975) and Hanusa and Schulz (1977).

Benson and Kennelly (1976) found that it is not noncontingency itself that generates the facilitative and inhibition effects on test task performance as Seligman proposed, but rather the experience of public failure. They found that noncontingent positive outcome feedback (feedback of success rather than failure) did not lead to any effect on test tasks as compared to controls who did not have the noncontingency training. Test performance deficit is seen only with subjects who receive failure feedback and who choose to guide observers to a conclusion of low effort to account for their failure. Koller and Kaplan (1978) found that the effect of failure from noncontingent feedback was entirely removed by informing subjects of the feedback deception and promising veridical feedback on the test trials.

DeVellis, DeVellis, and McCauley (1978) and Brown and Inouye (1978) found that the effects on test performance of repeated failure training also occur in the behavior of those who do not receive the failure training but simply observe the failure of another. Brown and Inouye had subjects observe another's failure training and gave the observers information that implied that the experimenter thought that the observers were either similarly competent or more competent than the person they observed. Those who thought they were similarly competent demonstrated the same significant performance decrement on test anagrams as did the subjects experiencing the failure feedback. On the other hand, subjects who received information that they were more competent than the subject they observed did not display a performance deficit on the test anagrams.

As a whole, studies of "learned helplessness" support the notion that many people respond to failure by trying to deflect others away from the conclusion that their failure is due to low capability. People's preferred solution to failure is to discount failure by focusing the observer's attention on task difficulty, some other feature of the situation, or luck. That failing, students feign low effort and lack of trying to lead the observer to an effort attribution. The results reveal that people protect their appearance of being capable, skilled, and able. People's concern about appearing incapable seems to be a common determinant of behavior. In another example, Fisher and Nadler (1976) found that people receiving help were sensitive to the ability implications of receiving help. They found that when subjects received help in an experimental task from another subject who had performed somewhat better than they had in the task, they rated themselves more positively and engaged in less self-help in a subsequent part of the experiment than did those who received help from subjects who appeared to perform much better than they had in the experimental task. Apparently, the threat to appearing able posed by receiving help from a similar other was best met by appealing to "low effort," while help from a superior other clearly implied lower capability, and subjects tried to remove the implication by improving their performance.

Failure and Malevolence

While the above considerations are well and fine for many college students, what about persons who endorse poor ability to account for failure rather than attempting to deflect the implications of failure through discounting and effort dissimulation? A very large body of research shows that persons with low self-esteem tend to attribute success to environmental or temporary states and failure to personal capability rather than the other way around. How can presenting oneself as unable be protecting a favorable image? The answer must be that in certain situations low effort has more negative social implications than low ability. When others depend on a person's performance, low effort is equivalent to lack of concern for others and implies and underlying motive to harm others—malevolence, the attribution found to be so earnestly avoided in the forced compliance literature. Also, appeal to low ability is a powerful strategy for countering others in the struggle for control in relationships. A person whose performance is attributable to low effort has the power to increase his or her performance value to others if he or she only would, and thus an appeal to low effort lays the person open to the efforts of others to "motivate" the person in whatever way they can. For example, we referred earlier to the finding that on a group interdependent task, students castigated poor performing students more when they perceived the poor performance to be due to effort than when they believed the performance was due to poor ability. The students' castigation of the other who let them down by not trying hard was the students' efforts to motivate the other to work harder. Their reaction suggests the virtue of appealing to low ability to account for failure—others' lose their ability to stimulate the performance of the failing person. Thus, appealing to low capability should be a common interaction strategy of the less powerful in relationships. Indeed, lower self-esteem is nearly a universal finding for females as opposed to males, as would be expected in a male-dominated society (Nicholls, 1975). Langer and Benevento (1978) have shown that low self-esteem is associated with social and employment roles of assistants and underlings and with persons in old-age homes.

Diener and Dweck (1978) studied the appeal to low ability in the face of failure among fifth-grade students. They looked at two groups, students who tended to emphasize effort as responsible for the outcomes of their endeavors and students who deemphasized effort—groups they called "mastery oriented" and "helpless."

They presented a series of concept formation discrimination tasks to the children individually. The experimental sessions began with several trials to teach the students to do such problems, during which time the students received veridical feedback and worked on the problems until they were correct. The students were then given more difficult problems of the same sort and received feedback that their answers were wrong. Deiner and Dweck were interested in the factors to which the students attributed their failure as reported on a questionnaire and as revealed by the children's remarks while they did the tasks.

Deiner and Dweck (1978) found that over 50% of the helpless children attributed their failure to low ability, while none of the mastery oriented children identified low ability as the reason for their failure. Instead, mastery children emphasized effort, luck, and experimenter unfairness—explanations few helpless children used. The students' vocalizations during failure were categorized, and the largest differences between helpless and mastery students were that the helpless students compared to the mastery children gave fewer self-monitoring and self-instruction statements, more solution irrelevant statements, fewer positive prognosis statements, more statements of negative affect, and more attributions to loss of ability. Deiner and Dweck comment:

> Helpless children ruminate about the causes of their failure and, given their attributions to uncontrollable factors, spend little time searching for ways to overcome failure. Mastery-oriented children, on the other hand, seem to be directed towards the attainment of a solution. They are less concerned with explaining past errors and more concerned with producing future successes. (p. 460)

Of the two operations that persons must simultaneously carry out, accomplishing the task and controlling the audience's perception of task performance, helpless children overfocus on the perception of others to the detriment of task performance. They seem to be quick to conclude that they have failed and quick to turn to convincing the observer that they should not try further by emphasizing the unchangeable features of their poor performance, their ability, and the difficulty of the task. Deiner and Dweck emphasized the speed of concluding failure by noting that many of the mastery oriented students seemed to not see themselves as having failed at all, but only as not having yet arrived at the correct conclusion.

Differences in the perception of failure and in the attribution of failure to low ability have been found in comparisons of college students and psychiatric rehabilitees (Menapace & Doby, 1976), fourth-grade male and female students (Nicholls, 1976), depressed and nondepressed female college students (Kuiper, 1978), and internals and externals (Lefcourt, Hogg, Struthers, & Holmes, 1975; Pittman & Pittman, 1979). An accompaniment of low ability attribution for failure is heightened self-awareness (Bockner, 1979a, 1979b; Bockner & Hulton, 1978; Deiner & Dweck, 1978; Dweck, 1975). Working with persons who rate themselves as high or low in ability (high and low self-esteem), Bockner found that when attention was focused on the person with mirrors, TV cameras, and direct observation, the performance of low self-esteem persons, as opposed to that of high self-esteem persons, was significantly lower on concept formation tasks following failure training. Without self-focus, the performance decrement effect for persons with low self-esteem was greatly attenuated and, with instructions to focus on the task, eliminated. His results reinforce Deiner and Dweck's observation that a major difference between helpless and mastery oriented persons is their focus on how they look to others during task performance versus concentration on the task. Deiner and Dweck proposed that helpless persons might be helped by encouraging them to focus on the task and think about strategies for accomplishing it, and thus turn their attention away from the observer and themselves. Dweck (1975) demonstrated the possible effectiveness of such a strategy in a study in which she gave helpless children extensive training on math problems in which they periodically failed so that the experimenter could encourage them to try harder and to put more effort into the task. Children receiving this "attributional" treatment responded to failure in test trials by working harder. Children who experienced training of equal length in which they did all problems right continued to demonstrate striking behavioral deteriorations on test trials, and they attributed their failure to poor ability.

Gaining a greater understanding of the strategy of covering failure with claims of poor ability is a matter of great importance, since many clients in counseling and psychotherapy use this strategy to insulate themselves from improvement. Client statements of "I can't help it" and "I want to but I can't" are all too familiar to therapists. Appeals to incapability cut off others' efforts to influence; the success of the strategy is attested to by our concern for depression, helplessness, negative attitudes, and so on. Many psychotherapies emphasize that client behavior reflects what they *want* to do rather than what they *can* do (will versus ability). Transactional analysis, rational emotive therapy, reality therapy, and other approaches refuse to entertain the statement "I can't" and insist on substituting the statement "I won't." They focus on eliminating overconcern for what others think. They emphasize "doing" rather than "doing well." These aspects of therapy are clearly strategies to encourage clients to decrease their focus on self and others' reactions and to encourage focus on the task and on doing; they are in line with the scanty but provacative research on how to counter helplessness control strategies (Bockner & Hulton, 1978; Dweck, 1975).

Egoism

Given people's readiness to discount failure through appeal to external circumstances or dissimulation of effort, findings that people are quick to claim success as representing the outworking of their personal capabilities are not surprising. For example, Johnson, Feigenbaum, and Weigby (1964) found that students attributed children's success in tasks the students were teaching the children to their capability as teachers, and they attributed the children's failures to the children's inability to learn. Arkin, Gleason, and Johnston (1976) found that students attributed the positive effects of the therapy they administered to their capabilities, but they attributed negative outcomes (the client's getting worse) to the nature of the treatment program when possible, and to their delivery of the program only when (*a*) they felt the experimenter believed they had freely chosen it and (*b*) the treatment had good results when others applied it. Schopler and Layton (1972) found that people perceived themselves to have influenced another only if the other succeeded at the problem they tried to influence. If the other failed, influence was denied. Freeman (1973) found that students, when presented with psychological test results that were discrepant from their own self-estimates, revised their self-estimates when the results were different in positive ways, and derogated the test interpreter when the results differed in a negative direction. Ross and Sicoly (1979) and Schlenker and Miller (1977) have shown in a variety of groups, including married couples, basketball teams, discussion groups, and problem -solving groups, that persons tend to take more credit for positive group outcomes than others are willing to assign to them, and they take less responsibility for the failures of the group. Ross and Sicoly have shown that giving persons information about others' contributions to group success attenuated the effect, as would be expected from persons' concerns for modesty and integrity as reviewed earlier.

Appearing Influenced

When a person is influenced by another, it can be presumed that the person has less social power than the other. The influenced person lacked the resources necessary to withstand the other's influence and has needs making him or her vulnerable to the other's resources. The social power implications of appearing to be influenced should make persons reluctant to appear so. They are likely to seek discounting factors such as expertise (Braver, Linder, Corwin, & Cialdini, 1977) to account for being influenced, or to present the appearance of changing autonomously of their own free will, for their own purposes, or to attempt to appear not changed at all.

The desirability of appearing to be influenced varies with circumstances and observers. In situations where the persuader has used rational and appealing methods of inviting change, appearing changed would be conforming to the persuader who might respond by seeing the influenced person as especially intelligent, personable, and attractive. A person who observed the change but did not agree with the content of the change might be threatened by the change and might respond by derogating the changer as lacking intelligence, easily led, and gullible. A person might be seen as lacking integrity if he or she is perceived to change to win the approval of another. If the persuader threatens coercion to gain compliance, the complier can seem weak and vulnerable and open to further exploitation. Compliance to threats and demands is very damaging to a person's appearance of capability, and discounting compliance to threats will occur only to the extent that others perceive that the threats were backed with real force.

Cialdini and his colleagues have studied the consequences of compliance under a variety of conditions. Cialdini, Braver, and Lewis (1974) asked students to attempt to persuade another student (a confederate) to adopt a particular position on an issue in the presence of another onlooking student. The confederate then indicated he did or did not change his opinion to that advocated by the persuader. Cialdini, Braver, and Lewis found that confederates who changed their opinions as urged were liked more and judged to be more intelligent by the persuaders than by observers, while the observers rated confederates who did not change as more likable and intelligent than did persuaders. In a later study, Braver, Linder, Corwin, and Cialdini (1977) assessed the amount students indicated they were changed when only the persuader was present, only an observer present, both were present, or when neither were present, and the experimenter presumably was the only one who knew whether the subject changed. As suggested by the relationship of change to ratings of liking found in the earlier study, the authors found that students presented themselves as most changed when the persuader was their only audience, less persuaded when both persuader and audience were aware of the extent of the subject's change, and little changed when only an observer or the experimenter was to know of the subject's degree of conformity to the persuasion attempt. Braver, Linder, Corwin, and Cialdini concluded:

> The interpretation of these results that we prefer is that targets know how persuaders and observers evaluate yielders and resisters. Further, they yield to or resist a persuasive attempt to maximize the positivity of the evaluation received for whomever is present when a public admission of social influence is made. (p. 573)

The same process underlies Brink's (1977) findings that students liked persons who were initially dissimilar after the students had an opportunity to attempt to persuade them to change, presumably because the students anticipated the dissimilar other would change as a result of the student's efforts.

These results suggest that under certain circumstances, an attempt to persuade provides the target with an opportunity to improve his or her perceived credibility in the eyes of the persuader. Conformity is a tactic of gaining power in some instances, especially in relationship with the persuader. Whether this is the result of yielding probably depends on the tactics of persuasion the persuader uses. Yielding to an "intelligent" and "rational" argument, responding to need, or being moved by personal testimony suggests desirable qualities that both the persuader and yielder can see as underlying the yielding. On the other hand, yielding to irrational argument, unknowledgeable sources, unscrupulous self-seekers, or unsubstantiated threats suggests undesirable qualities and contributes to the impression that the yielder is incapable, gullible, weak, inconsistent, and morally bankrupt.

Yielding or not yielding is problematic because different people look at the same events differently. Persuaders are likely to see their own efforts as rational and compelling and to see the yielding as a sign that they are right, and thus persuaders are likely to reward yielders with enhanced perceived capability. Observers, however, have an altogether different stake in the transaction. The fact that they themselves did not yield to the message means that it was not credible or emotionally compelling. Either the yielder is weak or the observer is wrong—people prefer to take the first alternative. Of course, yielding also involves an ever-present danger of being taken in by an insincere communicator and duped for his or her selfish personal gain. The thought of being laughed at behind one's back by an unscrupulous communicator and of appearing to others as gullible certainly restrains yielding.

One method of avoiding the many negative ramifications of being influenced is to deny that one has changed. For example, Goethals and Reckman (1973) found that high school students distorted their recall of their original stand on the issue of bussing after they took part in a group discussion of bussing that resulted in their changing their original opinions. They were thus able to change without appearing to change. Such a tactic becomes severely restricted when an audience has clear knowledge of the person's previous opinion. If an onlooker has the information, there is considerable danger that changing will make one appear gullible unless the circumstances seem compelling to the onlooker.

Another tactic of appearing unchanged, first identified by McGuire and Papageorgis (1962), is to change one's opinion before hearing the persuasive communication and thus avoid the danger of appearing to change as a result of the persuasive communication. Anticipatory belief change is an effective tactic of avoiding appearing gullible but only when the observer does not have knowledge of the person's position before the anticipatory shift. At the beginning of a school term Gaes and Tedeschi (1978) administered to one-third of an introductory psychology class a questionnaire in which was embedded an opinion question to be the target of persuasion in a later experiment. Later, a sample of the students reported for a study described for one-half of the students as intended to indentify what makes a certain set of messages persuasive (implicit persuasion condition) and, for the other half, as an effort to measure opinion change that results from listening to recorded messages (explicit persuasion condition). Half of the subjects were told that the communicator was a distinguished professor of physics and a member of the President's Select Council on Environmental Problems, while the other half were told that the communicator was another undergraduate at the university. They were then told what position the speaker would be taking on the issue. Before hearing the speech, the subjects were asked to indicate their opinion of the issue. Those who had indicated their opinions weeks earlier were reminded that "although their opinions were a matter of record, it would be appreciated if they would provide them once again" (p. 582). Extent of opinion change due to the experimental conditions was ascertained by subtracting the mean rating of a group of students (controls) who took the instrument at the same time as the subjects from the means of the subjects in each condition.

Gaes and Tedeschi found the largest changes in the "no reminder" conditions where subjects knew that the experimenter did not know their previous opinions, but only in two of the four conditions. The largest change was in the implicit persuasion—peer communicator condition, and the other statistically significant change was in the explicit persuasion—expert communicator condition. Subjects in the other two conditions did not significantly change their opinions in anticipation of the persuasive communications. Apparently, the threat of being persuaded and appearing gullible is greatest when faced with communications from a peer where persuasion is not the intent of the communication, and from an expert where persuasion is clearly intended. The patterns of anticipatory opinion changes were reversed when subjects were reminded of the experimenters' knowledge of their previous opinion. Students did not change their opinions in anticipation of the communications from a peer under implicit persuasion conditions or from an expert where opinion change was explicitly intended. Students did change their opinions significantly in anticipation of a communication from a peer where persuasion was explicit, and they tended to change, but not significantly, their opinions in anticipation of communications from an expert where persuasion was implicit.

Perhaps anticipatory change was not obtained with implicit intent—peer and explicit persuasion—expert conditions when the experimenter could detect change because the greater persuasive power of these communication circumstances could provide discounting factors for change after receiving the message. On the other hand, perhaps appearing inconsistent was preferable to appearing gullible and yielding to the persuasive efforts of the less persuasive communicators, experts not intent on persuasion and peers intent on persuasion. Gaes and Tedeschi concluded: "Thus, pretesting generally produced heightened concern about self presentation and a conflict between appearing consistent and hedging against appearing gullible" (p. 586).

Anticipatory change has been found in studies where students anticipated comparing their judgments of the appropriate sentence for criminal cases to that of an expert judge (Saltzstein & Sandberg, 1979), persuasive messages from experts (Cooper & Jones, 1970), and persuasive messages of peers (Cialdini, Levy, Herman, & Evenbeck, 1973). Hass and Mann (1976) found that anticipatory belief change occurred only when receipt of a persuasive message is anticipated. When subjects were led to anticipate receiving a message but then were told it would not be possible to present it to them, they did not shift their opinions in the direction of the message. Thus, anticipatory belief change is not a function of knowing that a discrepant message exists, but only of the anticipation of receiving and being influenced by the message. It is a strategy to avoid appearing to change when change is anticipated.

The above studies present a complex picture of persuasion. To avoid appearing gullible, persons seem ready to deny that their previous position differed from that held after persuasion by distorting their previous positions and by changing toward the expected message after receiving the message. A persuader would seem well advised to allow and even facilitate these methods of maintaining face to enable target persons to change as desired. Appeals to long-held underlying agreement in spite of the superficial appearances of differences and similar tactics would seem important to obtaining desired change. When it is difficult to deny change, persuaders need to provide rationales for change that enhance the good impression of the target person, such as providing an opportunity to appear insightful and informed through the possession of expert knowledge.

Threats

Appearing influenced when a persuader resorts to demands, imperatives, and threats gives the impression of not having the power to maintain equality in the relationship, of being weak, vulnerable, powerless, and fearful. Thus, persons are reluctant to appear influenced when others observe their responses to such tactics. Without the persuaders obviously having the power to back up tactics such as "You have no choice but to," the target person is likely to refuse to appear influenced even if he or she initially agrees with the persuader's desired behavior. For example, Worchel and Brehm (1970) had college students read persuasive speeches attributed to graduate students that advocated either a position held by the students, or a position opposed to the students' initial position. Half of the subjects read messages that were "liberally sprinkled with statements such as, 'you cannot believe otherwise,' or 'you have no choice but to believe this.' " The other half of the subjects received identical messages except that the threatening, demanding statements were omitted. Worchel and Brehm found that most students shifted their opinions (as measured after reading the messages) toward that urged by the messages in all conditions except the one in which students received threatening messages that advocated the opinion they held before the communication. In this condition, most of the students changed their opinions away from that advocated by the message and, in the process, away from their former opinion. This boomerang effect reflects the students' reluctance to appear helpless and without choice to the experimenter. Worchel and Brehm, using Brehm's reactance theory (1966), described the effect as reflecting the subjects' attempt to reestablish their freedom. Similar results are reported by Wicklund and Brehm (1968) and Brehm (1968).

Goodstadt (1971) provided another view of the boomerang effect. He found that students acted to reestablish their independence after the experimenter overstated their reactions of liking or disliking another student. The experiment had two parts. The first part created circumstances encouraging subjects to like or dislike another subject (a confederate), and the second part tested the willingness of subjects to do a favor for the liked or disliked other. Between the two parts, the experimenter looked at the student's rating of the other and (veridically) observed that, "It's very clear that you (dis)like the . . . (other student)," or made no statement. In a third condition the experimenter observed, "Apparently, you don't like the . . . (other student), but of course we don't put too much weight on measures like these." When the experimenter made no statement, many of the students who liked the other chose to help him, while few of those who disliked him chose to help. But when the experimenter made the "it's very clear" statement, the proportion of students helping or not helping was reversed so that few of those the experimenter stated liked the other chose to help him, and most of those the experimenter said disliked the other chose to help. The mild statement resulted in a high rate of helping for the liked and the disliked others. It appears that the experimenter's strong statement implied that the subject was predictable, easily controlled, and biased. Subjects used the opportunity to help the other as a means of dispelling the experimenter's apparent perception of bias and predictability. The helping opportunity served the function of correcting the experimenter's impressions of the subject's attitudes.

Heilman and Toffler (1976) found that perception of choice removed the boomerang effect of threats. They invited students to take part in a consumer research study. The students were told that they would work in pairs, one tasting the products and the other recording the results. Heilman and Toffler arranged for the tabulator to be able to increase or decrease the taster's payment for participation in the study, depending on whether the taster did what the tabulator requested. In some of the conditions, the tabulator threatened the taster with a substantial financial loss if she did not taste vinegar rather than orange juice. Some of the threateners offered the taster four vinegars to choose from, other tasters received a choice of vinegar as a function of a table of random numbers, and still others had no choice, as determined by either the tabulator or chance.

Significantly fewer of the tasters tasted the vinegar in the threat conditions than in conditions where the tabulators promised the taster higher payment for tasting vinegar, except in the threat condition in which the tabulator offered the taster a choice of type of vinegar. In that condition, the rate of compliance was the same as in conditions where higher payment was promised. Heilman and Toffler found that the subjects receiving the threats were more offended and defiant than those who received the promise of reward. Yet, those threatened subjects given a choice of how to comply were significantly less defiant than those not offered a choice. Importantly, threateners received much less favorable evaluations than promisers, disregarding whether the taster complied. Heilman and Toffler point out that the perception of being presented with a choice was effective because it gave the tasters a perception of independence and self-determination. The study suggests that defiance of a threat is based on the interpersonal consequences of appearing helpless, dependent, and without choice that accompany compliance rather than on an internal concern for restoring freedom. In the study, subjects given choice by an impersonal process (chance) did not comply more with the threats than did those given no choice at all.

Pallak and Heller (1973) provide another glimpse at factors affecting the results of threats. They found that students responded to messages from other students demanding that they endorse a particular point of view they initially agreed with by moving away from the demanded position, but only when the threatened students did not expect to work with the demanding student in the future. When they believed they would need to work in a cooperative manner with the demanding person in the future, they did not defy the demand, but did derogate the demander's competence on a rating available only to the experimenter. In the study, the demanding student was presented as having access to the complying student's ratings on opinions, and thus defiance and compliance communicated directly to the demander. The need to work cooperatively with the demanding student in the future attenuated the target subject's defiance in favor of a tactic of trying to gain the demander's favor through compliance to help establish a better working relationship in the future.

Taken as a whole, the above research suggests that threats are ineffective means of gaining compliance because of the implications of complying to a threat for the recipient's public impression: powerlessness, weakness, bias, control by others, and lack of self-determination. Overstating a person's opinions and trying to compel people do that which they are already doing results in mobilizing the persons in countermeasures to disqualify and disprove the threats and overstatements. Interestingly, a therapeutic method involves demanding that the client perform the symptomatic behaviors the client is already performing, with the frequent result that the client refuses to continue the symptoms (Haley, 1973). Milton Erickson has reported using the notion of offering alternatives of how to comply as a means of overcoming a person's resistance to a variety of therapeutic changes (Haley, 1973). Thus, it would appear that people's strong reactions against appearing helpless and controlled argue against trying to influence people to do or to believe something through threats, but provide fertile grounds for influencing people to stop doing or believing something by demanding that they continue doing it.

MANAGING OTHERS

Provoking Change

People are very sensitive to others' impressions of them and behave to impress others with their integrity and capability. Such impressions are instrumental in controlling relationships to meet needs. Because of people's interests in others' impressions of them, others can influence people's behaviors through feedback about the impressions their behaviors create. Feedback about the meaning of behavior influences future behavior. Perceptions, attributions, and reactions about another's behavior are attempts to influence the other. Orvis, Kelley, and Butler (1976) proposed this point of view in discussing the results of a study of attributions about disagreements between members of heterosexual couples. They stated, "We believe it will be necessary to deal with perception and communication as inseperable processes and, particularly, to view them in the context of relationship-maintaining processes" (p. 365). They suggest that a person's causal explanation of an interactant's behavior, though it must be constrained by conventions of plausibility and rationality, may not be rational, accurate, or complete in a scientific sense, or even given to change the partner's mind about the particular incident, but rather is intended to change what the interactant will do or how he or she will view the behavior next time. "At a more general level, as noted earlier, explanations acknowledge and reinstate the basic normative structure of the relationship regarding behavior. Thus, the discussion of causes, itself, acts as a causal influence on later behavior" (Orvis, Kelley, & Butler, 1976, p. 381).

If this point of view is true, or nearly so, objective perception and analysis of behavior (in the sense of disinterest about its effects on the other) should be impossible to give, much less to obtain. How a person perceives, analyzes, and responds to another should be a function of what he or she desires out of the relationship, how the other's behavior could contribute to that outcome, and what feedback is likely to encourage the other to change as desired. Obviously, people will differ in how they react to others, reflecting their needs, experiences, and cultural traditions.

A person's behavior with respect to another reveals as much about the person as it does about the other. Much of the counseling and psychotherapy interaction is spent studying the client's perceptions and causal attributions. The client's perceptions and attributions are seen as the causes of the client's problems in cognitive and insight therapies. Orvis, Kelley, and Butler (1976) comment:

> Meta-attributions will figure importantly in the evaluation of persons. When a given explanation is not credible to its hearer, he is likely to wonder why it was given. This raises questions about the speaker's candor, perceptiveness, and rationality. To the extent that the inadequacies of explanations can be attributed to properties of the explainer, serious doubt may be cast on the future of the given relationship. For how can one count on stable and productive interactions with a person who locates his behavior dishonestly or absurdly in the causal structure of the world? Hence, meta-attributions—explanations for explanations—will be a basic and important part of the evaluation of individuals. Further, the issue of why a given attribution is made may often, itself, become a matter of open discussion and conflict between close associates. (p. 381)

If we ignore how experimenters try to manage subjects in experiments, how people manage other people has not been studied much beyond the issues of how people manage others' impressions of them. Orvis, Kelley, and Butler broke ground in this important domain. They asked heterosexual couples who had been committed to one another for at least two years to complete a questionnaire about instances of conflict between them. They asked each person to identify several of his or her behaviors and those of his or her partner for which they had different explanations, and to describe the different explanations. Orvis, Kelley, and Butler categorized the behaviors and explanations and analyzed them in terms of frequencies of behavior and explanation types, differences in explanations for own and partners' behaviors, relationship of explanation to behavior type, and sex differences.

Most of the behaviors identified as sources of disagreement were negative and together provide a rather complete listing of ways to aggravate, anger, or embarrass another person. The behaviors were categorized into 19 groupings with labels such as "actor fails to behave warmly toward partner" and "actor has undesirable practices." "Actor" means the one performing the act, either the person or the person's partner. The most striking finding was that the explanations people gave for their own behaviors and the explanations they gave for their partner's behaviors were very different. Table 2 presents the frequencies of use of explanations for own and partner's behavior and the statistical significance of differences between them. Explanations people gave for their own behavior more than for their partner's behavior were circumstances and environment (9% versus 1.7%, respectively), objects (3% versus 0.1%), actor's psychological or physical state (8.1% versus 3.2%), actor's belief (8.2% versus 2.0%), actor's concern for mutual benefit (2.2% versus .3%), and activity is enjoyable (8.1% versus 3%). Explanations people gave for their partner's behaviors more frequently than for their own were actor's inability (3.0% versus 13% for self and partner respectively), Actor's characteristics (6.5% versus 19.7%), lack of concern for partner (0.4% versus 6.9%), and activity has good indirect consequences (2.2% versus 8.4%).

Table 2. Frequency of Use of Causes by Actors and Partners [a]

Causal Class or Category	Total (%)	Actors (%)	Partners (%)	ρ value
1. Circumstance/ environment	5.4	9.0	1.7	.001
a. Circumstance	2.1	3.5	0.07	—
b. State of environment	3.2	5.5	1.0	.001
2. People/objects	6.4	8.1	4.8	.02
a. People	4.8	5.1	4.6	—
b. Objects	1.6	3.0	0.1	.001
3. Actor's state	5.6	8.1	3.2	.001
a. Psychological state	3.8	5.1	2.5	.02
b. Physical state	1.8	3.0	0.6	.01
4. Actor's characteristics	22.6	11.4	33.9	.001
a. Inability	8.0	3.0	13.0	.001
b. Ability	0.3	0.6	0.0	—
c. Characteristics	13.1	6.5	19.7	.001
d. Habit	1.2	1.3	1.2	—
5. Actor's preference/belief	13.0	17.7	8.2	.001
a. Preference	7.8	9.4	6.3	.05
b. Belief	5.1	8.2	2.0	.001
6. Actor's concern	4.9	7.4	2.5	.001
a. Concern for partner	3.0	4.5	1.6	.01
b. Mutual benefit	1.2	2.2	0.3	.001
c. Concern for other people	0.6	0.7	0.6	—
7. Actor's intention to influence partner	4.2	4.2	4.2	—
a. To change partner's behavior	2.8	2.7	2.9	—
b. To define the relationship	1.4	1.4	1.3	—
8. Actor's negative attitude toward partner	8.1	3.3	12.9	.001
a. Lack of concern for partner	3.7	0.4	6.9	.001
b. Negative feelings toward partner	2.8	1.6	4.1	.01
c. Insecurity about the relationship	1.6	1.3	1.9	—
9. Partner is responsible	6.1	6.7	5.5	—
a. Partner's fault	3.0	3.8	2.3	—
b. Partner's influence	0.9	1.0	0.7	—
c. Partner's characteristics	1.7	1.9	1.4	—

Table 2. *(Continued)*

Causal Class or Category	Total (%)	Actors (%)	Partners (%)	p value
d. Partner's positive behavior	0.5	0.0	1.0	.05
10. Activity is desirable	11.4	15.8	6.9	.001
a. Activity is enjoyable	5.6	8.1	3.0	.001
b. Activity has good direct consequences	4.2	5.4	3.0	.05
c. Activity cuts costs	1.6	2.3	0.9	.05
11. Activity is undesirable	2.7	3.5	1.9	—
a. Not enjoyable	1.1	1.4	0.7	—
b. Bad direct consequences	1.6	2.0	1.2	—
12. Activity has desirable indirect consequences	7.0	3.3	10.7	.001
a. Good indirect consequences	5.3	2.2	8.4	.001
b. Response from other people	1.7	1.2	2.3	—
13. Uncodable	2.7	1.6	3.8	.02

[a] From Orvis, Kelley, and Butler, 1976, pp. 360−361.

Keeping in mind that most of the behaviors people listed were negative in tone, we see that the results reinforce the findings of research reviewed earlier on impression management. People discount much of their own disruptive behavior as due to external circumstances and temporary psychological states, and thus as not having implications for their personal characteristics. The explanation that they engaged in the behavior because of their beliefs sounds like the opinion moderation strategy found in the discussion of forced compliance—the person maintains integrity by attaching behavior to moderating beliefs to avoid the impression of having intended harm. The explanation "the activity is enjoyable" attaches the behavior to sincere motives, even if the other disagrees with the behavior. The actor's explanation of "concern for mutual benefit" seems to be an appeal to some deeper understanding of the couple's needs that, if the partner were just a little more enlightened, he or she would understand and appreciate. Overall, people presented a picture of not intending the disruptive behavior but of being innocent victims of external or temporary personal forces and of having sincere intentions for the disputed acts (certainly not malevolent although perhaps misguided). In short, they presented a picture of an altruistic but misunderstood person.

Partners, on the other hand, are not given much of a leg to stand on in their disagreements with the other person. One of the four explanations given more frequently for partner's behavior is generous and positive: "activity has good indirect consequences." The person may not like the behavior, but will allow that some good can come of it. But even here, the overall negative reaction to the act is clear, though somewhat masked in the pious hope that "surely some good can come out of it." The other explanations given for partner's behavior look a great deal like those that persons work to avoid in experiments. "Actor's inability" and "actor's characteristics" are attributions that directly attack the capability and integrity of the partner and that partners will strive to disavow in whatever ways available. Of course, this is exactly what a person wants to encourage the other to do when the other behaves in ways the person does not like. But note also how powerful the response, "You are right, I am incapable and stupid," is in countering the person's attributional attempts to create change. No wonder incapability is a common control tactic among the less powerful. The other frequently used attribution, "lack of concern for partner," strikes directly at the relationship and the other's sincerity and commitment to it. The attribution throws the other's affection, sincerity, and integrity directly into question. It implies that the relationship is founded on false premises and perhaps should be terminated. If the partner lacks caring for the person, what ulterior motives does he or she have for staying in the relationship? Surely the person should consider protecting himself or herself from the unscrupulous partner. In short, the attribution is a powerful attack at the other's integrity and should be very persuasive in terms of future behavior. And, according to these data, it is common.

Orvis, Kelley, and Butler's analysis of the frequency with which persons pair own and partner explanations for behavior reinforces the notion of persuasive nonsymmetry used by disputing couples. By far the most frequent pairs were "person's preference or belief" versus "partner's characteristics," "person's circumstances and environment" versus "partner's characteristics," and "activity desirable to the person" versus "the partner's concern for the activity's indirect consequences." The first two pairings pit the person's considered beliefs, preferences, and external circumstances against the partner's characteristics, usually inability and lack of integrity. The third pairing is more charitable: the person sees the disputed behavior as personally desirable, while the partner's objection concerns the activity's indirect consequences.

Orvis, Kelley, and Butler found some differences between male and female behaviors and attributions. Males were more frequently described as engaged in insensitive or unyielding behaviors toward their partners and in sports activity, while females were more frequently described as avoiding activities, especially self-help behaviors, engaging in emotional behavior, and doing things with their partners. Attributionally, both male and female raters attributed female behaviors more frequently than male behaviors to environment, other people, inability, and insecurity about relationships. Males, more often than females, were described as acting because the activity had good direct or indirect consequences. Orvis, Kelley, and Butler comment: "The attributions are clearly consistent with common stereotypes of the woman, that is, that she is the more dependent and weaker person. The weakness appears to be translated into her susceptibility to external control in the form of influence by the environment and other people" (p. 370). Conversely, males were seen as more actively controlling their lives by exercising choices among actions in terms of their consequences.

Passer, Kelley, and Michela (1978) explored the psychological dimensions underlying the attributions found by Orvis, Kelley, and Butler in a factor analysis of ratings of the similarity of causes. They presented college students with a series of situations drawn from the categories of behaviors found by Orvis et al. For each behavioral situation, students rated the similarities of causes from the standpoint of either the actor or the partner. Listed were the causes identified in the previous study. The students also rated the causes on a series of semantic differential scales. In interpreting the results, we must keep in mind that the behaviors "were overwhelmingly negative in character, representing ways in which the actor aggravated, angered, or embarrassed the partner" (Passer, Kelley, & Michela, 1978, p. 952).

Two dimensions best described the intercorrelations among the similarity ratings for both the actor's and the partner's view in the factor analyses; they are presented in Figures 6 and 7. Passer, Kelley, and Michela described the first dimension for both actor and partner ratings as "attitude toward partner." The first dimensions in the two solutions are very similar to one another and intercorrelate at $r = .84$. The causes most associated with the negative and positive poles of attitude toward partner in both solutions were "actor doesn't care for partner" at the negative pole and "actor thought the act was in partner's best interest" at the positive pole. In

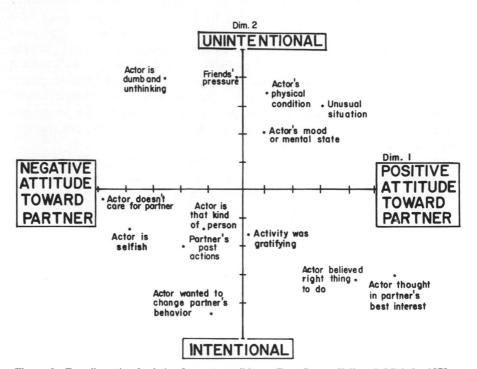

Figure 6 Two-dimensional solution for actor conditions. (From Passer, Kelley, & Michela, 1978, p. 955. Copyright 1978 by the American Psychological Association. Reprinted by permission.)

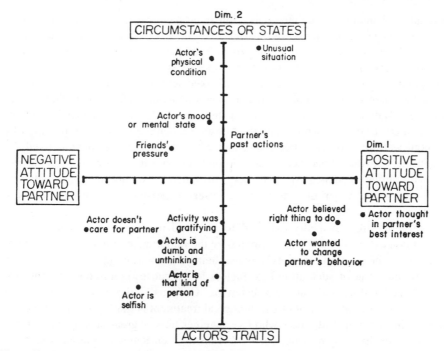

Figure 7   Two-dimensional solution for partner condition. (From Passer, Kelley, & Michela, 1978, p. 955. Copyright 1978 by the American Psychological Association. Reprinted by permission.)

addition, the following semantic differential items correlated between $r = .80$ and $r = .90$ with the attitude toward partner dimension in both actor and partner solutions: positive-negative attitude toward spouse, desire to benefit-harm spouse, good-bad, and appropriate-inappropriate.

The second factor in the actor solution was labeled intentional-unintentional. The two causes anchoring the unintentional pole of the dimension are "actor is dumb and unthinking" and "friend's pressure." The two causes anchoring the intentional pole are "actor wanted to change partner's behavior" and "actor thought [the action to be] in partner's best interest." Semantic differential scales that correlated between $r = .83$ to $r = .87$ with the dimension were accidental-deliberate, involuntary-voluntary, unintentional-intentional, and temporary-permanent. In the partner solution, the second factor was labeled "actor's traits versus circumstances or states." The factor is anchored on the "circumstances or states" pole with "actor's physical condition" and "unusual situation," and at the "actor's traits" pole with "actor is that kind of person" and "actor is selfish." Semantic differential items most highly correlated with the dimension ($r = .77$ to $r = .96$) were "temporary-permanent," "not actor's trait-actor's trait," "characteristic of situation-actor," and "outside-inside actor."

The most surprising finding in this study is the powerful and dominant first dimension in attribution for both actors and partners: attitude toward partner. Attribution theories have emphasized dimensions as stable-unstable, internal-external, and intentional-unintentional, but none have given much prominence to positive or negative attitude toward partner. But how we view the acts of another is very much conditioned by our attitude toward the person. If we like a person, their negative behavior is due to situational or temporary states, or perhaps misguided but sincere intentions. If we dislike them, the disliked act is but another example of why we dislike them—their deeply seated inclinations to do evil. Regan, Straus, and Fazio (1974) demonstrated this effect in a study in which they led students to like or dislike another student, whom they then observed behaving on a task in which he did both well and poorly. They found that when the observing students liked the person, they attributed his successful and good behavior to his personal characteristics. His failures and negative acts were attributed to situational constraints and temporary states. When they disliked the observed person, their attributions were opposite.

Counselors are repeatedly exhorted to like and even love their clients. In a broader context, religious systems emphasize the importance of loving others and of believing in the good of others even when their behavior is completely contrary. A dramatic outcome of such attitudinal factors is the causes counselors attribute for their clients' failing and antisocial behavior. Obviously, the attitudinal effect on attribution is a major element of psychological treatment. Finally, it is apparent that partners in marriage and others who live together have a great deal at stake in the attitudes they have toward one another. Marriage enrichment programs such as Marriage Encounter should and do reinforce loving attitudes toward one another as major targets of their interventions.

The major impact of the attitude diminension is on the "intentional" and "actor's traits" poles of the second dimensions in both actor and partner solutions. The "unintentional" and "circumstances and states" poles of the second dimensions are expressions of the discounting principle that has figured so prominently throughout this chapter. When the students rating the causes approached the causes from the actor's point of view, they clustered impelling environmental conditions such as "unusual situation" and "friend's pressure" and temporary physical or mental states such as "actor's physicial condition," "mood or mental states," and "dumb and unthinking" as causes the actor should not be held accountable for. It is significant that these are the causes actors used in the Orvis, Kelley, and Butler study to account for their disputed behavior, these plus the causes in the positive attitude–intentional quadrant (activity was gratifying, actor believed right thing to do, and actor thought that the action was in the partner's best interest). Clearly, these are the causes people would like to have others see as behind their behavior. The causes in the negative attitude–intentional quadrant are not those to which people will readily admit; they are ones that they avoid giving the impression of having: "I wanted to change partner's behavior" (manipulative and Machiavellian); "partner's past actions" (revenge); and "I am that kind of person," "I am selfish," and "I don't care for partner" (all malevolent).

The second dimension of the student's ratings of causes from the point of view of the partner receiving the action is somewhat different from that of the student's rating of causes from the actor's point of view. The discounting factors are situational and external factors (unusual situation, friend's pressure) and temporary states (mood and mental state and physical condition). Added to the discounting list is "partner's past actions." As we saw earlier, from the partner's point of view, retribution is a discounting principle. Students' ratings suggest that when partners have positive attitudes toward the actors, and the actors' behaviors are not discounted, the causes chosen by the partner reflect the belief in the good intentions of the actor to benefit the partner ("actor wanted to change partners," "actor thought the activity was in the partner's best interest"). Even though the actor's behavior was negative, the intention was not, and the positive-minded, believing partner looks to the deeper goodness of the actor to account for the action, along with viewing the behaviors as unfortunately distorted due to external pressures, temporary internal states, and misguided ideas. Note that the well-thinking partner identifies causes to account for the actor's negative behavior that are very similar to what the actor himself identifies. Both held the goodness of the actor sacrosanct and identify temporary disturbing factors as the culprits. Apparently, students saw a sincere desire to change the partner as a benevolent motive.

However, these discounting and benevolent motives were not those attributed by partners in the earlier study of Orvis, Kelley, and Butler to account for their partner's negative behaviors. Overwhelmingly, the partners referred to the causes that are in the negative attitude—actor's trait quadrant: they saw their partners as not caring for them, being dumb, unthinking, and selfish, as "that kind of person" (who would do such a rotten thing), and self-gratifying. In interpersonal conflict, persons are prone to imply that their interactants are uncaring and bad to the core. As all the research we have viewed testifies, such an assault on the person is calculated to lead the person to behave differently the next time to avoid the derision of their character and the loss of power in the relationship.

An implication of the two Kelley studies is that the basic attitude between spouses in a marriage is a major determinant of the harmoniousness of the marriage. When either partner behaves in a way that aggravates the other, the other's explanation of why the person behaved thusly is their immediate feedback to the spouse and is their attempt to curtail the behavior. Orvis, Kelley, and Butler's results show a clear preference for spouses to give negative feedback, suggesting that negative attitudes towards spouses may be common. In a study demonstrating the importance of attitude in marriage, Goffman, Notarius, Markman, Bank, Yoppi, and Rubin (1976) asked couples to discuss points of conflict with each other, to record the positive or negative intent of their statements, and to record their perception of the positive or negative intent of their spouses' remarks. As we would expect from the Kelley studies, couples with troubled marriages recorded much higher negative and lower positive ratings of the intents they perceived in their spouses remarks than did couples in harmonious marriages. No differences were recorded between the two groups of couples in spouse's self-rated intent, but only in perception of the other's intent. In marriage counseling, the spouses' attitudes toward one another are a major target for change, and perhaps the major point of difficulty in the marriage. Spouses in marriage counseling almost universally present their partners as wishing to injure them, being selfish, incapable, and so on, reflecting their basic attitude toward each other. Disabusing these damaging attributions requires changing their attitudes to one another as much as and even more than changing the provoking behaviors the attributions are intended to change.

Regan, Straus, and Fazio (1974) and Messé, Stollak, Larson, and Michaels (1979) also demonstrate the importance of the attitudinal dimension in relationships. Regan, Straus, and Fazio, described above, found that attributions for behavior depended on initial liking or dislike, Messé et al. had adults observe a child on video tape who exhibited either primarily positive or negative behaviors. In subsequent interaction with the child, the adults with a negative bias (those exposed to the negative behavior) dominated and structured the interaction more than those with the positive bias, while those with the positive bias tended to help the child more and to submit more to the child's demands. These results suggest that the negative-biased adults acted to counteract the negative traits of the child, while the positive-bias adults allowed the positive characteristics of the child to emerge, just as we would expect from the relationship of the attitudinal dimension to attribution of personal traits.

Discerning Liking

Given the importance of liking in interaction, how persons come to like or dislike others takes on a great importance. Byrne and associates (Byrne, 1961; Byrne & Blalock, 1963; Byrne, Griffitt, & Golightly, 1966) have shown that reciprocity is the ubiquitous principle of liking. We like persons who like us, and dislike persons who dislike us. We tend to like those we associate with (Berscheid & Walster, 1969) and those whom we perceive to be similar to us (Byrne, 1961). Napolitan and Goethals (1979) have shown that we tend to like persons who are friendly to us and become concerned about why they are friendly only when they are friendly one time and unfriendly another. Under these circumstances, interactants search for discounting factors to eliminate the inconsistency and perceive the other to be friendly or unfriendly depending on their findings. Lowe and Goldstein (1970) found that persons tend to like those who evaluate them positively and dislike those who evaluate them negatively. Drachman, DeCarufel, and Insko (1978) and Jones (1964) found the same tendency with the exception that those who evaluated a superior negatively in the face of the pressure to ingratiate themselves to the superior were also liked by the superior.

Jones and Gordon (1972) found that liking in response to self-disclosure depended on the facts and timing of the disclosures. Persons who disclosed their high abilities early in the conversation and did not disclose negative factors for which they were responsible until late into the conversation were not liked as well as persons who were quick to reveal their faults and withheld disclosure of their positive attributes until later. When the person was not responsible for the positive attributes, and when they were victims of negative events, the effect of disclosure timing on liking was reversed: greater liking occurred when good things over which the person had no control were revealed early, and bad things for which the person was not responsible were revealed later and reluctantly. It seems that persons are liked when they do not brag and are modest about their strengths, do not cry about their misfortunes, and are forthright about their faults. Nelson-Jones and Strong (1976) found the same effects of timing and content of self-disclosure on liking. Finally, Davis and Perkowitz (1979) have shown that persons like others who in conversation respond frequently to their statements and whose responses are related to the content of their productions. Persons like people who listen to them, respond to them, and show their attention to what they say by not changing the subject.

Discerning Personal Causes

What factors determine others' perception of the person's behavior as being due to traits and other stable personal characteristics or as due to unstable personal factors or external factors? People assume that behavior reflects the intentions and stable personal characteristics of the actor unless some outside force is evident, the person's behavior is inconsistent with expectation, or the person's behavior is inconsistent over time. Heider (1958) suggested that this assumption stems from the perceiver's desire for a stable and predictable environment, an objective that is greatly enhanced if people can be construed as controlled by stable personal dispositions a good deal of the time. For example, Miller, Norman, and Wright (1978) found that when persons expected to be interacting in the future with a stranger, they were much more concerned about discerning the stable characteristics of the person as evidenced by the person's behavior than when they did not expect future interaction. Sometimes people seem inclined to overlook external factors that are influencing a person's behavior. Yandell and Insko (1977) found that students were inclined to believe that other students delivering essays agreed with the positions the essays expressed, even when the students had been assigned to read the essays.

Persons use discounting and augmenting principles liberally. Napolitan and Goethals (1979), previously referred to, found that when a person's expressed liking for another was inconsistent, external, or temporary, internal states were sought and used to discount one set of behaviors. Messick and Reeder (1972) had students listen to a job interview of a person who was described as wanting or not wanting the job. Also, they were told that the job was congruent with an introverted personality (forester) or an extroverted personality (salesman). In the interview, the applicant presented himself as introverted. They found that when the applicant was presented as wanting the job and the job was as a forester, or the person did not want the job and the job was as a salesman, students drew few conclusions about the applicant. The person's desire to have or not have the job was sufficient explanation for the applicant to present himself as compatible or incompatable to the job. However, when the applicant behaved contrary to what the students saw as the reasonable way to manage the interviewer's impression of suitability for the job, they drew strong conclusions about the person's personality. The individual who wanted a job requiring an extrovert but presented himself as an introvert must be very introverted indeed. Likewise, a person who did not want to be offered the job yet presented a favorable impression of suitability must be very introverted. The results clearly show the role of both discounting and augmenting in the judgment of others' characteristics. An external inducement for a person to behave in a certain way is sufficient to account for their behavior when they do indeed so behave, and it makes it all the more remarkable when they fail to conform to the external inducement. A series of studies by Trope and colleagues (Trope, 1978; Trope & Burnstein, 1977) demonstrate the same principles. They found that students judge persons to have very little freedom to determine their behavior when external factors strongly favor one behavior over another, especially when the external factors favor behavior incongruent with the person's perceived disposition.

The discounting principle is apparent in a study reported by Kane, Joseph, and Tedeschi (1976). They asked students to judge the dispositions of a person doing harm to another within the contexts of the other having done more or less harm to the person previously. They found that the person was judged to be aggressive, negative, hostile, antagonistic, and so on, only when the other had previously not harmed or had harmed less. When the other previously had harmed the person as much or more, the person was not judged to be aggressive. The norms of reciprocity and equity provided external justification for the actor to act in revenge without being seen as aggressive, or even vengeful. Passer, Kelley, and Michela (1978) also found that a partner's previous negative behavior was a discounting factor for negative behavior to a spouse.

Lerner (1971) found the discounting effect of external factors in a study where students observed another student receive painful shocks in an experiment and then evaluated the characteristics of the victim. When the observers thought the student was not being compensated by the experimenter for being shocked or was not acting, they consistently evaluated the shock victim more negatively than when the discounting factors of compensation or acting were available. After all, what are the characteristics of someone who volunteers and allows others to painfully shock her for the fun of it?

Discerning How Others Perceive Us

The most important judgments persons in interaction with others make are about how others perceive them. Previously, we discussed research that showed that persons tend to respond reciprocally to others' liking and disliking of them. But it is clear that behavior cannot be taken at face value when ulterior motives might be responsible for the behavior. Persons in positions of authority are sitting targets for positive feedback from their subordinates when the superior can benefit the subordinate; and, in fact, all people are targets of ingratiation in interaction with others due to the positive effects for the other of being liked. Receiving negative feedback under such circumstances has special significance due to the augmentation principle. As discussed earlier, Drachman, DeCarufel, and Insko (1978) found that superiors liked those who gave them accurate negative feedback in spite of the obvious pressure to ingratiate them, a finding earlier reported by Jones (1964).

In spite of the clear problem of ingratiation, people still seem to readily receive and believe self-enhancing feedback in many circumstances (Sicoly & Ross, 1977). Some circumstances seem to heighten concern about discounting and augmenting factors behind positive and negative feedback. For example, Eagly and Whitehead III (1972) found that when students chose to receive feedback from others about their behavior, they discounted positive feedback and augmented negative feedback. However, when feedback was unsolicited, favorable messages had much greater effects on the persons self-ratings than did negative messages.

HELPING PEOPLE CHANGE

Characteristics of Psychological Symptoms

The results of research reviewed in this chapter depict people as prone to deny responsibility for negative events through defensiveness, rationalization, and appeals to weakness and inability, and eager to accept responsibility for positive events even remotely associated with them. Augment the positive and discount the negative seem to be the overriding rules in interdependence. For the most part, the picture is pessimistic, depicting people as self-centered, hedonistic, and superficial. Of course, we must keep in mind that the data are derived for the most part in experiments in laboratories in short-term interactions with psychologists under conditions that surely put people on their guard, and where people find themselves caught red-handed in the performance of disagreeable acts. Even so, the fact that Orvis, Kelley, and Butler's (1976) results fit the other results cautions against dismissing the other studies. Orvis et al. worked with couples who had been together two years or more, yet the nature of their attributions and how they were used are very much the same as found in the studies of short-term interactions.

The results support the notions that persons carefully defend their credibility in interactions and attack others' credibility as a means of stimulating change. When people behave in a way that others perceive as negative or harmful, the actors seem to avoid at all costs the correspondent implications of the behavior: that they intend to harm and are at the core malevolent. Likewise, when people fail, they avoid the correspondent implications that they are incapable or, when the failure represents harm to others, that they intended to fail. The results suggest a hierarchy of preferred solutions to harm-doing and failure. The most preferred solution to account for actions that attack one's credibility is to discount the behavior with some external circumstance. Responsibility for the action is lodged with the circumstance, while the actor was forced to so behave and had no choice. Other persons, circumstances, or luck forced the innocent victim to so act. When such factors are not available, persons turn to attitude moderation to defend against correspondent inferences. Their behavior reflects their belief that the act was not harmful. They had no intent to harm. They may have been wrong or misguided, but they certainly did not intend wrong. In the same category is the lack of trying. The person claims that the behavior does not reflect ability, but a lack of trying. For some reason, the person did not feel like an all-out effort just then, or some temporary mood state mitigated his or her normal performance. These two tactics can be called *justification* and *rationalization,* respectively.

The last stand against malevolence claims inability as a discount for harm-producing behavior. The individual did not intend to do harm, but could not help it due to his or her lack of ability, or some other factor of personality which cannot be willfully and intentionally controlled. Thus, the person cannot be held responsible. The appeal to uncontrollable personal factors as the cause of the harming behavior removes responsibility for one's own behavior and thus makes it impossible to willfully change. Thus, the person escapes the charge of malevolence at the cost of a loss of control over self. The strategy has the benefit of discouraging further pursuit by interactants, for the person cannot change nor can the person be held intentionally responsible. This strategy can be called *debilitation*.

Gaes, Kalle, and Tedeschi's (1978) results indicate that once launched in pursuit of avoiding the malevolence charge, persons will do what is necessary to protect themselves from exposure. Justifications will be found to cover justifications, rationalizations will be made to cover rationalizations, and helplessness developed to cover helplessness. The tactic chosen will be followed and elaborated upon to defend against detection and admission, for admitting the strategy would itself be admitting malevolence.

Orvis, Kelley, and Butler's (1976) results suggest that people attempt to get others to stop behaving in disagreeable ways by charging that the behavior reflects personal weakness or malevolent motives and intentions. As Orvis, Kelley, and Butler point out, the charge of malevolence is not so much intended to convince the other that he or she is evil as it is to lead the other to avoid further actions of the same sort in the future to avoid giving the impression of malevolence in the future. We do not know to what extent this change strategy is successful—it probably is relatively successful judging from its high frequence of use. That it is not always successful is attested to by the continued existence of conflict in Orvis, Kelley, and Butler's couples. While the change tactic frequently may be successful, it is probably countered often by strenuous tactics of justification, rationalization, and debilitation. Of Orvis, Kelley, and Butler's couples, the remarkable differences in their causal perceptions suggest that a charge of malevolence is countered by claims of justification, rationalization, and debilitation, and both tactics become more extreme in interaction. It is difficult to imagine that such interactions would not deteriorate with growing distrust and feelings of being misunderstood and disliked. Indeed, without other factors entering in, growing dislike should lead to more frequent charges and countercharges of malevolence and growing defensiveness. Within a relationship that cannot be easily dissolved, debilitation would seem a likely strategy for the weaker interactant because it is the only tactic that superior power cannot defeat. Justifications can be proven wrong and rationalizations exposed, but acceptance of blame with pitiful debilitation cannot be countered without resorting to paradox.

Many symptoms that lead to psychological treatment probably arise from the management of change in interdependence. It seems clear that the defensive strategy of claiming helplessness and inability is a common ingredient of many neurotic symptoms. Clients are depressed, anxious, unable to work, ulcerated, paralyzed, blind, and so on. Because of their inability or disability, they are unable to behave as others want them to. No amount of urging, pleading, demanding, or attacking will shake them because they cannot help themselves. However, the other defensive tactics also are symptomatic when they become dominant in the person's behavioral repertoire. To regularly deny responsibility because of external factors or to rationalize continuously leads to ineffectiveness and conflict with interactants. As responsibility for one's own actions is denied, feelings of being a pawn surely increase. On the other side, a partner attempting to obtain change is open to sliding into resentment, vengefulness, and depression. To be continuously seeing others as willfully evil and malevolent requires continuous anger, alertness to others' misdoing, and effort to reform others. The constant emotional alertness is likely to lead to physical breakdown to say nothing of the effects on one's relationships with others.

While strategies of defense and attack in pursuit of change in interaction do not account for all forms of psychological problems, they surely do account for some, perhaps many. Basically then, the following four targets for behavior change in counseling and psychotherapy emerge from the above considerations:

1. Justification—the practice of assigning negative, harmful, and failing behavior to external causes to avoid the behavior's correspondent implications to intentions and characteristics;

2. Rationalization—the practice of presenting, implying, feigning, or altering internal causes of behavior post hoc (after the behavior and its effects are known) to deny that harmful or failing effects were intended and thus to avoid the behavior's correspondent implications to intentions and characteristics;

3. Debilitation—the practice of assigning negative, harmful, and failing behavior to involuntary internal causes to avoid the behavior's correspondent implications to intentions and integrity; and

4. Vilification—the practice of believing, implying, and communicating to others that all negative, harmful, and failing behavior of others is correspondent with their malignant and malevolent intentions and characteristics.

These four behavior patterns are strategies of redirecting perceptions of the causes of behavior to enhance personal power and control in interaction. They are attributional strategies in which behavior is in the service of generating desired impressions for behavior control purposes. The behavior patterns are ways persons defend themselves against the loss of interpersonal power and control and are symptoms for psychological treatment only with extreme or overfrequent use. Overuse is probably the result of escalating cycles of efforts to change and to resist change.

Enhancing the Likelihood of Change

Change of interaction behavior is a tactic intended to gain credibility and control. Change is not a passive acceptance of another's wishes, but an active effort to gain control, mastery, and power given the circumstances. Therefore, efforts to change another will succeed to the extent that they create perceived opportunities for the other to gain control, mastery, and power by changing. Telling another to do what we want is often not very pragmatic, for the other will not do as we say unless the other believes that compliance will gain a more favorable circumstance for him or her than will noncompliance. The research of Cialdini and his colleagues (Cialdini, Braver, & Lewis, 1974; Braver, Linder, Corwin, & Cialdini, 1977) suggests that people are very sensitive to the negative implication of change: their power is weak relative to another. A person desiring to change another will be more successful if he or she (a) presents change as a way to enhance power, (b) arms the other with discounts to manage observers' perceptions of the change, (c) presents change as not really a change at all, and (d) presents change as coming from the others' autonomous processes rather than as a response to the greater power of the person.

The likelihood of change in counseling or psychotherapy is increased if the new position is presented as enhancing the client's power and control relative to the counselor. Perhaps the change would flatter, affirm, or otherwise favor and ingratiate the counselor and thus increase the counselor's view of the client's likeableness, intelligence, integrity, wisdom, maturity, and so on. The counselor might suggest that the change would render the counselor less powerful in the relationship and thus give the client the upper hand and perhaps cut off the counselor's further attempts to change the client. The counselor might suggest that the client does not have the strength, intelligence, or fortitude to change and thus present the client with an opportunity to show intelligence, strength, and cunning beyond what the counselor apparently believes is possible, and also to prove the counselor wrong and less able.

Through the use of modeling principles, the counselor should demonstrate the new behavior and show the positive consequences of its adoption. The counselor should identify the audience to whom the change would be favorable and make sure that this audience carries considerable weight with the client. The client would be responsive to learning how the new behavior would gain credibility and relationship control with liked and disliked interactants, as well as with idealized others, such as "rational man" or God. The counselor should present data supporting the correctness of the new position, data from scientific research, moral principles, and conduct codes of cathected others. The counselor should draw upon whatever credibility he or she has as an expert, a moral leader, a knowing peer, or other sources. The data and credibility of source will help the client discount the negative implications of change and help him or her defend the change as prudent, intelligent, rational, insightful, morally correct, and as a product of his or her strong capabilities to understand and reason rather than as a product of weak submission to the counselor's ideas. Such factors allow the client to present the change as a result of powerful personal factors rather than of weakness and submission to a more powerful other.

The counselor should make it possible for the client to change without appearing to change at all. The new behavior is best presented as an outgrowth of what the client is doing, feeling, and thinking already. By presenting the change as simply the next logical evolution of current behavior, the client changes without changing.

The client's intentions should be construed so that the new behavior is a better expression of what is already intended, and thus is a logical evolution of personal consistency that yields greater positive control of others through superior impression management and persuasion efforts. The new behavior should be presented as a product of an ongoing process of self-expression and development.

The counselor should avoid any expression that he or she has any real influence on the client, but should instead suggest that any change the client experiences comes from the client, from the emergence of his or her own characteristics such as basic rationality, organismic growth, the Holy Spirit, or released psychological energy. The counselor should suggest that changes that occur are to be expected with or without the counselor's intervention, are autonomous, self-generated growth, and that changes do not represent acquiescence to the influence of the counselor. Note that positing the change as a result of an autonomous growth process not only removes the stigma of changing in response to low power in the relationship, but also makes it difficult for the client to resist, for it is a process outside of the client's intentional control. The strategy of attributing change to growth places the change beyond intentional resistance and has the same interpersonal power in creating change in spite of resistance as does the debilitation strategy in resisting change in spite of the persuasive efforts of a more powerful other.

In summary, the counselor should keep in mind the following in order to create a climate conducive to change:

1. Demonstrate how the new position will enhance credibility and control;
2. Present factors the client can use to support and defend change;
3. Present the change as not a change; and
4. Present the change as caused by the client's autonomous internal growth processes.

Stimulating Change

When clients come to counselors, they present themselves in ways intended to control the behavior of the counselor, including the counselor's perception of the client's characteristics. Persons who make extreme use of the defensive and offensive strategies discussed earlier will use the same strategies to gain the counselor's aid against their enemies and will present themselves as innocent and misunderstood. The counselor can help the client present his or her symptoms in the counseling interaction by listening to the client's description of difficulties, showing special interest in emotional episodes, and agreeing with the client's accounts of the episodes, seeing them as understandable, reasonable, and natural. Such counselor behavior will help the client display the symptom pattern, facilitate the client's liking for the counselor, and communicate the counselor's liking for the client. The client's construction of events is intended to draw attention away from the conclusion that his or her behavior corresponds to basic characteristics and intentions, and toward the conclusion that other temporary and superficial factors are the operative causal elements behind his or her behavior. The counselor's agreement with the client's construances of events communicates a positive attitude toward the client. Basically, the counselor's attributional set for accounting for client behavior reflects the positive pole of the powerful attitudinal dimension of attribution found by Passer, Kelly, and Michela (1978).

The research reviewed in this chapter suggests that a powerful way to stimulate persons to change is to communicate that the impression their behavior creates for others is vastly different from what they had intended. Interactional behavior, especially when it achieves symptomatic proportions, has the major function of guiding others to causal attributions thought to be most facilitative of the person's credibility and control, given the circumstances. Thus, the person is very sensitive to feedback suggesting that the desired end has not been achieved, and the person is stimulated to change. This is the basic tactic used by most persons to stimulate others to change, as demonstrated in the studies of Orvis, Kelley, and Butler (1976), Goffman, Notarius, Markman, Bank, and Yoppi (1976) and Rubin (1975).

The attributional or causal significance of behavior is not a function of the acts themselves, but of the total context within which the behavior occurs. Thus, altering any aspect of the behavioral circumstances within which the client operates has the potential of significantly changing the causal significance of the client's behavior. The research reviewed here and elsewhere (Strong, 1978) suggests four tactics for stimulating clients to change:

1. Demand that the client perform the symptomatic behavior;
2. Exaggerate the attributional significance of the symptoms;
3. "Discover" previously unnoticed discounting and augmenting factors relevant to the client's symptomatic behaviors; and
4. Create meta-attributions for the client's symptomatic attributional strategies (behavior) that stimulate the abandonment of the symptomatic strategies.

Demanding Symptomatic Behavior

Several of the studies reviewed earlier showed that demanding that persons do what they are already doing surprisingly leads them to refuse to continue the behavior, at least under some conditions (Brehm, 1968; Wicklund & Brehm, 1968; Worchel & Brehm, 1970). Watzlawick, Beavin, & Jackson (1967) describe such a strategy in psychological treatment as a paradox, and many have reported good results using the strategy in treatment (L'Abate & Weeks, 1978). Demanding that a person do or think what he or she is already doing or thinking dramatically changes the causal structure of the behavior. The demand is a powerful discounting factor that argues against others seeing the behavior as intrinsically motivated and thus attacks the intrinsic support and significance of the behavior. To comply with the demand implies that the person is powerless in interaction with the demander, and thus it assaults the person's credibility. Finally, the symptomatic pattern is itself intended to control the other in the interaction. Performing the symptom on command makes the symptom the therapist's instrument for controlling the client rather than the other way around.

How the demand is given has a great effect on its effectiveness in stimulating the abandonment of the symptom. Heilman and Toffler (1976) showed that if the person perceives a choice in how to comply, the probability of compliance is increased. Pallak and Heller (1973) showed that when compliance gains power that may be needed in future interaction, compliance is more likely. More research is needed to understand how and when demand or paradox is an effective tactic in therapy. The sketchy data now available suggest that the use of paradox will be most successful (*a*) with persons greatly concerned about being controlled by others and (*b*) when the command allows the least autonomy possible in compliance.

Exaggerating the Symptoms

The results of the study by Goodstadt (1971) suggest that when another's understanding of the meaning of the person's behavior is much more extreme than the person intended, the person is stimulated to counter the exaggerated and credibility-threatening impression. It seems reasonable to hypothesize that exaggerating the interpersonal meaning of the client's symptoms should stimulate the client to counter the impression by moving away from the symptomatic behavior. In counseling and psychotherapy, three common ways of exaggerating symptom meanings are reflection of feeling, Gestalt exaggeration, and interpretation. Reflection or accurate empathy constantly probes for more extreme feelings, ideas, and reactions to events, and eventually it overshoots the person's intended impression, leading to denial of the extreme attitudes and feelings and emergence of corrective and moderate feelings and ideas. Gestalt exaggeration is patently intended to sharply identify the client's pattern of behavior and to push it to absurdity and abandonment. Interpretation is a bit more subtle. First the defensive pattern is identified, in itself a considerable escalation in extremity, unmasking the client and making continued use of the strategy much more difficult as it must now be done explicitly, openly, and obviously. The new meanings the therapist gives to the now explicit behavior can further increase and distort the perceived impact of the behavior on the counselor's impression of the client. The exact impact depends on the therapist's interpretative scheme and the client's values.

Discovering New Discounts and Augments

The studies reviewed in this chapter document a powerful effect of perceived circumstances on the personal significance of behavior. A major activity in counseling and psychotherapy is the discussion of events of significance to the client in search of the personal meaning of the client's behavior. This process of event analysis (Strong, 1978) presents many opportunities to discover heretofore unperceived causal factors in the client's and in others' behaviors. The analysis of events in search of causes and meanings is not objective but is a subjective and creative activity, although certain rules of evidence are observed, depending on social convention. Introducing new considerations can completely change the significance of behavior. For example, if a client sees aggressive behavior toward another as completely justifiable reciprocity for the other's aggression and thus of no personal significance, presenting evidence and argument that the other's behavior is situationally determined and not personally intended to harm removes the discount and opens the aggressive behavior to personal attribution. On the other hand, finding that one's behavior is only what might be expected under the circumstances removes its personal implications. For example, information about the widespread practice of masturbation can eliminate anxiety and debilitation for some clients.

The possibilities for reinterpreting behavior can be further increased by shifting the audience evaluating the meanings of the client's performance. Ellis' (1962) notions of what a "rational man" should do provide a distinctive set of rules; Roger's (1951) "actualized man" another set; the American college sophomore yet another; the Bible, the Torah, and the Koran yet others. Whether a factor is a discount depends on whose rules one uses. Add the prospect of shifting from audience to audience, and the possibilities of shifting the causal significance of any behavior are quite unlimited. One of the major effects of the counselor's preferred theory of counseling or psychotherapy is the rules of evidence used to determine the personal significance of behavior.

Creating Meta-Attributions

Drawing on the results of Orvis, Kelley, and Butler (1976), it has been argued that the major method of stimulating persons to change is to provide them with the feedback that the unwanted behavior implies a lack of ability or reflects malevolent motives and intentions. Counseling and psychotherapy do not differ in this regard from more homely interactions. In all approaches to verbal psychological treatment, the symptom pattern—itself an attributional strategy—is attributed to causes that are intended to stimulate the client to abandon the symptoms.

The meta-causes used in therapy operate on a number of levels in stimulating change. The causes to which the symptoms are attributed are not pleasant and imply weakness and disability. The causes are internal characteristics of the person, such as irrational ideas, distorted experiencing, unresolved complexes, self-defeating habits, and sinful desires (pride, lust, and so on). From these malignant internal characteristics, the client is seen as intending the harmful, destructive, and failing behavior entailed in the symptom strategy. Thus, the meta-attributions should stimulate client efforts to change the behaviors that led the counselor to have such an impression. However, the meta-attributions also provide clients with discounts for having such characteristics. The personal causes of the client's problem behaviors are themselves seem as created from the outside. Thus their existence is discounted. For example, irrational ideas are the natural results of growing up and functioning in an irrational world; distorted experiencing is accounted for by the conditional loving and valuation of the person by others during formative years; unresolved complexes are due to externally induced traumas during development; self-defeating habits come from inappropriate conditioning by parents and others; and sinful desires are the expected result of the Fall. As a result of the external discount factors provided by the meta-attributions, the person is not responsible for having the personal characteristics that are responsible for the symptomatic behavior.

Finally, the meta-attributions of therapy see the personal characteristics responsible for the symptoms as superficial and amenable to change. The troubling cause factors are externally induced and foreign residents in the person that inevitably will be dislodged by more basic forces unleashed in treatment. Irrational ideas will cease to rule the person as the person exercises his or her superior rational abilities that are intrinsically part of his or her makeup as a post-Renaissance human. Distorted experiencing will be sloughed off as the intrinsic actualization force is nourished in a completely accepting, loving environment. Complexes will be resolved through insight and transference, and the energies so released will enable the person to face current difficulties effectively. Self-defeating habits will be deconditioned and replaced with self-enhancing habits more reflective of the healthy hedonistic nature of the organism. Sinful desires will be eliminated as the person allows the Holy Spirit to redeem and remake his or her life in the image of the Redeemer and created perfection.

The meta-attributions used in therapy reflect the positive pole of the attitude dimension of attribution and are thus optimistic and incorporate a belief in the core goodness of the person, and in some manner see that goodness as inevitably growing to dominate and eliminate the more superficial and externally induced personal causes of symptomatic behavior. In therapeutic meta-attributions, while the undesired behavior is seen as purposively intended for distorted purposes due to the distorting influences of harmful past events, the person's more basic intentions and characteristics provide an unmistakable basis for change to behaviors that more correctly reflect the person's true self. In sum, the meta-attributional tactic allows change of the superficial to a better representation of what now exists more deeply at the core of the person. The change enhances consistency and is the outworking of the continuing and unchanged core of the person. The meta-attributional tactic creates change without change that is internally caused and has little to do with the therapist.

CHAPTER 5

Therapeutic Change As Spontaneous Compliance

Hodges and Brandt (1978) assessed the causes of behavior change that counselors communicated to clients and found that the communications were contradictory. They devised scales that reflected the internal or external locus of control implied by the causes communicated in the content of communications and causes implied by the style of communications. They found that scores on the content scale correlated negatively with scores on the style scale. Hodges and Brandt (1978) commented:

> Students were told that they have control over what happens to them while simultaneously being given answers to problems. An example of such a statement would be : "Only you can decide what you are going to do about college. Certainly you need to start studying more." It is internal with regard to content because it implies that the student has control over his future, but external with regard to style because it tells the student exactly what he needs to do. (pp. 346–347)

Hodges and Brandt imply that counselors should be consistent in their messages about client responsibility. An alternative interpretation is that contradictory messages are essential to the therapeutic process.

Most counseling and clinical psychologists endorse the philosophies that clients are responsible for the process of counseling, clients control how they change, and therapists are not to manipulate or influence clients in any way except to encourage client autonomy. In seeming contradiction, counselors and therapists in practice influence, manipulate, and encourage clients to change by differentially responding to clients' verbal behaviors (Truax, 1966), focusing on feelings (Rogers, 1951), interpreting, instructing, and rehearsing (Ellis, 1962), modeling (Rosenthal & Bandura, 1978), and behavior shaping and reinforcing (Krumboltz & Thoresen, 1969). The contradiction between what counselors and therapists say and what they do suggests that the intense concern for client autonomy is less a statement of what counseling is all about than it is part of the process of achieving change.

Jackson and Haley (1968) first pointed to contradictions in psychotherapy as an explanation for transference. Haley also analyzed hypnosis and schizophrenia as based on communication contradictions (Haley, 1968a, 1968b, 1968c). Communication contradictions are key components of therapeutic encounters because the contradictions are needed to bring about the kind of change desired from therapeutic

138

interaction. The problems brought to counseling often cannot be changed by will alone; that is, when a well-meaning friend or therapist tells a depressed person to be less depressed, the plea is usually met with a demonstration of helplessness to control depression (Watzlawick, Beavin, & Jackson, 1967). Change in counseling and psychotherapy often cannot be obtained by directly suggesting and requesting it; it requires more complex tactics (Jackson & Haley, 1968; Watzlawick, Weakland, & Fisch, 1974).

The nature of the change desired in therapy reflects the fact that clients seldom perform the behaviors they wish to change voluntarily with the phenomenological experience of full deliberateness and choice. Nor can they willfully behave differently with any regularity. The change desired in counseling is not simply for the client to act differently, but also for the client to want, need, be motivated, and impulsed to act differently. The depth of change desired in psychotherapy is a product of the view of behavior as caused by the characteristics of the person: behavior is a reflection of the internal makeup of the individual. Working from this theory, it is only sensible to change the internal determinants of behavior rather than focus on the superficial expression of the causes. With such a philosophy, it is insufficient that persons *act* different; they must *be* different. Thus, if a client behaves differently because a therapist told him or her to do so, the client can be said to be unchanged in a deeper sense, and the undesired behavior would be expected to reemerge as the therapist's influence wanes. If a client behaves differently because he or she wills to do so, the change would also be expected to be temporary, since willpower does not consistently win the battle with the motivational and impulsive causes of behavior (Bateson, 1972). The only lasting change is a change in the causes the symptom stems from, the uncontrollable and involuntary impulses of the deeper personality.

The therapeutic solution to the need for change deep within the personality is to induce the client to change along the lines the therapist models, instructs, reinforces, and interprets, within a context that requires the client to acknowledge the change as coming from deep within rather than from the therapist or from will alone, a change best described as *spontaneous compliance*. The client complies with the therapist's pressures to change (often delivered in the Hodges and Brandt style dimension) and misattributes the change to spontaneous internal causes. The change is spontaneous because it is not seen or presented as willful compliance to the therapist's demands, but as a result of change in the client's internal dynamics. The person is not *trying* to be different, not *willing* to be different, but *is* different.

For the person to *be* different, the change must be involuntary. Explanation of the nature of the processes of spontaneous compliance may lie in the concepts of voluntary and involuntary behavior. At one level, persons control everything they do. It is because they are alive that they breathe, hearts beat, stomachs digest, minds think, lips speak, and ears hear. In this sense and at this level, a person controls all that the body does. Perhaps better, a person *is* all that his or her body does. Surely, for example, the beating of a person's heart is due to the person's own processes rather than to something outside the person. Thus, the person controls his or her heartbeat behavior, and indeed all of his or her behavior.

At another level, a person's behavior is classified as voluntary or involuntary.

People are described and describe themselves as having willful control over some behaviors and not over others. Just what is voluntary and involuntary, however, is not entirely clear. Skinner (1953) identifies striate and smooth muscles as distinguishing the voluntary (operant) and involuntary (respondent) behavior systems. Yet emotions, controlled by smooth muscles, can be voluntarily controlled via cognitive methods developed by Ellis (1962), Meichenbaum (1975), and Goldfried and Goldfried (1975). Biofeedback research demonstrates that persons can control heartbeat and other involuntary behaviors willfully. Contrariwise, behaviors usually considered voluntary are frequently experienced as involuntary, such as habits, psychological symptoms, criminal behavior, speaking in tongues and prophesy, and hypnotic phenomena. While little about voluntary and involuntary behavior can be said with certainty, several assertions can be made that seem to underlie therapeutic change as well as spiritual behavior, hypnosis, healing, and similar phenomena:

1. Persons control all of their behavior. This statement ignores the concepts of will and voluntary and simply asserts that living organisms are the source of their behavior. This is substantiated by observing that inert materials such as stones do not act the same as living organisms. The differences in behavior are not in the conditions impinging on the bodies, but in the bodies.
2. The volume of behavior that occurs outside of consciousness is much greater than the volume of behavior of which the organism is aware or perceives as voluntarily controlled.
3. The organism is able to change many behaviors that are outside of conscious experience and voluntary control.

Control over behavior not experienced as voluntary requires acting outside of or beyond consciousness. It requires circumventing the rational, willful, conscious mind. This reaching beyond the conscious occurs very naturally as persons respond to the behavioral opportunities of circumstances without the intervention of conscious thought (Langer, 1978). It also occurs in special relationships where persons believe change agents are working in or on them, with hypnotists, witches, shamans, spiritual healers and mediums, animal magnetists, humanistic counselors, and so on. In these circumstances, persons do not consciously take deliberate actions but act at a deeper level and are not consciously aware of themselves as the agent controlling their behavior. The behavior is spontaneous compliance; the person responds to the situation, but responsibility for the behavior is lodged outside of the will and within involuntary determinants of behavior. The person attributes the behavior neither to compliance to external pressure nor to willful actions. Deeper components of the personality or of spiritual reality are seen as the causal agents of behavior.

SPONTANEOUS COMPLIANCE IN EVERYDAY INTERACTION

Causal attributions about behavior do not necessarily reflect the causes of behavior. Actions, and statements about the determinants of actions, are independently determined. Actions are guided by the requirements of the situation, and statements about actions are also guided by the requirements of the situation. Both actions and explanations of the causes of actions intend to control interactants. A situation may require that actions and the description of the causes of the actions be altogether different. People's explanations of why they act as they do need bear no resemblance to the determinants of their behavior. Inconsistencies between the causes of behavior and attributions about the causes of the behavior are common in human interaction. For example, the common American phrase, "Why don't you . . .?" is a compound of inconsistent messages that requires a brace of inconsistent responses. When a mother says to her son, "Why don't you make your bed?" she communicates two contradictory messages. On one hand, she communicates that she wants him to make his bed, a communication intended to influence him to make his bed that is supported by his dependence on her as well as norms of what one does in the morning. But in the form of the statement she does not demand that he make his bed. Instead, she has drawn attention away from her demand that he make his bed and suggests that he do so spontaneously. The "Why don't you . . .?" stem literally proposes that unless he can find reasons for not doing so, he will want to do so. The stem puts him on the defensive, for to not comply requires explanation and justification, while compliance can only be explained by his volition, not her demand: she did not demand!

Maintaining the appearance of volitional action seems to be a high priority in everyday interaction. People seldom demand that another do as they tell them. Instead, interactants invite spontaneous compliance to requests. "Would you like to . . .?" "Perhaps you would be so kind as to . . . ." "Why don't you . . .?" and other leads lodge compliance to communications in the volition of the complier and thereby mask the operation of social power and dependence in obtaining compliance. The requester avoids responsibility for the recipient's compliance, for the compliance occurs in the context of the recipient's volition. The recipient is left with responsibility for compliance.

Inconsistent messages avoid making an issue of the dependence of the message recipient on the requester so that the recipient is able to comply without conceding dependence on the other, a dependence that must be there or the person would not comply with the request. Research reviewed in the last chapter documents that Americans are very sensitive to being perceived as powerless and do not respond well to demands. Inconsistent messages may be an adaptation to interdependence where both parties are susceptible to the other's influence but are also able to resist being influenced due to the other's susceptibility to influence. Inconsistent messages are adapted to social norms that denigrate dependence, power, and the authoritarian exercise of power and exalt independence and autonomy. Inconsistent messages that generate spontaneous compliance allow the perception of autonomy within a context of dependence and control.

Inconsistent messages that invite spontaneous compliance generate more persistent and perservering behavior than do messages proposing compliance acknowledged to stem from dependence. In impression management terms, if we claim to act because of our desires, then others will expect us to continue to act whether the influence agent is present or not. If we claim to act because of the influence agent, there is no pressure for persistence. The "anti-tooth brushing" studies reviewed in the last chapter demonstrate that spontaneous compliance generates personally attributed and persistent change; students complied with the experimenter's request but changed how they presented themselves to appear to be independent of the experimenter. Miller, Brickman, and Bolen (1975) demonstrated the power of spontaneous compliance to generate persistent change. They asked teachers they assigned to a "persuasion" condition to persuade their students to pick up papers on the floor of the classroom and keep the room tidy using congruent persuasion methods of direct requests and commands such as, "Don't be so untidy! Pick up the papers!" In an "attribution" condition, teachers asked students to keep the rooms tidy in the context of praising the students for how tidy they were and how ecologically minded they were to be concerned about the tidiness of the room. Students in the persuasion condition kept the room tidy as long as teachers kept persuading them, but the rooms returned to their untidy states as soon as teachers stopped directing attention to untidiness. Students in the attribution condition also complied during the treatment phase, but the rooms remained tidy after the treatment was discontinued. The attribution treatment lodged the students' attribution of their tidying behavior in their own characteristics, and they continued the behavior after the teacher stopped, presumably to maintain the impression that their behavior was an expression of their volition and not of the teacher's social power.

HYPNOSIS AND RELATED PHENOMENA

Haley (1968a) proposed that hypnotic phenomena are a result of contradictory messages that require spontaneous compliance. According to Haley, in hypnosis the operator maintains control of the relationship and the subject is restrained from leaving or commenting on the operator's communication inconsistencies. In this context, the operator directs the subject to perform certain actions, like closing his or her eyes, raising an arm, or experiencing analgesia, but also insists through a series of challenges that the subject resist and not comply with the directives. The subject's solution to the contradictory communications is to respond on two levels. On one level, the subject complies with the requests, often performing behavior considered to be involuntary. On another level, subjects insist that they are not responsible for the behavior. While the subject's arm raises, he or she does not experience volitional control and reports the spontaneous incident as a bystander. The subject complies spontaneously. The behavior is spontaneous for it is not perceived to be a result of willful compliance to the operator's directives. At another level, it obviously is in response to the operator.

Many spiritual behaviors are of the same variety. Speaking in tongues and prophesy are performed by the believer, but are experienced as being controlled by spiritual forces. Spiritual behaviors are a result of expecting their occurrence (the person complies), but with the condition that the person is not responsible for the behavior: the spirit works through the believer. The behavior is formally similar to hypnotic behavior and includes behavior not considered to be under voluntary control. Many psychotic and neurotic symptoms are similar to hypnotic and spiritual behaviors. A victim of depression is obviously "doing" the depression, but the behavior is presented and experienced as not under the control of the sufferer. Hallucinations, delusions, paralyses, and other symptoms are of the same ilk. From the interactional point of view, all of these behaviors occur in circumstances in which control of the situation requires the behavior to occur but to come outside of the person's willful control. Spiritual prophesy that is experienced by the prophet as his or her own works and thoughts or is seen by others as the issue of the person is rejected as artificial and false. The hypnotic subject's productions are accepted only if everything about the subject's behavior suggests that he or she is genuinely not responsible for the behavior. Depression that appears to be "put on" is greeted with condemnation, sarcasm, and rejection.

THERAPEUTIC CHANGE

Therapeutic change is often spontaneous compliance. The therapeutic situation is fraught with contradictory communications necessary to generate persistent therapeutic change and to counter the contradictory messages conveyed in the client's symptomatic relationship behavior. Therapeutic change as spontaneous compliance is a result of the following factors:

1. The client is dependent on the therapist. If the therapist did not have social power, the therapist could not encourage therapeutic change.
2. The therapist maintains control of the relationship to establish the conditions needed for therapeutic change.
3. The therapist communicates on several levels to encourage the client to change his or her interaction behavior and to attribute change to causal factors beyond the voluntary realm.

Earlier chapters detail the character of social power. In therapy, clients comply with the relationship definitions therapists propose because of client dependence on therapists. Without dependence there would be no therapeutic change. Achieving therapeutic change also requires that the therapist maintain control of the relationship. Relationships can be categorized according to the pattern of control between the participants. Haley (1968a) dichotomized relationships as complementary or symmetrical. Complementary relationships are based on the differences between the parties, while symmetrical relationships are based on similarities. In a complementary relationship, one party overtly controls the behavior of the other party so that one tells while the other complies. In symmetrical relationships, the parties are equals or equivalents. Symmetrical relationships are often competitive with each party attempting to maintain equality with the other and, if possible, to place the other into an inferior role and thus transform the symmetrical relationship into a complementary relationship with themselves in overt control.

Therapy begins as a complementary relationship. Clients come to the expert to seek help with life problems. They expect the therapist to find out what the trouble nd tell them what to do. This arrangement is satisfactory if the client's difficulty not having necessary information or skills, often the case in educational and vocational counseling. The counselor can impart the required information much as a lawyer or physician would, and the client thus armed proceeds with life. However, when the problem is in the nature of how the client relates to others, this straightforward complementary relationship structure is not adequate because the required relationship change cannot be achieved through straightforward volitional compliance. These clients need to change perceptions of situations, objectives in relationships, and predictions about how others react. They need to change the internal equipment that guides their behavior. It is not enough for the therapist to establish a relationship in which the client will do what the therapist asks. The therapist must also establish a relationship in which the client does what the therapist proposes because of internal, nonvolitional self changes. The relationship must generate spontaneous compliance.

For therapeutic change to occur as spontaneous compliance, the client must be instructed to not comply with the therapist's requirements. This is accomplished by overtly placing the client in charge of the relationship. In a relationship in which the therapist is in charge, the therapist places the client in charge, and thus establishes what Haley (1968a) termed meta-complementary control of the relationship. When the client accepts the therapist's directive to take control of the relationship, he or she accepts the therapist's control of his or her control, or the therapist's metacontrol of the relationship. On one level, the therapist assumes complete control of the relationship by defining the client's efforts to control the relationship as compliance to the therapist's requests. As the client struggles to assert independence from the therapist and dominance over the therapist, the therapist consistently defines the client's actions as compliance to his or her requests and thus maintains control of the relationship. On the other hand, by defining the relationship as the client's responsibility, the therapist makes it very difficult for the client to attribute change to the therapist's influence. After all, the client is in charge, not the therapist. Thus, the client is given the opportunity to gain control of the relationship and the therapist by changing as the therapist proposes, but is led to attribute the change to internal changes, not to compliance to therapist activities.

Change is encouraged through the actions of opposing processes that work together, the affirmation paradox and the negation paradox. The processes are paradoxes because they are composed of communications on two levels that are contradictory if the levels are not distinguished. The communications of the affirmation paradox invite the client to adopt desired behavior as a spontaneous development, and the communications of the negation paradox encourage the client to abandon undesired behavior as a spontaneous involuntary adjustment to the therapeutic situation.

Affirmation Paradox

The affirmation paradox is made up of three elements:

1. The therapist presents desired behavior and insists that the behavior be adopted as part of the definition of the relationship.
2. The therapist communicates that change is a result of processes internal to the client and is not compliance with the therapist.
3. The therapist identifies an agent responsible for the change that acts beyond the client's volitional control.

In various approaches to counseling and psychothcrapy, dcsircd bchavior is presented more or less subtly in interpretations, counselor self-disclosures, examples of others, metaphors, reflections, questions, and verbal reinforcers. The therapist may also instruct the client about desired behavior in nonsubtle ways, as does Ellis (1962) and behavior therapists (Krumboltz & Thoresen, 1969) as they instruct clients on how to think and react in situations. Most subtle of all, and probably most powerful, is how the therapist behaves. The therapist is a live model to the client (Marlatt & Perry, 1975).

What is seen as appropriate behavior varies among therapy approaches and to some extent is idiosyncratic to the particular therapist, for what the therapist says and does is the most powerful message of desired behavior to the client. Therapy cannot proceed without some explicit or implicit model of behavior deemed desirable for clients to adopt. Therapy systems elaborate philosophies of life and of how life is best lived, for such information is essential to provide a direction for the client to change toward and a basis of judging whether the therapeutic effort is successful.

Therapy systems emphasize the necessity for clients to assume responsibility for their lives, actions, and the outcomes of therapy. However, the source or agent of change is not exclusively the willful, conscious processes of the client but rests on some deeper aspect of the personality. Roger's system exemplifies the causal attributions of the many humanistic systems popular today. The Rogerian system places the ultimate source of therapeutic change in the intrinsic processes of the core of the person. The person changes because of inevitable and intrinsic processes of personal development. The change is not basically volitional; it is deeper and more persistent and far reaching than momentary willful effort would allow. The person behaves differently because the person *is* different in such a deep way that the person is carried into change by his or her own processes. The change is experienced as new-found strength and new attitudes and motivations that affect behavior in relationships with others. The person behaves differently because the person *is* different. The change is carried into relationships with others beyond the therapist because the change is at the level of *being* rather than simply *doing,* as is characteristic of spontaneous compliance.

Clients adopt desired behavior because of their dependence on and thus vulnerability to therapists, because therapists require the behavior as part of achieving a congruent relationship, because therapists implicitly and explicitly instruct clients on what they are to do, and because therapists allow clients to gain control of the relationship by adopting the interactional behavior therapists propose but attributing the change to intrinsic personal processes. Counselors encourage client change by allowing clients to control them in the manner that requires the behaviors therapists want clients to emit. The change has pragmatic benefits to clients and is devised by clients because it gains them advantage in the relationship with therapists. The change gains control of the relationship, and clients deny that the change is compliance to therapists or, for that matter, is a willful response to the situation; clients see it instead as an expression of who they truly are. Because the change is autonomous, in principle it should extend into other relationships and situations, possibly because clients need to manage the impression of autonomy to therapists and others. Therapeutic change is in the same pattern as spiritual rebirth. The person becomes a new person because of the operation of a new spirit from within. This paradigm of change has the advantage of circumventing the vicissitudes of willpower and self-control. Self-control relies on conscious behavior control, while spontaneous compliance relies on control at the level of unaware doing, a level that is more basic and powerful than conscious, willful, volitional control.

Negation Paradox

The negation paradox is intended to discourage undesired symptomatic behavior through contradictory communications that require the abandonment of symptoms as a spontaneous event. Many symptoms are not experienced as under the client's volitional control, perhaps because of the relationship control afforded by the "uncontrollable" symptomatic behavior. Straightforward instruction to abandon symtpoms is seldom effective, for that which is not willfully controlled cannot be voluntarily abandoned (Watzlawick, Beavin, & Jackson, 1967). As in the affirmation paradox, the desired change is encouraged through interactive behavior in the interview, but it is presented as the expected outcome of nonvolitional changes in the client. Jackson and Haley (1968) pointed out that therapists are permissive and encouraging of the expression of symptomatic communication patterns in the therapeutic encounter but at the same time are unresponsive and punishing in reaction to clients' symptomatic behaviors. On the one hand, therapists encourage clients to talk about symptomatic behavior and to bring the behaviors into the therapeutic relationship. Therapists reflect feelings to draw out negative and traumatic feelings, show interest, question and make leading statements to encourage clients to talk about and act out their troubling experiences, and, in more extreme interventions, direct and assign clients to perform their symptoms.

Encouraging symptomatic behavior is part of the overall concern to maintain control over the interview. The purpose of the client's symptoms often is to control relationships, and asking the client to abandon the symptoms would result in increased helplessness and client control of the relationship through symptomatic behavior. Since clients will talk about symptoms and use them in the relationship, counselors maintain control of the relationship by requiring clients to do what they will do anyway, and thus bring symptomatic behavior under therapist control.

On another level, the therapist systematically discourages continuance of the symptoms. The therapist does not react to the symptoms with shock, withdrawal, fear, sympathy, or rescue, or whatever the client expects, and thus the functional utility of the symptoms is eliminated. The Gestalt concept of frustration is the clearest expression of removing the functional utility of symptoms. While the Gestalt therapist requires the client to perform the symptomatic behaviors in more and more extreme ways, the therapist steadfastly refuses to react with support or rescuing, or whatever complementary behavior the client expects, creating what Gestalt therapists call frustration (Eshbaugh, 1976).

Therapists focus on symptoms and make them increasingly prominent in the clients' attention and, at the same time, they do not respond to the symptoms appropriately. In impression management terms, counselors provide feedback to clients about the interpersonal meaning of client behaviors that is widely different from what clients expect to be the impact of the behavior; thus they stimulate clients to maneuver and change their interaction behavior in search of desired feedback and relationship control. It probably does not matter whether the feedback about the meaning of the behavior is positive or negative as long as it is plausible and different than expected. For example, Beck and Strong (1981) and Claiborn, Ward, and Strong (1981) demonstrated in short-term counseling that labeling client's negative mood states (Beck) or procrastination (Claiborn, Ward, & Strong) as positive assets or signs of personal weakness both lead to dramatic decreases in symptomatic behavior. Palazzoli, Boscolo, Cecchin, and Prata (1978) have demonstrated with schizophrenogenic families that labeling pathological family interaction as showing strength, sensitivity, and self-sacrifice leads to relatively rapid elimination of the symptomatic interaction patterns. Thus is appears that not reacting as expected to relationship behavior and giving feedback about the meaning of behavior that violates previous expectations stimulates persons to abandon the behavior in search of more effective behavior. When this is done within the context of permissiveness and apparent encouragement of behavior, the change cannot be seen as compliance with the unresponsive interactant, but as spontaneous change in the client's nonvolitional personality. It is spontaneous compliance.

Within therapy systems, change stimulated by the negation paradox is couched with the same causal agents as change stimulated by the affirmation paradox. In behavior therapy, old behavior drops out because of desensitization, extinction, or inhibition within the client's conditioning potentials, just as new behavioral relationships become embedded in the same conditioning potentialities. In humanistic theories, as distortions in the self-actualization potential of the person are healed and corrected, undesired behavior drops out and desired behavior emerges. In Ellis' system, irrationality yields to the more basic rational functioning of the mind, and the client ceases to be self-defeating and becomes rational and self-determining.

The negation and affirmation paradoxes work together to invite clients to capture control of the therapeutic relationship through change of undesired behavior to desired behavior as an expression of change in clients' deeper personalities. The paradoxes do not force clients to change but invite clients to take advantage of opportunities to control therapists. Clients are kept in the relationship by their needs, by the promise of needed resources through the therapeutic relationship, and by therapists' careful pacing of demands for change so that the demands are always within the limits of client dependence on the relationship. Clients are prevented from commenting on the incongruencies counselors present by the counselors' firm belief in the therapeutic entities they present and the sincerity with which they communicate. Clients are prevented from achieving symmetry with the therapists and control of the relationship by any tactic other than therapeutic spontaneous compliance by the therapists' meta-complementary maneuvers that place client challenges under the therapists' permissive authority.

Therapeutic change is the clients' active maneuver to seize the opportunity offered by the therapist to control the therapist and the relationship. It is not simply passive compliance to the therapists' maneuvers. The change is at the action level of behavior and goes beyond the conscious will. Thus, the change is more persistent and more extensive than is change due to conscious self-control and willpower. The contradictions noted by Hodges and Brandt (1978) are essential to the effectiveness of the therapeutic enterprise. The most successful therapy will pose most powerfully the contradictions leading to spontaneous compliance, the outcome of therapeutic encounters (Jackson & Haley, 1968).

CHAPTER 6

Processes and Techniques in the Therapeutic Encounter

This chapter reviews research and concepts related to the processes and techniques of the three phases of the therapeutic encounter of counseling and psychotherapy. In the first phase of the model presented in Chapter 2 (Figure 5), the therapist enters the client's system and draws out the client's symptomatic behaviors. The therapist establishes the pattern of the relationship which includes an intense focus on the client and therapist meta-complementary control. The therapist accepts and facilitates the client's descriptions of problems and related material, enhancing the client's trust in and dependence on the therapist. The therapist identifies the client's patterns of interaction from the client's descriptions of interactions with others, from behavior in the interview, and from the personal reactions the client's behavior stimulates in the therapist, and the therapist formulates a strategy to help the client change. In the second phase, the therapist systematically introduces incongruence into the relationship, creating and stimulating discrepancy to encourage the client to change interaction behavior. The therapist is careful to manage discrepancy so that the amount experienced by the client is never more than the client's dependence on the therapist can tolerate. Discrepancy is presented in many ways, including interpretations, directives, and self-disclosures. As the client accepts the therapist's invitation to establish control of the relationship through therapeutic change, incongruence in the relationship progressively diminishes, the power imbalance between the parties narrows, and the congruent but unstable relationship terminates in the third phase. The driving force of the relationship, the client's needs that brought him or her into counseling, cease to have high priority.

PHASE 1: ENTERING THE CLIENT'S SYSTEM

The basic structure of counseling and psychotherapy is a highly dissimilar involvement of its participants; the one seeking help exposes and describes his or her experiences, thoughts, and feelings, and the other listens, facilitates, and comments. Porter (1950) pointed out this basic structure:

> The aim [of counseling] . . . is to keep the client expressing and exploring his attitudes as freely as possible. The agreement seems general that unless the

client can bring himself both to express and explore the problems which are of concern to him there is little probability that he will achieve the help which he seeks, no matter how clear the problems may be to the counselor. (p. 4)

Therapeutic change occurs through the process of one person exposing actions, ideas, and feelings to another, and the other listening to and commenting on the exposition. This basic structure of therapy is generally understood. Kanfer (1965) had college students who were engaged in conversation role play therapy, one playing the role of client, the other of the therapist. The structure of the conversation shifted immediately from approximately equal talking to a highly disbalanced exchange, with the "client" talking much more than the "therapist." Lennard and Bernstein (1960) reported that the therapists in the eight therapist–client pairs they studied consistently contributed about 20% of the verbal output and clients contributed 80% throughout the eight months of observation. The talk ratios reported by Robinson (1950) are similar.

The interaction is structured around the client's disclosures, and the therapist conforms his or her less frequent but important contributions to the contributions of the client. Van Der Veen (1965) studied the behavior of each of six clients with four therapists in initial interviews and found that while both parties exerted a controlling influence on the other, therapists varied their behavior across clients more than did clients across therapists, a finding replicated by Moos and Clemes (1967), Houts, MacIntosh, and Moos (1969), and Moos and MacIntosh (1970). Ruzicka and Naun (1976) also report that in initial interviews, counselors vary their behaviors according to client problems and interaction styles rather than counselor philosophies of counseling. Therapists vary their behavior to that offered by the client as part of the process of entering the client's system.

The imbalance in frequency and volume of verbal productions is accompanied by an imbalance of attention to the behavior of the two participants. While the client focuses on describing how he or she feels, acts, and thinks, the therapist focuses on the meaning of the client's behavior to the client's characteristics. Crowder (1972) studied the transcripts of 25 counselor–client pairs over nine or more sessions each. He analyzed therapist and client responses according to Leary's (1957) interpersonal scheme and found that 40% of the clients' responses in the first three interviews could be classified as support seeking, 26% as passive resistant, 24% as hostile competitive, and only 9% as supportive interpretative. On the other hand, 90% of counselor responses classified as supportive interpretative, 8% as hostile competitive, 3% as passive resistant, and none as support seeking. He found these percentages to be reasonably characteristic throughout the interaction, with small but probably important change over time. Crowder's findings suggest that counselors focus exclusively on understanding clients and not at all on soliciting client observation and evaluation of themselves.

Counselors focus on interpreting the personal meanings of client behaviors. Batson (1975) found that professional helpers, as opposed to nonprofessional helpers, attributed a much higher percentage of client problems to the personal characteristics of the clients rather than to situational factors (70% versus 53%).

Snyder, Schenkel, and Schmidt (1976) found that when students role played counselors, they attributed clients' problems to the clients' personal characteristics more than did students role playing clients, and Shenkel, Snyder, Batson, and Clark (1979) found that this effect was accented when information suggested that the client had a previous history of difficulties. Patton, Fuhriman, and Bieber (1977) and Bieber, Patton, and Fuhriman (1977) analyzed the verb usage of a counselor and client pair in the first, eleventh, and twenty-fifth interviews and found a very rapid increase in the counselor's usage of stative verbs in the first interview (from less than 20% of all verbs in the first third of the interview to almost 40% by the last third) and an equivalent decrease in agentive verbs (from over 40% to 20%). Stative verbs denote the internal state of the person (forms of the verb "to be") while agentive verbs denote actions. Such a shift suggests a systematic focusing on the internal causes of client actions.

Rogers (1951) argued that counselors should focus on client internal experiencing, and counselors of a client-centered orientation and other therapists (Fischer, Paveza, Kickertz, Hubbard, & Grayston, 1975) respond with empathic and reflective remarks to the client's productions, counselor behaviors that increase the client's focus on and depth of self-exploration and relate to therapeutic outcome (Truax & Carkhuff, 1967; Truax & Mitchell, 1971). Lennard and Bernstein (1960) and Rice (1973) report significant increases over the course of treatment in the frequency of client statements describing internal affect, evidence of the impact of the counselor's focus on the internal causes and functioning of the client.

In the initial phase of counseling, the client must be taught the role of the client, and the counselor must establish control of the relationship. Lennard and Bernstein (1960, p. 65) found that therapist behavior characterized as "orientation" (asking for and giving repetitions, clarifications, and confirmations) accounted for nearly 70% of the therapists' propositions in the initial portion of therapy and diminished in frequency as therapy continued. Lennard and Bernstein also found that:

> The number of therapist questions is nearly seven times the number of patient questions. Questions are devices for turning the responsibility for communication over to the other partner in a communicational setting. We thus see that the therapist not only specializes in keeping his own communication low, but also in maximizing that of the patient. (pp. 83−85)

The fact that 90% of the therapist statements are supportive-interpretive (Crowder, 1972) attests to the counselor's control of the relationship. At a point early in the encounter, therapists explicitly place the client in charge by stating that what the client does with their time together is up to the client and that the client will determine what the outcome of their time together is. This is often done in a structuring statement near the beginning of the exchange (Blum & Balinsky, 1951). The high level of control exercised by the therapist is reflected in Lennard and Bernstein's finding that client spontaneous comments on the nature of the counselor's behavior rapidly diminish in therapy. In the first session, client comment on the therapist−client interchange follows counselor comment five times out of six and is spontaneous (initiated by the client) only one time out of six. By the third month, the ratio for spontaneous comments diminished to once out of 33 times. In other words, while client spontaneous comment on the nature of the therapist's behavior was infrequent at first, spontaneous comments on the therapist's behavior were practically nonexistent by the third month. Spontaneous therapist comment on the nature of the interchange was also unlikely in the first two sessions and became increasingly unlikely as therapy proceeded (one in seven in the first two sessions to one in 13 in the third month). This is a most striking example of control in therapy, for the client is essentially prohibited from commenting on the therapist's interview behavior directly, a prohibition necessary for the counselor's contradictory messages in therapy to lead to spontaneous compliance rather than meta-communicative comment.

The counselor establishes a very one-sided interchange with the client in the initial stage of counseling, rapidly shifts attention from a concern for what the client has done to a concern for the internal causes of the client's acts, orients the client to the client's role, and rapidly imposes an unspoken ban on client comment on the nature of counselor remarks. The counselor establishes complementary control, then meta-complementary control, and cuts off the client's option of discussing the nature of the counselor's tactics as a necessary condition for the generation of spontaneous compliance as the outcome of the exchange.

Consequences of the Structure of Therapy

The structure of therapy focuses intense attention on the client's behavior, on both descriptions of past events and in-therapy behavior. The client has an observer who listens carefully to what the client says, watches the client's behavior closely, and comments, evaluates, and questions. Even the most bland therapist comment conveys selective interest and provides feedback about the impression the client is creating. Add to this intense concentration the therapist's absorption in construing the client's behavior as caused by the client's internal characteristics, and it seems apparent that the structure of therapy promotes intense client awareness of the impression his or her behavior conveys.

The structure of therapy creates high objective self-awareness in the client. The concept of objective self-awareness was introduced by Duval and Wicklund (1972) to denote the circumstance of a person's attention directed toward self as opposed to focused outward to the environment. When attention is focused on the environment, the person is only aware of self subjectively and experientially. When persons focus attention on themselves, they are aware of themselves as objects, or are objectively self-aware. These two alternate focuses of attention are implied throughout this book especially in the concept of impression management, where attention is focused on the impressions actions create in the minds of other, versus a focus on the nonreactive elements of the environment. With proactive others, impression management is crucial to effective control of interactions. Duval and Wicklund's concept reflects the same concern, except they posit the phenomenon as an intrapsychic process. They report a number of studies showing that when persons are aware of themselves as the object of their attention, they are likely to experience lowered self-esteem, deteriorated performance in new skill tasks, enhanced consistency between attitudes and actions, and higher conformity to reference group standards (Wicklund, 1975). They argue that when a person is focused on self as object, the person becomes aware of shortfalls between desires for self and realities in behavior and characteristics, and thus suffers negative affect. If the person is unable to shift focus to the external environment, the person will act to diminish observed discrepancies through changes in behavior or standards.

Objective self-awareness reflects actor and observer differences in causal attribution, a difference first noted by Jones and Nisbett (1971). A great deal of attribution research shows that actors tend to see their behavior as a function of the situational factors impinging on them, while observers tend to see the same behavior as caused by the personal characteristics of the actors (Batson, 1975; Cialdini, Braver, & Lewis, 1974; Snyder & Jones, 1974). For example, Gruwitz and Panciera (1975) randomly assigned students to either a teacher or a student tole. The teacher presented the student with anagrams and rewarded or punished the student for right or wrong answers according to a schedule that the experimenter determined. On posttest, students believed that teachers' performances in the anagram task were more informative of the teachers' usual behaviors than did the teachers. On the other hand, teachers believed students' performances were more indicative of students' usual behavior than did students. Thus, both attributed more personal causation to the other as observers than they did to themselves as actors.

Differences between actors and observers seem to be a function of different information each has from which to infer causes, a difference largely due to their different focuses of attention. Changing the factors on which actors and observers focus changes their causal attributions. For example, Storms (1973) showed students videotapes of themselves engaged in short conversations with others. He showed other students, who had previously observed the actors in the conversations, tapes taken from the actors' perspective focused on the others. He found that both actor and observer attributions of situational or actor causes for the events in the interview were reversed by the reverse of perspective. Likewise, Eisen (1979) and Hansen and Lowe (1976) have found that with the same information, actors and observers do not differ in their construction of events.

Observers can be led to attribute the same level of responsibility to an actor as does the actor by showing him or her the interaction as observed by the actor (Storms, 1973), leading the observer to anticipate that he or she will be in the same role as the actor in the near future (Chaikin & Darley, 1972; Wolfson & Salancik, 1977) or by instructing the observer to place himself in the situation of the actor and focus on the situation from the actor's perspective (Regan & Totten, 1975; Wegner & Finstuen, 1977). Chaikin and Darley (1972) found powerful role-taking effects on perception of cause in a study where students observed a short interaction of two persons in which the work of one was destroyed by accident. Different students arrived at very different causal attributions about the accident, depending on whether their future role was to be that of the victim or of the other. Regan and Totten demonstrated the effects of empathy on attribution in a study of the causal ascriptions made for get-acquainted conversations. Without special instructions, observers ascribed much responsibility for the events in the conversation to the actor's dispositions. When observers were instructed to empathize with the actor, they ascribed events more to situational causes than to actor characteristics.

The structure of therapy begins with the usual actor—observer differences. Clients (the actors) concentrate on what they have done and the external determinants of their behaviors, and therapists (the observers) focus on the actions from the perspective of the client's personal characteristics as the causes of the client's behavior. Counselors, as typical observers, scrutinize client behavior for what it may reveal about the dynamic underlying personal causes of the client's troublesome behavior. But the therapists' focus of attention and feedback about reactions to the clients' productions leads clients to become observers of their own behavior; the counselors' attention pulls clients into objective self-awareness.

Research on the consequences of objective self-awareness indicates that persons greatly increase attribution of own behavior to personal causes when they are objectively self-aware (Carver & Scheier, 1978; Duval & Wicklund, 1973; Wicklund, 1975), increase their conformity to the opinions of reference groups (Diener & Srull, 1979), and change opinions in the direction of behavior to increase the consistency of attitudes and actions (Wicklund & Duval, 1971). For example, Gibbons (1978) found that subjects' reactions to sexual materials were more consistent with earlier self-rated attitudes about sexuality when the attention of the subjects was focused on themselves by a mirror while they reacted to the materials than when there was no mirror. In a related study, Cavior and Marabotto (1976) found that when subjects' attention was focused on their own behavior, either by instructions to monitor their own behavior or by instructions to interactants to monitor the subjects' behaviors, the frequency of behaviors the persons believed to be undesirable decreased, while the frequency of behaviors they believed to be desirable increased. Braucht (1970) obtained the same results when subjects observed themselves in videotaped replays. It has been observed that self-monitoring of a behavior that a person dislikes, such as smoking, decreases its frequency (Thoresen & Mahoney, 1974). This effect appears to be a result of the increased concern for impression management created by self-focused attention or objective self-awareness. That persons strive to look good when they are self-focused is also supported by Vallacher and Solodky (1979). They found that when subjects were self-focused, they were more inclined to cheat (cheating was presented as undetectable) on a task described as reflecting ability than when they were not self-focused. Conversely, when the task was not tied to ability, subjects cheated less when they were self-focused than when they were not. Thus, subjects were especially inclined to try to look good, either as competent or moral, when they were objectively self-aware.

The research reviewed earlier on turning observers into actors (Storms, 1973; Regan & Totten, 1975) suggests that the therapist's set to respond empathically to the client will increase the therapist's attributions to external causes of the client's behavior, but that seems to not be what happens in therapy according to Bieber, Patton, and Fuhriman (1977) and Batson (1975) (reviewed earlier in this chapter).

The effect of the therapist's set to empathize with the client seems to be closer to that demonstrated by Gould and Sigall (1977). They instructed observers in one condition of a study to empathize with a young man in a videotaped sequence trying to make a good impression on a female, and they instructed observers in another condition simply to observe. After the tape, observers were informed either that the man had been successful or unsuccessful and they were asked to account for the outcome. In the "simply observe" condition, subjects attributed both success and failure to the personal dispositions of the man. In the empathy condition, the man's success was attributed to his personal dispositions, while failure was attributed to situational factors.

It appears that empathizing shifts the observer to the positive pole of the attitude dimension of attribution that Passer, Kelley, and Michela (1978) identified, producing a particular pattern of personal and situational attributions rather than uniform situational attribution. Clinical training emphasizes seeing events in the client's life from the client's perspective, how the client must feel and think to react as she or he does. Clinicians are taught to focus on how clients must construe events to react as they do to them. The focus is on the client as the generator or cause of his or her own behavior. Yet, therapy theories have the built-in pattern that behaviors that are considered good and healthy (from the perspective of the theory) are seen as stemming from the deep, intrinsic core of the person, while behaviors that are considered to be unhealthy (from the perspective of the theory) are seen as caused by more superficial aspects of the client's personality, aspects that are themselves distortions caused by negative external factors in the client's development. Thus, the therapist's empathy set throws the therapist's attributions into the pattern of the positive pole of the attitudinal dimensions of Passer, Kelley, and Michela. This is consistent with the results of laboratory studies on the effect of empathy on attribution (Eisen, 1979; Gould & Sigall, 1977; Regan & Totten, 1975; Wegner & Finstuen, 1977). Turner and Keyson's (1978) results reinforce this interpretation of empathy; they found that therapists in charge of the treatment of clients were able to identify their client's internal experiences as measured on the *Private Self-Consciousness Scale*, a scale that reflects objective self-awareness (Carver & Scheier, 1978).

Results of self-awareness research imply that as therapists attend to clients' behaviors and encourage clients to disclose their experiences and feelings, clients will be inclined to evaluate themselves according to social desirability standards and to shift their behavior toward those standards. This process is subtle and apparently automatic. The counselor's empathy set results in a pronounced evaluative attributional set that sees the client's "positive' actions and effects as intrinsically caused and "negative" actions as (ultimately) situationally or externally induced. This evaluative set works in concert with the client's inclination to conform behavior to reference group standards when self-focused and encourages clients to increase desirable behavior and decrease undesirable behavior as evaluated from the counselor's frame of reference. Every counselor remark proposes social desirability standards for the client to conform to, finds fertile ground in the client's enhanced concern for managing impressions, and serves to pressure the client to modify behavior in the direction of the counselor's standards. Thus, it seems that attention focused on the client creates client focus on self, client self-disclosure, and therapeutic behavior change, much as Rogers postulated they would (Rogers, 1957).

Inducing Objective Self-Awareness

Inducing objective self-awareness is a matter of encouraging persons to focus attention on themselves. Focus on self is generally understood as appropriate client behavior in the counseling setting, and counselors reinforce that understanding when they initiate the encounter by asking clients to talk about why they are there. Asking persons to focus on their experiences and inner states explicitly reinforces self-focus. Therapist methods of reflection, questioning, interpretation, and instruction focus clients on themselves and encourage clients to describe how they feel, think, and act. Self-disclosure is a vital part of counseling and being asked to discuss one's self focuses attention on self.

Self-disclosure is a powerful tool for managing impressions on other. Recent research (reviewed in Chapter 4) shows that persons carefully select what they disclose to manage the impressions they want their audiences to have. Baumeister and Jones (1978), for example, found that subjects revealed characteristics to another to supplement and complement information the other already had to attain overall appearances of morality and competence. Self-disclosure is a delicate tool. Revealing socially desirable (positive) aspects might result in a good impression, but more likely it will lead others to see one as egotistical and vain, unless the disclosure is carried out with modesty and is balanced with acknowledgment of failings and inadequacies. Revealing negative facts (socially undesirable behavior) is likely to result in negative impressions unless it is done in the light of other positive information, or in the context of seeking help. Revealing negative self-information makes a person vulnerable to rejection, hostility, and loss of credibility. Because it has the probability of being negatively received, negative disclosure places the discloser in a position subordinate to the other, and thus increases the ability of the other to influence the discloser. Disclosure is a sensitive social tool. Persons who are considered in need of help are also likely to be indiscriminate in self-disclosure, disclosing at moderate, high, or low level indiscriminately to everyone (Chaikin, Derlega, Bayma, & Shaw, 1975; Cozby, 1973). In counseling, client self-disclosure, especially of socially undesirable aspects of self, increases the client's vulnerability to the counselor. The specific content of the disclosures is significant since it determines the areas in the client's life that the client makes vulnerable and that will be affected by the consequences of objective self-awareness and empathy described above.

Therapy is a setting in which disclosure of self is expected. Disclosure is greatly facilitated by the counselor's empathy set, in that an empathic counselor is prone to view the client's failings with compassion and as externally induced rather than as signs of personal weakness and wickedness. Aspects of the counselor's empathic set such as counselor warmth (Halpern, 1977; Pope and Siegman, 1968; Simonson,

1976), privacy and intimacy (Chaikin, Derlega, & Miller, 1976; Holahan & Slaikew, 1977), and physical touch (Pattison, 1973), have been found to be related to increased client self-disclosure. Extensive research literature on the effects of the therapeutic triad (empathy, positive regard, and congruence) on client self-exploration has established that warmth and reflection of feeling (accurate empathy) encourage deep client self-exploration and disclosure of feelings (Piaget, Berenson, & Carkhuff, 1974; Truax and Mitchell, 1971). Recent research in controlled experiments (Halpern, 1977; Highlen & Baccus, 1977; Hoffnung 1966) and field studies (Grater & Claxton, 1976; Kurtz & Grummon, 1972) have confirmed this relationship.

Questions, instructions, and modeling encourage client self-disclosure. In experiments in counseling-like situations, Hill and Gormally (1977), Highlen and Baccus (1977), and Barnabie, Cormier, and Nye (1974) have demonstrated that asking questions about subjects' statements about self increases subjects' statements about themselves and their feelings. McMullin (1972), Highlen and Voight (1978), and Highlen and Nicholas (1978) have shown that in counseling-like settings, instructing subjects on how to self-disclose increases self-disclosures, and exposure to others in precounseling sessions that model affective self-disclosure has been found to increase subject self-disclosures (Casciani, 1978; Highlen & Voight, 1978; McGuire, Thelen, & Amolsch, 1975; Thase & Page, 1977; Thelen & Brooks, 1976). Auerswald (1974) demonstrated in a counseling-like setting that receiving interpretations of disclosed material also increases the level of self-disclosure. It is apparent that just what is said would strongly affect subsequent disclosure. If questions reflected a negative reaction to disclosure, or if interpretations were hostile or models ridiculed, the effects of the interventions would be quite different. The positive reception of disclosure and reinforcement that disclosure is appropriate for the counseling setting are not doubt critical to encourage disclosure.

Therapist self-disclosure has been advocated as another method to encourage disclosure (Jourard & Jaffe, 1970). In the self-disclosure literature, the most common finding is that self-disclosure begets self-disclosure (Cozby, 1973). Yet, much of this research is on interactions between student peers. Also, the research is in a setting where the demand characteristics for reciprocal self-disclosure are high. Usually the experiments are presented as get-acquainted exercises. Considering the dynamic nature of self-disclosure, reciprocity is understandable. If one person discloses negative or socially undesirable aspects of self to another, the other must either reciprocate or accept vis-à-vis the discloser a superior power position either as a helper or condemner. If a person receives another's positive self-disclosure, the recipient must either reciprocate or accept an inferior role vis-à-vis the other. Thus, when self-disclosure occurs, symmetry or equality between interactants can be maintained only with reciprocity. The status effects of self-disclosure should cause therapists to pause before disclosing to clients. Therapist disclosure to encourage patient disclosure does not seem like a good use of the therapist's power unless some specific disclosure is needed. Patient disclosure is encouraged by the structural characteristics of the therapy situation and by many other therapist behaviors as noted above.

Therapist self-disclosure of personal items, especially of a negative or socially undesirable nature, results in client derogation of the therapist as disbalanced and in need of help (Simonson, 1976; Wiegel, Dinges, Dyer, & Straumfjord, 1972). In a carefully done study, Derlega, Lovell, and Chaikin (1976) found that therapist personal self-disclosure had positive effects (client self-disclosure) only when clients were informed before therapy that such therapist disclosure was appropriate. Almost all of the studies that suggest that interviewer disclosure has a beneficial effect on client disclosure were carried out in analogue settings with student subjects rather than clients and interviewers instead of counselors or therapists (Becker & Munz, 1975; Doster & Brooks, 1974; Johnson & Noonan, 1972; McAllister & Kiesler, 1975). Even so, these studies suggest that a modest frequency of disclosures (Giannandrea & Murphy, 1973; Mann & Murphy, 1975; Murphy & Strong, 1972) and disclosures of only moderately personal material (Simonson, 1976) are the most facilitative of client disclosures. Therapist self-disclosure is a potent therapeutic tool to modify client behavior, as is discussed later in this chapter. However, the structure of therapy and the need to maintain therapist credibility argue against heavy commitment by therapists to self-disclosure simply to facilitate client disclosure.

Diagnosis

Many psychological symptoms are behaviors intended to invite others to behave in ways that will create relationships clients believe will allow their needs to be met. People are seen as needing help when they behave in extreme and/or stereotyped ways. The extreme or stereotyped behavior is often the result of a significant relationship, a relationship not necessarily still present. The behavior pattern that is the symptom may no longer be adaptive in the relationship that generated it or in other relationships. The purpose of therapy is to change the pattern to be less extreme or more diversified. Thus, one of the first concerns of counseling is to identify the behavior pattern to be changed.

The problematic behavior does not have to be identified to be changed. Change requires only that the client be encouraged to abandon the symptomatic pattern and adopt a more adaptive one through interaction with the therapist. This can be done without the therapist being able to identify what is to be changed. Probably, however, therapist awareness of the target of change allows the therapist to proceed more efficiently.

A source of information in the effort to identify the target of change is the responses that the client's behavior evokes in the therapist. The client's behavior is intended to elicit certain behaviors from the interactant and likely will elicit that behavior from the therapist. Kiesler (1979) has written about therapy in these same terms:

> The priority tasks of the psychotherapist are two: to decode and identify the predominant self-defeating evoking style of the client as it shows up in the interactions during psychotherapy through identification of the predominant

impact responses being pulled from the therapist by his client; and to metacommunicate with the client about the client's rigid and extreme evoking style and its self-defeating consequences both with the therapist and with significant other persons in the client's life outside of therapy. (p. 307)

Identifying the pattern of behavior a client elicits from the therapist is a first priority and is a major step in identifying why the client is in therapy and the target of the therapeutic change. Kiesler and his colleagues have demonstrated that persons can reliably identify the behaviors others pull out of them and have developed *The Impact Message Inventory* as a means of measuring common evoking styles (Perkins, Kiesler, Anchin, Chirico, Kyle, & Federman, 1979).

A person's interaction style probably influences the person's reaction to another's interaction style and renders diagnosis somewhat idiosyncratic. Also, what one person sees as a troublesome interaction style or pattern may seem less troublesome to others with different interactional styles. Surely persons also differ in their ability to behave in beneficial ways with others: who any one person can treat is probably dependent on the person's own interaction style. Client symptoms are often so extreme as to render them diagnosable and treatable by a wide range of therapists. On the other hand, therapists probably need interaction styles that are adaptable to a wide variety of others' styles, much as the studies by Van Der Veen (1965), Moos and Clemes (1967), and Moos and MacIntosh (1970) reviewed earlier suggest.

PHASE 2: MANAGING INCONGRUENCE

Phase 2 is the heart of counseling where the process of behavior modification is carried out. The basic structure of counseling has been established, client dependence is secured, and counselor control is in hand. While these matters continue to require attention, they no longer are the primary focus. Phase 2 is potentially a long struggle as the counselor carefully presents discrepant information to the client to nudge the client to change. The counselor's power is limited, so that progress can only be made in small steps. The counselor needs to be tenacious and to continue efforts with the client until the desired change is achieved. The counselor needs to pose the elements of the affirmation and negation paradoxes as powerfully as possible, always inviting the client to spontaneously change and take control of the relationship. Interventions during this period strike at the client's interaction behaviors that need to be changed by giving them negative personal meanings, frustrating them, and removing their controlling effects. Desired behaviors are nourished within the attributional context of the spontaneous emergence of already existing basic characteristics of the client. The process is marked with an experimental flavor, as the counselor tries a tactic, receives information on its effectiveness, and modifies his or her approach as seems most effective. This middle period in counseling is certainly the most difficult phase due to the need to maintain a consistent thrust and at the same time to constantly shift to capitalize on opportunities and repair and adjust to setbacks. The counselor's constant empathic attitude toward the client, and the consistent influence of the counselor's notions of "the good life," guide the counselor in moment to moment interaction with the client and constantly press the client for therapeutic change through objective self-awareness and the attributional matrix established in the first phase and carried throughout therapy. Other interventions increase the pressure on the client to change. Alternatively stated, other interventions further enhance the advantages to the client to be gained through change.

Not much research has been reported on the process of Phase 2 beyond the social psychological research in opinion, attitude, and action changes reviewed in Chapters 3 and 4. What research there is reinforces the idea that it is a period of increased incongruence and discrepancy. Lennard and Bernstein (1960) report a constant increase in the frequency of therapist evaluation statements from less than 20% of all propositions in the first three sessions to over 40% by the third month. They describe evaluative behavior as "asking for and giving opinions, evaluations, analysis, and expression of feeling" (p. 65). Dietzel and Abeles (1975) studied early, middle, and late interviews with 20 client–counselor pairs, analyzing the extent to which counselor–client complementary behavior characterized the interaction. Complementary behaviors were considered high probability pairings of responses of persons in interaction drawn from Leary's interpersonal circumplex (1957), such as "dominance followed by submissive behavior, submissive behavior followed by dominance, friendliness followed by friendliness, and hostility followed by hostility" (p. 64). Note that some of these pairings are complementary while others are symmetrical (friendly-friendly, hostile-hostile). They are by any standard the expected pairings in social interaction. They found significantly lower levels of complementarity in the middle interviews of counseling than in early or late interviews, especially for client–therapist pairs judged successful. Interestingly, they found greatest complimentarity in early interviews with clients judged to be more disturbed. Both findings support the phase notions of the counseling model. In the case studied by Bieber, Patton, and Fuhriman (1977), the largest discrepancy between the counselor and client usage of verb types occurred at the eleventh (middle) interview. Percentages of stative verbs in total verb use by counselor and client were 36% and 28%, respectively. It appears that the greatest lack of tracking between counselor and client occurred in the middle phase of counseling.

Interventions in the second phase of counseling encourage the client to abandon symptoms and endorse alternative interaction strategies. Clients are encouraged to abandon symptoms when the counselor does not respond to the client as the client's behavior is intended to induce the counselor to behave. Counselor interventions disrupt the client's interaction patterns, make the client's behaviors more painful to carry out, or change the patterns so that the behaviors cannot have their usual effects. Desirable behaviors are evoked by teaching them to clients, presenting them in desirable contexts, modeling the behaviors, and yielding control to the client when he or she performs the behaviors. The changes the counselor hopes to induce the client to make must occur in a context that encourages the client to attribute behavior change to changes in core personality and not to compliance to the counselor or to environmental pressures, nor to the exclusive effects of self-control, as described in Chapter 5.

Most therapeutic interventions can be classified as reframing techniques or as directives. *Reframing techniques* are therapist efforts designed to change clients' perceptions of the meaning of their behaviors. Reframing is proposed in therapist communications that explicitly or implicitly identify the meanings, intentions, or functions the therapist perceives in the client's behavior. Reframing is communicated to the client through the therapist's feedback to the client in the interaction. *Directives* are counselor communications that propose that the client behave in a particular way. Directives are of many kinds, including instructions to the client on how to behave in the interview, homework assignments, questions, commands, and reflections. Therapist self-disclosure is discussed as a separate technique, although self-disclosure performs both reframing and directive functions. It is discussed separately because of its special functions in the therapeutic encounter.

Reframing Techniques

Reframing is the therapeutic tactic of changing clients' perceptions of the meaning of their behavior. The term is preferable to interpretation in that interpretations are but one technique of reframing, the technique of using explicit statements to posit or define the meaning of client behaviors. Any therapist communication to the client could be a source of reframing if it provides feedback to the client that differs from what the client had expected or had previously received. New or unusual feedback can alter the perceived interactional context of behavior and thus stimulate clients to change their perception of the interpersonal meanings of their behaviors.

Leon Levy (1963) described interpretation as a method of changing the meaning of the client's problem so that it is solvable. Levy suggests that the client has defined his or her problem in a way that does not allow solution, and that the utility of an interpretation is in changing the meaning of the problem to render it solvable. This view of interpretation clearly falls within the concept of reframing; but it also implies that the content of an interpretation is intrinsically significant and it suggests that some contexts or meanings of problems are more amenable to solution than are others. Is the content of reframing intrinsically significant? Most theories of counseling and psychotherapy posit that certain understandings and concepts are intrinsically related to psychological health, and client insight into and integration of these concepts is essential for recovery. Within psychoanalysis, client insight into psychological defenses and traumatic events is essential for recovery, and the goodness of any analytic interpretation is judged by its conformance to psychoanalytic theory (Bordin, 1968). In Ellis' (1962) system, the key to health is recognition of irrational ideas and their replacement with rational ideas. Mechenbaum (1975) and Goldfried and Goldfried (1975) believe that certain cognitive notions are essential for improvement. Behaviorists instruct their clients in behavioral theory so that clients know the significance of desensitization and behavior control programs (Thoresen & Mahoney, 1974). Bandler and Grinder teach persons about the linguistic components of thought that they say have been lost, whose absence accounts for the problem, and whose recovery intrinsically promotes psychological health (Bandler, Grinder, & Satir, 1976).

None of the above notions could have intrinsic value, for if one did the others would not. Yet all of the mentioned approaches, and many not mentioned, are effective (Bergin & Lambert, 1978). In Chapter 1 it was proposed that it is not the reality, truth, or existential validity of the tenets of a theory that accounts for its effectiveness in helping people change, but rather it is belief in the reality of the tenets of a theory that accounts for its effects on people (Frank, 1961). The utility of a theory of therapy partially lies in its ability to engender the client's belief in its tenets. In the history of mental healing, it is clear that theories have come and gone on the wings of the belief systems of contemporary society.

If, in fact, the existential reality of the tenets of a theory or of an interpretation that stems from them is not significant in accounting for its effectiveness, then what does, beyond simple belief? Within the interactional framework, reframing communications have their effects through their function as feedback to the client about the interpersonal impression his or her behavior creates in the eyes of the interactant. If we assume that clients, like anyone else, behave as they do to create certain impressions of their characteristics to induce interactants to act in ways that yield them and the interaction to the client's control, interpretations and other reframing behaviors have their effects by informing the client that desired or expected impressions were not achieved. Implicitly, the feedback of the reframing communication may also provide cues to the client about how the client could achieve the desired control through other tactics.

The interaction view of the mechanism through which reframing encourages behavior change does violence to many tenets of personality psychology and to the beliefs in folk psychology about the causes of behavior (Heider, 1958). Deducing the enduring personal causes of behaviors has the utility of rendering persons predictable and thus aids in the task of controlling relationships (Heider, 1958). Also, assigning personal causes to account for another's behavior influences the other to change, and thus is a control strategy (Kelley, 1971). Essentially, reframing is the therapist's use of the second function of attribution to personal causes: interpretations and the theoretical systems they spring from function to stimulate change. As might be expected, interpretations offered by psychologists are largely uncomplimentary to clients, and thus they carry the meaning that unless clients change, their behavior reveals that they are immoral or incompetent. Being driven by impulses and complexes from the past implies incompetence (Bordin, 1968); guiding one's behavior with irrational ideas implies incompetence (Ellis, 1962); continuing to distort reality and experiencing is incompetent (Rogers, 1951), relying on incomplete and distorted linguistic patterns is incompetent (Bandler, Grinder, & Satir, 1976); continuing to live in selfish and irresponsible ways is incompetent and immoral (Glasser, 1965; Strong, 1980).

From an impression management point of view, the effectiveness of reframing in stimulating change is as much a function of feedback that implies that a different impression was achieved than that desired as it is a function of feedback that a negative or socially undesirable impression was achieved. A very positive and socially desirable impression resulting from a behavior intended to create the impression of helplessness and incompetence would seem as distressing and in need of correction as are the predominantly socially undesirable impressions communicated in the interpretations referred to above. Recent research on reframing supports this hypothesis. Palazzoli, Boscolo, Cecchin, and Prata (1978) report success in working with families of identified schizophrenic patients using reframing statements that positively connote the family system and reframe symptomatic behavior as reflecting sensitivity and self-sacrifice. In discussion of their results, they suggest that the unhealthy family interaction patterns result from each individual's determination to dominate the others (hubris), and thus the positive connotation feedback is an unacceptable impression to be seen to have conveyed. Palazzoli and colleagues report relatively rapid and complex beneficial changes in interaction patterns, including the elimination of the schizophrenic symptoms, following the positive connotation feedback. A considerable body of case studies and antidotal reports also attest to the effectiveness of positive reframing of symptomatic behavior in eliminating symptomatic behaviors (L'Abate & Weeks, 1978). In an experimental study of short-term therapy, Beck and Strong (1981) attributed depressive symptoms to self-sacrifice, sensitivity, and an ability to tolerate loneliness; they found that clients decreased their depression symptoms in this positive connotation treatment as much as did clients receiving traditional negative connotation treatments, and significantly more than did clients not receiving therapy. Feedback that implied incompetence and feedback that implied competence both disrupted the clients' expectations sufficiently to stimulte change. They also found that the clients receiving the positive connotation feedback retained the benefit of the intervention beyond the time when those receiving negative connotation feedback were experiencing symptom relapse, suggesting that positive reframing was more effective in promoting long-term change than was negative reframing. Perhaps the effect was a result of the lack of justification for eliminating depression symptoms provided by the positive connotation reframing. The positive interpretations posed the negation paradox most powerfully, and this resulted in the most resilient spontaneous compliance (see Chapter 5).

Reframing also disrupts undesirable behavior patterns by destroying the utility of the behavior with others because the others come to interpret the behavior in altered ways. In group and family therapy, and in individual therapy, when behavior is labeled as having manipulative, illicit, and implicit intentions, interactants no longer respond to the behavior as they did before. For example, if a person used a shrug of the shoulder, a raised eyebrow, and a snort of disgust to get others to placate him and reverse their unwanted former positions, drawing attention to the pattern and labeling it as an attempt to intimidate greatly diminishes interactants' likelihood to continue to respond the same way, for to do so would be for the interactants to admit that they are helpless and controlled by the person. After labeling the behavior, the other is more likely to point to the person's behavior and ridicule the person than he or she is to comply with it. The effectiveness of the behavior is lost. The behavior pattern has become a symbol of incompetence and immorality rather than a useful control strategy.

One of the main differences between individual and family therapy is the multiple audiences for each therapist statement. Not only does a message to one party affect that party, but it also affects everyone else. For this reason, interpretations that imply incompetence are less useful in family therapy than in individual counseling. In family counseling, a statement implying the incompetence of one member implies that another member is more competent, and it aligns the therapist with the latter against the former. Family members often come to therapy with the hidden agenda of gaining the support of the powerful therapist to prove that they are right in their struggle for dominance with their spouses and other family members. Negative statements must be made by the therapist with great care, and positive statements have similar difficulties unless they positively connote the entire system and all its members equally (Palazzoli, Boscolo, Cecchin, & Prata, 1978).

The impression management view of reframing argues that reframing encourages clients to abandon symptomatic behavior and endorse other behavior because of the undesired interpersonal implications of the behavior created by reframing and the disruption of interaction patterns the new meanings generate. The intrinsic meaning of the content of the interventions would seem to be important only insofar as it renders the intervention believable. On the other hand, the content will determine what clients think about their behavior and how they explain themselves and any possible changes they make. Many contents of interventions should be equally feasible and effective in generating change, although differences in content should create differences in what clients say about themselves and in what behaviors they choose as alternatives to the symptoms. The results of the Temple study (Sloane, Staples, Cristol, Yorkston, & Whipple, 1976) support these notions in that the study found that behavioral and insight approaches were about equally effective in an overall sense, but resulted in differences in the specifics of the changes obtained. For example, behaviorally treated clients were more likely to make specific changes in particular behaviors, while insight clients were more likely to change their views of broader concerns, such as the meaning of life. Bednar and Parker (1969) found that different treatment procedures resulted in different kinds of changes, but were equally effective. Strong, Wambach, Lopez, and Cooper (1979) and Claiborn, Ward, and Strong (1981) likewise found that treatment espousing that procrastination was controllable and treatment espousing that procrastination was uncontrollable resulted in clients' adopting opposite views of the nature of their procrastination but in the same levels of symptom reduction. Likewise, Beck and Strong's (1981) positive and negative interpretation condition clients had strikingly different notions of the meaning of their depression, but changed similarly. The Strong et al. study is especially significant to the impression management point of view in that it was conceived with the notion that the intrinsic content of an interpretation was critical to its effectiveness. The study was drawn from Strong's (1978) theory of social influence that hypothesized that to be effective, an interpretation must equip the client to control problem behavior. The treatments were designed to render clients in a "controllable" condition able to control their proscrastination, while clients in the "uncontrollable" condition received interpretations that explicitly denied that they could control their proscrastination. Therefore, it was expected that clients in the controllable condition would be able to change, while clients in the uncontrollable condition would not be able to change. Unfortunately for the "intrinsic value" hypothesis, while the clients in the controllable condition changed more rapidly, the clients in the uncontrollable condition also changed. They could not have done so if the theory had been correct. The study also demonstrated that interpretations function to encourage clients to change: clients in both interpretation conditions were more motivated to control their procrastination than were clients in a noninterpretative condition.

The acceptance of an interpretation is encouraged by presenting evidence supporting the validity of the causal inference (see Chapter 3 for research evidence). Strong (1970, 1978) reviewed research on attribution that suggests how evidence is evaluated to deduce personal causes of events. For a behavior to be open to ascription to a particular personal cause, it must be seen as due to the person and not to the situation. Because clients are objectively self-aware in therapy, clients often readily accept personal responsibility for their actions and the consequences of their actions. Kelley (1967) proposed that persons determine the causes of events by a kind of mental analysis of variance of the evidence. When a person is associated with an effect over time (consistency), it is seen as caused by the person. When an effect occurs only in the presence of a distinctive stimulus, it is seen as caused by that stimulus (distinctiveness). When an effect occurs the same for all people (consensus), it is seen as caused by the situation; if it occurs differently for different persons, it is seen as caused by the persons. McArthur (1972) and Orvis, Cunningham, and Kelley (1975) tested these notions by asking students to assign causes for events described in short vignettes in which the evidence was systematically varied. The implications of these results for the task of changing the clients' causal inferences are described by Strong (1978) as follows:

> The information required to change a client's causal atrributions depends on the original inference. If the client believes his behavior is due to a special circumstance, event, or person, showing him a consistent pattern of similar actions over a wide spectrum of other persons or events would free the action for stable personal attribution. On the other hand, if the client views his actions as personally caused, information that suggests he responds in that way only to a particular individual or circumstance, or that he had never behaved that way before or since, leads to external or circumstantial attribution. (p. 126)

Of the rules of consistency, distinctiveness, and consensus, consensus has been found to be the weakest (Borgida, 1978; Nisbett & Borgida, 1975; Wells & Harvey, 1977, 1978). Consensus is the notion that if everybody does the same thing in a situation then the cause of the behavior is the situation. Thus, base rates of behavior in settings are of importance to attribution. However, if some persons or even one person behaves differently than the others, can the situation be said to be entirely responsible for the person's behavior? Strong, Matross and Danser (1981), Nisbett and Borgida (1975), and others (Hansen & Donoghue, 1977; Nisbett, Borgida, Crandall, & Reed, 1976) have found that the actions of a few are more important than base rates of a population. The existence of alternatives to committed action and the possibility that another might have chosen a different alternative eliminates the claim of situational determination and opens the behavior to personal ascription (Harvey & Johnston, 1973). When the therapist generates alternative actions to that performed by the client and suggests that he or she (the therapist) or another would have behaved the alternative way, the therapist forces the client to reattribute to personal causes actions previously attributed to situational causes. Client causal ascriptions can be directed away from personal attribution by the therapist's analysis of the overpowering and compelling nature of the situational restraints and speculation that anyone else would have behaved in the same fashion.

Given that a behavior is freed for personal attribution, the case for a particular personal attribute as the cause needs to be built on evidence of consistency of action in a variety of situations and from the content of the behavior and situations. Effects repeatedly achieved that are unique to the events achieved as compared to events not achieved provide evidence to support an inference of a specific intention, motive, or deeper personal causal entity (Jones & Davis, 1965). Proposing specific personal causes without having learned about the client and his or her experiences in living opens the way for the client to reject the interpretation on the basis of the counselor's lack of understanding. For example, Taylor (1975) has shown that persons are reluctant to accept personal causes (motives, intentions, and so on) based on one piece of information when the attribution has important personal consequences, certainly the case in therapy. Research with brief therapy has shown, however, that attributions will be accepted by the client in a very short time, even within one or two interviews (Beck & Strong, 1981; Bednar & Parker, 1969; Claiborn, Ward, & Strong, 1981; Lopez and Wambach, in press; Strong, Wambach, Lopez, & Cooper, 1979; Wambach, 1980). In the above studies, as well as in Kiesler, Pallak and Kanouse (1968) and Pallak and Heller (1973), difference between one and two interviews is marked and suggests that the prospect of facing the therapist again enhances the client's acceptance of interpretations, perhaps to avoid an argument with the therapist or to avoid appearing incompetent and lacking in intelligence to the therapist by a failure to accept logical interpretations. It also seems likely that the seriousness with which the therapist delivers a reframing comment affects its acceptance. Many reframes, especially positive connotations, appear ridiculous, and if they are not presented with an air of solemnity and thoughtfulness, they could be rejected easily as jests. Overall, personal attribution is greatly enhanced in therapy because of the focus on the client as the salient actor in his or her own experiences. Salience has been found repeatedly to be the major factor in causal attribution (Newtson, Engquist, & Bois, 1977; Pryor & Kriss, 1977; Taylor, Crocker, Fiske, Sprinzen, & Winkler, 1979).

Directives

A *directive* is a "specific communication from someone in authority that serves to direct and guide an action, attainment, or goal" (*Webster's Dictionary*, 1967). The counselor is responsible for the attainment of the therapeutic goals of counseling and guides and directs the actions of the client so that the counselor—client interaction generates the fulfillment of therapeutic goals. The counselor is the authority in the interaction, and his or her communications carry that authority with the client (Chapters 2 and 3). However, some counseling authorities argue against the use in counseling of directives that explicitly advise, instruct, or direct (Rogers, 1951) and, according to the notions described in Chapter 5, achieving change that the client acknowledges to be compliance to the counselor's directives is an unacceptable outcome of counseling. At issue is not whether the counselor has the responsibility to direct the therapeutic encounter or to be acknowledged as authoritative, but how to direct and use authority to achieve compliance that is attributed to deep-level changes in the client's personality rather than to a voluntary response to the demands of the authority.

If a directive is a communication that guides the behavior of another and is effective partially because of the social power of authority of the source of the communication, then most counselor responses are directives. The counselor subtly or blatantly directs the client to certain behaviors in the interview and guides the client's behavior between interviews through implicit suggestions or explicit commands. The client's response to each counselor communication is partially a function of how it is stated and the implications of complying with or defying the directive. From the interactional point of view, the debate over whether counselors should be directive or nondirective is a matter of the pragmatics of what directives, given the client's current behavior, will successfully invite the client to respond in the direction of the therapeutic goals of the interaction. What is needed is an understanding of the client's current behavior, the impact of different forms of directives, and the goals of counseling.

Choice

Choice, personalism, and explicit-implicit meaning are major aspects of the form of a directive that determine its impact on another. A major determinant of the outcome of a directive is whether the recipient perceives choice in how to respond. If a person perceives no choice but to do exactly as directed, the person will attribute his or her compliance and any result of the compliance to the communicator. The person will not take personal responsibility for the action or its consequence. On the other hand, if the person believes he or she has a choice to comply, compliance is attributed to self. In Chapter 4 it was noted that the key variable probably is whether the person believes another believes he or she had a choice. In laboratory studies of spontaneous compliance (forced compliance), whether the experimenter asks the subject what to do makes the difference between compliance with personal attitude change or compliance with external attribution of cause. Since all subjects choose to be helpful, doubts creep in about the validity of the perception of choice. The implications of the results, however, are powerful: by phrasing a directive so that the person perceives he or she has a choice as to behaving as directed or not, the person can be led to do as the communicator wishes and to accept personal responsibility for having done so.

This is not an unknown fact. Parents typically begin their attempts to get their children to do as they wish by phrasing their directives as requests rather than as orders: "Please go to bed now." "Would you like to clean up your room now?" "Perhaps you would be willing to get to your homework now?" and on it goes. These are the forms that generate spontaneous compliance. Counselors almost never tell clients what to do directly. Everything is couched in indirect and permissive forms such as: "Perhaps you would like to begin by telling me why you are here?" "I was just wondering how you felt about that." "Maybe, if you feel like it, you might consider trying this approach the next time you see her." "Well, it's up to you—if you want to keep on feeling lousy, then go ahead and keep on saying those irrational thoughts!" The counselor's ultimate form of avoiding explicitly telling the client what to do and thus of discouraging the client from vesting cause in the counselor's commands is to phrase communications in forms that on the face of it are not requests at all. The statement, "I was just wondering how you might feel about that," makes a statement about what the counselor is thinking but does not explicitly command or request the client to talk about how he or she feels. Clients almost always respond to such statements with self-focused disclosures like, "Well, I really felt lousy about that." Clients seldom, if ever, say, "Wondering were you? How curious!" As discussed earlier, the set of the client is that he or she is to reveal him or herself. Comment on the counselor's behavior is covertly forbidden. These expectancies allow the counselor to direct the client's actions and at the same time leave the client vulnerable to accepting responsibility for just about everything he or she does in or out of counseling at the counselor's direction.

Reflections are directives to continue talking about the topic reflected. Usually a reflection accents or magnifies a part of the client statement it reflects, and thus it serves to guide the client in a particular way. Yet, a reflection is not explicitly directive. Statements like, "You seem to be saying, 'I really did not want to be there!' " or "It does not seem that you could hurt more, but you do, is that right?" direct the clients to specific aspects of their experiences, encourage continuation and deepening of the inquiry, and suggest ways of feeling and thinking, but they do so without giving a shred of evidence the client could use to justify his or her next statement as compliance to the counselor's authority.

Counselors can enhance the client's responsibility and personal attribution for change by questioning whether the client should change or should go through with planned efforts to change. "Are you sure you want to do this?" or "You know, this will be difficult—I'm not sure you are ready for it," and similar statements accent further the client's perception of responsibility for compliance to therapist suggestions, and thus they serve to commit the client to change and to increase the likelihood of change being implemented and maintained. Haley (1976) has discussed such statements as paradoxes; the counselor stimulates the client into change by doubting that the client should or could do so. Here the counselor's directives begin to take on a different function than is usually considered, that of increasing commitment to a course of behavior the directives supposedly discourage, and thus lodging responsibility for the behavior firmly within the client.

Research discussed in Chapter 4 suggested that the perception of choice was a determinant of compliance to a directive. Perhaps the negative interpersonal implications of appearing helpless in the face of another's power stimulate persons to resist and reject directives that are so worded as to imply that they have no choice but to do as commanded. Related to this phenomena is the finding that attribution to personal factors as causes of an action is diminished when external factors such as rewards or explicit directives are applied to the performance of the behavior (Deci, 1975). Thus, explicit directives to do what one is now doing can result in refusal to continue to do so. This paradoxical result of a directive may be partially a function of the degree of choice implied in the directive. The less choice implied in the form of a directive, the less likely a person is to continue to perform the behavior. Thus, to tell a client that he or she must continue to worry exactly as he has been doing should diminish the worrying, while a statement implying choice such as "If you would like, you might continue worrying as you have been doing," would likely lead to compliance (continued worrying). Choice can also be in how to comply. The study by Heilman and Toffler (1976) reviewed in Chapter 4 showed that giving students alternatives of how to comply led to high levels of compliance compared to when they were given no alternative. Thus, a request such as, "You must continue worrying either as you have been or by worrying more or less than you have, whatever you choose," should lead to compliance (continued worrying) rather than defiance and diminished worry. A recent study of this hypothesis compared the results of two directives differing in choice (Wright & Strong, in press). In one condition people wishing help with procrastination were instructed, "You *must* continue procrastinating *exactly* as you have been. . . ." The interviewer then detailed how the client was to continue to procrastinate based on the discussion of how the client procrastinated. In the other condition, the client was instructed, "You *must* continue procrastinating in *some* of the ways you have been doing. You might_____ or _____or _____, whatever you choose." Preliminary results suggest that clients in the first condition (who were not given alternatives in how to carry out the directive) immediately defied it, and so rapidly decreased their procrastination. Clients in the second condition tended to comply more with the directive and decreased their procrastination more slowly than did clients in the first condition.

The client who does not follow the counselor's directive (to continue doing as he or she has) cannot attribute discontinuance to the counselor's directive, since the counselor directed the client to continue. Nor is the client likely to attribute noncompliance to a rational decision or willful choice, because that would require confronting the counselor with a direct refusal to do as instructed. Thus, defiance of an explicit directive can be expected to be attributed to spontaneous change in the inner characteristics of the client. Unfortunately, neither Wright and Strong (in press) nor Lopez and Wambach (1981) carried out their data lines far enough to assess the relative persistance of changes from paradoxical and nonparadoxical directives.

It is apparent that a counselor should not direct a client to do something the counselor wants the client to do using explicit directive forms that do not imply choice, for the client will find himself or herself spontaneously unable to comply, or will comply but hold the counselor responsible for the change. This is probably what is behind the concern in therapy that therapists do not explicitly direct or advise clients to get better. If the therapist did so, the client would likely respond by finding himself or herself unable to comply, and thus be even less in control of his or her problem behavior than before (Watzlawick, Beavin, & Jackson, 1967). Becvar (1978) reports the same results with counselors in training. When he required students to behave according to the new theories they were learning, they reported themselves unable to do so because the new procedures were strange and unnatural. When he cautioned them not to use any of the new techniques just yet, because they would be strange and disruptive, they reported being unable to prevent new behaviors from spontaneously occurring in their counseling efforts.

Personalism

Impression management theory suggests that complying to another's demands without the semblance of choice will be avoided because it implies low interpersonal power. However, if the request stems not from the communicator's desires, but from the requirements of the situation, compliance may imply less interpersonal powerlessness than intelligence and understanding of what is required (Friedland, 1976). For example. Heilman and Toffler (1976) found that students refused to comply with another's personal demand to taste vinegar, but they were willing to do so when the demand was presented as a result of computer-generated randomization. Complying with the personal demand of the other implied powerlessness, while compliance with the computer-generated condition had no such implications. Compliance to a directive is enhanced by making it an impersonal request based on the requirements of the situation. Surely, some of the effectiveness of directives rests on the assumption that the directive is based on a reliable body of scientific knowledge or informed judgment. For example, Lopez and Wambach (in press), in a short-term counseling experiment with clients concerned about procrastination, directed clients in one condition to procrastinate for a set period of time every day, and in another directed clients to study a set period of time every day. Both directives were supported with scientific explanations: careful observation of procrastination will allow greater understanding and thus greater control; setting goals and rewarding oneself builds effective self-control. Both directives were followed and both led to rapid and significant drops in procrastination. Physicians, lawyers, and psychologists may not have difficulties getting many people to do what they wish. However, compliance may not carry the attributional impact needed for spontaneous compliance. Thus, when a counselor wishes a client to comply with a directive, it would seem best to present it as stemming from the scientific understanding of what is required for the client to improve, and to present it also in the context of the client's responsibility to choose whether to comply, or even in the context that the client should be cautious about adopting such behavior and should reconsider if he really wishes to change. On the other hand, if the counselor wishes the client to defy the directive, as would be the case in the assignment of the symptoms, the counselor should imply that the directive is a result of the personal whim of the counselor with no particular scientific rationale. While there are no studies on it, this hypothesis suggests that when assigning symptoms with the hope of generating defiance, the rationale should not be very solid or elaborate. If the rationale is solidly scientific and based on good authority, it may be followed and thus lead to an increase in the symptomatic behavior.

Implicit versus Explicit

Directives can be placed on a continuum from implicit to explicit. Reflections are implicit directives in that the intent of the communication to control is not explicit, and neither client nor counselor is likely to readily agree that a reflection is an attempt to exert control. On the other hand, a personal, no-choice directive is explicitly understood to be an effort to influence and control. The more explicit the directive, the less likely it is to generate compliance.. To an even greater degree, the implicit-explicit dimension affects the attributions clients make for compliance and noncompliance. The more implicit a directive is, the more likely compliance is to be attributed to the characteristics of the complier. For example, innuendos and metaphors and other very implicit directives should be very effective in generating personality changes in clients. On the other hand, the more explicit a directive is, the less likely the client is to experience spontaneous change through compliance with the directive. For example, in the Lopez and Wambach (in press) study described earlier, the decreased procrastination in the "procrastinate" condition would be expected to be longer lasting following the termination of treatment because the directive only implied that the client was to stop procrastinating, and thus the client should have attributed the decreased procrastination to internal changes. The "stop procrastinating and study" directive should have been less effective in the long run because of its more explicit nature. While Lopez and Wambach's data imply such a relationship, the data line was not carried long enough beyond treatment to test the hypothesis. The same observations can be made for the Claiborn, Ward, and Strong (1981), Strong, Wambach, Lopez, and Cooper (1979), and Wright and Strong (in press) studies. Change in the "uncontrollable" condition should have been more persistent than in the "controllable" condition. Again, while the data suggest such a result, the data line is too short to fully assess the hypothesis. On the other hand, Beck and Strong (1981) followed up their clients one month after therapy was terminated and found that the implicit directive condition (positive reframing), which seemed to encourage rather than discourage depression, resulted in longer lasting change than the explicit directive condition (negative reframing), which cast depression in a negative light and implied that the counselor wanted the client to stop it. While clients in both conditions gave up depression in the course of treatment, clients in the positive reframing condition did so without clear justification from the counselor's remarks, remarks that explicitly labeled depression as a good thing. They were thus forced to see their change as a spontaneous, personal change. Clients in the negative reframing condition, on the other hand, received criticism and derogation from their therapists and could see their change as partially a compliance with their therapist's wishes. As in Miller, Brickman, and Bolen (1975), the difference in attribution shows up after the termination of treatment—where it counts.

Defiance of an implicit directive probably has little effect on the client's self-attributions or other behaviors. However, defiance of explicit directives should generate spontaneous attributions to account for the failure to comply, including spontaneous accounting for the disappearance of previous behaviors such as symptoms.

It seems clear that directives are the counselor's main tools for modifying the behavior of the client. The therapeutic effects of counseling are derived from a complex pattern of directives, some intended to invite compliance, others intended to invite defiance; some stated to generate attribution to the self, others stated to invite attribution to external and nonspontaneous circumstances; some stated to invite attribution to the self for abandoning behavior. The old controversy between directive and nondirective points of view was stated too simply. Yet, in terms of the subtleties of obtaining internal attribution for the changes counselors invite, the nondirective advocates seem to have had their hands on the more crucial part of the elephant of counseling.

The recent controversy over whether clients prefer explicit directives as reflections would seem to be focused on a minor concern (Claiborn, 1979; Helner & Jessell, 1974; Hagebak & Parker, 1969; Reisman & Yamokoski, 1974; Venzor, Gillis, & Beal, 1976). It is not a question of whether people prefer a certain kind of communication, but an issue of what role a particular kind of communication has in stimulating therapeutic change. Likewise, studies comparing the effectiveness of directive and nondirective counseling were looking for differences between explicit and implicit directives at too gross a level. The question is how such differences affect the process of change and thus how they can contribute to the outcome of counseling. Outcome is the result of a complex pattern of communications tailored to fit the change needs of a particular client. Surely, different mixes of explicit and implicit directives can combine to generate equivalent outcomes through rather different processes. Serious research on directives in counseling and psychotherapy has but begun.

Therapist Self-Disclosure

Attention in counseling is focused on the client as the counselor and client concentrate on the personal meanings of the client's behavior. Yet, the counselor's behavior is the client's source of information about the counselor's reactions to and interpretations of the client's behavior. The client can interpret the meaning of the counselor's behavior only in the context of inferences about the characteristics of the counselor. Another's behavior is meaningful feedback about the impact of one's own behavior only in the context of inferences about the situation to which the other responds and about the other's attributional practices and motives (Goethals, 1976). Attributions about another's characteristics largely determine the meaning of feedback from the other and thus reactions to the feedback of another. A client actively construes the characteristics of the therapist while simultaneously deciphering the impact of his or her own behavior from the therapist's reactions.

Everything the therapist does informs the client about whom the client is dealing with. The counselor cannot not communicate to the client about who he or she is, for even not responding is feedback to the client (Watzlawick, Beavin, & Jackson, 1967). The counselor communicates his or her characteristics to the client in every look, movement, emotional response, and sound, as well as with every word. Clients actively construe the personal characteristics, meanings, and causes behind counselor's behaviors in order to evaluate the personal significance of the counselor's remarks.

In a sense, therapist self-disclosure begins when the client first receives information about what therapists are like (Gelso & McKenzie, 1973) and then what this therapist is like; it continues with every contact with the therapist. This sense of self-disclosure, however, is too inclusive to be useful. Self-disclosure is usually understood in a narrower sense as communications about how the communicator feels, thinks, or acts, or has felt, thought, or acted in the past. Self-disclosures identify aspects of a person's experiencing that another could only infer from observing the person's behaviors, or from observations of the person in some other place or time. Through self-disclosure, the communicator is able to identify historical or current factors that bear on behavior another has observed, factors that give the behavior specific meaning and significance. As reviewed in Chapter 4, Quattrone and Jones (1978) and Baumeister and Jones (1978) have demonstrated that persons use discounting and augmenting principles with self-disclosures to alter the significance of information others already have to achieve desired impressions on the others. The effort to guide another's impressions of self not only serves the purpose of determining the other's views, but also invites the other to behave in desired ways and thus gains the other's participation in desired interaction patterns. A person does not always want to create a positive impression on another, but rather the person reveals aspects of self that encourage the other to behave as desired. The ultimate aim in interaction is not good impression, but relationship control.

Counselor self-disclosures serve the functions in the counseling interaction that self-disclosures do in other interactions. Counselors self-disclose to control clients' impressions of the counselor's characteristics and to encourage clients to behave in ways the counselors believe will lead to therapeutic consequences. Thus, some counselor self-disclosures might be expected to encourage clients to perceive counselors as expert, attractive, and trustworthy, characteristics presented in Chapter 3 as crucial to a counselor's ability to effect client behavior change. Counselor remarks have impact on the client only in so far as the client infers that the remarks come from a motivation to benefit the client and not a motivation to manipulate the client for some personal gain for the counselor (trustworthiness). The client's inference that the counselor is expert allows the client to infer that counselor remarks have validity and stem from scientific facts, theories, informed professional opinion, and a clear understanding of the client. Counselor efforts to gain an understanding of the client assure the client that the counselor's remarks and recommendations are a unique integration of scientific knowledge with a deep personal understanding of the client. Inferring that the counselor likes the client (attractiveness) assures the client that the counselor's perceptions come from an orientation of good will, favorable bias, and sympathetic understanding, and would seem to facilitate the other elements—trust and expertness.

Counselor self-disclosures can directly encourage the client to behave in helpful ways by providing social comparison and social desirability data from an audience (the counselor) to whom the client attributes unusual knowledge and understanding of the social meanings of behavior, and by modeling how it is best to act with others, think about issues, and react emotionally to situations. The counselor is a model with (presumably) impeccable credentials. Counselor self-disclosures about current experiences in the interview propose appropriate interview behavior, and disclosures of out-of-interview past and present behaviors model appropriate behavior in other settings. Counselor reactions to the client's productions in the interview model other ways to think, feel, and act in the situations under discussion. In sum, counselor self-disclosure affects the client's perceptions of the counselor's remarks, the client's judgments about the desirability of certain behaviors, and models of desirable behavior both within and outside of the interview.

Credibility

Many of the studies reviewed in Chapter 4 deal with people's attempts to present themselves as competent through their actions; they are relevant to self-disclosure only as it is broadly defined. Some of the studies are on self-disclosure as more narrowly defined, as most tests, questionnaires, and ratings are specific self-disclosures. From this research, we know that college students in psychology experiments attempt to appear competent and moral. Quattrone and Jones (1978) and Baumeister & Jones (1978), reviewed earlier, show that persons use self-disclosure to affect others' perceptions of their competence. These studies suggest that a person begins with an inference about the implications of what he or she presumes the other already knows, and then the person presents evidence that alters the overall picture to the impression the person desires the other to have. If the other knows of some act of competence, the discloser presents evidence that discounts possible external and miscellaneous causes of the competent performance and that augments the personalogical inference by showing how external causes were working against competent performance. The whole enterprise rests on judgments of what the audience will see as competent and how the audience will evaluate the evidence. If a person believes an audience has evidence of low competence, the actor will present information that will supplement and discount the implications of that existing information.

Research evidence is lacking on what counselors do to augment their being perceived as expert, trustworthy, and attractive, but the above reasoning suggests what counselors should do to enhance client perception of their competence. Clearly, any self-disclosure intended to enhance competence must be based on an assessment of what the client already thinks about the counselor. If the client already perceives the counselor as competent (which is highly likely), self-disclosures about competence are probably unnecessary and in fact probably would work to generate client dislike of the counselor. Jones and Gordon (1972) and Nelson-Jones and Strong (1976a) have shown that persons do not react well to another's declarations of skills and competencies; they are inclined to see the other as a braggart, full of himself, a bore, and mentally unbalanced. While clients may not deprecate the skills and training of bragging counselors, they will dislike them and question their personal stability. It would seem likely that a counselor might gain more from indirect disclosures, such as offhanded references to personal experiences in training, or statements of deductions from extensive work with others or from one's research. Statements like, "My experience in working with persons with problems similar to yours suggests that . . . ," should increase perceived expertness and boost a probable acceptance of the content of the statement attached to the self-disclosure.

Direct reference to training and experience is probably appropriate only when the client does not know about it. For example, when a counselor is working in an unusual setting such as a church or a community drop-in center where clients might be unaware of the counselor's credentials and are likely concerned to learn about the competence of the counselor, some self-disclosure of training and experience would seem appropriate. Again, however, direct reference runs the risk of appearing egotistical and of generating dislike. Self-disclosure would no doubt be most appropriate when given in response to a client's inquiry about the counselor's background. Such inquiry reflects the client's attempt to calibrate the significance of statements of the unknown counselor, and so it must be handled carefully. Modest recounts of training and experience that are somewhat general probably would carry the greatest effect. Disclosures that are specific may run into the difficulty of revealing details the client will find to be reasons to discount the counselor. For example, working in a religious setting always raises tension of possible secular contamination through extensive training and experience in secular settings, and self-disclosures probably should be detailed enough to imply sound training and experience, but should be accompanied with subtle discounts of secular training in favor of cues to devotion to the religious beliefs of the client. Of course, the opposite tact is best when the client is likely to see religious dedication as an indicant of incompetence. There also is the question of the client using inquiry into credentials as a tactic to put the counselor on the defensive. In such a situation, a brief statement of credentials should be followed by inquiry into the meaning of the client's questioning credentials. The client's inquiry needs to be redirected to the client to maintain the counselor's meta-complementary control of the relationship. When it is unclear whether the client has a grasp of the counselor's credentials, the counselor might say, "You may be uncertain about my experience in counseling. I was trained at _____ and have worked as a counselor at _____ for _____ years. I am very pleased to have the opportunity to talk with you. You were describing your mother's demands on you. Could you tell me more about that?"

Strong and Schmidt (1970b) demonstrated that counselor self-disclosures that violated the confidentiality of the interaction were ways of inducing low trustworthiness. In an experiment with counseling-like interviews, interviewers disclosed confidences revealed by students to student-clients and indicated that they were going to use the disclosures to the others' disadvantages. While the interviewers' disclosure reduced ratings of the interviewers' trustworthiness, they did not lead to ratings of untrustworthiness. The subject-clients in the experiment apparently attributed the interviewers' behavior to the requirements of the experiment and therefore attributed expertness to the interviewers rather than untrustworthiness. In counseling with clients, such self-disclosures probably would not be so attributed and would encourage clients to refrain from disclosing anything that might work against them in the wrong hands.

Derlega, Harris, and Chaikin (1973) and others (Archer & Berg, 1978; Chaikin & Derlega, 1974a, 1974b; Nelson-Jones & Strong, 1976; Wiegel, Dinges, Dyer, & Straumfjord, 1972) have shown that anyone, even counselors, who reveals deviant experiences will likely be derogated and seen as in need of help. Such relevations by counselors would seem to diminish perception of the counselor's competence, unless the self-disclosure is about problems of the past which are now resolved. Such testimonials may encourage the client and inspire confidence in the counselor. They also may not. Such disclosures need to be used with care and for specific purposes. An example of the power of self-disclosure to affect perceptions of competence and of the importance of the perception of competence to the therapy enterprise is reported by Yalom (1970). Two counselors began a group encounter they were leading with disclosures of uncertainty and self-doubt in their ability to lead the group. The group completely dissolved in the next few weeks.

Self-disclosure to enhance the perception of liking (attractiveness) has been the subject of much research, which has revealed one principle: disclosure of similarity enhances liking and the perception of being liked (Byrne, 1961). Schmidt and Strong (1971), Strong and Dixon (1971), Daher and Banikiotes (1976), and Lawless and Nowicki, Jr. (1972) found that counselors' statements indicating similar experiences and characteristics or dissimilar experiences and characteristics to the client contribute to the client's liking or disliking of the counselor. Murphy and Strong (1972) found disclosure of similar experiences, thoughts, and feelings to enhance positive perceptions of the counselor; so did Hoffman-Graff (1977) and Hoffman and Spencer (1977). In the Hoffman studies, counselor self-disclosures of having the problem the client reported (procrastination) or not having experienced the problem strongly affected the client's liking for the counselor.

Liking is closely tied to similarity. Revelation of unshared positive behavior (strengths, skills, abilities) leads to dislike, and revelation of negative self-aspects that are unshared leads to derogation (Jones & Gordon, 1972; Nelson-Jones & Strong, 1976). Positive effects are obtained only when self-disclosures are of characteristics the client shared (Levine, Ranelli, & Valle, 1974). For example, Nielsen (1979) found that therapist revelation of demographic material such as place of residence and education decreased the clients' liking for the therapist, apparently because it enhanced the clients' awareness of the discrepancies between them and the therapist.

Use of self-disclosure as a means of enhancing attractiveness must be carefully tailored to knowledge of the client's experiences. Great care in using similarity self-disclosure is needed, for such disclosures also affirm the client and diminish motivation and the probability of change (Hoffman-Graff, 1977; Johnson & Noonan, 1972). The search for attraction can diminish the prospects of therapeutic change.

To some extent, many of the studies reviewed here miss the point of liking in counseling. What affects the client's reaction to the counselor's statements is the client's perception that the counselor likes (or does not like) him or her rather than the client's liking for the counselor. Research reviewed in Chapter 4 shows that persons attribute liking to persons who listen to and track what one says and who share similar experiences, certainly major parts of therapist behavior. Also, Byrne (1961) has established that liking another leads to attributing that the other likes us. Thus, the above studies probably imply the effects of the client's perceptions of counselor's liking for them. Still, these studies have not clearly examined the hypothesized effects of attributed liking.

Normative Effects

Counselor self-disclosure provides clients with feedback about the desirability and undesirability of the behaviors disclosed from the perspective of therapists, certainly powerful authorities on social desirability in clients' lives (Lowe, 1976). If the counselor discloses having problems similar to those of the client, the client's perception of the negative implications of his or her own behavior is assuaged. If the therapist, presumably an expert on getting along with others and on mental health, has the same problems as the client, the problems must not be as important or as negative as the client had presumed. Also, therapist revelation of the same feelings or experiences as the client reveals removes the possibility of the client being discredited and losing face from disclosing the dangerous or negative aspects of the client's experience. On the other hand, therapist disclosure of experiences or feelings different from what the client experiences and discloses immediately reveals the client's behavior to be deviant and in need of change and correction and carries implications of the loss of face and credibility with the counselor and others. Thus the client is encouraged to abandon unshared and thus deviant behavior.

Hoffman explored the above hypothesis in two studies (Hoffman-Graff, 1977; Hoffman & Spencer, 1977) in which students concerned with procrastination were interviewed by counselors. After a client had been led to discuss his or her procrastination, the counselor disclosed similar difficulties with procrastination when he or she was a student, or disclosed he or she had never been troubled with procrastination (the counselor always got papers in on time, always did her or his work before playing, and so on). The effect of the disclosures on the student-clients was that those receiving the similarity self-disclosures later rated their procrastination to be less of a problem than they had before the interview, and they studied less during the next week. Those receiving the dissimilarity self-disclosure rated themselves as having a more serious problem in procrastination after the interview than they had before, and they studied more in the subsequent week.

Surely clinicians at least occasionally use self-disclosures to diminish client anxiety about the horribleness of their behavior, or to propose changes in thinking, feeling, and acting. Disclosing similar thoughts, feelings, actions, or experiences to clients serves to reassure clients that their experiences are not abnormal, or at least are not unshared by important others. On the other hand, exposure of differences in experiencing suggests that the client is indeed unusual and needs to consider changing. Exposure of differences through self-disclosure stimulates motivation and change but also diminishes attraction. Disclosure of similarities diminishes motivation and the likelihood of change and increases attraction. Therapists need to consider carefully the effects of disclosure in terms of therapeutic goals before they self-disclose anything.

Modeling Effects

Therapist behaviors in the interview provide feedback to the client about the therapist's evaluation of the client's behavior and about what the client should do. As discussed earlier, telling the client what to do in a direct way often is not the best way to encourage the client to change. Indirect methods often are superior in that they carry the force of the therapist's social power in defining the nature of behavior that should take place in the interview, but they cannot be directly opposed as attempts to influence as can be direct approaches to influence.

Therapist self-disclosure may be the most powerful method of indirectly suggesting to the client how he or she should behave. As described earlier, the self-disclosure, "I'm wondering how you feel," directs the client's behavior without the appearance of directing. Statements like, "I used to feel that way also. I have found, however, that I am much better off if I look at situations like this . . . .," suggest behavior changes to clients without directly proposing that the clients change. Therapist self-disclosures propose how the client should think, feel, and act by example and implication. The counselor is a powerful model for the client. What the counselor discloses about his or her own actions, feelings, and thinking should be powerfully formative to the client. Unfortunately, there is no research on this effect beyond studies of the impact of therapist self-disclosure on client self-disclosure in the interview.

Studies reviewed by Cozby (1973) and more recent studies (Davis, 1977, 1978; Davis & Skinner, 1974; Rubin, 1975) show that, under certain circumstances, self-disclosure begets self-disclosure. When persons are inducted into experiments and requested to get acquainted with another, they carefully match the behavior of the other in disclosure content, intimacy, and duration (Becker & Munz, 1975; Cozby, 1973; Davis, 1978). Several have commented on the experimental demand characteristics that lead to such precise matching (Becker & Munz; Rubin) and indeed, studies in which the demand was not so stringent reveal that recipients of self-disclosures use other response strategies at times, such as derogating the discloser and offering help (Archer & Berg, 1978; Nelson-Jones & Strong, 1976a). Also, videotaped examples of peer models of self-disclosing behavior in counseling have been shown by many to increase the self-disclosing tendencies of potential clients in subsequent interviews (Casciani, 1978; Gelman & McGinley, 1978; Highlen & Voight, 1978; McGuire, Thelen, & Amolsch, 1975; Thase & Page, 1977; Thelen & Brooks, 1976); the examples also have shown the effects of variables like sex, age, success, and so on that moderate the effectiveness of models (Marlatt & Perry, 1975).

Does therapist self-disclosure encourage client self-disclosure? The dynamics of the therapeutic situation are different from those of many of the studies that are used to support the notion that it does (Jourard & Jaffe, 1970), and the results of studies by Derlega, Lovell, and Chaikin (1976), Simonson (1976), and Simonson and Bahr (1974) suggest that it may not. Yet, the client should be anxious to reciprocate counselor self-disclosures to maintain the social structure of the exchange (Davis & Skinner, 1974; Lynn, 1978). Client self-disclosure to counter counselor self-disclosure and thus maintain the structure of the exchange could be used to encourage the client to disclose specific items of interest, and to encourage clients in groups to self-disclose.

Research on the utility of therapist self-disclosure as a means of inducing therapeutic change in thinking, acting, and feeling is urgently needed. It should be noted that self-disclosure is not usually considered part of the therapist's role, and extensive self-disclosure, especially of negative personal material, has been found to be associated with diminished therapist credibility (Derlega, Lovell, & Chaikin, 1976; Simonson, 1976; Simonson & Bahr, 1974). Derlega, Lovell, and Chaikin's findings suggest that if the therapist's use of self-disclosure is presented to prospective clients as usual therapeutic practice, the negative effect on credibility is removed. One might question if the significance of therapist self-disclosure in terms of affecting the client is also altered by explicit identification of therapist self-disclosure as part of the therapist's work.

Extensive use of therapist self-disclosure would probably have negative effects on the interaction because it would focus the attention of the members of the interaction on the therapist, forcing the client to focus attention on the therapist and away from himself or herself as the cause of behavior. Probably occasional and short therapist self-disclosures are interpreted by the client as implicit messages about how the client should think, feel, or act, as messages to the client about the client rather than messages about the therapist, and as messages that have considerable power in suggesting to the client what the client should do without any explicit recognition of the therapist's attempt to persuade or influence. This dynamic probably lies behind the effects of therapist self-disclosure in changing clients' evaluations of their own behavior and in inducing different behaviors.

PHASE 3: DISSOLUTION

The therapeutic encounter enters the third phase as the client accepts the counselor's invitation to gain control through therapeutic change. The client's behavior converges on the counselor's definition of how the client ought to behave. The maneuver enhances the client's power in the relationship, and the power differential progressively diminishes. The counselor relinquishes meta-complementary control, and the relationship experiences a transition into symmetry. The needs that brought the client into the relationship and had been the driving force behind the relationship are lessened and/or become less important to the client, and the relationship dissolves.

Chapter 3 discussed evidence that clients become more like counselors in successful counseling, the phenomenon of psychological convergence between counselor and client as an outcome of counseling. Lennard and Bernstein (1960) found that clients and therapist became increasingly alike in their verbal behavior as therapy proceeded. Correlations between the percentage of therapist and patient statements concerning the primary system, evaluation, and affect in the first two sessions, the fifth and sixth sessions, and two sessions from the third and fourth months were, for comments on the primary systems, $r = .72$, $r = .66$, and $r = .88$, respectively; for evaluation remarks, $r = .36$, $r = .45$, and $r = .58$, respectively; and for statements of affect, $r = .23$, $r = .43$, and $r = .70$, respectively. Lennard and Bernstein comment:

> there is over time an increase in correlation, with an especially marked increase in the correlations for affective propositions. These findings suggest that there is over time an increase in similarity of patient and therapist behavior with regard to those three areas. (p. 93)

Dietzel and Abeles (1975) also report increased complimentariness of counselor and client behaviors in the later sessions as opposed to the middle sessions of counseling.

Other than convergence between counselor and client, what kinds of interview behavior might accomplish the changes in the structure of the encounter, or reflect the changes? Self-disclosure might be one tool because of its impact on the power balance between interactants. Counselors might engage in heavy self-disclosure as a means of equalizing the power balance in the encounter (or as a reflection of an evening power balance?) and establishing symmetry. Counselor self-disclosure also signals a significant change in the counselor's tactics of relationship control, for responding to client statements with statements about self rather than statements about the client or the client's statements breaks the unspoken ban on meta-communication about counselor behaviors, diminishes attention on the client, and establishes symmetry. Such a change in tactics forces the client's attention to his or her environment, namely the counselor, and ends the intensive focus on the client which is characteristic of the first and second phases of counseling.

In the third phase of counseling, the counselor might increasingly respond directly to client statements, giving opinions, experiences, and thoughts and yielding to the client as an equal. In the last session especially, the participants would probably review the accomplishments of the encounter. Both might discuss the client's growth, probably with the counselor sharing similar experiences and effects in his or her own growth. We would expect them to justify ending the encounter with statements of goals accomplished or "in progress." Plans for how to handle anticipated future challenges might be discussed. Finally, both would wish the other well, and the encounter would come to an end.

Some of the above notions about the likely events of the third phase of counseling are drawn from the seminal work of Albert and Kessler (1978) on ending social encounters. They have found that structured interactions, interactions with purpose such as counseling, begin the termination of the encounter with summary statements that recount the history of the encounter. Next in the termination sequence are statements that justify the termination of the encounter. Structured conversations between friends are characterized by reference to internal justifications for ending the encounter, such as having achieved the goals of the encounter, fatigue, and so on. Such statements are followed by testimonials of the positive benefits from the encounter, perhaps partially to smooth over any hard feelings that may have been aroused by justification statements. Finally, statements about continuing contact are made, and the parties wish each other well.

In support of the above notions, Crowder (1972) found that counselors increased their support-seeking statements and decreased supportive-interpretative statements in the last interviews. But the best evidence concerning counselor behaviors during the terminal phase of counseling is reported by Bieber, Patton, and Fuhriman (1977) in their analysis of language usage in counseling. Their analysis, though based on only one counselor and client pair over a 25-session counseling encounter, conforms precisely to the above description of the third phase of counseling. They report that:

> In the 25th (last) interview, the counselor did a great deal more talking than he had done in the first and eleventh interviews. Moreover, he talked a great deal about himself and did so by using a majority of experiencer verbs that identified himself as the experiencer of some process of feeling, sensing, or knowing. . . .
> He had begun this interview by making the majority of his direct references to the client using the benefactor case, itself signalling a dramatic change in his choice of verbs. [The benefactor case denotes possession, and probably indicates the counselor's identification of the client's assets and characteristics as a consequence of counseling.] His talk about himself using the experiencer case was then interspersed with references to the client that exhibited an initial increase in defining her as either an agent or an experiencer, followed by a slight decrease in his use of both these case assignments. At the close of the final interview, he had increased his use of stative verbs when referring directly to the client. The point we wish to make here is that following both a great deal of counselor ''self-talk'' using the experiencer case and the counselor's direct referencing of the client as a benefactor of many things, the client exhibits a striking increase in talk about herself using verbs that take the experiencer case. In fact, her use of the experiencer case to identify herself with processes of feeling, sensing, and knowing eclipses her use of all other cases in the final third of the last interview. . . . In short, the client talks as if she were someone who now feels, perceives, and knows many things about herself. (p. 269)

CHAPTER 7

Group Counseling

Counseling and psychotherapy are group processes. When the therapist meets with one client to form a group of two, the process is called *individual counseling* or *psychotherapy*. When therapists meet with more than one client to form a group of three or more, the process is called *group counseling, family counseling,* or *couple counseling*. Group counseling is distinguished from family and couple counseling by the nature of the preexisting relationships among the clients with whom the therapist forms a therapeutic relationship. Group counseling is a therapeutic effort with two or more clients who are relative strangers. Family and couple counseling is a therapeutic effort with two or more clients who have a preexisting intimate relationship with one another.

The effects of successful therapy are felt in the client's ongoing relationships whether the relationships are present in therapy or not. If therapy does not lead clients to change behavior in ongoing relationships, it has failed. Clients seek therapy because of dysfunctional interaction behaviors in ongoing relationships, and the purpose of therapy is to change how clients interact in ongoing relationships. Whether clients receive therapy individually, in concert with relative strangers, or in concert with others with whom they frequently interact is a matter of strategy and pragmatics. The dynamics of change are the same in all therapeutic strategies, and therapists operationalize the dynamics according to the strategy for behavior modification they choose and the opportunities and resources available to them.

GROUP DYNAMICS

Change is a product of the search for a congruent relationship and occurs through the process of negotiating a relationship definition that meets the needs of the participants in the relationship. People change because they experience discrepancies between what they desire others to do and the feedback they receive from others on whom they are dependent. The sum of the dependencies of all parties in a relationship on each other is the *cohesion* of the group. Cohesion is the quality of a group that determines how resilient it is in face of disagreements about what the relationship definition of the group should be and outside forces that compete with the group for the presence of group members. Cohesiveness is the power of the members of a group on each other; it underlies the extent that they attempt to influence one another and the success of their influence efforts (Back, 1951). High cohesiveness denotes a high level of dependence of all or most members of a group on each other. Low cohesiveness denotes low dependence of all or most group members on each other.

Discrepancy is the personal experience of receiving feedback that is at variance with one's desired definition of a relationship. A relationship in which one or more participants experiences discrepancy is incongruent. The magnitude of the incongruence of a relationship is the sum of the discrepancies the members of a relationship experience. Incongruence in a relationship among any number of persons knit together in a highly cohesive group will result in changes in some of the members of the group as the group relationship strives toward congruence. If an individual experiences greater discrepancy than dependence on the other members of the group, the group will approach congruence by losing that member.

The definition of a relationship is composed of numerous elements, referred to as *norms,* that specify aspects of the relationship. An individual's behavior in a group tends to conform to the norms of the group. Members of a group may conform to norms but not be able to identify the norms verbally or to recognize their behavior as conformity to norms. In fact, some norms that define a relationship specify whether parties of the relationship are to be aware of and to note the constraints on their behavior. An example is the unspoken ban on client meta-communications about therapist contradictory behaviors described in Chapter 6, a norm of the therapeutic situation that is unspoken and unknown by the participants. Norms, congruence, and cohesiveness are the dynamics of groups of two or more persons. They are group expressions of the individual dynamics of definition, discrepancy, and dependence.

Whether therapy in groups of three or more members is operationally different from therapy in two-person groups depends on the therapist's decision about the communication pattern most beneficial for the client members of the group. In the two-person group, communications flow between therapist and client; therapist and client participate unequally in the interchange; therapist and client focus attention on the client. Therapist communications are feedbacks to the client that may disrupt undesired relationship behavior and facilitate desired relationship behavior. Cohesion results from the interdependence of client and therapist. In the two-person group, therapists have close control of the outcome of client discrepancy and dependence as they affect both with their communications to the client. Therapists can function much the same in a group of three or more members by channeling their communications to each client individually, dealing with individual clients in turn, and discouraging direct communications between clients. This pattern of group communication is called the *wheel* (Shaw, 1964). The therapist is the hub, and each client is a spoke. Traditional forms of psychoanalytic, Gestalt, transactional analysis, behavioral, and many other schools of group therapy conform to this pattern. Operationally, therapy groups of three or more members organized in the wheel pattern and therapy groups with two members differ very little. In fact individual therapy, the two-person group, is a wheel pattern of group therapy.

In the wheel pattern, some factors are affected by an increase in the number of clients from one to two or more. For example, as the number of clients becomes larger, individual client satisfaction with therapy no doubt decreases. Much research has documented that the spoke members of a wheel communication pattern become increasingly disenchanted with the arrangement as the number of spokes increases (Cohen, 1962; Lawson, 1965; Leavitt, 1951; Shaw & Rothschild, 1956). Another factor is the impact of observers. For the client interacting with the therapist, the waiting clients are an onlooking audience. Each client statement must be suited to impact all the observers, not just the therapist. The fact that the group members are strangers may attenuate this effect somewhat, but the concern for managing the impressions of the observing audience surely changes the nature of the client's disclosures to the therapist. Without the audience, self-disclosures and other interaction behaviors are intended to manage the impressions and channel the behaviors of the therapist. It seems likely that the addition of an audience makes the client more reserved and conservative in disclosures and other presentations of self and less conforming to the therapist's remarks (Cialdini, Braver, & Lewis, 1974; Cialdini & Mirels, 1976). On the other hand, any behavior the client emits in the presence of the onlooking audience is likely to be attributed to personal causes, for the client will have committed himself or herself to behavior in front of observers and will feel pressuure to be consistent (Riess & Schlenker, 1977). Thus, while less change is likely to be generated with observers, the obtained change is more likely to be generalized and maintained than in the two-person group.

The wheel communication style of group therapy probably facilitates client acceptance of and conformity to the client role, as each client will have the benefit of observing the others and using them as models of appropriate client behavior. Clients also probably compete with one another for the therapist's attention and favor and develop little attraction for each other. Thus, group cohesiveness is probably limited to the client–therapist pair dependencies. Perhaps this is an aspect of the robust finding noted above that the spoke members of large wheel groups are relatively dissatisfied with the experience. They probably drop out more and experience less change as a consequence of group membership than do members of two-person groups. On the other hand, the therapist retains direct control of the discrepancy experienced by each member of the group and of the dependence against which discrepancy interacts in the change process.

Another communication pattern a therapist might choose for the three or more person group is the *comcon* (Shaw, 1964) in which each person communicates with every other person. Here, the impact of the group experience on each member depends on the norms of the relationship worked out by the entire group and his or her dependence on all of the other members. In this pattern, therapeutic change is a joint function of discrepancy and dependence, but both discrepancy and dependence stem from all other members of the group. The therapist's tasks in the comcon to achieve therapeutic change for clients are different from those in the wheel. In the comcon, the therapist's primary tasks are to mold group cohesion and norms and to manage incongruence so that the group functions therapeutically. The therapist indirectly facilitates individual client therapeutic change by forming the group as a therapeutic community. While the therapist retains the role of directly interacting with individual clients to facilitate therapeutic change, direct intervention occurs in the context of the actions of a (more-than-equal) member rather than of the hub of the group. Direct therapeutic interactions with individuals in the group must function primarily to mold the group as a therapeutic tool and only secondarily as direct therapeutic interventions with individual clients.

Descriptions of therapy in the two-person group (individual therapy) presented in previous chapters are applicable to the wheel pattern of group counseling and to the direct therapeutic efforts of therapists in the comcon pattern. The functions of the therapist in forming a group of comparative strangers into a therapeutic community are discussed below in terms of therapist tasks, cohesion, and discrepancy management.

Therapist Tasks in Comcon Groups

Group psychotherapy in the comcon pattern evolved from the work of Kurt Lewin and the National Training Laboratories (Bradford, Gibb, & Benne, 1964) and the encounter group movement (Lieberman, Yalom, & Miles, 1973). A major tenet of this tradition of group therapy is that the group leader (therapist) does not direct the group but allows the group to form its own organization. The rationale for this tenet first revolved around the purpose of the groups: to teach community leaders how groups form and function. The groups were conceived of as training experiences on group processes. Many of the current exponents of the "nondirection" point of view base their notions on other ideas, such as the democracy of the leaderless group and the need to allow actualization processes of group members to evolve without interference from a structuring and controlling leader.

For a group to form as a therapeutic community in the comcon pattern, the therapist cannot overtly direct the group or the communication pattern will develop as a wheel with the directing therapist as the hub. Also, participants will see their actions in the group as direct compliance with the therapist's demands, and spontaneous compliance as the therapeutic outcome will be inhibited. However, to conclude that the therapist must not direct the group or provide leadership is wrong. Rather, the type of leadership and direction must allow and foster perceptions of group processes as developing spontaneously and individual changes as spontaneous personal expressions. Groups in the comcon pattern rely heavily on the notion of spontaneous compliance discussed in Chapter 5. The major responsibility of the therapist is to form and shape the behavior of the individuals in the group and the group processes so that they appear to participants as spontaneous occurrences for which the participants must accept responsibility. This leadership style has been identified as that of a social engineer and provider rather than the popularly perceived stereotype of laissez-faire (Lieberman, Yalom, & Miles, 1973).

The therapist's ability to form and shape the group's processes stems from the therapist having greater power than any of the other members of the group. Chapter 3 describes the sources of the therapist power in individual counseling, and the same variables operate in group therapy. Social psychological research has shown that no matter what the high power member of a group does, he or she has a major impact on the formation and functioning of the group (Torrance, 1954). Most of the communications in groups are directed to the higher power members of the group

(Cohen, 1958; Hurwitz, Zander, & Hymoritch, 1960; Stephan & Mishler, 1952).

The therapist has a dramatic impact on the group no matter what he or she chooses to do. Whatever the therapist does is interpreted by other members of the group as messages about what they should or should not do, whether the therapist's communications are explicit, overt, and direct or implicit, covert, and indirect. The therapist can direct the behavior of the other members of the group through covert and indirect communications, low profile modeling, reinforcement, and innuendos just as much as through overt and direct instructions and commands. The therapist cannot prevent himself or herself from having a profound impact on the group. Groups do not just evolve or develop on their own. Whether group members perceive that their group evolved and developed on its own or at the direction of the therapist is itself an outcome of the therapist's method of shaping the group. Whatever happens in the group, the therapist is responsible.

An important aspect of the therapist's task of forming a group as a therapeutic community is to create the perception that all members are responsible for the processes of the group and for their own behavior. To engender these norms, the therapist rejects the overt role of the leader, refuses to provide much direct structure, reinforces the ban on client meta-communications on the therapist's behaviors, and packages most of his or her interventions in the group as the responses of one (more-than-equal) member to other members of the group. The need for a high level of cohesiveness in the therapeutic group requires that the therapist encourage norms of personal interaction, caring and acceptance, self-disclosure of high risk material, and empathic responding to self-disclosures. The need for incongruence requires norms of attending and responding to here-and-now behaviors and providing feedback that attributes undesirable behaviors to external causes and desirable behaviors to personal causes. In addition to the overall responsibility to develop the norms of group process that create therapeutic change, the therapist must monitor each individual's experience of dependence and discrepancy on a moment to moment basis. The therapist must push some members and protect and support other members and shift attention to some and away from others to prevent dropouts and negative changes and to maximize therapeutic grains.

The therapist never behaves in a particular way just because he or she feels like it but gauges each intervention in light of the need to develop, strengthen, and extend norms and keep the experiences of each individual within a therapeutic balance of dependence and discrepancy. Yet, all of the therapist's interventions must appear to be spontaneous and based on his or her feelings at the moment in order to model openness, honesty, and transparency. While this seems like a contradiction, in practice it is seldom a problem. Therapists have a multitude of interventions at high strength at any particular moment and simply select the genuine response that will most facilitate group functioning. The major function of the therapist's behavior is to model what he or she wishes client members to do. As therapist modeling, facilitating, and reinforcing have their inevitable effects of shaping the member's behaviors so that they conform to necessary process norms, the therapist can increasingly turn to expanding and deepening norms, supporting and confronting particularly needy clients, and acting to change the therapeutic norms rather than to perpetuate them.

Cohesion in Comcon Groups

Cohesiveness is one of the two power variables determining therapeutic change in groups. Studies have shown that as the cohesiveness of a group increases, conformity to the norms of the group increases and members of the group increase their efforts to influence one another (Back, 1951; Sherif, Harvey, White, Hood, & Sherif, 1961). Cohesiveness is the relationship expression of individual member dependence on other members in the group. Dependence is presented in Chapters 2 and 3 as a function of an individual's needs and his or her presumption that the needs can be met through a relationship with the other. Cohesiveness of a group is built by increasing the members' perceptions that they have needs for which relationships with others in the group can provide resources. Client needs related to symptomatic behaviors are the drivers of the therapeutic relationship in individual and group therapy.

A basic need of every human is to be accepted and liked by others. Many of the peculiar methods of interaction control that clients present in therapy can be seen as methods to defend against the personal rejection and denigration that would result if others held the person responsible for his or her reprehensible behavior. Because of this, the single most important norm in group therapy is caring for and acceptance of members of the group. Lieberman, Yalom, and Miles (1973) found that caring was the single most important quality of leader behavior in encounter groups. The norm of caring for the person independent of his or her behavior removes much of the force of undesirable interaction behaviors in groups because such behaviors are often intended to elicit caring. The norm of caring is especially powerful in conjunction with the norm of high risk self-disclosures. Disclosures of negative thoughts about others, personal failures, socially undesirable behaviors, and abilities and competencies have the likely social effect of generating rejection, dislike, and loss of status and power (Nelson-Jones & Strong, 1976a, 1976b, 1977). Disclosures of such information increase the vulnerability of group members to each other and, if the disclosures are met with caring and empathy, individual attraction to and dependence on the group are greatly increased. Evolving and deepening norms of caring and self-disclosure in therapy groups increase the dependence of individuals on the groups and thus increase their vulnerability to influence and change.

The norms of caring and empathy automatically introduce an attributional set in those that hear self-disclosures to attribute undesirable behavior to superficial personal causes that are ultimately externally based and positive and desirable behavior to deep personal causes. The attributions free undesirable behavior for change and commit the discloser to behavior seen as desirable by group members. The therapist shapes the norms of what behaviors are seen as desirable and undesirable through self-disclosures, reactions to members of the group, and instructions and thus controls the automatic effects of empathy in the matrix of caring, disclosure, and growing cohesivenesss.

Group therapy fosters *deindividuation* of the members of the group. Deindividuation is a concept introduced by Festinger, Pepitone, and Newcomb (1952) and Zimbardo (1970) to describe the effects of decreased social accountability on the behavior of individuals. A common phenomenon in groups is the progressive development of behaviors that the individuals involved would not perform without the influence of the group. Deindividuation is fostered by the following characteristics of group therapy:

1. Because the proceedings of therapy are private and confidential, and the members of the group are relative strangers, the behavior of individuals in the group is neither observable nor available to the people outside the group who normally monitor the individuals' behavior. The individual is anonymous.
2. Responsibility for the behavior of the group is diffused among its participants so that no one person can be held responsible. Therapeutic rhetoric emphasizes personal responsibility, yet responsiblility is in fact diffused among the members of the group.
3. Attention is focused on the present, and the past and future are distanced. The focus on the present is a consequence of the therapy group's primary focus on the here-and-now.
4. Group therapy is a novel and unstructured situation that stimulates high arousal. The situation is designed to be different and novel in order to change usual behavior.
5. While some attention is focused on cognitive variables in group therapy, much more than ordinary attention is given to feelings and nonverbal communications. The therapist instructs the group mostly through doing rather than saying. There is a heavy reliance on noncognitive interaction and feedback.

The above circumstances result in several subjective and behavioral changes in the participants in group therapy:

1. Concern for social evaluation by those outside the group and for related self-evaluation is minimized.
2. Controls based on guilt, shame, fear, and commitment to those outside the group are weakened.
3. The threshold for expressing inhibited behaviors is lowered.
4. Behavior becomes less controlled by the restrictions and evaluations of outside reference groups and becomes more emotional, impulsive, irrational, regressive, and intense.
5. Behaviors released by the circumstances of the group become more and more extreme and intense as they repeat and cycle among members.
6. Extreme levels of liking and attraction to the group occur. The group becomes difficult to terminate.
7. The behavior of participants becomes highly influenceable by those present in the group and unresponsive to other reference groups and norms not represented in the group.

The impact of the norms of caring and self-disclosure and the processes and consequences of deindividuation have the potential of generating very high levels of group cohesiveness, higher than can be achieved in a two-person therapy group. Thus, when the conditions for group development are favorable, the potential for therapeutic change is higher than achievable in individual therapy. Whether high cohesiveness leads to therapeutic change, decompensation, or simply a "high" experience depends crucially on the management of discrepancy and the norms for behavior developed in the group under the therapist's subtle guidance.

Discrepancy Management in Comcon Groups

People change in groups that are highly cohesive and highly incongruent. In group therapy, managing incongruence is a key therapist activity. Incongruence must always be kept within the bounds of the cohesiveness of the group and, even more exacting, individual member experiences of discrepancy must be kept within the bounds of his or her dependence on the group.

A first concern is to draw into group process the behaviors to be changed. The need to attract typical behavior into groups argues for beginning groups ambiguously without much structure so that clients can impose their own structures on the situation and thus reveal their control styles. Yet, it is probably not damaging for a therapist to take a more active role in structuring the therapy task. When the therapist later decreases the structure, clients will impose their own patterns on the interaction. Recent research suggests that high structure at the beginning of therapy groups gets them into meaningful interaction more quickly but makes little difference in the long run (Bednar & Kaul, 1978). The amount of structure may be best determined by considerations of how much time is available for the group's life and how much ambiguity the clients' initial dependencies on the group will tolerate. Inducing individuals to demonstrate their symptomatic behaviors requires only that they be induced to behave in the group. Clients demonstrate their symptoms in nearly all relationships. That is one of the reasons their interaction behaviors are labeled symptomatic. Even in groups of nonclients, participants can be expected to behave typically in the group, and attention is focused on their means of controlling others in the group.

The focus of therapy is always on the client's methods of controlling others with his or her relationship behavior and is thus always on the here-and-now meaning of the client's behavior. Even with therapeutic systems and philosophies that do not emphasize the here-and-now, the object of change is the client's means of interacting with others. Changing here-and-now behavior does not require focusing explicitly on here-and-now behavior but can be accomplished by using client here-and-now behavior to generate personality interpretations and historical inferences whose final consequence is change in client here-and-now behavior.

Drawing attention to what a person is doing to others through his or her behavior is a very strong intervention and generates much discrepancy for the person, perhaps too much at first. Thus, the therapist may need to begin by drawing attention to relatively trivial interaction patterns, or even by taking refuge in the metaphors of Berne, Freud, or others to soften the here-and-now confrontation. As the objective of comcon group therapy is to shape the group as a therapeutic community, the therapist needs to model the here-and-now focus and reinforce other members' efforts to focus on here-and-now behaviors.

The major intervention of group therapy is providing feedback to clients about the interactional implications of their behavior. Feedback usually is shaped to include two components: a description of what the other did and a description of how the person giving the feedback responded to the other's behavior. The first part of the intervention is seen as the responsibility of the one receiving the feedback and the second portion as the responsibility of the one giving the feedback. The interventions are powerful because they not only bring attention and awareness to the control tactics of the recipient of the feedback, but they also present a veiled attribution about the personal meaning of the behavior. The unsaid message in the second half of feedback is that, "Your behavior suggests that you are the kind of person who wants to achieve these kinds of effects in others." In Chapter 4, feedback of this type is discussed as the most common form of behavior modification intervention. The rhetoric that a person's reaction to the behavior of another is the responsibility of the person (the one providing feedback) makes it more difficult for the recipient of feedback to retaliate with defensiveness or to counterattack because the feedback is presented as not being an effort to change the recipient. The reactions of the one giving the feedback to the pattern he or she points out are revealing about his or her tactics of controlling others, tactics now being applied to the one receiving the feedback. Providing feedback reveals interaction control behaviors and forms fertile ground for further interventions.

An important companion to the emphasis on the here-and-now is emphasis on disclosures of past and current experiences that relate to exposed here-and-now patterns. Behavior has little meaning without the context of past and present experiences. The functions and dynamics of self-disclosure in therapy are discussed in Chapter 6, and the only revision necessary to generalize that discussion to groups is to note that disclosures are directed to all the members of a group and thus are modified from what the client would reveal to the therapist alone. Therapists are alert to what clients are trying to achieve through disclosing specific perceptions and memories and encourage confrontative feedback on these objectives when such confrontation will foster therapeutic change.

The therapist responds to here-and-now behaviors and to the self-disclosures intended to give meaning to the behaviors with meaning frameworks of his or her own, frameworks that foster therapeutic change. The therapist models placing undesired interaction behavior in the context of being acquired to defend against unfortunate experiences and of not being representative of the client's core personality. Such attributes dislodge undesired behaviors and make them vulnerable to change. Desirable interaction behaviors are framed with personal meanings of deep significance and are cast as behaviors flowing from the core of the person that truly represent his or her deepest personhood. Such attributions encourage the maintenance and generalization of the desirable behaviors (Beck & Strong, 1981; Miller, Brickman, & Bolen, 1975).

A great variety of interventions are available to the therapist to encourage change, including paradoxical assignments both within the group and between group meetings, interpretations, and structured exercises (Schutz, 1967). However, the primary concern of the therapist in all interventions is to equip and facilitate the group as a therapeutic tool and only secondarily to directly intervene in the symptomatic behavior of a specific client. A therapist must always consider what impact a particular intervention with a specific client will have on the other members of the group and on overall group processes and let his or her individual interventions serve these purposes first. Gaining another's intervention is always preferable to direct therapist intervention.

As in individual therapy, the group therapist leads the group to endorse the norms of healthy interaction behavior as he or she defines it. The norms for group behavior must begin close to where the clients are and evolve to their final demand for healthy behavior as the members of the group are able to respond therapeutically to the final norms within the cohesive strength of the group. Successful outcome of therapy is client compliance to the final process norms of the therapeutic relationship. As in individual therapy, when clients adopt interaction behaviors the therapist believes are healthy, clients are quietly urged to assume a therapist role and are increasingly treated as equals. The extent that a therapist is able to relax the ban on client meta-communication on therapist behaviors and to behave without editing for impact on group processes may be good indicators of the degree that a group has achieved its therapeutic objectives with all client members. Individual differences among clients probably condemn most group therapy efforts to incomplete dissolution no matter how long their duration.

STRENGTHS AND WEAKNESSES OF GROUP THERAPY

Psychotherapy in the comcon group has the potential for powerful effects on participants, more powerful than are possible in wheel arrangements including individual therapy. This potential is a consequence of the deindividuation process and other factors that potentially can develop powerful cohesiveness and thus dramatic behavior changes as participants conform to the norms of the highly cohesive group. Yet, research suggests that group therapy outcomes are about the same as individual therapy outcomes (Bednar & Kaul, 1978; Hartman, 1979). Lieberman, Yalom, and Miles' (1973) study of 17 encounter groups suggests that the modest effectiveness of comcon groups is a result of the difficulty of getting cohesiveness and norms to function therapeutically. One of their groups was very effective in generating positive outcomes, a group that emphasized caring, disclosure, and meaning attribution. Some of the other groups resulted in no effects at all and a few in numerous casualties without any positive outcomes. Their study makes it clear that developing caring as a basic norm of group functioning and the therapist's management of discrepancy and dependency for each member are crucial to prevent casualties in group therapy. Equally clearly, learnings in the here-and-now must be integrated into a meaning framework to facilitate generalization and maintenance of therapeutic change. Managing the development of cohesiveness, behavioral norms, incongruence, and the individual discrepancy experiences of participants is a demanding task, especially when therapists are not aware that these are the crucial dynamics of group counseling.

Even when the therapist is focused on cohesion, norm, and incongruence dynamics, success in generating a therapeutic community is limited by the therapist's relative influence in the group. Perhaps other members of the group are able to counter the therapist's influence and instill other norms that sabotage the therapeutic functioning of the group. The therapist must have adequate power in the group to guide and foster its development as a therapeutic community. The most serious issue for the therapeutic functioning of comcon groups is the ability of participants to respond to the interventions of the therapist and the group norms the therapist guides the group into adopting. Persons with very deviant interaction control tactics can sabotage the therapist's efforts. Group research shows that a single deviant from group norms can effectively counteract the compliance pressures of cohesiveness so that many others will also deviate and thus eliminate the desired behavior pattern as a norm (Asch, 1955). Including clients in comcon groups whose behaviors are very abnormal, aggressively nonconformist, or withdrawn and unresponsive to social influence eliminates the prospect of achieving therapeutic gains in comcon groups. Clients whose behavior deviates widely from usual relationship control patterns are better helped through group or individual wheel organizations of therapy. In the wheel, the therapist is much more able to manage dependence and discrepancy experiences for each client than in the comcon for he or she does not need to be concerned about the development of group cohesiveness or about the negative impact of one client's behavior on the group's functioning.

Comcon groups draw their strength from group processes and can far surpass individual therapy or wheel groups in power and impact. On the other side of the coin, comcon groups are extremely vulnerable to deviants and can be rendered at best ineffective and at worst destructive by participants who will not or cannot conform to the therapist's covert influence and the group processes.

THOUGHTS ON THE ROLE OF AWARENESS IN BEHAVIOR CHANGE

The role of awareness in behavior change is drawn into question by the concept of spontaneous compliance, the ban in therapy on awareness of and comment on contradictory therapist behaviors, and the group therapist's tactic of drawing attention away from his or her influence to foster misattribution of the causes of group processes and individual therapeutic change. Hoyt, Henley, and Collins (1972) noted the misattribution aspects of therapy in their exploration of the implications of forced compliance research to group psychotherapy:

> Many change, growth, and therapy techniques often use social pressure to entice a participant to behave in a counterattitudinal (novel or healthy) way. The source of change often is, in fact, social pressure from the group, but every effort is made to conceal this fact and to lead the participant to believe that he,

himself, is personally responsible for his independent and significant behaviors. Since most of us tend to deny the importance of social influence in determining our behavior, social pressure may be a special kind of external pressure for behavior change which leads the individual to (a) engage in the act and (b) infer that he is personally responsible for his actions. This internal attribution, whether correct or incorrect, will maximize the probability that the act will produce lasting personal change. (p. 209)

What then is the function of awareness in behavior? Most therapists believe that a major benefit of their activities is to increase client awareness and that awareness is a major curative and existentially valuable outcome of therapy. But it may be a mistake to view awareness as existentially valuable. Life, the quality of being alive, is mysterious. Living beings are by definition needful and driven to manipulate their environment to yield the qualities that are essential for continued survival and growth. It is doubtful that living creatures are privy to their internal processes of needs, drives, and motives that form the seething cauldron Freud dubbed the unconscious and the source and captain of behavior. Behavior is the means of environmental manipulation for the unknowable purposes of the living creature. Behavior is shaped by its success in molding the environment to the purposes of the unknowable core of the living being. Perhaps awareness is but another component of behavior, and people are aware whenever awareness is essential to the successful accomplishment of the purposes of the core being and unaware whenever not being aware is essential to the successful accomplishment of the purposes of the core being. Since an awake being is always aware of something, the management of attention, shifting attention to those efforts that require awareness for success and away from those efforts that require unawareness for success, is simply a fact of the functioning being.

This conception of awareness fits the facts of psychotherapy. Therapists draw attention and awareness to interaction behavior patterns clients use to control others that are by some standard undesirable. Incredibly, such attention often has the function of eliminating the behaviors! Surely the explanation is that many interaction control tactics labeled symptomatic are successful because they occur outside of awareness, and attention robs them of their effectiveness. Yet, the behaviors substituted for symptomatic behaviors are not the opposite of those they replace. Through therapeutic rhetoric emphasizing awareness and choice, the source and cause of new behavior is systematically removed from attention and awareness. Attention is drawn to supposed internal sources of the behavior, sources that clearly are not the causes of the behavior. Focusing attention on supposed internal sources of behavior allows the person to be unaware of the source and utility of his or her new behavior, enables the person to behave effectively and desirably in interactions, and allows the behavior to be generalized and maintained. The behavior is effective because its source and utility are kept outside of awareness, just as symptomatic behavior, now removed, has been.

CHAPTER 8

Family and Couple Counseling

Family counseling has emerged in the last two decades as an expression of the growing interest in the function of behavior in its social context. As a sign of its youth, 9 of the 11 journals dealing with families and couples have been started in the last 15 years (Gurman & Kniskern, 1978). The development of family therapy is a result of thinking about psychological problems as interaction control strategies:

> symptoms, defenses, character structure and personality can be seen as terms describing the individual's *typical interactions which occur in response to a particular interpersonal context*. Since the family is the most influential learning context, surely a more detailed study of family process would yield valuable clues to the etiology of such typical modes of interaction. (Jackson, 1977a, p. 2)

This notion is expressed by Palazzoli (1974) as follows:

> if we take a transpersonal view of the family, *all forms of mental illness must be considered logical adaptations to a deviant and illogical transpersonal system.* (p. 193)

THE DYNAMICS OF FAMILY FORMATION, SELF-REGULATION, AND TRANSFORMATION

The family is a rule-governed system. The members of the system "behave among themselves in an organized, repetitive manner and . . . [the] patterning of behaviors can be abstracted as a governing principle of family life" (Jackson, 1977b, p. 6). As a system, the family is characterized by wholeness, self-regulatory processes, and transformation:

1. Wholeness, in the sense that the system is not only more than the sum of its parts, but it is *independent* of its parts. What is primary is the arrangement between the elements, not the elements; system parameters will predominate over initial conditions. The relationships have an objective, independent existence in the changing organization of interaction.

2. Self-regulatory processes (cybernetics): a family is a rule-governed system, which tends to constancy within a defined range (homeostasis). All families that

stay together must have a certain degree of negative feedback, that is resistance to change, in order to withstand the stresses imposed by the environment and individual members. This resistance to change is organized into rules that are often neither conscious nor explicit. Of these rules, the most universal is what I would call the 'rule of rules,' that is the rule that it is forbidden to make comments, or to metacommunicate, about the rules. Disturbed families are peculiarly refractory to change and demonstrate a remarkable ability to maintain the *status quo*, often ensnaring the therapist in rules which, in fact, he ought to be trying to change.

3. Transformation. A family is a system of transformations. As Rabkin has put it so well: the best example of a family as a system of transformations comes from myths. When the princess kissed the frog, she *transforms* him into a prince. Marriage is also a powerful transformation. Suddenly, if the formula is pronounced correctly, you are husband and wife and possibly transformed from a frog to a prince, or from a prince to a frog (Palazzoli, 1974, p. 196)

Marriage has other characteristics that make it a unique system of human interaction:

1. It is a *voluntary* relationship, even though undertaken in a culture which views marriage as almost compulsory.

2. It is a *permanent* relationship; that is, it is supposed to be a lifetime contract. ('Till death do us part').

3. Marriage in the western world is an *exclusive* relationship, in which the parties are supposed to be virtually sufficient each unto the other, with a marked exclusion of third parties and outside relationships.

4. It is a broadly *goal-oriented* relationship with many vital mutual tasks to be carried out on a long-term basis and marked by time-bound eras—each with its special problem. (Jackson, 1977a, p. 22)

Formation

Families spontaneously evolve out of marriages which are formed when people voluntarily decide to take the monumental step of melding their individual fates into a mutual fate through the formation of an exclusive and permanent relationship. The attraction of male and female to one another is impossible to explain but is readily observed. Walster and Walster (1969) and Berscheid and Walster (1978) have shown that, while individuals are desirous of becoming linked with the most attractive person of the opposite sex possible, dating occurs according to the rules of equity in that men and women of about the same attractiveness are most likely to affiliate and forge lasting relationships with one another. Equitable mating is a logical outcome of the competitive market as each person maximizes his or her outcomes (need satisfaction) given the resources to attract another each has.

Having made the initial step of contacting each other, a man and woman enter an extended or short-lived effort to negotiate a congruent relationship that meets many of both parties' needs. The continuing importance of attractiveness is apparent in studies that show that couples imbalanced in attractiveness tend to experience one-sided relationships with the less attractive giving more and the more attractive getting more. The frequent outcome of unbalanced attractiveness in couples is the dissolution of the relationship due to the more attractive party seeking partners with greater resources or the less attractive party becoming disenchanted with being exploited (Aldous, 1977; Hill, Rubin, & Peplau, 1976; Kelley, 1979; Walster, Walster, & Traupmann, 1978).

Congruence is forged through thousands of exchanges of ploy and counterploy in the struggle to define the relationship. In the process, each party is willing to give to the other due to his or her dependence on the other. Interdependence grows as each gives to the other because accommodating to the other's wishes increases the resources in the relationship that meet the other's needs. Dependence on the other makes each party concerned about the discrepancies the other experiences in the interaction. If the other's discrepancies are too large, the other will terminate the relationship and the person will lose the real and potential resources in the relationship that correspond to his or her needs. Thus, the formation of a relationship characterized by high interdependence necessarily means the transformation of its participants as they seek resources for their own needs and adjust their expectancies to take into account the other's needs as is necessary for the relationship to survive and grow in interdependence. Kelley (1979) has proposed that a partner's concern for the other's desires in a relationship results from a synthesis of the partner's original self-oriented matrix of desired outcomes and a transformation matrix of the other's desired outcomes that produces a third matrix, the "effective" matrix, that controls the partner's behavior.

A person enters a new relationship with interpretations, definitions, predictions, and operational tactics generated in previous relationships. The person adopted these characteristics to shape previous relationships to meet his or her needs in the context of former interactants' needs. The person maintains or changes these characteristics in the process of forming a new relationship in response to the discrepancies he or she experiences in the context of dependence on the new partner. Personal transformation, marked change in the person's interactional characteristics, is likely only in the context of high dependence. The attraction men and women unaccountably have for one another's company generates the high levels of dependence required to transform both parties.

The step of entering a permanent relationship is based to a great extent on each party's attributions of the causes of the other's accommodations to his or her needs. Is the other accommodating on a tactical level for some short-term gain, such as sexual experience, or is the other expressing a deep and abiding disposition to subordinate or modify his or her desires to take into account the needs of the person? This issue can be resolved only through extended interaction with another and observation of the other's consistent behavior, especially in events where the other's interests and the partner's interests conflict. Such events give the partner the opportunity to observe the depth of the other's willingness to forgo for the sake of the partner (Kelley, 1979). When couples develop high levels of interdependence, develop exclusiveness in relation to other potential partners, and develop a level of trust in the other's concern for their welfare, they take the step of forming an exclusive and relatively permanent marriage relationship. They may not have resolved all aspects of the definition of their relationship and may still experience considerable incongruence. Yet, the interdependence forged in the process and behavioral agreement on many issues (norms) makes them hopeful that congruence is possible and they bravely commit themselves to the future, a future filled with inevitable change as each party changes, other persons (as children) become part of their relationship, and the environment in which the new unit functions changes.

Self-Regulation

People survive by behaving to render their environments to their needs. The patterns of behavior people strive to bring about in others are the patterns they have found to provide resources and qualities that meet their needs. In highly interdependent relationships, people change their behaviors and supporting internal equipment as a strategy to maintain the relationships and render them fruitful of their needs in the long term. Altruism, giving of self for the benefit of another, is but a long-term strategy for forming relationships to meet needs. In relationships of high and balanced interdependence, a critical characteristic of participants is their willingness to accept self-change as an intermediate sacrifice for the long-term satisfactoriness of the relationship. Changes can be absorbed by one party, or both may accept some loss in compromise solutions. If both parties are not willing to accept self-change, the relationship is doomed to continual incongruence as each party struggles to have his or her own way. When the parties are willing to accept dissolution of the relationship as a possible outcome, conflict (incongruence) escalates only until someone gives in, a compromise is forged, or the relationship dissolves. If both parties are unwilling to change *and* are unwilling to risk losing the relationship, the stage is set for the development of a stable incongruent relationship characterized by tenacious maintenance and continual conflict.

The struggle for supremacy in relationship definition is waged in the realm of attribution. Chapter 4 presented the concept of persuasive asymmetry that describes interaction patterns of attempts to stimulate the other to change and to counter such attempts. Attempts to stimulate change often take the form of claiming the other has a negative attitude toward the partner and attacking the credibility of the other by implying that the other's unwanted behaviors are a consequence of negative and disgusting personal dispositions. Resisting change often takes the forms of attributing disputed behaviors to circumstances, misunderstood platonic motives, and personal (but peculiar) attitudes and beliefs. People also resist change by attributing disputed behaviors to personal causes over which they have no control, such as depression, fatigue, paralysis, and headaches (Kelley, 1979).

Attempts to stimulate change that imply a lack of caring assert that the other is not to be trusted to take the person's needs into consideration and thus draw the wisdom of continuing the relationship into question. The tactics are effective because the other is dependent on the person and is unwilling to lose the relationship. A tactic that relies on veiled questions about the other's willingness to sacrifice for the person is meekly surrendering to the other's demands and implying that one has no choice but to give in. The tactic implies that the other is selfish. He or she is unwilling to benefit the partner but looks out only for himself or herself in a predatory and selfish way. The implication that one is selfish is unacceptable because it implies that one is unwilling to make personal sacrifices for the other and thus that the other has no choice but to reconsider the wisdom of continuing the relationship. This tactic also denies that accepting the other's proposal is motivated by a concern for the other, a concern that would have consistent beneficial effects on the person's treatment of the other in the relationship. It thus presents the other with the dilemma of having won the battle but lost the war. Because each party is necessarily concerned about achieving a stable relationship that will consistently meet his or her needs, each is highly sensitive to attributional cues about the causes of the other's behavior with respect to him or her and the causes the other sees of one's own behavior with respect to the other. Both find compliance without signs of permanent personal change unacceptable grounds for conflict resolution.

The process of negotiation results in redundancies in the patterns of behavior in the relationship. The redundancies may represent points of congruence in the relationship where the parties have changed to accommodate each other, and thus the relationship may be mutually satisfactory and without high levels of tension. In congruent relations, the parties maintain the pattern of the relationship and resist changes that result from natural changes in the parties, changes in relationship membership, and changes induced from the outside. As long as the parties are willing at some level to accept personal change, these disruptions in the pattern of relationship can be resolved through negotiation.

Negotiations for change are not usually carried out in an explicit way with meta-communication about the changes but occur through a process of ploy and counterploy, and personal adjustments result from the matrix of attributional conflict. It is tempting to suggest that meta-communication about the rules of the relationship and the necessity of change is a superior way to resolve relationship incongruencies. However, meta-communication is itself a powerful strategy to gain advantage in the relationship. Each person necessarily looks at the relationship from his or her point of view, punctuates events in ways that are favorable to him or herself, and attributes causes for behaviors that stimulate the other to change. Breaking Palazzoli's rule of rules is a powerful attributional strategy of persuasion and results in more attributional conflicts with little prospect of change if the parties are unwilling to accept personal change as a possible outcome of negotiations.

In negotiations, it is crucial that each party not explicitly demand that the other change in order that the other be left the opportunity to comply with the pressure to change and attribute the change to spontaneous personal causes. Only if the changes wrought in negotiation are personally attributed will the parties experience "being" different rather than merely "acting" different and thus experience changes that are generalized to other behaviors and are maintained over the longer term of the relationship. Explicitly demanding that the other change is a dangerous tactic. It removes the possibility of a successful outcome from negotiation. A person who behaves differently because he or she "has" to cannot be perceived by the other as having really changed, and the changer cannot experience him or herself as being changed. The process of negotiating change is fraught with difficulties and can only be managed successfully if the parties generate conditions in their strategies that allow spontaneous compliance. It may well be that negotiation for change is best carried out in ploy and counterploy without insight and meta-communication (Haley, 1976). If meta-communication is used as a strategy for inducing change, it must draw attention away from the compliance aspects of change and to some quality of spontaneous personal change as the agent of accommodation.

All conflicts between marriage partners are not resolved through accommodation and personally attributed dispositional change. Some incongruencies remain in all relationships if for no other reason than the elements of the system are living creatures who are subject to continual change as a given condition of their quality of being alive. But for relationships among parties who are unwilling to change and defer to one another and are unwilling to risk the dissolution of the relationship, incongruence, with its continual cycles of ploy and counterploy in persuasive asymmetry, becomes their defining characteristic. Incongruence is the most notable characteristic of the relationships Palazzoli (1974), Palazzoli, Boscolo, Cecchin, and Prata (1978), Haley (1968d), and Jackson and Yalom (1977) describe in their studies of relationships that produce symptoms such as schizophrenia, anorexia nervosa, and ulcers.

Relationships that remain highly incongruent but stable are marked with behavioral redundancies or family rules, but the rules are not manifestations of accommodations of the parties to each other. Rather, they are the lines of battle around which the continual struggle for supremacy is waged. In incongruent stable relationships, the redundancies in the patterns of behavior are not nodes of strength and sources of growing interdependence but are constant threats to the relationships' maintenance, threats of schismatic disintegration. In the context of such rules or redundancies, the rule of rules has the vital function of drawing explicit attention away from the danger of disruption posed by the struggle. Explicit focus on the conflict would serve to escalate the battle, possibly to intolerable levels. The behaviors that mark redundancy in stable incongruent relationships are heavily flavored with efforts to manage the impressions the opposition gains from one's behavior and to communicate impressions of the other's behavior that are intended to finally bring the other to spontaneously change and allow one to emerge victorious. In dealing therapeutically with such patterns of interaction, Palazzoli (1974) eloquently describes the necessity of abandoning the attributional practice of making correspondent inferences to dispositional causes on the basis of the behavior of the struggling parties. In such a battle, the parties are experts at managing impressions of their ''being'' as a major part of their tactics intended to stimulate the other to change. Only when the therapist eliminates the verb ''to be'' from his or her descriptions of the interactant's behaviors and substitutes the verb ''to show'' is he or she able to formulate effective intervention strategies (Palazzoli, 1974; Palazzoli, Boscolo, Cecchin, & Prata, 1978).

Family participants in the process of negotiating and maintaining a relationship are linear theorists who conceive of their own behavior and the behavior of the others in linear cause and effect sequences and punctuate the events as suits their advantage in the struggle. Thus, they often see and present the other's behavior as the cause of their own behavior and attribute the conflict to the other's behavior and to underlying dispositional qualities they select as most likely to induce the other to change.

While the interaction develops out of each party's efforts to render the relationship to his or her advantage in the short or long term, the behavior of individuals in stable interactions is better conceived of as emergent from the interaction and not strictly caused by either party. How the parties come to behave in their relationship is a function of their interdependence and the strategies each uses to counter or accommodate to the strategies of the other. Thus, how a person behaves in an interaction is a function of the interaction and is not strictly under individual control. This is true not only on the specific behavior level but also on the level of the dispositions the individual comes to attribute to himself or herself. Spontaneous compliance to the other's demand forms the person's pattern of behavior and supporting personal characteristics. The strategies the person adopts to influence and counter the other form the basis of the other's attributions of qualities to the person. Interactions characterized by high interdependence truly transform the person and are experiences that forge the individual's behavioral characteristics and personality.

Stable relationships characterized by a high level of incongruence are constantly threatened with schism and generate extreme efforts to correct and eliminate the threat. The ploys meant to stimulate change are extreme and are countered with extreme ploys intended to prevent change. The interactants live in a constant state of tension, alertness, and alarm (Palazzoli, Boscolo, Cecchin, & Prata, 1978). New entrants into the relationship are inducted into the struggle as each party attempts to use the third party to gain advantage with the other. In families with parents in a stable and incongruent struggle, children are inducted into the struggle and become willing parties in the effort. Each parent attempts to form coalitions with the child against the other and each also makes strenuous efforts to block coalitions of the other with the child, creating a constant "domino" effect of shifting coalitions and denial of coalitions.

Children are totally dependent on the family system to meet their needs and thus conform to the family rules more completely than either parent. They play the rules harder in their effort to maintain the system and gain advantage in it. As a result, family systems that generate distinguishable psychological symptoms do so most effectively in the child members of the systems. For the children, their extreme behavior is their attempt to gain advantage in the relationship through conformity to its rules. As a result, the identified patient in the family system is often one of the children, and the family seeks therapy in an effort to ward off the threat of schism that the identified patient's extreme behavior poses to the family system.

Transformation

In a stable relationship, change in the pattern of system behavior results from a violation of the rules of the system by one or more of the parties in the relationship. One person's bid for change in a relationship is countered by another member of the relationship in an effort to maintain his or her position relative to that person, resulting in increased incongruence in the relationship that may or may not resolve into system transformation and the establishment of a new point of balance. The new point of balance may represent a new norm or a new line of battle. A bid for change may result in homeostatic change in the system or in system transformation. In homeostatic change, the oscillation of ploy and counterploy becomes more (or less) extreme, but the point of balance does not change, giving rise to the often noted observation: "Plus ça change, plus c'est la meme chose." On the other hand, the bid to change may result in system transformation in which the old norm or line of battle is abandoned and a new norm or line of battle emerges as a reflection of the transformation of behavior patterns in the system and the transformation of the behavior and attributed characteristics of its participants.

Change is inevitable in systems composed of living members. Family systems fall prey to the fallacy of attempting to maintain constancy in the face of the contrary and deeper characteristic of living, the constancy of change. Forces for change may be shifts in the balance of power or dependence among members brought about by changes in needs, resources, or alternative relationships possibilities, or changes in interpretations, definitions, predictions, or behavior strategies. Members may experience changes in behavior and supporting internal characteristic induced in relationships outside the family, such as in psychotherapy. Children enter the system, grow, and constantly change in needs, capabilities, and dependence on the family system. Grandparents may enter the system or leave it through their needs for family care, death, or other means.

Many efforts to induce change fall victim to the powerful self-corrective features of the family system, features rooted in each party's determination to render the system to his or her purposes. System transformation occurs only when the parties of the relationship determine that behaving in new ways better serves their purposes than the old ways and thus is always based ultimately on self-interest. Transformation in relationships composed of parties willing to accept self-change and the prospect of relationship dissolution results from shifts in the power balance of the relationship and coordinated shifts in behavior as the more powerful party introduces incongruencies that stimulate change. Persistent effort, negotiation, and attributional strategies that invite spontaneous compliance stimulate changes in behavior and self-attribution that increase the resources available to the more powerful party and thus rebalance the dependencies between or among the parties of the relationship.

In families composed of members who will not accept change and will not consider dissolution of the relationship, the most powerful cause of transformation of the system is dialectical synthesis. The struggle of ploy and counterploy basic to the incongruence in a relationship can be conceptualized as thesis and antithesis. Communications that assert that the pattern of behaviors give the impression not of efforts to assert superiority and avoid subordination but of mutual subordination and self-sacrifice that further the collective goal of maintaining the relationship radically violate the parties' search for supremacy. Thesis and antithesis are synthesized and reframed as cooperative and self-sacrificial acts subordinate to the goal of relationship maintenance. Such a changed understanding of the meanings of behaviors generates dramatic changes that create a new order in the relationship as each party strives to regain intended unilateral control of the relationship definition for his or her purposes. Dialectical synthesis is possible in relationships in which the parties are unwilling to give in to each other but are also unwilling to risk dissolution of the relationship. When faced with feedback that implies that behaviors intended to stimulate the other to change and to resist the other's efforts to stimulate change are in fact self-sacrificial accommodations to the other's needs, participants abandon the battle and pursue the effort to subordinate the other through different tactics.

Family system transformation takes time. Change is the out-working of ploy and counterploy in which the participants adjust their behaviors to each successive feedback in search of advantage in the relationship. The new point of balance is not immediately achieved but evolves in time as the parties adjust and refine their individual strategies to the other's changed strategies. Palazzoli's research (Palazzoli, 1974; Palazzoli, Boscolo, Cecchin, & Prata, 1978) with families with stable and highly incongruent patterns of interaction suggests that new behavior balance points often require one or more months to emerge.

SYMPTOMS

Psychological symptoms are interaction behaviors devised by the person to gain supremacy in a stable and incongruent relationship. While the individual enacts the behaviors, the behaviors are a product of the interaction and emerge in the struggle to gain advantage in the relationship as part of the fabric of ploy and counterploy characteristic of incongruent relationships. Symptoms are an expression of the participant's hubris, his or her overweaning desire to gain unilateral control over interactants (Palazzoli, 1974). The behaviors are intended both to counter the others' efforts to stimulate the person to change and to stimulate the others to change. They not only maintain the current pattern of incongruent interaction but also threaten the family system with schism. Symptomatic behaviors are products of a system whose participants refuse to change and refuse to risk dissolution of the system. The stronger the hubris and fear of system collapse generated and expressed in the relationship, the more extreme the symptoms. Extreme threat of schism motivates the family to seek assistance to regain a more tolerable level of oscillation along the existing lines of battle.

What makes symptom control strategies so powerful and what renders them beyond the autocorrective abilities of the system is the individual's recourse to the attributional strategy of claiming that his or her behavior is beyond self-control. The individual presents himself or herself as a victim of the behavior and of a perplexing and uncontrollable "demon" that now controls his or her behavior. The victim is thus rendered unable to change or to be changed by the efforts of others. Through this extreme strategy, the individual makes a powerful bid to at last gain advantage on the others while at the same time presents himself or herself as not intending to achieve such an end. After all, he or she does not control the behavior.

The linear attributional practices of the interaction participants lead them to attribute the victim's behavior to perverse dispositions as they attempt to stimulate the victim to change. The victim undercuts their influence attempts by completely agreeing with them and disqualifying their efforts to stimulate change by claiming to have no control over the disposition. From the victim's point of view, his or her current disability is a function of the others not being what they should have been, implying that if they only were what they are not, the victim would not be who he or she is, itself a powerful indictment intended to stimulate change and submission. While the victim owns the symptom, it is but a reciprocal of the strategies employed by the other members of the relationship to assert their dominance in the relationship. The pattern of behavior is a function of the system. The symptom is but a "logical adaptation to a deviant and illogical transpersonal system" (Palazzoli, 1974, p. 231). None of the participants in the illogical transpersonal system can change without breaking the rules of the relationship, rules that are protected by the rule of rules. All of the participants are trapped in the system they jointly created. Brilliant descriptions of the transpersonal systems that generate symptoms labeled schizophrenic are presented by Palazzoli, Boscolo, Cecchin, and Prata (1979) and Haley (1968d); anorexia nervosa, by Palazzoli (1974); and ulcers, by Jackson and Yalom (1977).

Less extreme forms of symptoms are produced by systems whose participants are victims of less extreme hubris and fear of relationship dissolution than those the above authors describe. Yet, the dynamics behind the symptoms and the generating transpersonal systems differ only in extremity. When the participants in a relationship are reasonably willing to lose the battle for relationship definition, accommodate to the others, and accept the dissolution of the relationship as a possible outcome of relationship incongruence, the strategies intended to gain unilateral control of the relationship are developed to a less extreme level, are less refractory to change, and are often amenable to negotiated settlement.

INTERVENTION STRATEGIES

Identified patients, family members whose chosen behavior strategies for relationship control threaten the family system with schism, can be treated psychologically in individual therapy, therapy groups of relative strangers, or in family system therapy. Results of studies of the effectiveness of the three intervention strategies in facilitating therapeutic change for persons whose symptoms are embedded in ongoing family interactions clearly indicate that family system intervention is the treatment of choice over individual and group interventions. In their excellent review of research on marital and family psychotherapy, Gurman and Kniskern (1978) concluded the following:

> 1. *Individual therapy for marital problems is a very ineffective treatment strategy and one that appears to produce more negative effects than alternative approaches.* . . .

2. *Couples benefit most from treatment when both partners are involved in therapy, especially when they are seen conjointly. . . .*

3. *Family therapy appears to be at least as effective and possibly more effective than individual therapy for a wide variety of problems, both apparent individual difficulties and more obvious family conflicts.* (p. 883)

Gurman and Kniskern found that family system interventions for couples produced success rates of about 66%, while individual interventions produced success rates of less than 50%. Further, deterioration effects have been found to be twice as frequent in individual treatment of marital problems (about 12%) as in family system interventions (about 6%). In evaluation studies of interventions with children who are identified patients, individual interventions, including behavioral interventions, have seldom been found to be effective in the long term, while family system interventions have been found to be highly effective in over two-thirds of the cases reported.

These clear findings are not surprising if we consider the options available to a family member successfully treated in individual interventions. If he or she is to maintain therapeutic change, the person is faced with the task of stimulating change in the redundant patterns of family interaction of which his or her symptomatic behavior is a part. The person's changed behaviors increase incongruence in the family system. Family members respond to the person's changed behaviors with efforts to maintain the status quo and in the process increase the discrepancies the person experiences, increasing still further system incongruence. Unless the therapeutically improved family member is able to exert greater power on family members and/or has greater skills in stimulating family members to change than previously, the likely outcome is the collapse of therapeutic change and the reemergence of symptomatic behaviors, often at more extreme levels. Success for the more dependent members of a family system such as young children is unlikely, and even for husband or wife it is problematic at best. A likely outcome of individual marital counseling is dissolution of the family. Individual therapy strengthens the spouses' abilities to present each other with discrepancies in their feedback to each other and induces greater willingness to dissolve the relationship, a likely formula for schism. Gurman and Kniskern (1978) document that individual therapy for marital problems does indeed increase the frequency of divorce as compared to family system interventions.

Individual treatment is the treatment of choice when the individual is not strongly embedded in an ongoing family system (older adolescents, young adults, singles, and separated, divorced, and surviving spouses), or when the continuation of the family system is not a valued outcome.

Family System Interventions

Family system interventions are described ably and in detail with many case examples by Haley (1976), Minuchin (1974), Palazzoli (1974), and Palazzoli, Boscolo, Cecchin, and Prata (1978). The discussion below focuses only on some of the more critical processes of family system interventions: entering the family system, uncovering symptom-embedded communication patterns, stimulating dialectical synthesis, and using directives.

For the family counselor to have any impact on a family's interaction patterns, the counselor must gain a position of power within the system. The family's dependence on the therapist stems most significantly from the family members' concern for the schismatic threat to the family system posed by the symptoms of the identified patient or, more generally, by the high level of conflict in the system. Therefore, the therapist must take the family's complaints seriously and not openly attempt to redefine their problem as one of communication or reciprocal interaction. The therapist must use the presenting problem or symptom as a lever to induce change in the system. Studies reviewed by Gurman and Kniskern (1978) make it clear that the therapist qualities of empathy, positive regard, and gentleness are critical especially in the beginning of therapy. Such therapist behaviors assure family members that the therapist is genuinely committed to helping them and can be trusted to view their problems and behaviors from a positive and sympathetic perspective. Introducing interventions that greatly increase the discrepancy one or more members experience before the members trust the therapist is associated with negative outcomes in therapy and loss of family members from the therapy encounter (Gurman & Kniskern, 1978, p. 875). The therapist must avoid forming a coalition with one or more family members against another member in the beginning of the encounter and must avoid implicit or explicit labeling of one or another member as in the wrong. These strategies risk stimulating the victim of the coalition or of the labeling to discontinue therapy. Family members usually come to therapy with the hidden objective of at last proving themselves right in their conflict with other members and are only too willing to draw the therapist into validating their claims. Faced with the powerful therapist sided against them, family members nullify the therapist's power by breaking off therapy.

In couple and family therapy, traditional individual therapeutic procedures intended to generate insight, such as interpretations and process meta-communications, are of negative value. These procedures implicitly or explicitly cast the recipient of the therapist's communication in a negative light by branding one behavior wrong and another right. Recourse to negative attribution to stimulate change is the bread and butter of family members in conflict. The therapist's use of such interventions traps the therapist in maneuvers in which the family members are expert and stimulates denial, disqualification, and resistance as family members react against the therapist's bid for change in order to maintain the stability of their system. Traditional interpretative interventions stimulate the system's autocorrective mechanism (already at a high level) and enmesh the therapist in the family game without prospect of stimulating transformation. The therapist must avoid being inducted into the family game and at the same time must express empathy and understanding to each member. Palazzoli, Boscolo, Cecchin, and Prata (1978) have emphasized that the therapist needs to be detached in his or her encounter with the family, noting the effects of the members' communications on each other and on his or her thoughts, feelings, and response potentials for diagnostic purposes, but not acting on them. Being drawn into the family conflict negates the therapist's ability to stimulate the family into transformation.

A critical therapist task is to identify the redundancies in the family communication pattern that are associated with identified symptoms. In order to do this, the therapist must induce the family members to communicate with one another so that they can display their communication patterns in the here-and-now interaction of the therapy setting. No matter what the content of communications, the therapist's interest is in the impact of each individual's message on the other members of the group and the patterns of communication that emerge in interaction. All family members that have a part in the behavioral redundancies that include the symptomatic behaviors need to be present in the interview. All members must be drawn into the interaction, and the therapist must direct the family members' communications to each other rather than allow them to use the therapist as a go-between, as the hub of the interaction. Haley (1976) decribes methods of inducing family interaction, drawing symptomatic behaviors into the interview, and drawing all members into the interaction.

When the therapist has identified what appears to be the communication patterns that entail symptomatic behavior, the most powerful initial intervention to begin the process of system transformation is positive connotation (Palazzoli, 1974; Palazzoli, Boscolo, Cecchin, & Prata, 1978). Positive connotation communications denote the symptom-embedded patterns of communication as positive aspects of family interaction that clearly show all parties to have the objective of maintaining the system regardless of personal cost. Positive connotation communications explicitly comment on the behaviors and motivations of all parties of the family. Positive connotation communications frame each member's part of the symptom-embedded communication pattern as positive, self-sacrificial, and sensitively intended to benefit the other members. Finally, positive connotation communications attribute each person's behavior to his or her spontaneous efforts to maintain the system and to serve the others and avoid any hint that the behaviors are compliance to the others' strategies. Palazzoli, Boscolo, Cecchin, and Prata (1978) richly describe many examples of positive connotation communications in family therapy.

The notion of positively reframing delinquency, schizophrenic behaviors, self-starvation, depression, and their interaction reciprocals in family communication patterns seems sarcastic and dynamically incorrect from the perspective of most clinical theories of abnormal behavior and psychotherapy. Symptoms are not viewed in most pathology descriptions and therapeutic systems as self-sacrificial, generous, sensitive, and spontaneous gestures intended to benefit others, nor are the often abusive, contradictory, and defensive messages of the others in the system so viewed. The reciprocal behaviors of the nonvictims in the family interaction are often seen in traditional theories as causes and intentional efforts to victimize the identified patient. However, in system interaction terms, all of these behaviors serve the function of maintaining the system and preventing its collapse. From the system interaction perspective, identifying one party's behavior as bad, as the cause of another's behavior, imposes a linear cause model of arbitrary event punctuation on the circular causal system. Positive connotation correctly identifies the circular nature of the communication pattern and its hidden function of maintaining the system. While connotating the overall pattern and the behaviors of each member negatively conforms to most theories of pathology and therapy, it directly attacks the maintenance function of the symptom-embedded communication pattern and serves to stimulate resistance, denial, and disqualification as the members rally to one another's aid to protect the system from the schismatic threat posed by the therapist's negative connotation. Even worse are statements that moralize by identifying one or another as to blame, for they stimulate countermaneuvers that increase the extremity of the symptom-embedded pattern as the members attempt to protect the system from collapse. Any statement that implicitly or explicitly connotates one member's behavior as bad automatically vindicates the others' side of the persuasive asymmetry communication pattern as correct and stimulates redoubled efforts by the accused party to avoid loss. Redoubled efforts mean a deepening of the symptom behaviors and their reciprocals in the interaction pattern.

Positive connotation places all members of the family on an equal footing as complementary and subordinate to the system. Positive connotation implies that the pattern of persuasive asymmetry in which symptomatic behaviors are embedded is in reality a pattern of accommodation. In persuasive asymmetry, each person intends to win unilateral dominance in defining the relationship by finally bringing the others to change as the person desires. Each person's behaviors are intended to stimulate the others to change and to resist the others' attempts to stimulate the person to change. Positive connotation implies that these influence strategies, including the strategies of the identified patient, are generous, spontaneous, and self-sacrificing behaviors sensitively intended to serve the needs of the others. Thus, the behaviors intended to force the others to change are cast as accommodations to the others' needs. Each finds that they are deferring to the needs of the others, and the recipients of the generous and spontaneous behaviors find that they are seen as having needs for which the generous behaviors sensitively provide resources. The recipients of the generous behaviors are thus faced with the prospect of the other person gaining power on them in the relationship by providing resources for their mysterious and unexpected needs.

Accommodating to the others is the last thing family members caught up in persuasive asymmetry intend to do, for doing so admits that the others are more powerful in the relationship and have won the struggle to define the relationship. Each unexpectedly finds him or herself to have deferred to the others rather than to have stimulated the others to defer to him or her. Each finds that he or she has unwittingly made himself or herself vulnerable to the others by having needs operative in the relationship that provide the others means for increasing his or her dependence.

The power of positive connotation communications is in the implication that symptom-related behaviors are spontaneous, generous, and sensitive accommodations that acknowledge the greater power of the other, increase interdependence, and render the recipients of the accommodations more vulnerable to future influence. Since the intentions of parties caught up in persuasive asymmetry are to be invulnerable to the others' efforts to influence them and to force the others to change, they react to positive connotation by terminating the generous behaviors and denying that they have needs for which the others can provide resources. Resistance, denial, and disqualification are directed against the continuation of the symptom-embedded pattern and are converted into forces and strategies that transform the relationship rather than maintain the symptom-embedded pattern.

Family members accept the positive connotation feedback from the therapist because of the therapist's power in the relationship, the therapist's heartfelt sincerity and obvious intent to benefit the members of the family, and his or her unquestionable expertise in deciphering the psychological meanings of behavior.

Positive connotation is a form of paradoxical symptom assignment in that it implies that the therapist wishes the parties to continue their good and generous behavior. The impact of positive connotation communications in stimulating transformation through dialectical synthesis can be intensified by directly assigning family members the task of maintaining and intensifying their symptom-related behaviors. When symptom assignment occurs in the context of positive connotation, the meaning of continued symptom-related behaviors has been shifted to that of deferring to others, and thus continuing the behaviors violates the family member's intent to unilaterally define the relationship. As a result, family members resist, deny, and disqualify the therapist's paradoxical assignments and find themselves strangely unable to continue the behaviors. In order to disqualify the therapist's attempt to make them continue their symptom-related behaviors, family members present their changed behaviors as spontaneous personal changes over which they have no control. Thus, therapeutic change is generalized and likely to be maintained in the long run. It is not only the therapist that members seek to control through their spontaneous change; they primarily seek to control each other. They present their change in their responsive treatment of each other as involuntary and spontaneous and not intended to control the others. Usually, the conflict among interactants has simply shifted to other areas and different patterns. As new patterns emerge, they in turn are subjected to dialectical synthesis, until the exasperated family members are finally willing to accept change and/or system dissolution and thus at last are equipped to negotiate accommodations to achieve more congruence in their relationship.

Haley (1976) introduced a variant of positive connotation and paradoxical symptom assignment, the technique of restraining change by doubting its wisdom. The technique partially relies on the couple's desire to manage the therapist's impression of them as competent and capable people by implying that the therapist believes that they could not tolerate behaving in a nonsymptom-related way. The technique also implies that symptom-related behaviors are accommodations that serve the needs of recipients as in positive connotation. The therapist implies that there are negative consequences of changing the symptom-embedded pattern and that such a change would be inadvisable for this particular family. To accelerate the impression that the couple cannot manage without the presenting symptoms and that the symptom-related pattern of communication serves the needs of the family's members, the therapist assigns the couple the task of drawing up lists of the possible negative consequences of therapeutic change. When the couple next appears for therapy, the therapist inquires about their list and usually finds that the couple has failed to identify any reasons why they should not change. They usually protest that they are already changing. The therapist persists in his or her sincere concern, produces a list of possible negative repercussions, and presents them to the couple. They on their part disqualify, deny, and resist the therapist's suggestions and, in the process, their resistance produces therapeutic transformation.

Directives are a key intervention tool in stimulating therapeutic change in couple and family counseling. Directives are used to stimulate changes in communication patterns and function either to induce desired behaviors through obtaining compliance with the directive or to eliminate undesired behaviors by stimulating family members to resist the directive. Haley (1976) uses directives in the interview to begin changing the communication patterns and makes out-of-therapy assignments to create new family communication patterns through their following or resisting the directives. In a similar vein, Palazzoli (1974) and Palazzoli, Boscolo, Cecchin, and Prata (1978) describe the use of family rituals, essentially extra-interview assignments based on directives, as a means of changing family communication patterns at the level of doing. The use of directives in couple and family counseling is similar to their use in individual counseling and is discussed in detail in Chapter 6.

Positive connotations, paradoxical directives, change-restraining maneuvers, and directives in couple and family counseling powerfully invoke the negation paradox and lead to the remission of symptom-related behaviors that is attributed to changes in the personal dispositions of family members. The affirmation paradox in family counseling is less evident in the writings of family system theorists and practitioners but is surely invoked through the therapist's abiding positive belief in the family and its members and the therapist's persistent efforts to stimulate the members to negotiate accommodations for their conflicts. The therapist also communicates in his or her interventions the importance and value of spontaneous self-sacrifice and generous giving to others and the ultimate truth of each family member as complementary and subordinate to a larger system—the family and, by extension, a power greater than themselves such as God (Bateson, 1972).

Therapy may be terminated with the disappearance of the symptoms early in the therapeutic encounter. The parties may begin the process of negotiating accommodation at any point, at which time the need for continuing therapy is over. Palazzoli, Boscolo, Cecchin, and Prata (1978) identify a series of transformations of the family system likely to be experienced in the process of achieving the ability to negotiate relationship accommodations. Likewise, Haley (1978) has introduced the notion of needing to stimulate one or more different abnormal family communication patterns before achieving the desired pattern that allows the negotiation of accommodations. The following is Palazzoli, Boscolo, Cecchin, and Prata's (1978) description of the stages of therapy typical with families caught up in illogical transpersonal systems that have produced schizophrenic symptoms in one of their members:

> 1. The therapists enter the family system as full-right members, owing to their avoidance of a critical attitude. Rather, they approve of and in some cases prescribe the very behavior they have observed in the family, avoiding any

judgment or definition of what or who is good or bad. Interest is shown in the relations between the parents and their respective extended families; and the family may react in three ways: with floods of information, endless trivialities, or frozen attitudes and avoidance, stupidity, and amnesia. Whatever the case, conflicts with the factions within the extended families slowly become apparent.

2. Each parent continues his attempts to make a coalition with the therapists with the purpose of differentiating between the good and the bad in the family system.

3. The therapists repulse this maneuver with a countermaneuver, declaring the identified patient to be the real leader, both good and generous, who has sacrificed himself of his own will for what he believes to be the good of the family, or of one or more of its members. The symptoms of the identified patients are thus qualified and approved of as being spontaneous behavior, decreed by his sensitivity and altruism.

4. The parents, in their relationship with the therapist, who are increasingly parentified, immediately become competitive not only with each other, but also with the identified patient. At the same time, they speak less of their respective families of origin.

5. The identified patient changes in his relationship with his parents from the position of parent to that of sibling, and begins to abandon his symptoms.

6. The parents intensify their respective attempts to create a coalition with the therapists and to receive some preferential judgment.

7. The therapists refuse to make any such statement, and are increasingly parentified.

8. The identified patient abandons his symptoms and takes a more secondary role during the sessions as well as in his home life.

9. If the family consists of more than one child, one of the identified patient's siblings often produces symptoms at this point.

10. The therapists praise this behavior, attributing it to the child's perception of his parent—fear of terminating therapy.

11. The family presents itself with all the children free of symptomatic behavior. The parents, however, escalate their competitive battle in a last attempt to induce the therapist to continue treatment.

12. At this point the therapists abdicate the role of parents, which, until now, they have accepted, and paradoxically prescribe it to the member or members of the last generation. (Palazzoli, Boscolo, Cecchin, & Prata, 1978, pp. 165–166)

CHAPTER 9

The Transformation of Therapeutic Psychology

Therapeutic psychology, both counseling and psychotherapy, is in the midst of revolutionary change. Goldfried (1980) has pulled together statements of disaffection by leading proponents of all approaches to psychotherapeutics that publicly air self-doubts, doubts that their chosen point of view has all the answers, and call for integration and cross-fertilization. Such statements would have been unspeakable even a decade ago. The inventive minds of therapeutic psychologists have created over 130 distinct approaches to therapy (Parloff, 1976; Corsini, 1981). Each system has legions of therapists who are committed to the ultimate truth of their approach and are certain of the basic erroneous perceptions of their competitors. Yet, beams of a greater truth are being seen by many adherents of every approach: despite competing claims of sole ownership of the truth, it is increasingly clear that "everybody has won and all must have prizes" (Luborsky, Singer, & Luborsky, 1975). As a result of research on therapeutic processes and outcomes, research fostered by the Boulder model of training counseling and clinical psychologists as scientist-practitioners, the evidence is in on the effectiveness of the various forms of psychotherapy, and the evidence supports only one conclusion: all systems are about equally effective! Psychoanalytic, behavioristic, and humanistic forms of psychotherapy are, in the final analysis, interchangeable. None can claim unique superiority over their competitors. While the approaches appear on the surface to be remarkably different, in function they are not. They are interchangeable.

It is important to note that the conclusion is not that psychotherapy is no more effective in fostering therapeutic change than no treatment at all, as was first asserted by Eysenck (1952). Most if not all approaches are more effective than no therapy at all. All can claim effective outcomes for two-thirds or more of their clients, well above rates of spontaneous remission (Bergin & Lambert, 1978). But on the horizon are shapes taking clearer form that contradict the claim that all are equally effective. Gurman and Kniskern (1978) amassed evidence brought together for the first time that counters the equality claim: "Everyone has *not* won, and only some must have prizes" (p. 835). For a number of problems, systems-based approaches emerge clearly superior to traditional approaches. Palazzoli, Boscolo, Cecchin, and Prata (1978) provide stunning evidence of the effectiveness of the systems interactional approach with schizophrenia, a collection of psychological problems that has been notoriously intractable to treatment with traditional therapeutic approaches.

THE FORM OF REVOLUTION: FROM THE INTRAPSYCHIC TO THE INTERACTIONAL

All traditional forms of psychotherapy rest on the premise of linear causality. They attribute aberrant behavior to intrapsychic causes, to the dispositional characteristics of the victim, and each theory presents elaborate schemes of intrapsychic dynamics to account for psychological symptoms. Each claims that the function of psychotherapy is to change these dynamics to stimulate therapeutic change. They have erroneously taken the dispositional consequences of persuasive asymmetry in interactions of persons engaged in battle for supremacy in relationship definition to be the cause of deviant interactional behavior, rather than correctly seeing the dispositional consequences as part and parcel of the deviant interactional behavior. Astute clinical observers, themselves in bondage to linear causality, have been taken in by the strategies of their clients and have accepted the impressions clients offer as their true being. Clinical theorists have focused on elaborating the intrapsychic meanings and causes of interactional behavior and have waged their own battles for supremacy against other theorists on attributional (intrapsychic) grounds, just as their clients have in their troubled interactions. They have been trapped by the tyranny of language (Palazzoli, Boscolo, Cecchin, & Prata, 1978).

If this is so, one might inquire how any system of therapy is more effective than spontaneous remission. All traditional approaches would seem to be trapped by their linear premise into joining their clients who are likewise trapped and thus to serve mainly to perpetuate the symptomatic games. The answer lies in communication paradoxes that have been intrinsic to psychotherapeutics since Freud and indeed long before Freud in the practices of supernatural healers and magnetists. The effectiveness of every traditional approach rests in its operationalization of the negation and affirmation paradoxes and the therapeutic double bind. The basic therapeutic paradoxes can be operationalized in many ways, and the agents of disease and restoration can take uncountable forms, including demons, spirits, magnetism, psychological hydraulics, irrational and rational ideas, learning potentials, distorted experiencing, various forms of cognitions, and parent, adult, and child states. The only requirement is that the therapist be able to generate client belief in the reality of the identified entities. Thus, the search for the final therapeutically true system has been carried out in the jungle of change agents, in the morass of attributed dispositional entities in which no answers lie. The real causes of effective psychotherapy, the communication paradoxes, have been protected by Palazzoli's rule of rules: one must not be aware of and must not comment on the rules of the interaction system.

The seeds for the transformation of therapeutic psychology were planted by those who turned to the transpersonal system of the family for answers about mental illness. Any therapist who ventures into the beckoning battleground of marital and family conflict armed with negative interpretations and meta-communication interventions intended to stimulate insight, armament drawn from professional training in the traditional arts of therapeutic intervention, soon learns that he or she is helpless against the highly skilled combatants in family conflict. While traditional approaches provide satisfying outcomes with families who do not have serious problems, it is with just those who need help most that the traditionally armed clinician fails most spectacularly. Two years of family and couple counseling in a parish setting thoroughly disheartened the senior author as he began to perceive that those most in need of help did not benefit from his best efforts. Instead of his well-intended efforts facilitating problem resolution, they stimulated wider swings of conflict. So often, first one, then the other spouse would present himself or herself as much improved while the other, then the one, reciprocally became more intractable, hostile, resistant, and symptom laden. In the final analysis, his efforts served to worsen the conflict. After deeply troubled families managed to extrude him from their systems, they frequently experienced dramatic schism, several times carried out with physical assault and alcoholic binges. Such behaviors managed to draw public authorities into the conflict who forceably negotiated the dissolution of the family system. Armed with traditional therapeutic skills, the therapist becomes enmeshed in the highly incongruent family system and becomes but another perpetrator and victim of the family game.

The originator of the transformation of therapeutic psychology was Gregory Bateson and his schizophrenia project at Palo Alto in the early 1950s. Bateson, himself an anthropologist, put together a most unlikely team, including Don Jackson, a psychiatrist who was writing about family homeostasis, and Jay Haley, a communication specialist (Jackson, 1968a, 1968b). Their brilliant concept of the double bind has been largely ignored or attacked as senseless by the mainstream of therapeutic psychology for three decades (Watzlawick, 1968). Current attention to their innovations is largely attributable to the introduction of paradoxical interventions, interventions that violate all rationality from the standpoint of traditional linear model clinical theories. In fact, such interventions are contra-indicated: only a sadistic clinician would openly encourage the victims of psychological problems to continue and intensify their problems! Yet, paradox works (L'Abate & Weeks, 1978; Beck & Strong, 1981; Lopez and Wambach, in press; Wright & Strong, in press). If anything exposes the limitations of traditional clinical thinking, paradoxical intervention does.

While Gregory Bateson can be credited with introducing the notion of circular causation into psychotherapeutic thinking, the same concept is embedded in behaviorism. Response chaining contains the notion that each response is at once an effect and a cause of previous and subsequent responses, and early efforts to apply behavior principles to therapeutic processes clearly presented the notion that each participant's verbal responses are at once the result of and the cause of the other's responses (Strong, 1964). Yet, these early premonitions of circular causality fell victim to arbitrary punctuation, and behavioral analysis failed to capitalize on the concept and became yet another linear approach to psychotherapeutics.

Systems level thinking leads to the observation of interaction processes. By viewing the participants in interaction as determined to control their relationships and to define them according to their purposes, their reliance on attributional and impression management tactics is exposed. Attributional differences in conflict are identified and cast into the model of persuasive asymmetry. The perceptions and behaviors of the parties are seen as influence efforts, both to persuade the other and to counter the other's persuasion. The perceptions and behaviors are seen as indicants of the participants' efforts to control others through managing impressions of their being rather than as indicants of their intrapsychic being. Interaction behaviors judged to be pathological are transformed from symptoms of puzzling intrapsychic entities needing to be excised to control strategies in need of change. While clients are trapped in their linear causal beliefs, clinicians are equipped with the higher-order concept of circular causality that allows them to generate interventions that directly stimulate therapeutic changes.

Paradoxical interventions are paradoxical (puzzling) only from the vantage of linear intrapsychic causation. The systems interaction perspective of circular causation exposes the relationship maintenance function of symptomatic behavior, and paradoxical interventions are seen to reinforce system maintenance and at the same time to undercut the persuasive asymmetry maintaining the symptomatic behavior. Paradoxical interventions generate change in the system by stimulating individuals to change tactics in their search for more effective means to gain unilateral control of the definition of the relationship. Individuals change tactics because (a) the symptoms are recast as behaviors that defer to the greater power of others in selfless service and sacrifice, (b) the symptoms are recast as accommodations that render their recipients more vulnerable in the relationship, and (c) the symptoms are stripped of their effectiveness in influencing others (therapists, family members, and others). An individual's change in tactics changes the feedback in the interaction system, and the system and its participants transform. Paradox stimulates and forces dialectical synthesis in the ongoing relationship.

The transformation of therapeutic psychology will occur as theorists and practitioners recognize the operation of the negation and affirmation paradoxes and the therapeutic double bind in the therapeutic process and devise interventions to maximize their impact in individual therapy. But in all likelihood, the transformation will also see the emergence of family and couple system interventions as the treatment of choice when feasible. Surely directly intervening in the interactions of which symptomatic behaviors are a part offers greater hope of long-term effectiveness than individual intervention, particularly when the identified patient is immersed in a family system and the continuation of the family is a valued outcome. Yet, because of the difficulties of involving all family members and the fact that all individuals spend parts of their lives outside of close family relationship, individual interventions will be frequent. With clear identification of the dynamics of individual interventions, their effectiveness should be enhanced, and spontaneous compliance with therapeutically desirable interaction behaviors should increasingly be the outcome of individual psychotherapy.

INTERACTION CONCEPTS

The transformation of therapeutic psychology requires that concepts of the basic variables controlling human behavior in transpersonal interactions be evolved and applied. Three major concepts have evolved in this book: congruence, interdependence, and attributional and impression managmnet tactics of relationship control.

Congruence

Congruence describes the extent to which the behaviors of participants in a relationship are intended to maintain or to change the current pattern of behavior in their relationship. The more that interaction behaviors are intended to stimulate change, the greater the incongruence of the relationship. Each party in a relationship endeavors to bring the relationship into congruence in line with his or her definition of what the relationship should be like because the definitions are ultimately based on the needs each wishes to have met through the relationship.

Incongruence in a relationship is a function of individual experiences of discrepancy between the other's behavior (as he or she interprets it) and the behavior the individual desires from the other (his or her definition). Discrepancy stimulates efforts to change the other, efforts that increase relationship incongruence. The impact of relationship incongruence is a function of the level and balance of interdependence in the relationship as well as elusive personal qualities such as hubris. The less the interdependence the more likely incongruence will result in the termination of the relationship. The greater the interdependence, the more likely incongruence will resolve into behavioral accommodation by one or both parties and thus result in the transformation of the relationship and of the characteristics of the parties in the relationship. The greater the hubris of the parties in the relationship— their determination to establish congruence on unilateral grounds—the less likely incongruence will resolve into accommodation and the more evident persuasive asymmetry will be in the relationship. While accommodation increases the strength of the relationship through increased interdependence, persuasive asymmetry threatens the stability of the relationship and stimulates individual behaviors that diminish the likelihood of achieving congruence. The persuasion and counterpersuasion tactics employed by the parties in persuasive asymmetry progressively increase relationship incongruence and transform both parties into self-righteous *provocateurs* and victims of unaccountable dispositional forces that prevent them from accommodating to the other's wishes. They generate hubris. To generate interaction behaviors that are classified as psychological symptoms, a relationship must be characterized by high incongruence, persuasive asymmetry, hubristic participants, and extreme interdependence often generated by an unwillingness to terminate the relationship.

Every relationship is subjected periodically to incongruence because the members of the relationship constantly change as living beings, others enter into and exit from the relationship, and the environment in which the relationship exists changes. Incongruence in a relationship provides opportunities for the participants to change, grow, and develop in positive or pathological directions (Riegel, 1976).

Interdependence

The balance of interdependence of parties in interaction is the relative levels of dependence of each participant on the other or others in the interaction. Dependence is a function of the needs of the person that are met or potentially can be met by resources available or potentially available from the other through the relationship. The balance of interdependence determines who will be most affected by incongruence in the relationship; the behavior of the most dependent party will be most affected. Greater dependence in incongruent relationships results in one of the following four behavior changes: (*a*) changes that comply to the other's wishes but are attributed to the other's greater power and thus are temporary; (*b*) changes that comply to the other's wishes but are attributed to uncontrollable (spontaneous) personal dispositions and thus will be maintained; (*c*) changes that resist the wishes of the other but are attributed to temporary external or internal causes and thus are temporary; or (*d*) changes that resist the wishes of the other but are attributed to ongoing causes that are spontaneous and beyond the person's control and thus will be maintained. The greater and more balanced the interdependence between parties, the more both will be transformed by incongruence in the relationship as they either negotiate accommodations to each other's needs or attempt to influence and counter one another in persuasive asymmetry.

Attributional and impression management tactics in incongruent relationships affect interdependence by influencing the parties' perceptions of the resources and needs available and operative in the relationship. Accommodation, behavioral compliance attributed to personal dispositions, is one of the most powerful tactics. Accommodation increases resources congruent with the more powerful member's needs, increases the dependence of the more powerful member, and thus decreases the imbalance of interdependence. Accommodation decreases incongruence in the relationship, increases the overall level of interdependence, and thus increases the likelihood of continuation of the relationship to the satisfaction and growth of all parties.

Stimulating the other into accommodation is a high priority for interactants in incongruent relationships and might be accomplished by a number of tactics, tactics that change the balance of interdependence in the relationship. A person might attempt to increase the resources the other perceives to be potentially available from the person to increase the other's dependence and thus encourage the other to accommodate with the person's wishes. A person might attempt to minimize the needs the other perceives the person to have, a tactic that might stimulate the other into accommodating to the person's wishes in an effort to increase the person's dependence on the relationship. Attempts to maximize the needs of the person that the other perceives to correspond to the other's resources might encourage the other to believe that the person can be relied upon to accommodate to the other's needs in the future and thus increase the other's dependence on the relationship. Attempts to minimize the resources the other perceives to be available from the person might encourage the other to intensify his or her presentation of deep and multifarious needs for which the person has correspondent resources, an attempt by the other to strengthen the relationship through showing his or her dependence.

A powerful subset in the management of interdependence is the use of coalitions. Parties showing coalitions in a relationship against a third combine their resources and thus intensify their collective power over the hapless victim of the coalition. Impressions of having coalitions with outside parties diminish the needs the other perceives the person showing the coalition to have that correspond to the resources of the other in the relationship and thus shift the balance of interdependence in favor of the person.

No doubt, experienced tacticians in interaction use even more subtle tactics than those described above to manage the other's impressions of needs and resources to stimulate changes in interdependence for their own purposes. The effort to manage interdependence is overlaid with concerns for sincerity as each party must be alert to purposive manipulation. Thus, tactics must be cast in powerful protestations of sincerity and heartfelt honesty. The participants must make every effort to create the impression of "being" rather than of "showing."

Attributional and Impression Management Tactics

The struggle to form and maintain a relationship is waged with attributional and impression management tactics. The utterly basic social nature of human beings is revealed in their indefatigable efforts to relate to one another, to form and maintain relationships. While the urges that give rise to this indefeasible struggle are unknowable, the effort itself is waged on attributional and impression management grounds, and the tactics used within the context of interdependence and incongruence form the personality and behavioral characteristics of each individual (Riegel, 1976).

Many attributional and impression management tactics related to interdependence and relationship incongruence are described above. The attributional tactic of spontaneous change is critical to relationship formation and maintenance. Spontaneous compliance is the tactic of accommodation. The person complies to the wishes of the other through self-adjustments that strengthen the interdependence of the relationship and set the stage for long-term congruent interaction in a mutually agreeable and growth-producing relationship. Spontaneous defiance is the most extreme tactic arising out of persuasive asymmetry. The individual defies the other's wishes through self-adjustments that render the victim impervious to the other's efforts to stimulate accommodation. While the other is prevented from rendering the relationship to his or her needs, the tactic also removes the potential for the victim to achieve his or her own purposes. Both are prevented from accommodating.

A critical issue is what tactics invite and prevent accommodation. Attributional tactics that invite accommodation draw awareness away from the forces of compliance and to positive personal dispositions that can be seen as the causes of change, like growing maturity, capabilities, responsibility, and selfless giving. Tactics that encourage accommodation propose that unwanted behaviors are motivated by a sincere desire to benefit the other, or perhaps are due to external causes or misguided but superficial personal causes that are themselves results of unfortunate experiences. Such attributions undercut persuasive asymmetry, free undesired behaviors for change, and provide the person the opportunity to gain personal esteem through accommodation. Empathy, with its automatic attributional bias that frames unwanted behaviors as results of underlying positive intentions or external temporary causes and desired behaviors as expressions of positive dispositions, carries out the attributional tactics necessary to invite accommodation. Empathy is a function of a positive affectional disposition toward the other. Little wonder that accommodation is prevalent in affectionate marital and parent−child relationships. Persons with positive attitudes toward us are the sources of positive personal development and the architects of positive personal self-perception and growth. The source of the indefatigable human search for affectionate interactants lies here, as well as the transforming power of a personal relationship with a loving supreme being.

Attributional tactics that prevent accommodation directly and obviously demand compliance, imply that the behavior to be changed is caused by intrinsic and disgusting personal dispositions, or imply that the behavior to be desired is beyond the spontaneous capacities of the individual. Little wonder that persuasive asymmetry tends to grow in troubled relationships. The very tactics chosen to stimulate change prevent accommodation and allow the other to change only as direct and acknowledged compliance to the person or as spontaneous defiance. The tactics generate hubris. Direct demands to change may generate compliance, but they prevent the attribution of compliance to personal and spontaneous causes and thus form no basis for a continuing and growing relationship or for positive self-attribution.

The above notions suggest that indirection and covert strategies should be dominant in effective relationships, and that participants should be reluctant to see themselves as manipulating and influencing others. Palazzoli's rule of rules would seem to have the function of allowing personal attribution of interaction behaviors, behaviors that are in fact compliance or defiance to others. Strongly bonded voluntary relationships simply cannot be developed and maintained unless attention is diverted away from the influence process. Nor can persons acquire valued *or* destructive personal dispositions.

INTERACTION INTERVENTION STRATEGIES

The application of interaction concepts to individual, group, and family system interventions is described in detail in Chapters 6, 7, and 8 and elsewhere (Strong, 1982). All interventions begin with establishing a working level of interdependence between therapist and client. The major source of client dependence on the therapist is the client's needs associated with the symptoms and the resources the client perceives to be available to meet these needs through a relationship with the therapist. Client needs arise from threats of relationship schism created by the symptoms as well as from the personally punishing aspects of symptomatic interaction behaviors. The thearpist's dependence on the client is a function of the therapist's evangelical fervor to convert the suffering other to his or her version of the good life.

In the initiation of the encounter, the therapist shows sincere interest in the welfare of the client and in hearing his or her story and avoids feedback to the client that would arouse discrepancy. The therapist complies initially with the relationship definition proposed by the client to increase the client's dependence in the relationship. Such compliance promises the resources the client desires from the relationship. The therapist pays careful attention to the client's interaction behaviors and the feelings, thoughts, and action potentials the client's behaviors stimulate in the therapist, but the therapist does not act on these behaviors. Instead, the therapist shows interest in and empathy with the client's plight. The therapist searches for redundancies in the patterns of interaction among the client's behavior, the behavior aroused in the therapist, and, if the client collectivity is composed of more than one person, the behaviors of the others. The client's presentation of past events provides further opportunities to observe redundancies in behavior, both in the patterns described and in the description itself. The initiation of the encounter enhances client dependence on the therapist and provides information for a tentative diagnosis of the nature of the problem and how it might be resolved.

The structure of the encounter is cast during its initiation. Attention is focused on the client and drawn away from the therapist. Focusing on the client and redirecting client statements about the therapist's behavior invoke an unspoken ban on meta-communication about the therapist's behavior. As the ban is successfully developed, the therapist gives the impression that the client is responsible for his or her own change, and attention is drawn to the uncontrollable causal agent that will inevitably lead to change. This redirection of responsibility for change further draws attention away from the therapist's role in generating change and establishes a context for spontaneous compliance.

As the structure of the encounter is formed, the therapist begins the task of transforming the relationship to requiring healthy client interaction behaviors and thus the transformation of the client. The therapist introduces incongruence into the relationship within an attributional context that encourages the client to accommodate the therapist's wishes. The therapist violates the persuasive asymmetry the client proposes and expects to develop in his or her interaction with the therapist. If the collective client is composed of more than one individual, they strive to induct the therapist into their ongoing pattern of persuasive asymmetry. The therapist is careful to violate persuasive asymmetry in ways that reinforce the maintenance of the relationship among clients and between client and therapist and stimulate dialectical synthesis.

The therapist's positive attitude toward the client, made operative through his or her empathic responses, and the implicit and/or explicit structuring of the relationship in the initiation of the encounter, introduce the negation and affirmation paradoxes. The therapist escalates the power of the paradoxes by positively connoting the symptom-laden redundant behavior patterns observed in the interaction between client and therapist and with others present or not present in the interaction. The therapist introduces positive connotation with heartfelt sincerity but is careful not to positively connote client behavior until the client and therapist have interacted for a sufficient duration for the client to believe that the therapist's impressions are based on a careful analysis of the situation. The therapist enhances the negation paradox further by directing the client to continue in his or her self-sacrificing symptomatic behaviors both within and outside of the interview. The directives may be explicit and overt symptom assignments, or implicit and covert symptom assignments such as abiding and intent interest in the client's suffering and empathic responses that deepen the client's symptomatic feelings. The therapist may direct the client to behave in and out of the interview in ways that require the client to violate the symptom-embedded behavior patterns, being careful to draw attention away from the intended effect of the directives, perhaps by emphasizing the need to observe and explore communications between the client and others.

In interventions with individual clients, the therapist might meta-communicate about the client's behavior patterns and interpret their meanings with negative attributions. These techniques must occur in the context of implicit and/or explicit directives to continue symptomatic patterns. Negative interpretations posit causes for behaviors that are not intrinsic to the client's core person but are distortions of the client's basic character induced by external historical experiences. The implicit and/or explicit directives to continue the symptoms disrupt the persuasive asymmetry maintaining the symptoms. Drawing attention to changeable personal causes of the behaviors and away from the therapist's efforts to discourage the continuation of the undesired behaviors further enables spontaneous compliance.

The therapist intensifies the affirmation paradox by teaching the client what behaviors are desirable in interactions through modeling the behaviors in the interview and through self-disclosure, metaphors, and direct instruction. The teaching includes identification of a personal and spontaneous agent, such as an emerging capability or actualization, that is responsible for the client's adoption of the desired behaviors, and thus draws attention away from the therapist's role in gaining client compliance and to an agent that works beyond the client's will and effort.

Because the client is prevented from being aware of and commenting on the therapist's influence and the therapist's contradictory and paradoxical communications, and due to the greater power of the therapist in the relationship, the client adopts the behaviors proposed by the therapist and attributes the change to the agent identified in the process. The client extracts himself or herself from the therapeutic encounter with the tactic of accommodation and thus neutralizes the therapist's power advantage. The client is changed in fundamental ways and is a new and different person whose personal strengths no longer require the services of a therapist, and the therapeutic relationship dissolves. The impact of interaction strategies on clients was well expressed by a client treated for depression with brief psychotherapy that emphasized positive connotation: ''I am a different person now, at a different place, so (I am) not distressed'' (Beck & Strong, 1981).

References

Abelson, R. P., Aronson, E., McGuire, W. J., Newcomb, T. M., Rosenberg, M. J., & Tannenbaum, P. H. (Eds.). *Theories of cognitive consistency: A sourcebook.* Chicago: Rand McNally, 1968.

Adams, J. E. *Competent to counsel.* Grand Rapids, MI: Baker Book House, 1970.

Adams, J. S. Inequity in social exchange. In L. Berkowitz (Ed.) *Advances in experimental social psychology,* Vol. 2. New York: Academic Press, 1965.

Albert, S., & Kessler, S. Ending social encounters. *Journal of Experimental Social Psychology,* 1978, 14, 541−553.

Aldous, J. Family interaction patterns. *Annual Review of Sociology,* 1977, 3, 105−135.

Anchin, J. C., & Kiesler, D. J. (Eds.) *Handbook of interpersonal psychotherapy.* New York: Pergamon, 1981.

Archer, R. L., & Berg, J. H. Disclosure reciprocity and its limits: A reactance analysis. *Journal of Experimental Social Psychology,* 1978, 14, 527−540.

Arkin, R. M., Gleason, J. M., & Johnston, S. Effect of perceived choice, expected outcome, and observed outcome of an action on the causal attributions of actors. *Journal of Experimental Social Psychology,* 1976, 12, 151−158.

Aronson, E. The theory of cognitive dissonance: A current perspective. In L. Berkowitz (Ed.) *Advances in experimental social psychology,* Vol. 4. New York: Academic Press, 1969.

Aronson, E., & Carlsmith, J. M. Experimentation in social psychology. In G. Lindzey & E. Aronson (Eds.) *The handbook of social psychology,* Vol. 2, 2nd ed. Reading, MA: Addison-Wesley, 1968.

Aronson, E., Turner, J., & Carlsmith, J. M. Communicator credibility and communication discrepancy as determinants of opinion change. *Journal of Abnormal and Social Psychology,* 1963, 67, 31−36.

Asch, S. Opinions and social pressure. *Scientific American,* 1955, 11, 32.

Atkinson, D. R., & Carskaddon, G. A prestigious introduction, psychological jargon, and perceived counselor credibility. *Journal of Counseling Psychology,* 1975, 22, 180−186.

Auerswald, M. C. Differential reinforcing power of restatement and interpretation on client production of affect. *Journal of Counseling Psychology,* 1974, 21, 9−14.

Austin, A. W. The functional autonomy of psychotherapy. In J. R. Braun (Ed.) *Clinical psychology in transition.* Cleveland: Howard Allen, 1961.

Back, K. Influence through social communication. *Journal of Abnormal and Social Psychology,* 1951, 46, 9−23.

Bandler, R., Grinder, J., & Satir, V. *Changing with families*. Palo Alto, CA: Science and Behavior Books, 1976.

Barnabie, F., Cormier, W. H., and Nye, S. Determining the effects of three counselor verbal responses on client verbal behavior. *Journal of Counseling Psychology*, 1974, 21, 355–359.

Bateson, G. *Steps to an ecology of mind*. New York: Ballantine Books, 1972.

Batson, C. D. Attribution as a mediator of bias in helping. *Journal of Personality and Social Psychology*, 1975, 32, 455–466.

Baumeister, R. F., & Jones, E. E. When self-presentation is constrained by the target's knowledge: Consistency and compensation. *Journal of Experimental Social Psychology*, 1978, 36, 608–613.

Bayes, M. A. Behavioral cues of interpersonal warmth. *Journal of Consulting and Clinical Psychology*, 1972, 39, 333–339.

Beck, J. T., & Strong, S. R. *Positive Connotation: Stimulating Therapeutic Change with Paradoxical Interpretations*. Unpublished manuscript, Virginia Commonwealth University, 1981.

Becker, J. F. & Munz, D. C. Extraversion and reciprocation of interviewer disclosures. *Journal of Consulting and Clinical Psychology*, 1975, 43, 593.

Becvar, R. Paradoxical double binds in human-relations training. *Counselor Education and Supervision*, 1978, 18, 36–44.

Bednar, R. L., & Kaul, T. J. Experiential group research: Current perspectives. In S.L. Garfield & A. E. Bergin (Eds.) *Handbook of psychotherapy and behavior change: An empirical analysis*, 2nd Ed. New York: Wiley, 1978.

Bednar, R. L., & Parker, C. A. Client susceptibility to persuasion and counseling outcome. *Journal of Counseling Psychology*, 1969, 16, 415–420.

Bem, D. J. Self-perception theory. In L. Berkowitz (Ed.) *Advances in experimental social psychology*, Vol. 6. New York: Academic Press, 1972.

Benson, J. S., & Kennelly, K. J. Learned helplessness: The result of uncontrollable reinforcements or uncontrollable aversive stimuli? *Journal of Personality and Social Psychology*, 1976, 34, 138–145.

Benware, D., & Deci, E. L. Attitude change as a function of the inducement for espousing a proattitudinal communication. *Journal of Experimental Social Psychology*, 1975, 11, 271–278.

Bergin, A. E. The effect of dissonant persuasive communications upon changes in a self-referring attitude. *Journal of Personality*, 1962, 30, 423–438.

Bergin, A. E., & Lambert, M. J. The evaluation of therapeutic outcomes. In S. L. Garfield & A. E. Bergin (Eds.) *Handbook of psychotherapy and behavior change: An empirical analysis*, 2nd ed. New York: Wiley, 1978.

Berscheid, E. Opinion change and communicator-communicatee similarity and dissimilarity. *Journal of Personality and Social Psychology*, 1966, 4, 670–680.

Berscheid, E., & Walster, E. *Interpersonal attraction*. Reading, MA: Addison-Wesley, 1969.

Berscheid, E., & Walster, E. H. *Interpersonal attraction*, 2nd ed. Reading, MA: Addison-Wesley, 1978.

Beutler, L.E. Attitude similarity in marital therapy. *Journal of Consulting and Clinical Psychology*, 1971, 37, 298–301.

Beutler, L. E., Jobe, A. M., & Elkins, D. Outcomes in group psychotherapy: Using persuasion theory to increase treatment efficiency. *Journal of Consulting and Clinical Psychology,* 1974, 42, 547−553.

Beutler, L. E., Johnson, D. T., Neville, C. W., Jr., Elkins, D., & Jobe, A. M. Attitude similarity and therapist credibility as predictors of attitude change and improvement in psychotherapy. *Journal of Consulting and Clinical Psychology,* 1975, 43, 90−91.

Bieber, M. R., Patton, M. J., & Fuhriman, A. J. A metalanguage analysis of counselor and client verb usage in counseling. *Journal of Counseling Psychology,* 1977, 24, 264−271.

Binderman, R. M., Fretz, B. R., Scott, N. A., & Abrams, M. H. Effects of interpreter credibility and discrepancy level of results on responses to test results. *Journal of Counseling Psychology,* 1972, 19, 399−403.

Blum, M. L., & Balinsky, B. *Counseling and psychology.* New York: Prentice-Hall, 1951.

Bochner, S., & Insko, C. A. Communicator discrepancy, source credibility, and opinion change. *Journal of Personality and Social Psychology,* 1966, 4, 614−621.

Bockner, J. Self-esteem, self-consciousness, and task performence: Replications, extensions, and possible explanations. *Journal of Personality and Social Psychology,* 1979a, 37, 447−461.

Bockner, J. The effects of self-esteem, success & failure, and self-consciousness on task performance. *Journal of Personality and Social Psychology,* 1979b, 37, 1732−1741.

Bockner, J. & Hulton, B. How to reverse the vicious cycle of low self-esteem: The importance of attention focus. *Journal of Experimental Social Psychology,* 1978, 14, 564−578.

Bohn, Jr., M. J. Therapist responses to hostility and dependency as a function of training. *Journal of Consulting Psychology,* 1967, 31, 195−198.

Bordin, E. S. *Psychology counseling,* 2nd ed. New York: Appleton-Century-Crofts, 1968.

Borgida, E. Scientific deduction—Evidence is not necessarily informative: A reply to Wells and Harvey. *Journal of Personality and Social Psychology,* 1978, 36, 477−482.

Bradford, L. P., Gibb, J. R., & Benne, K. D. (Eds.) *T-group therapy and laboratory method.* New York: Wiley, 1964.

Braucht, G. N. Immediate effects of self-confrontation on the self-concept. *Journal of Consulting and Clinical Psychology,* 1970, 35, 95−101.

Braver, S. L., Linder, D. E., Corwin, T. T., & Cialdini, R. B. Some conditions that affect admissions of attitude change. *Journal of Experimental Social Psychology,* 1977, 13, 565−576.

Brehm, J. *A theory of psychological reactance.* New York: Academic Press, 1966.

Brehm, J. W. Attitude Change from threat to attitudinal freedom. In A. G. Greenwald, T. C. Brock, and T. M. Ostrom (Eds.) *Psychological foundations of attitudes.* New York: Academic Press, 1968.

Brehm, J. W., & Cohen, A. R. *Exploration in cognitive dissonance.* New York: Wiley, 1962.

Brehm, J. W., & Crocker, J. C. An experiment on hunger. In J. W. Brehm & A. E. Cohen, *Explorations in cognitive dissonance.* New York: Wiley, 1962. Pp. 133−137.

Brehm, J. W., & Leventhal, G. S. An experiment on the effect of commitment. In J. W. Brehm & A. R. Cohen, *Explorations in cognitive dissonance.* New York: Wiley, 1962. Pp. 192−198.

Brink, J. H. Effect of interpersonal communication on attraction. *Journal of Personality and Social Psychology,* 1977, 35, 783–790.

Brock, T. C. Cognitive restructuring and attitude change. *Journal of Abnormal and Social Psychology,* 1962, 64, 264–271.

Brock, T. C., & Buss, A. H. Dissonance, aggression, and evaluation of pain. *Journal of Abnormal and Social Psychology,* 1962, 65, 197–202.

Brown, I. Jr., & Inouye, D. K. Learned helplessness through modeling: The role of perceived similarity in competence. *Journal of Personality and Social Psychology,* 1978, 36, 900–908.

Browning, G. J. An analysis of the effects of therapist prestige and levels of interpretation on client response in the initial phase of psychotherapy. Doctoral dissertation, University of Houston, 1966. *Dissertation Abstracts,* 1966, 26, 4803.

Bulman, R. J., & Wortman, C. B. Attributions of blame and coping in the "real world": Severe accident victims react to their lot. *Journal of Personality and Social Psychology,* 1977, 35, 351–363.

Byrne, D. Interpersonal attraction and attitude similarity. *Journal of Abnormal and Social Psychology,* 1961, 62, 713–715.

Byrne, D., & Blaylock, B. Some similarity of attitudes between husbands & wives. *Journal of Abnormal and Social Psychology,* 1963, 67, 636–640.

Byrne, D., Griffitt, W., & Golightly, C. Prestige as a factor in determining the effect of attitude similarity–dissimilarity on attraction. *Journal of Personality,* 1966, 34, 434–444.

Calder, B. J., Ross, M., & Insko, C. A. Attitude change and attitude attribution: Effects of incentive, choice and consequences. *Journal of Personality and Social Psychology,* 1973, 25, 84–99.

Carlsmith, J. M., Collins, B. E., & Helmreich, R. L. Studies in forced compliance: I. The effect of pressure for compliance on attitude change produced by face-to-face role playing and anonymous essay writing. *Journal of Personality and Social Psychology,* 1966, 4, 1–13.

Carlson, E. R. Attitude change through modification of attitude structure. *Journal of Abnormal and Social Psychology,* 1956, 52, 256–261.

Carver, C. S., & Scheier, M. F. Self-focusing effects of dispositional self-consciousness: mirror presence, and audience presence. *Journal of Personality and Social Psychology,* 1978, 36, 324–332.

Casciani, J. M. Influence of model's race and sex on interviewers' self-disclosure. *Journal of Counseling Psychology,* 1978, 25, 435–440.

Cash, T. F., Begley, P. J., McCown, D. A., & Weise, B. C. When counselors are heard but not seen: Initial impact of physical attractiveness. *Journal of Counseling Psychology,* 1975, 22, 273–279.

Cash, T. F., & Kehr, J. Influence of nonprofessional counselors' physical attractiveness and sex on perceptions of counselor behavior. *Journal of Counseling Psychology,* 1978, 25, 336–342.

Cash, T. F., & Salzbach, R. F. The beauty of counseling: Effects of counselor physical attractiveness and self-disclosures on perceptions of counselor behavior. *Journal of Counseling Psychology,* 1978, 25, 283–291.

Cavior, N., & Marabotto, C. M. Monitoring verbal behaviors in a dyadic interaction. *Journal of Consulting and Clinical Psychology,* 1976, 44, 68–76.

Chaikin, A. L., & Darley, J. M. Victim or perpetrator? Defensive attribution of responsibility and the need for order and justice. *Journal of Personality and Social Psychology*, 1972, 25, 268–275.

Chaiken, A. L., & Derlega, V. J. Liking for the norm breaker in self-disclosure. *Journal of Personality*, 1974a, 42, 117–129.

Chaiken, A.L., & Derlega, V. J. V. Variables affecting the appropriateness of self-disclosure. *Journal of Consulting and Clinical Psychology*, 1974b, 558–593.

Chaikin, A. L., Derlega, V. J., Bayma, B. & Shaw, J. Neuroticism and disclosure reciprocity. *Journal of Consulting and Clinical Psychology*, 1975, 43, 13–19.

Chaikin, A. L., Derlega, V. J., & Miller, S. J. Effects of room environment on self-disclosure in a counseling analogue. *Journal of Counseling Psychology*, 1976, 23, 479–481.

Cialdini, R. B., Braver, S. L., & Lewis, S. K. Attributional bias and the easily persuaded other. *Journal of Personality and Social Psychology*, 1974, 30, 631–637.

Cialdini, R. B., Levy, A., Herman, C. R., & Evenbeck, C. Attitude politics: The strategy of moderation. *Journal of Personality and Social Psychology*, 1973, 25, 100–108.

Cialdini, R. B., & Mirels, H. L. Sense of personal control and attributions about yielding and resisting persuasive targets. *Journal of Personality and Social Psychology*, 1976, 33, 395–402.

Claiborn, C. D. Counselor verbal intervention, nonverbal behavior and social power. *Journal of Counseling Psychology*, 1979, 26, 378–383.

Claiborn, C. D., & Schmidt, L. D. Effects of presession information on the perception of the counselor in an interview. *Journal of Counseling Psychology*, 1977, 24, 259–263.

Claiborn, C. D., Ward, S. R., & Strong, S. R. Effects of congruence between counselor interpretations and client beliefs. *Journal of Counseling Psychology*, 1981, 28, 101–109.

Cohen, A. R. Upward communication in experimentally created hierarchies. *Human Relations*, 1958, 11, 41–53.

Cohen, A. R. An experiment on small rewards for discrepant compliance and attitude change. In J. W. Brehm & A. R. Cohen, *Explorations in cognitive dissonance*. New York: Wiley, 1962. Pp. 73–78.

Cohen, A. R. Changing small-group communication networks. *Administrative Science Quarterly*, 1962, 6, 443–462.

Cohen, A. R., Greenbaum, C. W., & Mansson, H. H. Commitment to social deprivation and verbal conditioning. *Journal of Abnormal and Social Psychology*, 1963, 67, 410–422.

Cohen, A. R., & Latané, B. An experiment on choice in commitment to counterattitudinal behavior. In J. W. Brehm & A. R. Cohen, *Explorations in cognitive dissonance*. New York: Wiley, 1962. Pp. 88–91.

Cook, T. E. The influence of client–counselor value similarity on change in meaning during brief counseling. *Journal of Counseling Psychology*, 1966, 13, 77–81.

Cooper, J., Fazio, R. H., & Rhodewalt, F. Dissonance and humor: Evidence for the undifferentiated nature of dissonance arousal. *Journal of Personality and Social Psychology*, 1978, 36, 280–285.

Cooper, J., & Jones, R. A. Self-esteem and consistency as determinants of anticipatory opinion change. *Journal of Personality and Social Psychology*, 1970, 14, 312–320.

Cooper, J., Zanna, M. P., & Taves, P. A. Arousal as a necessary condition for attitude change following induced compliance. *Journal of Personality and Social Psychology,* 1978, 36, 1101−1106.

Corsini, R. (Ed.). *Handbook of innovative psychotherapies.* New York: Wiley, 1981.

Cozby, P. C. Self disclosure: A literature review. *Psychological Bulletin,* 1973, 79, 73−91.

Crowder, J. E. Relationship between therapist and client interpersonal behaviors and psychotherapy outcome. *Journal of Counseling Psychology,* 1972, 19, 68−75.

Daher, D. M., & Banikiotes, P. G. Interpersonal attraction and rewarding aspects of disclosure content and level. *Journal of Personality and Social Psychology,* 1976, 33, 492−496.

Darley, S. A., & Cooper, J. Cognitive consequences of forced noncompliance. *Journal of Personality and Social Psychology,* 1972, 24, 321−326.

Davis, J. D. Effects of communication about interpersonal processes on the evolution of self-disclosure in dyads. *Journal of Personality and Social Psychology,* 1977, 35, 31−37.

Davis, J. D. When boy meets girl: Sex roles and the negotiation of intimacy in an acquaintance exercise. *Journal of Personality and Social Psychology,* 1978, 36, 684−692.

Davis, J. D., & Perkowitz, W. T. Consequences of responsiveness in dyadic interaction: Effects of probability of response and proportion of content-related responses on interpersonal attraction. *Journal of Personality and Social Psychology,* 1979, 37, 534−550.

Davis, J. D., & Skinner, A. E. G. Reciprocity of self-disclosure in interviewers: Modeling or social exchange? *Journal of Personality and Social Psychology,* 1974, 29, 779−784.

DeCarufel, A., & Schopler, J. Evaluation of outcome improvement resulting from threats and appeals. *Journal of Personality and Social Psychology,* 1979, 37, 662−673.

Deci, E. L. Effects of externally mediated rewards on intrinsic motivation. *Journal of Personality and Social Psychology,* 1971, 18, 105−115.

Deci, E. L. Intrinsic motivation, extrinsic reinforcement, and inequity. *Journal of Personality and Social Psychology,* 1972, 22, 113−120.

Deci, E. L. *Intrinsic motivation.* New York: Plenum Press, 1975.

Dell, D. M. Counselor power base, influence attempt, and behavior change in counseling. *Journal of Counseling Psychology,* 1973, 20, 399−405.

Dell, D. M., & Schmidt, L. D. Behavioral cues to counselor expertness. *Journal of Counseling Psychology,* 1976, 23, 197−201.

Derlega, V. J., Harris, M. S., & Chaikin, A. L. Self-disclosure reciprocity, liking, and the deviant. *Journal of Experimental Social Psychology,* 1973, 9, 277−284.

Derlega, V. J., Lovell, R., & Chaikin, A. L. Effects of therapist disclosure and its perceived appropriateness on client self-disclosure. *Journal of Consulting and Clinical Psychology,* 1976, 44, 866.

DeVellis, R. F., DeVellis, B. M., & McCauley, C. Vicarious acquisition of learned helplessness. *Journal of Personality and Social Psychology,* 1978, 36, 894−899.

Diener, C. I., & Dweck, C. S. An analysis of learned helplessness: Continuous changes in performance, strategy and achievement cognition following failure. *Journal of Personality and Social Psychology,* 1978, 36, 451−462.

Diener, E., & Srull, T. K. Self-awareness, psychological perspective, and self-reinforcement in relation to personal and social standards. *Journal of Personality and Social Psychology,* 1979, 37, 413−423.

Dienstbier, R. A. Attribution, socialization, and moral decision making. In J. H. Harvey, W. Ickes, & R. F. Kidd (Eds.) *New directions in attribution research,* Vol. 2. Hillsdale, NJ: Erlbaum, 1978.

Dietzel, C. S., & Abeles, N. Client−therapist complementarity and therapeutic outcome. *Journal of Counseling Psychology,* 1975, 22, 264−272.

Dixon, D. N., & Claiborn, C. D. *Effects of perceived need and commitment on influence in career counseling.* Unpublished manuscript, University of Nebraska-Lincoln, 1980.

Dollinger, S. J., & Thelen, M. H. Overjustification and children's intrinsic motivation: Comparative effects of four rewards. *Journal of Personality and Social Psychology,* 1978, 36, 1259−1269.

Doster, J. A., & Brooks, S. J. Interviewer disclosure modeling, information revealed, and interviewer verbal behavior. *Journal of Consulting and Clinical Psychology,* 1974, 42, 420−426.

Drachman, D., DeCarufel, A., & Insko, C. A. The extra credit effect of interpersonal attraction. *Journal of Experimental Social Psychology,* 1978, 14, 458−465.

Durant, W. *The age of faith.* New York: Simon & Schuster, 1950.

Durant, W., & Durant, A. *The age of reason begins.* New York: Simon & Schuster, 1961.

Duval, S., & Wicklund, R. A. *A theory of objective self awareness.* New York: Academic Press, 1972.

Duval, S., & Wicklund, R. A. Effects of objective self-awareness on attribution of causality. *Journal of Experimental Social Psychology,* 1973, 9, 17−31.

Dweck, C. S. The role of expectations and attributions in the alleviation of learned helplessness. *Journal of Personality and Social Psychology,* 1975, 31, 674−685.

Dyck, R. J., & Rule, B. G. Effect on retaliation of causal attributions concerning attack. *Journal of Personality and Social Psychology,* 1978, 36, 521−529.

Eagly, A. H., & Whitehead, G. I. III. Effect of choice on receptivity to favorable and unfavorable evaluations of oneself. *Journal of Personality and Social Psychology,* 1972, 22, 223−230.

Edwards, B. C., & Edgerly, J. W. Effects of counselor−client congruence on counseling outcome in brief counseling. *Journal of Counseling Psychology,* 1970, 17, 313−318.

Ehrlich, H. J., & Graeven, D. B. Reciprocal self-disclosure in a dyad. *Journal of Experimental Social Psychology,* 1971, 7, 389−400.

Eisen, S. V. Actor-observer differences in informational inference and causal attribution. *Journal of Personality and Social Psychology,* 1979, 37, 261−272.

Ellis, A. *Reason and emotion in psychotherapy.* New York: Lyle Stuart, 1962.

Enzle, M. E., & Ross, J. M. Increasing and decreasing intrinsic interest with contingent rewards: A test of cognitive evaluation theory. *Journal of Experimental Social Psychology,* 1978, 14, 588−597.

Eshbaugh, R. N. Frustration, fun and folly. In C. Hatcher & P. Himelstein (Eds.) *The handbook of gestalt therapy.* New York: Jason Aronson, 1976.

Eysenck, H. J. The effects of psychotherapy: An evaluation. *Journal of Consulting Psychology,* 1952, 16, 319−324.

Festinger, L. *A theory of cognitive dissonance.* Evanston, IL: Row, Peterson, 1957.

Festinger, L. A., & Carlsmith, J. M. Cognitive consequences of forced compliance. *Journal of Abnormal and Social Psychology,* 1959, 58, 203–210.

Festinger, L., Pepitone, A., & Newcomb, T. Some consequences of deindividuation in a group. *Journal of Abnormal and Social Psychology,* 1952, 47, 382–389.

Festinger, L., Riecken, H. W., & Schachter, S. *When prophecy fails.* New York: Harper, 1956.

Firestone, I. J. Insulted and provoked: The effects of choice and provocation on hostility and aggression. In P. G. Zimbardo (Ed.) *The cognitive control of motivation.* Glenview,IL: Scott, Foresman, 1969.

Fischer, J., Paveza, G. J., Kickertz, N. S., Hubbard, L. J., & Grayston, S. B. The relationship between theoretical orientation and therapists' empathy, warmth, and genuineness. *Journal of Counseling Psychology,* 1975, 22, 399–403.

Fisher, J. D. & Nadler, A. Effect of donor resources on recipient self-esteem and self-help. *Journal of Experimental Social Psychology,* 1976, 12, 139–150.

Folger, R., Rosenfield, D., & Hays, R. P. Equity and intrinsic motivation: The role of choice. *Journal of Personality and Social Psychology,* 1978, 36, 557–564.

Frank, J. D. *Persuasion and healing.* Baltimore: Johns Hopkins, 1961.

Frank, J. D. *Persuasion and healing,* rev. ed. Baltimore: Johns Hopkins, 1973.

Frankel, A., & Snyder, M. L. Poor performance following unsolvable problems: Learned helplessness or egotism? *Journal of Personality and Social Psychology,* 1978, 36, 1415–1423.

Freedman, J. L. Involvement, discrepancy, and change. *Journal of Abnormal and Social Psychology,* 1964, 69, 290–295.

Freeman, H. R. Effects of positive and negative feedback and degree of discrepancy on responses to test results. *Journal of Counseling Psychology,* 1973, 20, 571–572.

French, J., & Raven, B. The bases of social power. In D. Cartwright (Ed.) *Studies in social power.* Ann Arbor: Institute for Social Research, 1959.

Frey, D. Reactions to success and failure in public and private conditions. *Journal of Experimental Social Psychology,* 1978, 14, 172–179.

Friedland, N. Social influence via threats. *Journal of Experimental Social Psychology,* 1976, 12, 552–563.

Fromm, E., & Shor, R. E. (Eds.) *Hypnosis: Research developments and perspectives.* Chicago: Aldine, 1972.

Gaes, G. G., Kalle, R. J., & Tedeschi, J. T. Impression management in the forced compliance situation. *Journal of Experimental Social Psychology,* 1978, 14, 439–510.

Gaes, G. G., & Tedeschi, J. T. An evaluation of self-esteem and impression management theories of anticipatory belief change. *Journal of Experimental Social Psychology,* 1978, 14, 579–587.

Gelman, R., & McGinley, H. Interpersonal liking and self-disclosure. *Journal of Consulting and Clinical Psychology,* 1978, 46, 1549–1551.

Gelso, C. J., & McKenzie, J. D. Effect of information on students' perceptions of counseling and their willingness to seek help. *Journal of Counseling Psychology,* 1973, 20, 406–411.

Gerard, H. B. Basic features of commitment. In R. P. Abelson, E. Aronson, W. J.

McGuire, T. M. Newcomb, M. J. Rosenberg, & P. H. Tannenbaum (Eds.) *Theories of cognitive consistency: A sourcebook*. Chicago: Rand McNally, 1968.

Giannandrea, V., & Murphy, K. Similarity self-disclosure and return for a second interview. *Journal of Counseling Psychology*, 1973, 20, 545−548.

Gibbons, F. X. Sexual standards and reactions to pornography: Enhancing behavioral consistency through self-focused attention. *Journal of Personality and Social Psychology*, 1978, 36, 976−987.

Glass, D. C. Changes in liking as a means of reducing cognitive discrepancies between self-esteem and aggression. *Journal of Personality*, 1964, 32, 531−549.

Glasser, W. *Reality therapy: A new approach to psychiatry*. New York: Harper & Row, 1965.

Goethals, G. R. Consensus and modality in the attribution process: The role of similarity and information. *Journal of Personality and Social Psychology*, 1972, 21, 84−92.

Goethals, G. R. An attributional analysis of some social influence phenomena. In J. H. Harvey, W. J. Ickes, and R. F. Kidd, *New directions in attribution research*, Vol. 1. Hillsdale, NJ: Erlbaum, 1976.

Goethals, G. R., & Cooper, J. Role of intention and post behavioral consequence in the arousal of cognitive dissonance. *Journal of Personality and Social Psychology*, 1972, 23, 293−301.

Goethals, G. R., & Nelson, R. A. Similarity in the influence process: The belief−value distinction. *Journal of Personality and Social Psychology*, 1973, 25, 117−122.

Goethals, G. R., & Reckman, R. F. The perception of consistency in attitudes. *Journal of Experimental Social Psychology*, 1973, 9, 491−501.

Goffman, E. Embarrassment and social organization. *American Journal of Sociology*, 1956, 62, 264−271.

Goffman, E. *The presentation of self in everyday life*. Garden City, NY: Doubleday, 1959.

Goffman, E. *Encounters: Two studies in the sociology of interaction*. Indianapolis: Bobbs-Merrill, 1961.

Goffman, J., Notarius, C., Markman, H., Bank, S., Yoppi, B., & Rubin, M. E. Behavior exchange theory and marital decision making. *Journal of Personality and Social Psychology*, 1976, 34, 14−23.

Goldfried, M. R. Toward the delineation of therapeutic change principles. *American Psychologist*, 1980, 35, 991−999.

Goldfried, M. R., & Goldfried, A. P. Cognitive change methods. In F. H. Kanfer & A. P. Goldstein (Eds.) *Helping people change*. New York: Pergamon, 1975.

Goldstein, A. P. Psychotherapy research by extrapolation from social psychology. *Journal of Counseling Psychology*, 1966, 13, 38−45.

Goldstein, A. P. *Psychotherapeutic attraction*. New York: Pergamon Press, 1971.

Goldstein, A. P., Heller, K., & Sechrest, L. B. *Psychotherapy and the psychology of behavior change*. New York: Wiley, 1966.

Goodstadt, M. S. Helping and refusal to help: A test of balance and reactance theories. *Journal of Experimental Social Psychology*, 1971, 7, 610−622.

Goranson, R. E., & Berkowitz, L. Reciprocity and responsibility reactions to prior help. *Journal of Personality and Social Psychology*, 1966, 3, 227−232.

Gould, R., & Sigall, H. The effects of empathy and outcome on attribution: An examination of the divergent-perspectives hypothesis. *Journal of Experimental Social Psychology,* 1977, 13, 480—491.

Gouldner, A. W. The norm of reciprocity: A preliminary statement. *American Sociological Review,* 1960, 25, 161—178.

Grater, H., & Claxton, D. Counselor's empathy level and client topic changes. *Journal of Counseling Psychology,* 1976, 23, 407—408.

Green, R. G., Stonner, D., & Shope, G. L. The facilitation of aggression by aggression: Evidence against the catharsis hypothesis. *Journal of Personality and Social Psychology,* 1975, 31, 721—726.

Greenberg, M. S., & Frisch, D. M. Effect of intentionality on willingnss to reciprocate a favor. *Journal of Experimental Social Psychology,* 1972, 8, 99—111.

Greenberg, R. P. Effects of presession information on perception of the therapist and receptivity to influence in a psychotherapy analogue. *Journal of Consulting and Clinical Psychology,* 1969, 33, 425—429.

Greenstein, T. Behavior change through value self-confrontation: A field experiment. *Journal of Personality and Social Psychology,* 1976, 34, 254—262.

Greenwald, H. J. The involvement-discrepancy controversy in opinion change. (Doctoral dissertation, Columbia University, 1964). *Dissertation Abstracts,* 1964, 25, 1380.

Greenwald, H. J. *The involvement controversy of persuasion research.* Unpublished manuscript, Columbia University, 1965.

Greenwood, J. *Some effects of counselor expertness upon the client's perception of the counseling relationship.* Unpublished master's thesis, The Ohio State University, 1973.

Gruwitz, S. B., & Panciera, L. Attributions of freedom by actors and observers. *Journal of Personality and Social Psychology,* 1975, 32, 531—539.

Gurman, A. S., & Kniskern, D. P. Research on marital and family therapy: Progress, perspective, and prospect. In S. Garfield & A. Bergin (Eds.) *Handbook of psychotherapy and behavior change: An empirical analysis,* 2nd ed. New York: Wiley, 1978.

Guttman, M. A., & Haase, R. F. Effect of experimentally induced sets of high and low 'expertness' during brief vocational counseling. *Counselor Education and Supervision,* 1972, 11, 171—178.

Haccoun, D. M., & Lavigueur, H. Effects of clinical experience and client emotion on therapists' responses. *Journal of Consulting and Clinical Psychology,* 1979, 47, 416—418.

Hagebak, R. W., & Parker, G. V. Therapist directiveness, client dominance, and therapy resistance. *Journal of Consulting and Clinical Psychology,* 1968, 33, 536—540.

Haley, J. *Strategies of psychotherapy.* New York: Grune & Stratton, 1963.

Haley, J. An interactional explanation of hypnosis. In D. Jackson (Ed.) *Therapy, communication, and change. Human communication,* Vol. 2. Palo Alto, CA: Science and Behavior Books, 1968a.

Haley, J. Control in psychotherapy with schizophrenics. In D. Jackson (Ed.) *Therapy, communication and change. Human communication,* Vol. 2. Palo Alto, CA: Science and Behavior Books, 1968b.

Haley, J. An interactional description of schizophrenia. In D. Jackson (Ed.) *Communication, family, and marriage. Human communication,* Vol. 1. Palo Alto, CA: Science and Behavior Books, 1968c.

Haley, J. The family of the schizophrenic: A model system. In D. Jackson (Ed.) *Communication, family and marriage. Human communication,* Vol. 1. Palo Alto, CA: Science and Behavioral Books, 1968d.

Haley, J. *Uncommon therapy.* New York: Norton, 1973.

Haley, J. *Problem-solving therapy.* San Francisco: Jossey-Bass, 1976.

Halpern, T. P. Degree of client self-disclosure as a function of past disclosure, counselor disclosure, and counselor facilitativeness. *Journal of Counseling Psychology,* 1977, 24, 41–47.

Halverson, R. R., & Pallak, M. S. Commitment, ego-involvement, and resistance to attack. *Journal of Experimental Social Psychology,* 1978, 14, 1–12.

Hamid, P. N., & Flay, B. R. Change in locus of control as a function of value modification. *British Journal of Social and Clinical Psychology,* 1974, 13, 143–150.

Hansen, R. D., & Donoghue, J. M. The power of consensus: Information derived from own and others behavior. *Journal of Personality and Social Psychology,* 1977, 35, 294–302.

Hansen, R. D., & Lowe, C. A. Distinctiveness and consensus: The influence of behavioral information on actors' and observors' attributions. *Journal of Personality and Social Psychology,* 1976, 34, 425–433.

Hanusa, B. H., & Schulz, R. Attributional mediators of learned helplessness. *Journal of Personality and Social Psychology,* 1977, 35, 602–611.

Hart, R. J. Crime and punishment in the army. *Journal of Personality and Social Psychology,* 1978, 36, 1456–1471.

Hartman, J. J. Small group method of personal change. In M. R. Rosenzweig & L. W. Porter (Eds.) *Annual Review of Psychology, 1979.* Palo Alto, CA: Annual Reviews Inc., 1979.

Harvey, J. H., & Johnston, S. Determinants of the perception of choice. *Journal of Experimental Social Psychology,* 1973, 9, 164–179.

Harvey, J., & Mills, J. Effects of a difficult opportunity to revoke a counter attitudinal action upon attitude change. *Journal of Personality and Social Psychology,* 1971, 18, 201–209.

Hartley, D. L. Perceived counselor credibility as a function of the effects of counseling interaction. *Journal of Counseling Psychology,* 1969, 16, 63–68.

Hass, G., & Mann, R. Anticipatory belief change: Persuasion or impression management? *Journal of Personality and Social Psychology,* 1976, 34, 105–111.

Heider, F. *The psychology of interpersonal relations.* New York: Wiley, 1958.

Heilman, M. E., & Toffler, B. L. Reacting to reactance: An interpersonal interpretation of the need for freedom. *Journal of Experimental Social Psychology,* 1976, 12, 519–529.

Helmreich, R., Aronson, E., & LeFan, J. To err is humanizing—sometimes: Effects of self-esteem, competence, and a pratfall on interpersonal attraction. *Journal of Personality and Social Psychology,* 1970, 16, 259–264.

Helner, P. A., & Jessell, J. C. Effects of interpretation as a counseling technique. *Journal of Counseling Psychology,* 1974, 21, 475–481.

Heppner, P. P., & Dixon, D. N. Effects of client perceived need and counselor role on clients' behaviors. *Journal of Counseling Psychology,* 1978, 25, 514–519.

Heppner, P. P., & Pew, S. Effects of diplomas, awards, and counselor sex on perceived expertness. *Journal of Counseling Psychology,* 1977, 24, 147−149.

Heslin, R., & Amo, M. F. Detailed test of the reinforcement-dissonance controversy in the counter-attitudinal advocacy situation. *Journal of Personality and Social Psychology,* 1972, 23, 234−242.

Highlen, P. S., & Baccus, G. K. Effect of reflection of feeling and probe on client self-referenced affect. *Journal of Counseling Psychology,* 1977, 24, 440−443.

Highlen, P. S., & Nicholas, R. P. Effects of locus of control, instructions, and verbal conditioning on self-reference affect in a counseling interview. *Journal of Counseling Psychology,* 1978, 25, 177−183.

Highlen, P. S., & Voight, N. L. Effects of social modeling, cognitive structuring, and self-management strategies on affective self-disclosure. *Journal of Counseling Psychology,* 1978, 25, 21−27.

Hill, C. E., & Gormally, J. Effects of reflection, restatement, probe, and nonverbal behaviors on client affect. *Journal of Counseling Psychology,* 1977, 24, 92−97.

Hill, C. T., Rubin, Z., & Peplau, L. A. Breakups before marriage: The end of 103 affairs. *Journal of Social Issues,* 1976, 32, 147−168.

Hodges, K. K., & Brandt, D. Measurement of attribution of causality in counselor behavior. *Journal of Counseling Psychology,* 1978, 25, 343−348.

Hoehn-Saric, R., Frank, J. D., & Gurland, B. J. Focused attitude change in neurotic patients. *Journal of Nervous and Mental Diseases,* 1968, 147, 124−133.

Hoehn-Saric, R., Liberman, B., Imber, S. D., Stone, A. R., Pande, S. K., & Frank, J. D. Arousal and attitude change in neurotic patients. *Archives of General Psychiatry,* 1972, 26, 51−56.

Hoffman, M. A., & Spencer, G. P. Effect of interviewer self-disclosure and interviewer−subject sex pairing in perceived and actual subject behavior. *Journal of Counseling Psychology,* 1977, 24, 383−390.

Hoffman-Graff, M. A. Interviewer use of positive and negative self-disclosure and interviewer−subject sex pair. *Journal of Counseling Psychology,* 1977, 24, 184−190.

Hoffnung, R. .J. Conditioning and transfer of affective self references in a role-played counseling interview. *Journal of Consulting and Clinical Psychology,* 1966, 33, 527−531.

Holahan, C. J., & Slaikew, K. A. Effects of contrasting degrees of privacy on client self-disclosure in a counseling setting. *Journal of Counseling Psychology,* 1977, 24, 55−59.

Hollen, C. C. Value change, perceived instrumentality, and attitude change. (Doctoral dissertation, Michigan State University, 1972.) *Dissertation Abstracts International,* 1972, 33, 899b.

Holmes, J. G., & Strickland, L. H. Choice freedom and confirmation of incentive expectancy or determinants of attitude change. *Journal of Personality and Social Psychology,* 1970, 14, 39−45.

Houts, P. S., MacIntosh, S., & Moos, R. H. Patient−therapist interdependence: Cognitive and behavioral. *Journal of Consulting and Clinical Psychology,* 1969, 32, 40−45.

Hovland, C. I., Janis, I. L., & Kelley, H. H. *Communication and persuasion: Psychological studies of opinion change.* New Haven: Yale University Press, 1953.

Hoyt, M. G., Henley, M. D., & Collins, B. E. Studies in forced compliance: Confluence of choice and consequences on attitude change. *Journal of Personality and Social Psychology*, 1972, 33, 205–210.

Hurwitz, J., Zander, A., & Hymoritch, B. Some effects of power on relations among group members. In D. Cartwright & A Zander (Eds.) *Group dynamics: Research and theory*, 2nd ed. Evanston, IL: Row, Peterson, 1960.

Jackson, D. D. (Ed.) *Communication, family and marriage*. Palo Alto, CA: Science and Behavior Books, 1968a.

Jackson, D. D. (Ed.) *Therapy, communication and change*. Palo Alto, CA: Science and Behavior Books, 1968b.

Jackson, D. D. Family interaction, family homeostasis, and some implications for conjoining family therapy. In D. Jackson (Ed.) *Therapy, communication, and change. Human communication*, Vol. 2. Palo Alto, CA: Science and Behavior Books, 1968c.

Jackson, D. D. The study of the family. In P. Watzlawick & J. Weakland (Eds.) *The interactional view*. New York: Norton, 1977a.

Jackson, D. D. Family rules: Marital quid pro quo. In P. Watzlawick & J. Weakland (Eds.) *The interactional view*. New York: Norton, 1977b.

Jackson, D. D., & Haley, J. Transference visited. In D. Jackson (Ed.) *Therapy, communication, and change. Human communication*, Vol. 2. Palo Alto, CA: Science and Behavior Books, 1968.

Jackson, D., & Yalom, I. Family research on the problems of ulcerative colitis. In P. Watzlawick & J. Weakland (Eds.) *The interactional view*. New York: Norton, 1977.

Johnson, D. W. Attitude modification methods. In F. H. Kanfer and A. P. Goldstein (Eds.) *Helping people change*, 2nd ed. New York: Pergamon, 1980.

Johnson, D. W., & Noonan, M. P. Effects of acceptance and reciprocation of self-disclosures on the development of trust. *Journal of Counseling Psychology*, 1972, 19, 411–416.

Johnson, T. J., Feigenbaum, R., & Weiby, M. Some determinants and consequences of the teacher's perception of causation. *Journal of Educational Psychology*, 1964, 55, 237–246.

Jones, E. E. *Ingratiation: A social psychological analysis*. New York: Appleton-Century-Crofts, 1964.

Jones, E. E., & Davis, K. E. From acts to dispositions: The attribution process in person perception. In L. Berkowitz (Ed.) *Advances in experimental social psychology*, Vol. 2. New York: Academic Press, 1965.

Jones, E. E., & DeCharms, R. Changes in social perception as a function of the personal relevance of behavior. *Sociometry*, 1957, 20, 75–85.

Jones, E. E., & Gordon, E. M. Timing of self-disclosure and its effects on personal attraction. *Journal of Personality and Social Psychology*, 1972, 24, 358–365.

Jones, E. E., & Nisbett, R. E. *The actor and the observer: Divergent perceptions of the causes of behavior*. Morristown, NJ: General Learning Press, 1971.

Jourard, S. M., & Jaffe, P. E. Influence of an interviewer's disclosure on the self-disclosing behavior of interviewees. *Journal of Counseling Psychology*, 1970, 17, 252–257.

Kahn, A., & Tice, T. E. Returning a favor and retaliating harm: The effects of stated intentions and actual behavior. *Journal of Experimental Social Psychology*, 1973, 9, 43–56.

Kane, T. R., Joseph, J. M., & Tedeschi, J. T. Person perception and the Berkowitz paradigm for the study of aggression. *Journal of Personality and Social Psychology,* 1976, 33, 663−673.

Kanfer, F. H. Structure of psychotherapy: Role playing as a variable in dyadic communication. *Journal of Consulting Psychology,* 1965, 29, 325−332.

Kaul, T. J., & Schmidt, L. D. Dimensions of interviewer trustworthiness. *Journal of Counseling Psychology,* 1971, 18, 542−548.

Kell, B. L., & Mueller, W. J. *Impact and change: A study of counseling relationships.* New York: Appleton-Century-Crofts, 1966.

Kelley, H. H. Attribution theory in social psychology. In D. Levine (Ed.) *Nebraska symposium on motivation, 1967.* Lincoln: University of Nebraska Press, 1967.

Kelley, H. H. Attribution in social interaction. In E. E. Jones, D. E. Kanouse, H. H. Kelley, R. E. Nisbett, S. Valins, & B. Weiner (Eds.) *Attribution: Perceiving the causes of behavior.* Morristown, NJ: General Learning Press, 1971.

Kelley, H. H. *Personal relationships: Their structure and processes.* Hillsdale, NJ: Lawrence Erlbaum, 1979.

Kelly, G. A. *The psychology of personal constructs.* New York: Norton, 1955.

Kelman, H. C., & Baron, R. M. Inconsistency as a psychological signal. In R. P. Abelson, E. Aronson, W. J. McGuire, T. M. Newcomb, M. J. Rosenberg, and P. H. Tannenbaum (Eds.) *Theories of cognitive consistency: A sourcebook.* Chicago: Rand McNally, 1968.

Kerr, B. A., & Dell, D. M. Perceived interviewer expertness and attractiveness: Effects of interviewer behavior and attire and interview setting. *Journal of Counseling Psychology,* 1976, 23, 288−292.

Kiesler, C. A., & Corbin, L. H. Commitment, attraction, and conformity. *Journal of Personality and Social Psychology,* 1965, 2, 890−895.

Kiesler, C. A., Pallak, M. S., & Kanouse, D. E. The interactive effects of commitment and dissonance. *Journal of Personality and Social Psychology,* 1968, 8, 331−338.

Kiesler, C. A., & Sakumura, J. A. A test of a model for commitment. *Journal of Personality and Social Psychology,* 1966, 3, 349−352.

Kiesler, C. A., Zanna, M., & DeSalvo, J. Deviation and conformity: Opinion change as a function of commitment, attraction, and presence of a deviate. *Journal of Personality and Social Psychology,* 1966, 3, 458−467.

Kiesler, D. J. An interpersonal communication analysis of relationship in psychotherapy. *Psychiatry,* 1979, 42, 299−311.

Kimble, C. E., Fitz, D., & Onorad, J. R. Effectiveness of counter aggression strategies in reducing interaction aggression by males. *Journal of Personality and Social Psychology,* 1977, 35, 272−278.

Klir, G. J., & Valach, M. *Cybernetic modeling.* Princeton, NJ: Van Nostrand, 1967.

Koller, P. S., & Kaplan, R. M. A two-process theory of learned helplessness. *Journal of Personality and Social Psychology,* 1978, 36, 1177−1183.

Kruglanski, A. W. Lay epistemo-logic-process and contents: Another look at attribution theory. *Psychological Review,* 1980, 87, 70−87.

Kruglanski, A. W., Alon, S., & Lewis, T. Retrospective misattribution and task enjoyment. *Journal of Experimental Social Psychology,* 1972, 8, 493−501.

Krumboltz, J. P., & Thoresen, C. E. (Eds.) *Behavioral counseling: Cases and techniques.* New York: Holt, Rinehart & Winston, 1969.

Kuiper, N. A. Depression and causal attributions for success and failure. *Journal of Personality and Social Psychology,* 1978, 36, 236–246.

Kulik, J. A., & Brown, R. Frustration, attribution of blame, and aggression. *Journal of Experimental Social Psychology,* 1979, 15, 183–194.

Kurtz, R. R., & Grummon, D. L. Differential approaches to the measurement of therapist empathy and their relationship to therapy outcomes. *Journal of Consulting and Clinical Psychology,* 1972, 39, 106–115.

L'Abate, L., & Weeks, G. A bibliography of paradoxical methods in psychotherapy of family systems. *Family process,* 1978, 17, 95–98.

LaCrosse, M. B. Nonverbal behavior and perceived counselor attractiveness and persuasiveness. *Journal of Counseling Psychology,* 1975, 22, 563–566.

Landfield, A. W. *Personal construct systems in psychotherapy.* Chicago: Rand McNally, 1971.

Langer, E. J. Rethinking the role of thought in social interaction. In J. H. Harvey, W. J. Ickes, & R. F. Kidd (Eds.) *New directions in attribution research,* Vol. 2. Hillsdale, NJ: Lawrence Erlbaum, 1978.

Langer, E. J., & Benevento, A. Self-induced dependence. *Journal of Personality and Social Psychology,* 1978, 36, 886–893.

Lawless, W., & Nowicki, S. Jr. Role of self-disclosure in interpersonal attraction. *Journal of Consulting and Clinical Psychology,* 1972, 38, 300.

Lawson, E. D. Change in communication nets, performance, and morale. *Human Relations,* 1965, 18, 139–147.

Leary, T. *Interpersonal diagnosis of personality.* New York: Ronald Press, 1957.

Leavitt, H. J. Some effects of certain communication patterns on group performance. *Journal of Abnormal and Social Psychology,* 1951, 46, 38–50.

Lefcourt, H. M., Hogg, E., Struthers, S., & Holmes, C. Causal attributions as a function of focus of control, initial confidence, and performance outcomes. *Journal of Personality and Social Psychology,* 1975, 32, 391–397.

Legant, P., & Mettee, D. R. Turning the other cheek versus retaliation: vengeance, equity, and attraction. *Journal of Personality and Social Psychology,* 1973, 25, 243–253.

Lennard, H. L., & Bernstein, A. *The anatomy of psychotherapy: Systems of communications and expectation.* New York: Columbia University Press, 1960.

Lepper, M. R., & Greene, D. Turning play into work: Effects of adult surveillance and extrinsic rewards on children's intrinsic motivation. *Journal of Personality and Social Psychology,* 1975, 31, 479–486.

Lerner, M. J. Observer's evaluation of a victim: Justice, guilt, and veridical perception. *Journal of Personality and Social Psychology,* 1971, 20, 127–135.

Lerner, M. J., & Lichtman, R. R. Effects of perceived norms on attitudes and altruistic behavior toward a dependent other. *Journal of Personality and Social Psychology,* 1968, 9, 226–232.

Leventhal, G. S., Weiss, T., & Long, G. Equity, reciprocity, and reallocating rewards in a dyad. *Journal of Personality and Social Psychology,* 1969, 13, 300–305.

Leventhal, G. S., & Whiteside, H. D. Equity and the use of reward to elicit high performance. *Journal of Personality and Social Psychology,* 1973, 25, 75–83.

Levine, J. M., Ranelli, C.J., & Valle, R. S. Self-evaluation and reaction to a shifting other. *Journal of Personality and Social Psychology*, 1974, 29, 637−643.

Levy, L. H. *Psychological interpretation*. New York: Holt, Rinehart & Winston, 1963.

Lieberman, M. A., Yalom, I. D., & Miles, M. B. *Encounter groups: First facts*. New York: Basic Books, 1973.

Lopez, F. G., & Wambach, C. Effects of Paradoxical and Self-Countrol Directive in Counseling. *Journal of Counseling Psychology*, in press.

Lowe, C. A., & Goldstein, J. W. Reciprocal liking and attributions of ability: Mediating effects of perceived intention and personal involvement. *Journal of Personality and Social Psychology*, 1970, 16, 291−297.

Lowe, C. M. *Value orientations in counseling and psychotherapy: The meanings of mental health*. 2nd ed. Cranston RI: Carrell Press, 1976.

Luborsky, L., Singer, B., & Luborsky, L. Comparative studies of psychotherapies: Is it true that "everybody has won and all must have prizes"? *Archives of General Psychiatry*, 1975, 32, 995−1008.

Lynn, S. J. Three theories of self-disclosure exchange. *Journal of Experimental Social Psychology*, 1978, 14, 466−479.

Mann, B., Murphy, K. C. Timing of self-disclosure, reciprocity of self-disclosure, and reactions to an initial interview. *Journal of Counseling Psychology*, 1975, 22, 304−308.

Mansson, H. H. The relation of dissonance reduction to cognitive, perceptual, consummatory, and learning measures of thirst. In P. G. Zimbardo (Ed.) *The cognitive control of motivation*. Glenview, IL: Scott, Foresman, 1969.

Marlatt, G. A., & Perry, M. A. Modeling methods. In F. H. Kanfer & A. P. Goldstein (Eds.) *Helping people change*. New York: Pergamon, 1975.

Matross, R. P. Socratic methods of counseling and psychotherapy. Office for Student Affairs Research Bulletin, University of Minnesota, 1974.

McAllister, A., & Kiesler, D. J. Interviewer disclosure as a function of interpersonal trust, task modeling, and interviewer self-disclosure. *Journal of Consulting and Clinical Psychology*, 1975, 43, 428.

McArthur, L. A. The how and what of why: Some determinants and consequences of causal attribution. *Journal of Personality and Social Psychology*, 1972, 22, 171−193.

McCarthy, P. R., & Betz, N. E. Differential effects of self-disclosure versus self-involving counselor statements. *Journal of Counseling Psychology*, 1978, 25, 251−256.

McGuire, D., Thelen, M. H., & Amolsch, T. Interview self-disclosure as a function of length of modeling and descriptive instructions. *Journal of Consulting and Clinical Psychology*, 1975, 43, 356−362.

McGuire, W. J. Cognitive consistency and attitude change. *Journal of Abnormal and Social Psychology*, 1960, 60, 345−353.

McGuire, W. J. The nature of attitudes and attitude change. In G. Lindzey & E. Aronson (Eds.) *The handbook of social psychology*, Vol. 3, end ed. Reading, MA: Addison-Wesley, 1969.

McGuire, W. J., & Papageorgis, D. Effectiveness of forewarning in developing resistance to persuasion. *Public Opinion Quarterly*, 1962, 26, 29−34.

McMullin, R. E. Effects of counselor focusing on client self experience under low attitudinal conditions. *Journal of Counseling Psychology*, 1972, 19, 282−285.

Meichenbaum, D. Self-instructional methods. In F. H. Kanfer & A. P. Goldstein (Eds.) *Helping people change*. New York: Pergamon, 1975.

Menapace, R. H., & Doby, C. Causal attribution for success and failure for psychiatric rehabilitees and college students. *Journal of Personality and Social Psychology*, 1976, 34, 447−454.

Merluzzi, T. V., Banikiotes, P. G., & Missbach, J. W. Perceptions of counselor characteristics: Contributions of counselor sex, experience, and disclosure level. *Journal of Counseling Psychology*, 1978, 25, 479−482.

Messé, L. A. Stollak, G. E., Larson, R. W., & Michaels, G. Y. Interpersonal consequences of person perception processes in two social contexts. *Journal of Personality and Social Psychology*, 1979, 37, 369−379.

Messick, D. M., & Reeder, G. Perceived motivation, role variations, and the attribution of personal characteristics. *Journal of Experimental Social Psychology*, 1972, 8, 482−491.

Miller, D. T., Norman, S. A., & Wright, E. Distortion in person perception as a consequence of the need for effective control. *Journal of Personality and Social Psychology*, 1978, 36, 598−607.

Miller, R. L., Brickman, P., & Bolen, D. Attribution versus persuasion as a means for modifying behavior. *Journal of Personality and Social Psychology*, 1975, 31, 430−441.

Mills, J., & Harvey, J. Opinion change as a function of when information about the communicator is received and whether he is attractive or expert. *Journal of Personality and Social Psychology*, 1972, 21, 52−55.

Minuchin, S. *Families and family therapy*. Cambridge: Harvard University Press, 1974.

Moos, R. H., & Clemes, S. R. Multivariate study of the patient therapist system. *Journal of Consulting Psychology*, 1967, 31, 119−130.

Moos, R. H., & MacIntosh, S. Multivariate study of the patient-therapist system: A replication and extension. *Journal of Consulting and Clinical Psychology*, 1970, 35, 298−307.

Morse, S. J., Gruzen, J., & Reis, H. T. The nature of equity restoration: Some approval-seeking considerations. *Journal of Experimental Social Psychology*, 1976, 12, 1−8.

Murphy, K. C., & Strong, S. R. Some effects of similarity self-disclosure. *Journal of Counseling Psychology*, 1972, 19, 121−124.

Napolitan, D. A., & Goethals, G. R. The attribution of friendliness. *Journal of Experimental Social Psychology*, 1979, 15, 105−113.

Nelson-Jones, R., & Strong, S. R. Positive and negative self-disclosure, timing and personal attraction. *British Journal of Social and Clinical Psychology*, 1976a, 15, 323−325.

Nelsen-Jones, R., & Strong, S. R. Rules, risk and self-disclosure. *British Journal of Guidance and Counseling*, 1976b, 4, 202−211.

Nelsen-Jones, R., & Strong, S. R. British students' positive and negative evaluations of personal characteristics. *Journal of College Student Personnel*, 1977, 18, 32−27.

Newtson, D., Engquist, G., & Bois, J. The objective basis of behavior units. *Journal of Personality and Social Psychology*, 1977, 35, 847−862.

Nicholls, J. G. Causal attributions and other achievement-related cognitions: Effects of task outcome, attainment, value, and sex. *Journal of Personality and Social Psychology*, 1975, 31, 379−389.

Nielson, S. K. *Functional impact of therapist self-disclosure on change in therapy.* Unpublished doctoral dissertation, University of Nebraska-Lincoln, 1979.

Nisbett, R. E., & Borgida, E. Attribution and the psychology of prediction. *Journal of Personality and Social Psychology,* 1975, 32, 932–943.

Nisbett, R. E., Borgida, E., Crandall, R., & Reed, H. Popular induction: Information is not always informative. In J. S. Carroll & J. W. Payne (Eds.) *Cognitive and social psychology.* Hillsdale, NJ: Erlbaum, 1976.

Norman, R. When what is said is important: A comparison of expert and attractive sources. *Journal of Experimental Social Psychology,* 1976, 12, 294–300.

Orne, M. T. The nature of hypnosis: Artifact and essence. *Journal of Abnormal and Social Psychology,* 1959, 58, 277–299.

Orne, M. T. On the social psychology of the psychology experiment. *American Psychologist,* 1962, 17, 776–783.

Orne, M. T. Demand characteristics and the concept of quasi-controls. In R. Rosenthal & R. Rosnow (Eds.) *Artifact in behavioral research.* New York: Academic Press, 1969.

Orne, M. T. Hypnosis, motivation, and the ecological validity of the psychological experiment. In D. Levine (Ed.) *Nebraska symposium on motivation, 1970.* Lincoln: University of Nebraska Press, 1970, pp. 187–265.

Orvis, B. R., Cunningham, J. D., & Kelley, H. H. A closer examination of causal inference: The roles of consensus, distinctiveness, and consistency information. *Journal of Personality and Social Psychology,* 1975, 32, 605–616.

Orvis, B. R., Kelley, H. H., & Butler, D. Attributional conflict in young couples. In J. H. Harvey, W. J. Ickes, & R. F. Kidd (Eds.) *New directions in attribution research,* Vol. 1. Hillsdale, NJ: Erlbaum, 1976.

Ostrom, T. M., & Brock, T.C. *A cognitive model of attitudinal involvement.* Unpublished manuscript. Ohio State University, 1968.

Page, M. M. Demand characteristics and the verbal operant conditioning experiment. *Journal of Personality and Social Psychology,* 1972, 23, 372–378.

Page, M. M. Demand characteristics and the classical conditioning of attitudes experiment. *Journal of Personality and Social Psychology,* 1974, 30, 418–476.

Page, M. M., & Kahle, L. R. Demand characteristics in the satiation-deprivation effect on attitude conditioning. *Journal of Personality and Social Psychology,* 1976, 33, 553–562.

Page, M. M., & Scheidt, R. J. The elusive weapons effect: Demand awareness, evaluation apprehension, and slightly sophisticated subjects. *Journal of Personality and Social Psychology,* 1971, 20, 304–318.

Palazzoli, M. S. *Self-starvation: From the intrapsychic to the transpersonal approach to anorexia nervosa.* London: Human Context Books, 1974.

Palazzoli, M. S., Boscolo, L., Cecchin, G., & Prata, G. *Paradox and counterparadox.* New York: Jason Arouson, 1978.

Pallak, M. S., & Heller, J. F. Interactive effects of commitment to future interaction and threat to attitudinal freedom. *Journal of Personality and Social Psychology,* 1973, 17, 325–331.

Pallak, M. S., Sogin, S.R., & Van Zante, A. Bad decisions: Effect of volition, focus of causality, and negative consequences on attitude change. *Journal of Personality and Social Psychology,* 1974, 30, 217–227.

Parloff, M. B. Shopping for the right therapy. *Saturday Review,* February 21, 1976, pp. 14–16.

Passer, M. W., Kelley, H. H., & Michela, J. L. Multidimensional scaling of the causes for negative interpersonal behavior. *Journal of Personality and Social Psychology,* 1978, 36, 951–962.

Pattison, J. E. Effects of touch on self-exploration and the therapeutic relationship. *Journal of Consulting and Clinical Psychology,* 1973, 40, 170–175.

Patton, M. J. Attraction, discrepancy, and responses to psychological treatment. *Journal of Counseling Psychology,* 1969, 16, 317–324.

Patton, M. J., Fuhriman, A., & Bieber, M. R. A model and a metalanguage for research on psychological counseling. *Journal of Counseling Psychology,* 1977, 24, 25–34.

Patty, R. A., & Page, M. M. Manipulations of a verbal conditioning situation based upon demand characteristics theory. *Journal of Experimental research in personality,* 1973, 6, 307–313.

Pepinsky, H. B., & Karst, T. O. Convergence: A phenomenon in counseling and psychotherapy. *American Psychologist,* 1964, 19, 333–338.

Perkins, M. J., Kiesler, D. J., Anchin, J. C., Chirico, B. M., Kyle, E. M., & Federman, E. J. The impact message inventory: A new measure of relationship in counseling/ psychotherapy and other dyads. *Journal of Counseling Psychology,* 1979, 26, 363–367.

Perls, F. S. *Gestalt therapy verbatim.* Moab, Utah: Real People Press, 1969.

Persons, R. W., & Pepinsky, H. B. Convergence in psychotherapy with delinquent boys. *Journal of Counseling Psychology,* 1966, 13, 329–334.

Petoney, P. Value change in psychotherapy. *Human Relations,* 1966, 19, 39–45.

Piaget, G. W., Berenson, B. G., & Carkhuff, R. R. Differential effects of the manipulation of therapeutic conditions by high- and moderate-functioning therapists upon high- and low-functioning clients. *Journal of Consulting Psychology,* 1964, 31, 481–486.

Pittman, N. L., & Pittman, T. S. Effects of amount of helplessness training and internal-external locus of control on mood and performance. *Journal of Personality and Social Psychology,* 1979, 37, 39–47.

Podmore, F. *From Mesmer to Christian Science: A short history of mental healing.* New York: University Books, 1963.

Pope, B., & Siegman, A. W. Interviewer warmth in relation to interviewer verbal behavior. *Journal of Consulting and Clinical Psychology,* 1968, 32, 588–595.

Porter, E. H. Jr. *An introduction to therapeutic counseling.* New York: Houghton Mifflin, 1950.

Pryor, J. B., & Kriss, M. The cognitive dynamics of salience in the attribution process. *Journal of Personality and Social Psychology,* 1977, 35, 49–55.

Quattrone, G. A., & Jones, E. E. Selective self-disclosure with and without correspondent performance. *Journal of Experimental Social Psychology,* 1978, 14, 511–526.

Regan, D. T. Effects of a favor and liking on compliance. *Journal of Experimental Social Psychology,* 1971, 7, 627–639.

Regan, D. T., Straus, E., & Fazio, R. Liking and the attribution process. *Journal of Experimental Social Psychology,* 1974, 10, 385–397.

Regan, D. T., & Totten, J. Empathy and attribution: Turning observers into actors. *Journal of Personality and Social Psychology,* 1975, 32, 850–856

Reis, H. T., & Gruzen, J. On mediating equity, equality, and self-interest: The role of self presentation in social exchange. *Journal of Experimental Social Psychology,* 1976, 12, 487−503.

Reisman, J. M., & Yamokoski, T. Psychotherapy and friendship: An analysis of the communications of friends. *Journal of Counseling Psychology,* 1974, 21, 269−273.

Rhine, R. J., & Severance, L. J. Ego-involvement, discrepancy, source credibility, and attitude change. *Journal of Personality and Social Psychology,* 1970, 16, 175−190.

Rhodewalt, F., & Comer, R. Induced-compliance attitude change: Once more with feeling. *Journal of Experimental Social Psychology,* 1979, 15, 35−47.

Rice, L. N. Client behavior as a function of therapist style and client resources. *Journal of Counseling Psychology,* 1973, 20, 306−311.

Riegel, K. F. The dialectic of human development. *American Psychologist,* 1976, 31, 689−700.

Riess, M., & Schlenker, B. R. Attitude change and responsibility avoidance as modes of dilemma resolution in forced compliance situations. *Journal of Personality and Social Psychology,* 1977, 35, 21−30.

Rivera, A. N., & Tedeschi, J. T. Public versus private reactions to positive inequity. *Journal of Personality and Social Psychology,* 1976, 34, 895−900.

Robinson, F. P. *Principles and procedures in student counseling.* New York: Harper, 1950.

Rogers, C. *Client-centered therapy.* Boston: Houghton Mifflin, 1951.

Rogers, C. R. The necessary and sufficient conditions of therapeutic personality change. *Journal of Consulting Psychology,* 1957, 21, 95−103.

Rokeach, M. *The nature of human values.* New York: Free Press, 1973.

Rokeach, M., & Cochrane, R. Self-confrontation and confrontation with another as determinants of long-term value change. *Journal of Applied Social Psychology,* 1972, 2, 283−292.

Rokeach, M., & McLellan, D. D. Feedback of information about values of self and others as determinants of long-term cognitive and behavioral change. *Journal of Applied Social Psychology,* 1972, 2, 236−251.

Roll, W. V., Schmidt, L. D., & Kaul, T. C. Perceived interviewer trustworthiness among black and white convicts. *Journal of Counseling Psychology,* 1972, 19, 537−541.

Rosen, N. A., & Wyer, R. S., Jr. Some further evidence for the "Socratic effect" using a subjective probability model of cognitive organization. *Journal of Personality and Social Psychology,* 1972, 24, 420−424.

Rosenberg, M. J. Cognitive reorganization in response to the hypnotic reversal of attitudinal affect. *Journal of Personality,* 1960, 28, 39−63.

Rosenberg, M. J. When dissonance fails: On eliminating evaluation apprehension from attitude measurement. *Journal of Personality and Social Psychology,* 1965, 1, 28−42.

Rosenberg, M.J. The conditions and consequences of evaluation apprehension. In R. Rosenthal & R. Rosnow (Eds.) *Artifacts in behavioral research.* New York: Academic Press, 1969.

Rosenthal, D. Changes in some moral values following psychotherapy. *Journal of Consulting Psychology,* 1955, 19, 431−436.

Rosenthal, T., & Bandura, A. Psychological modeling: Theory and practice. In S. Garfield & A. E. Bergin (Eds.) *Handbook of Psychotherapy and Behavior Change,* 2nd ed. New York: Wiley, 1978.

Ross, L. The intuitive psychologist and his shortcomings: Distortions in the attribution process. In L. Berkowitz (Ed.) *Advances in experimental social psychology,* Vol. 10. New York: Academic Press, 1977.

Ross, M., & Sicoly, F. Egocentric biases in availability and attribution. *Journal of Personality and Social Psychology,* 1979, 37, 322−336.

Rothmeier, R. C., & Dixon, D. N. Trustworthiness and influence: A reexamination in an extended counseling analogue. *Journal of Counseling Psychology,* 1980, 27, 315−319.

Rubin, Z. Disclosing one self to a stranger: Reciprocity and its limits. *Journal of Experimental Social Psychology,* 1975, 11, 233−260.

Ruzicka, M. F., & Naun, R. Range of verbal behavior as a function of counselor philosophy and coached-client role behavior. *Journal of Counseling Psychology,* 1976, 33, 283−285.

Saltzstein, H. D., & Sandberg, L. Indirect social influence: Change in judgement process or anticipating conformity? *Journal of Experimental Social Psychology,* 1979, 15, 209−216.

Sapolsky, A. Effect of interpersonal relationships upon verbal conditioning. *Journal of Abnormal and Social Psychology,* 1960, 60, 241−246.

Savitsky, J. C., Zarle, T. H., & Keedy, N. S. The effect of information about an interviewer on interviewee perceptions. *Journal of Counseling Psychology,* 1976, 23, 158−159.

Schachter, S., & Singer, J. Cognitive, social and physiological determinants of emotional state. *Psychological Review,* 1962, 69, 379−399.

Scheid, A. B. Clients' perception of the counselor: The influence of counselor introduction and behavior. *Journal of Counseling Psychology,* 1976, 23, 503−508.

Schlenker, B. R., & Miller, R. S. Egocentrism in groups: Self-serving biases or logical information processing? *Journal of Personality and Social Psychology,* 1977, 35, 755−764.

Schmidt, L. D., & Strong, S. R. "Expert" and "inexpert" counselors. *Journal of Counseling Psychology,* 1970, 17, 115−118.

Schmidt, L. D., & Strong, S. R. Attractiveness and influence in counseling. *Journal of Counseling Psychology,* 1971, 18, 348−351.

Schneider, D. J., Hastorf, A. H., & Ellsworth, P. C. *Person perception,* 2nd ed. Reading, MA: Addison-Wesley, 1979.

Schopler, J. Social power. In L. Berkowitz (Ed.) *Advances in experimental social psychology,* vol. 2. New York: Academic Press, 1965.

Schopler, J., & Layton, B. Determinants of the self-attribution of having influenced another person. *Journal of Personality and Social Psychology,* 1972, 22, 326−332.

Schopler, J., & Thompson, V. D. Role of attributive processes in mediating amount of reciprocity for a favor. *Journal of Personality and Social Psychology,* 1968, 10, 243−250.

Schutz, W. C. *Joy.* New York: Grove Press, 1967.

Seligman, M. E. P. Depression and learned helplessness. In R. J. Friedman & M. M. Ketz (Eds.) *The psychology of depression: Contemporary theory and research.* Washington: Winston-Wiley, 1974.

Seligman, M. E. P. *Helplessness.* San Francisco: Freeman, 1975.

Sell, J. M. Effects of subject self-esteem, test performance feedback, and counselor attractiveness on influence in counseling. *Journal of Counseling Psychology,* 1974, 21, 324−344.

Shaw, M. E. Communication networks. In L. Berkowitz (Ed.) *Advances in experimental social psychology*, Vol. 1. New York: Academic Press, 1964.

Shaw, M. E., & Rothschild, G. H. Some effects of prolonged experiences in communication nets. *Journal of Applied Psychology*, 1956, 40, 218—286.

Shenkel, R. J., Snyder, C. R., Batson, C. D., & Clark, G. M. Effects of prior diagnostic information on clinician's causal attributions of a client's problems. *Journal of Consulting and Clinical Psychology*, 1979, 47, 404—406.

Sherif, M., Harvey, O., White, B., Hood, W., & Sherif, C. *Intergroup conflict and cooperation: The robber's cove experiment*. Norman: Institute of Group Relations, University of Oklahoma, 1961.

Sherif, M., & Hovland, C. I. *Social judgement: Assimilation and contrast effects in communication and attitude change*. New Haven: Yale University Press, 1961.

Sherman, S. J. Effects of choice and incentive on attitude change in a discrepant behavior situation. *Journal of Personality and Social Psychology*, 1970, 15, 245—252.

Sicoly, F., & Ross, M. Facilitation of ego-biased attributions by means of self-serving observer feedback. *Journal of Personality and Social Psychology*, 1977, 35, 734—741.

Siegel, J. C., & Sell, J. M. Effects of objective evidence of expertness and nonverbal behavior on client-perceived expertness. *Journal of Counseling Psychology*, 1978, 25, 188—192.

Simons, H. W., Berkowitz, N. N., & Moyer, R. J. Similarity, credibility, and attitude change: A review and a theory. *Psychological Bulletin*, 1970, 73, 1—16.

Simonson, N. R. The impact of therapist disclosure on patient disclosure. *Journal of Counseling Psychology*, 1976, 23, 3—6.

Simonson, N. R., & Bahr, S. Self-disclosure by the professional and paraprofessional therapist. *Journal of Consulting and Clinical Psychology*, 1974, 42, 359—363.

Skinner, B. F. *Science and human behavior*. New York: Macmillan, 1953.

Skinner, B. F. *Verbal behavior*. New York: Appleton-Century-Crofts, 1957.

Sloane, R. B., Staples, F. R., Cristol, A. H., Yorkston, N. J., & Whipple, K. *Psychotherapy versus behavior therapy*, Cambridge, MA: Harvard University Press, 1975.

Smith, T. W., & Pittman, T. S. Reward, distraction, and the overjustification effect. *Journal of Personality and Social Psychology*, 1978, 36, 565—572.

Snyder, C. R., Shenkel, R. J., & Schmidt, A. Effects of role perspective and client psychiatric history on locus of problem. *Journal of Consulting and Clinical Psychology*, 1976, 44, 467—472.

Snyder, M. Attribution and Behavior: Social perception and social causation. In J. H. Harvey, W. J. Ickes, & R. F. Kidd (Eds.) *New directions in attribution research*, Vol. 1. Hillsdale, NJ: Erlbaum, 1976.

Snyder, M., & Jones, E. E. Attitude attribution when behavior is constrained. *Journal of Experimental Social Psychology*, 1974, 10, 585—600.

Snyder, M., & Swann, N. B. Jr. Behavioral confirmation in social interaction: From social perception to social reality. *Journal of Experimental Social Psychology*, 1978, 14, 148—162.

Spiegel, S. B. Expertness, similarity, and perceived counselor competence. *Journal of Counseling Psychology*, 1976, 23, 436—441.

Stephan, F. F., & Mishler, E. G. The distribution of participation in small groups: An exponential approximation. *American Sociological Review,* 1952, 17, 598–608.

Steieper, D. R., & Wiener, D. N. *Dimensions of psychotherapy.* Chicago: Aldine, 1965.

Storms, M. D. Videotape and the attribution process: Reversing actors' and observers' points of view. *Journal of Personality and Social Psychology,* 1973, 27, 165–175.

Strong, S. R. Verbal conditioning and counseling research. *Personnel and Guidance Journal,* 1964, 42, 660–669.

Strong, S. R. Counseling: An interpersonal influence process. *Journal of Counseling Psychology,* 1968, 15, 215–224.

Strong, S. R. Causal attribution in counseling and psychotherapy. *Journal of Counseling Psychology,* 1970, 17, 388–399.

Strong, S. R. Social Psychological Approach to Psychotherapy Research. In S. L. Garfield & A. E. Bergin (Eds.) *Handbook of psychotherapy and behavioral change,* 2nd ed. New York: Wiley, 1978.

Strong, S. R. Christian counseling with homosexuals. *Journal of Psychology and Theology,* 1980, 8, 279–287.

Strong, S. R. Emerging integrations of clinical and social psychology: A clinician's perspective. In G. Weary & H. Mirels (Eds.) *Integration of clinical and social psychology.* New York: Oxford University Press, 1982.

Strong, S. R., & Dixon, D. N. Expertness, attractiveness, and influence in counseling. *Journal of Counseling Psychology,* 1971, 18, 562–570.

Strong, S. R., & Matross, R. P. Change processes in counseling and psychotherapy. *Journal of Counseling Psychology,* 1973, 20, 25–37.

Strong, S. R., Matross, R. P., & Danser, D. B. Interview methods of affecting self-attribution. *Perceptual Motor Skills,* 1981, 53, 451–455.

Strong, S. R., & Schmidt, L. D. Expertness and influence in counseling. *Journal of Counseling Psychology,* 1970a, 17, 81–87.

Strong, S. R., & Schmidt, L. D. Trustworthiness and influence in counseling. *Journal of Counseling Psychology,* 1970b, 17, 197–204.

Strong, S. R., Taylor, R. G., Bratten, J. C., & Loper, R. G. Nonverbal behavior and perceived counselor characteristics. *Journal of Counseling Psychology,* 1971, 18, 554–561.

Strong, S. R., Wambach, C. A., Lopez, F. G., & Cooper, R. K. Motivational and equipping functions of interpretation in counseling. *Journal of Counseling Psychology,* 1979, 26, 98–107.

Tannenbaum, P. H. Comment: Models of the role of stress. In R. P. Abelson, E. Aronson, W. J. McGuire, T. M. Newcomb, M. J. Rosenberg, & P. H. Tannenbaum (Eds.) *Theories of cognitive consistency: A sourcebook.* Chicago: Rand McNally, 1968a.

Tannenbaum, P. H. Summary: Is anything special about consistency? In R. P. Abelson, E. Aronson, W. J. McGuire, T. M. Newcomb, M. J. Rosenberg, & P. H. Tannenbaum (Eds.) *Theories of cognitive consistency: A sourcebook.* Chicago: Rand McNally, 1968b.

Taylor, S. E. On inferring one's attitude from one's behavior: Some delimiting conditions. *Journal of Personality and Social Psychology,* 1975, 31, 126–131.

Taylor, S. E., Crocker, J., Fiske, S. T., Sprinzen, M., & Winkler, J. D. The generalizability of salience effects. *Journal of Personality and Social Psychology,* 1979, 37, 357–368.

Taylor, S. E., & Fiske, S. T. Salience, attention and attribution: Top of the head phenomena. In L. Berkowitz (Ed.) *Advances in experimental social psychology,* Vol. 11. New York: Academic Press, 1978, pp. 249–288.

Tedeschi, J. T., Horai, J., Lindskold, S., & Faley, T. The effects of opportunity costs and target compliance on the behavior of a threatening source. *Journal of Experimental Social Psychology,* 1970, 6, 205–213.

Tedeschi, J. T., Schlenker, B. R., & Bonoma, T. V. Cognitive dissonance: Private ratiocination or public spectacle? *American Psychologist,* 1971, 26, 685–695.

Tennen, H., & Eller, S. J. Attributional components of learned helplessness and facilitation. *Journal of Personality and Social Psychology,* 1977, 35, 265–271.

Thase, M., & Page, R. A. Modeling of self-disclosure in laboratory and nonlaboratory interview settings. *Journal of Counseling Psychology,* 1977, 24, 35–40.

The Jerusalem Bible. Garden City, NY: Doubleday, 1966.

Thelen, M. H., & Brooks, S. J. Social desirability and self-disclosure: Both independent of psychopathology. *Journal of Consulting and Clinical Psychology,* 1976, 44, 868.

Thibaut, J. W., & Kelley, H. H. *The social psychology of groups.* New York: Wiley, 1959.

Thibaut, J., & Ross, M. Commitment and experience as determinants of assimilation and contrast. *Journal of Personality and Social Psychology,* 1969, 13, 322–329.

Thoresen, C. E., & Mahoney, M. J. *Behavioral self-control.* New York: Holt, Rinehart & Winston, 1974.

Torrance, E. P. Leadership training to improve aircrew group performance. *USAF ATC Instructor's Journal,* 1954, 5, 25–35.

Trope, Y. Extrinsic rewards, congruence between dispositions and behaviors, and perceived freedom. *Journal of Personality and Social Psychology,* 1978, 36, 588–597.

Trope, Y., & Burnstein, E. A disposition-behavior congruity model of perceived freedom. *Journal of Experimental Social Psychology,* 1977, 13, 357–368.

Truax, C. Reinforcement and non-reinforcement in Rogerian psychotherapy. *Journal of Abnormal and Social Psychology,* 1966, 71, 1–9.

Truax, C. B., & Carkhuff, R. R. *Toward effective counseling and psychotherapy.* Chicago: Aldine, 1967.

Truax, C. B., & Mitchell, K. M. Research on certain therapist interpersonal skills in relation to process and outcome. In A. E. Bergin & S. L. Garfield (Eds.) *Handbook of psychotherapy and behavior change: An empirical analysis.* New York: Wiley, 1971.

Turner, R. G., & Keyson, M. *Journal of Consulting and Clinical Psychology,* 1978, 46, 1586–1587.

Uranowitz, S. W. Helping and self-attributions: A field experient. *Journal of Personality and Social Psychology,* 1975, 31, 852–854.

Valins, S. Cognitive effects of false heart-rate feedback. *Journal of Personality and Social Psychology,* 1966, 4, 400–408.

Vallacher, R. R., & Solodky, M. Objective self-awareness, standards of evaluation, and moral behavior. *Journal of Experimental Social Psychology,* 1979, 15, 254–262.

Van Der Veen, F. Effects of the therapist and patient on each other's therapeutic behavior. *Journal of Consulting Psychology,* 1965, 29, 19–26.

Venzor, E., Gillis, J. S., & Beal, D. G. Preference for counselor response styles. *Journal of Counseling Psychology*, 1976, 23, 538–542.

Verhaeghe, H. Mistreating other persons through simple discrepant role playing: Dissonance arousal or response contagion? *Journal of Personality and Social Psychology*, 1976, 34, 125–237.

Von Bertalanffy, L. *General system theory: Foundation, development, application*. New York: G. Braziller, 1968.

Walster, E., Aronson, E., & Abrahams, D. On increasing the persuasiveness of a low prestige communicator. *Journal of Experimental Social Psychology*, 1966, 2, 325–342.

Walster, E., Berscheid, E., & Barclay, A. M. A determinant of preference among modes of dissonance reduction. *Journal of Personality and Social Psychology*, 1967, 7, 211–216.

Walster, E., Berscheid, E., & Walster, G. W. New directions in equity research. *Journal of Personality and Social Psychology*, 1973, 25, 151–176.

Walster, E., & Walster, G. W. The matching hypothesis. *Journal of Personality and Social Psychology*, 1969, 6, 248–253.

Walster, E., Walster, G. W., & Traupmann, J. Equity and premarital sex. *Journal of Personality and Social Psychology*, 1978, 36, 82–92.

Wambach, C. A. *Interpretation and attribution methods of stimulating change in counseling*. Unpublished doctoral dissertation. University of Minnesota, 1980.

Watzlawick, P. A review of the double bind theory. In D. Jackson (Ed.) *Communication, family, and marriage*. Palo Alto, CA: Science and Behavior Books, 1968.

Watzlawick, P., Beavin, J., & Jackson, D. *Pragmatics of human communication*. New York: Norton, 1967.

Watzlawick, P., Weakland, J., & Fisch, R. *Change: Principles of problem formation and problem resolution*. New York: Norton, 1974.

Webster's seventh new collegiate dictionary. Springfield, MA: Merriman, 1967.

Wegner, D. M., & Finstuen, K. Observers' focus of attention in the simulation of self-perception. *Journal of Personality and Social Psychology*, 1977, 35, 56–62.

Wells, G. L., & Harvey, J. H. Do people use consensus information in making causal attributions? *Journal of Personality and Social Psychology*, 1977, 35, 279–293.

Wells, G. L., & Harvey, J. H. Naive attributors' attributions and predictions: What is informative and when is an effect an effect? *Journal of Personality and Social Psychology*, 1978, 36, 483–490.

Wicklund, R. A. Objective self awareness. In L. Berkowitz (Ed.) *Advances in experimental social psychology*, Vol. 8. New York: Academic Press, 1975.

Wicklund, R. A., & Brehm, J. W. Attitude change as a function of felt competence and threat to attitudinal freedom. *Journal of Experimental Social Psychology*, 1968, 4, 64–75.

Wicklund, R. A., & Brehm, J. W. *Perspectives on cognitive dissonance*. Hillsdale, NJ: Lawrence Erlbaum, 1976.

Wicklund, R. A., & Duval, S. Opinion change and performance facilitation as a result of objective self awareness. *Journal of Experimental Social Psychology*, 1971, 7, 319–342.

Wiegel, R., Dinges, N., Dyer, R., & Straumfjord, A. Perceived self disclosure, mental health, and who is liked in group treatment. *Journal of Counseling Psychology*, 1972, 19, 47–52.

Winett, R. A. Attribution of attitude and behavior change and its relevance to behavior therapy. *The Psychological Record,* 1970, 20, 17–32.

Wixon, D. R., & Laird, J. D. Awareness and attitude change in the forced compliance paradigm: The importance of when. *Journal of Personality and Social Psychology,* 1976, 34, 376–384.

Wolfson, M. R., & Salancik, G. R. Observer orientation and actor observer differences in attributions for failure. *Journal of Experimental Social Psychology,* 1977, 13, 441–451.

Worchel, S., Arnold, S. E., & Harrison, W. Aggression and power restoration: The effects of identifiability and timing on aggressive behavior. *Journal of Experimental Social Psychology,* 1978, 14, 43–52.

Worchel, S., & Brehm, J. W. Effect of threats to attitudinal freedom as a function of agreement with the communicator. *Journal of Personality and Social Psychology,* 1970, 14, 18–22.

Wortman, C. B., & Brehm, J. W. Responses to uncontrollable outcomes: An integration of reactance theory and the learned helplessness model. In L. Berkowitz (Ed.) *Advances in experimental social psychology,* Vol. 8. New York: Academic Press, 1975.

Wortman, C. B., Panciera, L., Shusterman, L., & Hibscher, J. Attributions of causality and reactions to uncontrollable outcomes. *Journal of Experimental Social Psychology,* 1976, 12, 301–316.

Wright, R. M., & Strong, S. R. Stimulating therapeutic change with directives: An exploratory study. *Journal of Counseling Psychology,* in press.

Yalom, I. D. *The theory and practice of group psychotherapy.* New York: Basic Books, 1970.

Yandell, B., & Insko, C. A. Attribution of attitudes to speakers and listeners under assigned-behavior conditions: Does behavior engulf the field? *Journal of Experimental Social Psychology,* 1977, 13, 269–278.

Zagona, S. V., & Harter, R. Credibility of source and recipient's attitude: Factors in the perception and retention of information on smoking behavior. *Perceptual and Motor Skills,* 1966, 23, 155–168.

Zanna, M. P., Higgins, E. T., & Taves, P. A. Is dissonance phenomenologically aversive? *Journal of Experimental Social Psychology,* 1976, 12, 530–538.

Zillmann, D., & Cantor, J. R. Effect of timing of information about mitigating circumstances on emotional responses to provocation and retaliatory behavior. *Journal of Experimental Social Psychology,* 1976, 12, 38–55.

Zimbardo, P. G. Involvement and communication discrepancy as determinants of opinion conformity. *Journal of Abnormal and Social Psychology,* 1960, 60, 86–94.

Zimbardo, P. G. Cognitive dissonance and the control of human motivation. In R. P. Abelson, E. Aronson, W. J. McGuire, T. M. Newcomb, M. J. Rosenberg, & P. H. Tannenbaum (Eds.) *Theories of cognitive consistency: A sourcebook.* Chicago: Rand McNally, 1968.

Zimbardo, P. G. *The cognitive control of motivation.* Glenview, IL: Scott, Foresman, 1969.

Zimbardo, P. G. The human choice: Individuation, reason and order versus deindividuation, impulse, and chaos. In W. J. Arnold & D. Levine (Eds.) *Nebraska Symposium on Motivation, 1969.* Lincoln: University of Nebraska Press, 1970.

Zimbardo, P. G., Ebbesen, E. B., & Maslach, C. *Influencing attitudes and changing behavior,* 2nd ed. Reading, MA: Addison-Wesley, 1977.

Author Index

Subject Index

Psychology and Psychiatry in Courts and Corrections: Controversy and Change
  by Ellsworth A. Fersch, Jr.
Restricted Environmental Stimulation: Research and Clinical Applications
  by Peter Suedfeld
Personal Construct Psychology: Psychotherapy and Personality
  edited by Alvin W. Landfield and Larry M. Leitner
Mothers, Grandmothers, and Daughters: Personality and Child Care in
Three-Generation Families
  by Bertram J. Cohler and Henry U. Grunebaum
Further Explorations in Personality
  edited by A. I. Rabin, Joel Aronoff, Andrew M. Barclay, and Robert A. Zucker
Hypnosis and Relaxation: Modern Verification of an Old Equation
  by William E. Edmonston, Jr.
Handbook of Clinical Behavior Therapy
  edited by Samuel M. Turner, Karen S. Calhoun, and Henry E. Adams
Handbook of Clinical Neuropsychology
  edited by Susan B. Filskov and Thomas J. Boll
The Course of Alcoholism: Four Years After Treatment
  by J. Michael Polich, David J. Armor, and Harriet B. Braiker
Handbook of Innovative Psychotherapies
  edited by Raymond J. Corsini
The Role of the Father in Child Development (Second Edition)
  edited by Michael E. Lamb
Behavioral Medicine: Clinical Applications
  by Susan S. Pinkerton, Howard Hughes, and W. W. Wenrich
Handbook for the Practice of Pediatric Psychology
  edited by June M. Tuma
Change Through Interaction: Social Psychological Processes of Counseling and Psychotherapy
  by Stanley R. Strong and Charles D. Claiborn